W9-BZU-356

PEARSON
BACCALAUREATE

History

20th Century World

Causes, practices and effects of wars

KEELY ROGERS • JO THOMAS

ALWAYS LEARNING

PEARSON

Pearson Education Limited is a company incorporated in England and Wales, having its registered office at Edinburgh Gate, Harlow, Essex, CM20 2JE. Registered company number: 872828.

www.pearsonbaccalaureate.com

Pearson is a registered trademark of Pearson Education Limited

Text © Pearson Education Limited 2010

First published 2010

20 19 18 17 16 15 14 13
IMP 12 11 10 9 8 7 6 5

ISBN 978 0 435994 43 3

Edited by Chris McNab
Designed by Tony Richardson
Typeset by TechType
Original illustrations © Pearson Education Limited 2010
Illustrated by Oxford Designers & Illustrators and TechType
Cover design by Tony Richardson
Picture research by Joanne Forrest Smith
Cover photo © Corbis / Dmitri Baltermants / The Dmitri Baltermants Collection
Printed in Malaysia (CTP-PJB)

Acknowledgements
The authors and publisher would like to thank the following individuals and organizations for permission to reproduce photographs:

(Key: b-bottom; c-centre; l-left; r-right; t-top)
Alamy Images: akg-images 55, Bettmann 58tc, Imagestate Media Partners Limited - Impact Photos 185, Photos 12, 164, 297, Pictorial Press Ltd 304, Tim Graham 197; Bridgeman Art Library Ltd: Kollwitz, Kathe Schmidt (1867–1945) / Deutsches Historisches Museum, Berlin, Germany / © DACS 63; British Cartoon Archive, University of Kent www.cartoons.ac.uk: 46, 62, 78, Express Syndication 191, Solo Syndication 31, 91, 102, 103, 106, 121, 123t, 136, 166, 242, 287; Camerapress: IWM 196; Corbis: 4, 27b, 57, 129, Archives Barrat-Bartoll 289, Archives Barrat-Bartoll / Sygma 281, 283, Archives Barrat-Bartoll / Sygma 281, 283, Atlantide Phototravel 306, Bettmabb 255, Bettmann 2, 12t, 12c, 14, 27c, 29, 48, 51b, 53, 58tl, 71, 117, 135, 141, 149, 170, 188cl, 201t, 239, 254bl, 257, 270, 286, 294, 300, 303, 307, Bettmann 2, 12t, 12c, 14, 27c, 29, 48, 51b, 53, 58tl, 71, 117, 135, 141, 149, 170, 188cl, 201t, 239, 254bl, 257, 270, 286, 294, 300,

303, 307, Christel Gerstenberg 111, Galen Rowell 199t, Horacio Villalobos 188tl, Hulton-Deutsch 64, Hulton-Deutsch Collection 16, 52, 88, 97, 147, 153, Hulton-Deutsch Collection 16, 52, 88, 97, 147, 153, Hulton-Deutsch Collection 16, 52, 88, 97, 147, 153, Hulton-Deutsch Collection 16, 52, 88, 97, 147, 153, Hulton-Deutsch Collection 16, 52, 88, 97, 147, 153, J. Howard Miller 171, Jacques Pavlovsky / Sygma 209, Juan Guzman / EFE 246bc, Rykoff Collection 21t, Salvador Dali, Gala-Salvador Dali Foundation / Artists Philadelphia Museum of Art / Philadelphia Museum of Art Rights Society (ARS), New York / Philadelphia Museum of Art 234, Succession Picasso / The Art Archive 244, Swim Ink 43, 167l, Swim Ink 43, 167l, Ted Spiegel 219, Whisson / Jordan 305; Mary Evans Picture Library: 18, 41, 51cr, 301; FotoLibra: Jackie Fox 79; Getty Images: Hulton Archive 123b; Ronald Grant Archive: 246t, CASBAH FILM / IGOR FILM 285; Magnum Photos Ltd: 235; The National Library of Wales: 275, Solo Syndication 174; ; or courtesy www.psywarrior.com: Major Ed Rouse, US Army (Retired) 220; Pearson Education Ltd: 1, 68, 120, 130, 156, 183, 226, 252, 279; Punch Cartoon Library: 22, 105; Randall Bytewrk: 98; Rex Features: 195br; Telegraph Media Group: Nicholas Garland 201b, 205, Nicholas Garland 201b, 205, Nick Garland 224; TopFoto: 145, 151, 195c, 199b, 230, 265, 145, 151, 195c, 199b, 230, 265, AP 231, PA 194, Roger Violett 216, The Granger Collection 167r, The Print Collector / HIP 254c, Topham Picturepoint 21b, ullsteinbild 94.
All other images © Pearson Education Limited

The publisher and authors would also like to thank the following for permission to use © material:

From Anthony Adamthwaite, *The Making of the Second World War* (Routledge, 1989), used by permission of Anthony Adamthwaite. From Nick Alchin, *Theory of Knowledge* (Hodder Murray, 2002), reproduced by permission of Hodder & Stoughton Limited. Translation of the "Kruger Telegram", from Michael Balfour, *The Kaiser and his Times* (Cresset Press, 1964), used by permission of Mrs G. Balfour. From Ian Beckett, *The Great War* (Longman, 2001), used by permission of Pearson Education Ltd. From Anthony Beevor, *The Battle for Spain* (Weidenfeld & Nicolson, 2006), used by permission of Weidenfeld & Nicolson, an imprint of The Orion Publishing Group, London © Anthony Beevor, 1982. From Philip Michael Hett Bell, *Twentieth-century Europe: unity and division* (Hodder Arnold, 2006), © Bloomsbury Academic, an imprint of A&C Black Publishers Ltd. From David Bergamini, *Japan's Imperial Conspiracy* (William Morrow, 1971), © HarperCollins Publishers Ltd 1971. From Antony Best, Jussi M. Hanhimaki, Joseph A. Maiolo, and Kristen E. Schulze, *International History of the Twentieth Century* (Routledge, 2004), p.208 and p.453, used by permission of Routledge, a division of the Taylor & Francis Group. From Raymond Betts, *France and Decolonisation* (Macmillan, 1991), reproduced with permission of Palgrave Macmillan. From Jeremy Black, *Introduction to Global Military History* (Routledge, 2005), p.1 and p.239, used by permission of Routledge, a division of the Taylor & Francis Group. From an interview with Karl Blenk, in Martin Middlebrook, *The First Day of the Somme* (Allen Lane The Penguin Press, 1971), used by permission of Martin Middlebrook. From Peter Calvocoressi, *Total war: The Story of World War II* (Pantheon Books, 1972), used by permission of Paul Calvocoressi. From Peter Calvorocessi, *World Politics 1945–2000* (Pearson 2001), used by permission of Pearson Education Ltd. From Ian Cawood and David McKinnon-Bell, *The First World War* (Routledge, 2001), p.89, used by permission of Routledge, a division of the Taylor & Francis Group. From a radio broadcast by Maurice Challe, April 1960, translated by Alan Sheridan in Jean Lacouture, *De Gaulle, the ruler, 1945–1970* (Harvill, 1991), © Harvill Secker, a division of Random House. From Chen Yi, "Guerrillas in Southern Kiangsi" in *The Unquenchable Spark* (Foreign Languages Press, 1963), © Foreign Languages Press. From an interview with Chu Teh, in Agnes Smedley, *The Great Road: the Life and Times of Chu Teh* (Monthly Review Press, 1972), used by permission of Oneworld Classics. From Winston Churchill, speech in Parliament of 18 June 1940. From Norman Davies, *Europe at war 1939–1945: No Simple Victory* (Pan books, 2006), reproduced with permission of Palgrave Macmillan (also published as *No Simple Victory: World War II in Europe 1939–1945*). From Graham Darby, *Europe at War 1939–45* (Hodder Education, 2003), reproduced by permission of Hodder & Stoughton Limited. From Alistair Finlan, *The Gulf War* (Osprey, 2003), used by permission of Osprey. From Charles de Gaulle, *Major addresses, statements, and press conferences, May 19, 1958--January 31, 1964* (French Embassy, Press and Information Division, 1964), used by permission of the Embassy of France in the United States. From Brad DeLong, "Review of Akrira Irire's, *The Origins of the Second World War in Asia and in the Pacific*" (http://www.j-bradford-delong.net/Econ_Articles/reviews/iriye_origins.html), used by permission of Brad DeLong. From THE WAR OF THE WORLD by Niall Ferguson, Copyright © 2007 Niall Ferguson. Reproduced by permission of Penguin Books Ltd. From Fritz Fischer, *Germany's Aims in the First World War* (Chatto & Windus, London, 1967), © Chatto & Windus, a division of Random House. From Michael Foot, Introduction to *Years of Wrath, Cartoons by David Low* (Gollancz Paperbacks, 1986), © Michael Foot. Lawrence Freedman and Efraim Karsh, *The Gulf Conflict* (Faber & Faber, 2007), © Lawrence Freedman and Efraim Karsh. From Robert Goldston, *The Road Between the Wars* (Fawcett Cress, 1978), used by permission of Max Goldston. From June M. Grasso, Jay P. Corrin, and Michael Kort, *Modernization and Revolution in China: From the Opium Wars to World Power* (M.E. Sharpe, 1997), reproduced by permission of M.E. Sharpe. From Jack Gray, *Rebellions and Revolutions: China from the 1800s to the 1980s* (Oxford University Press, 1990), used by permission of Oxford University Press. From A MORTAL FLOWER by Han Suyin © 1969. Reprinted by kind permission of Han Suyin. From Ruth Henig, *The Origins of the First World War* (Lancaster pamphlets, Routledge, 2nd edition 1993), p.42 and p.54, used by permission of Routledge, a division of the Taylor & Francis Group. From Ruth Henig, *Versailles and after 1919–1933* (Routledge, 1995), p.35, used by permission of Routledge, a division of the Taylor & Francis Group. From a speech by Ernst von Heydebrand of 9 November 1911, translated by Isabella Massey in Luigi Albertini, *The Origins of the War of 1914 Volume 1* (Oxford University Press, 1986), used by permission of Oxford University Press. From a statement of Adolf Hitler of 7 January 1942, translated in Norman Cameron, R. H. Stevens, and Hugh Trevor-Roper, *Hitler's Table-Talk* (Weidenfeld and Nicholson, 1973), used by permission of Weidenfeld & Nicolson, an imprint of The Orion Publishing Group, London. From Alistair Horne, *A Savage War of Peace: Algeria 1954–1962* (New York Review Books, 2006), used by permission of New York Review Books. From an interview with Charles Horner on the *Washington Post* website (http://www.washingtonpost.com/wp-srv/inatl/longterm/fogofwar/hornertext.htm), reproduced by permission of The Washington Post. From Immanuel Hsu, *The Rise of Modern China* (Oxford University Press, 4th ed. 1990), used by permission of Oxford University Press. From Saburo Ienaga, *The Pacific War: World War II and the Japanese, 1931–1945* (Pantheon Books, 1978), translated by Frank Baldwin and reproduced by permission of Random House USA. From the IBO Online curriculum centre (http://occ.ibo.org/ibis/occ/guest/home.cfm), used with permission of the IBO. From Akira Iriye,

Websites
There are links to relevant websites in this book. In order to ensure that the links are up to date, that the links work, and that the sites are not inadvertently linked to sites that could be considered offensive, we have made the links available on the Pearson Hotlinks website at www.pearsonhotlinks.com. When you access the site, the express code is 4433P.

Contents

Introduction

How will this book help you in your IB examination?

This book is designed to be your guide to success in your International Baccalaureate examination in History. It covers a range of the prescribed wars from Topic 1 and emphasizes the key themes that the IB has identified within the wars topic. This book also aims to equip you with the knowledge and skills that you will need to answer essay questions on Paper 2, and document-based questions on Paper 1.

Within most chapters we have included:
- Analysis of the key causes/events/results of each war
- Discussion of major themes/issues relating to each war
- A summary of, or reference to, up-to-date historiography
- Discussion on how to answer essay and document questions
- Essay planning techniques for each war
- Timelines to help you put events into context
- Review and research activities to help you develop your understanding of the key issues and concepts.

How this book works
Information boxes

You will see a number of coloured boxes interspersed throughout each chapter. Each of these boxes provides different information and stimulus as follows.

Theory of Knowledge

There are ToK boxes throughout the book. These boxes will enable you to consider ToK issues as they arise and in context. Often they will just contain a question to stimulate your thoughts and discussion.

ToK Time
How far do historians 'revise' their views of leaders and their actions with the benefit of hindsight?

Interesting facts

These boxes contain information that will deepen and widen your knowledge, but which does not fit within the main body of the text.

Diktat
A harsh unilateral settlement imposed by the victors on the defeated.

Key terms

These important terms or concepts are highlighted in the main body of the text and explained in the glossary at the end of the book.

Examiner's hints

These boxes can be found alongside questions, exercises and worked examples and they provide insight into how to answer a question in order to achieve the highest marks in an examination. They also identify common pitfalls when answering such questions, and suggest approaches that examiners like to see.

To access worksheet 1.1 on total war and the Geneva Conventions, please visit www. pearsonbacconline. com and follow the on-screen instructions.

● **Examiner's hint**
When you are asked to look for an answer in a source, underline the relevant points and then focus on the information that you need to answer the question. Don't list everything, only what is relevant.

Online resources

Online resources boxes indicate that online resources are available that relate to this section of the book. These resources might be extension exercises, additional practice questions, interactive online material, suggestions for IA, EE and revision, or other sources of information. Some of the content on this site may be password protected for copyright reasons. When prompted for a password, please use PearsonBaccWars exactly as shown.

Weblinks

Relevant websites are recommended in the Further Reading section at the end of the book. On these web pages you will find video simulations and background information to support the topic.

IB Learner Profile sections

These are to identify the skills that you are developing as an IB learner (see p.x).

IB History: assessment objectives

In this book, we cover the six IB assessment objectives that are relevant to the core externally examined papers. Thus, although this book is essentially designed as a textbook to accompany the Paper 2 topic: Wars, it addresses all of the assessment objectives required for both Paper 1 and Paper 2. In other words, as you work through this textbook, you will be learning and practising the skills that are necessary for each of the core papers. In addition, as you will see below, the book also covers assessment objectives relevant to Paper 3 and the Internal Assessment (IA).

Specifically, the assessment objectives are:
- To demonstrate historical understanding through the acquisition, selection and effective use of knowledge (Papers 1, 2 and IA)
- To demonstrate an understanding of historical context; cause and effect; continuity and change (Papers 1, 2, 3 and IA)
- To evaluate different approaches to, and interpretations of, historical events and topics (Papers 1, 2, 3 and IA)
- To comprehend, analyze and evaluate historical sources as evidence (Paper 1)
- To present historical explanations using arguments that are clear, coherent, relevant and well substantiated (Papers 2 and 3)
- To compare and contrast issues or events across time and space (Papers 2 and 3).

There is one more assessment objective for both Standard and Higher students:
- To undertake individual research and present results using a formal plan of organization and presentation (IA).

This objective is focused on the Internal Assessment, and although we suggest research activities, we do not do this within the formal 'plan of organization' and 'presentation' that the IB requires.

Higher-level students also have to cover Objective 8:
- To demonstrate in-depth historical understanding of a period of regional history through the critical evaluation and synthesis of appropriate knowledge and concepts (Paper 3).

We do not cover this objective directly in this book, although there may be some overlap of material that is relevant to each regional in-depth paper.

Mark schemes

For Paper 1 there are individual paper-specific mark schemes for each examination; this is also true for Papers 2 and 3. However, for Papers 2 and 3 there are also generic 'mark bands' that should be used by teachers and students when planning and writing their essays. These are essential 'rubrics' that offer students a better understanding of what is wanted from their essays in the examination. The mark bands for Paper 2 are on pp.x–xi.

Causes, practices and effects of wars: the key themes

As you read and work through this book, you will be covering the major themes for this History topic. At the end of the book, we will review these themes by considering how to answer possible thematic essay questions.

Different types of warfare

The different types of war – total, limited, civil and guerrilla – are explained in Chapter 1 and then discussed further in each relevant case study. This book has two examples of each of the different types of war to give you enough material for essay questions.

Origins and causes of wars

The origins and causes of each war in the book are divided into long-term, short-term and immediate causes. In addition, the economic, ideological, political and religious causes are discussed where relevant.

The nature of 20th-century wars

For each war, the characteristics of the fighting are discussed. Depending on the war, this discussion could include an analysis of the tactics and weaponry used in the fighting on land, on sea and/or in the air. Where relevant, there will also be discussion of the impact of technological developments on the course and the outcome of the war. The economic and social impact of wars is also considered.

The effects and results of wars

The results of the wars are analyzed at the end of each chapter.

Theory of Knowledge

History is a Group 3 subject in the IB Diploma. It is an 'area of knowledge' that considers individuals and societies. In historical investigation, many different ways of obtaining knowledge are used, for example: data collection, use of observations and experiments, and **inductive** and **deductive** reasoning. When working through this book, you should reflect on the 'Ways of Knowing' utilized not only by professional historians, but also by you as a student of history.

The methods used by historians are important to highlight, as you will need to be able to compare and contrast these with other areas of knowledge, such as the Group 4 Sciences (Physics, Chemistry and Biology).

IB LEARNER PROFILE CHARACTERISTICS

Below you can find the IB Learner Profile characteristics, which will be referred to throughout this book.

Inquirers	They develop their natural curiosity. They acquire the skills necessary to conduct inquiry and research and show independence in learning. They actively enjoy learning and this love of learning will be sustained throughout their lives.
Knowledgeable	They explore concepts, ideas and issues that have local and global significance. In so doing, they acquire in-depth knowledge and develop understanding across a broad and balanced range of disciplines.
Thinkers	They exercise initiative in applying thinking skills critically and creatively to recognize and approach complex problems, and make reasoned, ethical decisions.
Communicators	They understand and express ideas and information confidently and creatively in more than one language and in a variety of modes of communication. They work effectively and willingly in collaboration with others.
Principled	They act with integrity and honesty, with a strong sense of fairness, justice and respect for the dignity of the individual, groups and communities. They take responsibility for their own actions and the consequences that accompany them.
Open-minded	They understand and appreciate their own cultures and personal histories, and are open to the perspectives, values and traditions of other individuals and communities. They are accustomed to seeking and evaluating a range of points of view, and are willing to grow from the experience.
Caring	They show empathy, compassion and respect towards the needs and feelings of others. They have a personal commitment to service, and act to make a positive difference to the lives of others and to the environment.
Risk-takers	They approach unfamiliar situations and uncertainty with courage and forethought, and have the independence of spirit to explore new roles, ideas and strategies. They are brave and articulate in defending their beliefs.
Balanced	They understand the importance of intellectual, physical and emotional balance to achieve personal well-being for themselves and others.
Reflective	They give thoughtful consideration to their own learning and experience. They are able to assess and understand their strengths and limitations in order to support their learning and personal development.

From *History Guide* © International Baccalaureate Organization, 2007

IB MARK BANDS FOR ESSAYS FOR PAPER 2

Here are the mark bands for Paper 2. Check your essays against these to ensure that you are meeting the criteria for the top bands.

Marks	Level Descriptor
0	The work does not reach a standard described by the descriptors below.
1–3	Answers lack understanding of the demands of the question or accurate/relevant historical knowledge.
	Answers show little or no evidence of appropriate structure and consist of little more than vague, unsupported assertions.
4–5	Answers reveal little understanding of the question.
	While historical details are present, they are largely inaccurate and/or of marginal relevance to the task.
	There is little or no understanding of historical context or historical processes.

6–7	Answers indicate some understanding of the question.
	There is some relevant historical knowledge, but it is limited in terms of quantity and quality.
	There may be some attempt to place events in their historical context. Understanding of historical processes and (where appropriate) comparison and contrast may be present but underdeveloped.
	While there may be a recognizable essay structure, the question is only partially addressed.
8–9	Answers indicate that the demands of the question are generally understood.
	Relevant historical knowledge is present and applied, but is not full or accurately detailed and is presented in a narrative or descriptive manner. Alternatively, there is coherent argument that requires further substantiation. Relevant critical commentary is implicit.
	There has been an attempt to place events in their historical context and to show an understanding of historical processes and (where appropriate) comparison and contrast.
	There is evidence of an attempt to follow a structured approach, either chronological or thematic.
10–12	Answers indicate that the demands of the question are understood and addressed, though not all implications are considered.
	Relevant, largely accurate historical knowledge is present and applied as evidence. Answers may attempt some critical commentary.
	Events are generally placed in their historical context. There is an understanding of historical processes and (where appropriate) comparison and contrast.
	There may be some awareness of different approaches to, and interpretation of, historical issues and events. However, responses that mainly summarize the views of historians and use these as a substitute for, rather than a supplement to, the deployment of relevant historical knowledge cannot reach the top of this band.
	There is a clear attempt to structure answers either chronologically or thematically.
13–15	Answers are clearly focused responses to the demands of the question.
	Relevant historical knowledge is applied as evidence. Critical commentary using the evidence base is present, but not always used consistently.
	Events are placed in their historical context. There is a sound understanding of historical processes and (where appropriate) comparison and contrast.
	There may be awareness and some evaluation of different approaches to, and interpretations of, historical issues and events. These are used to supplement, in a relevant manner, the arguments presented.
	Answers are structured (either chronologically or thematically) using relevant evidence to support historical arguments.
16–20	Answers are clearly focused responses, showing a high degree of awareness of the demands of the question. Where appropriate, answers may challenge the question successfully.
	Detailed and accurate historical knowledge is applied as evidence and used consistently and effectively to support critical commentary.
	Events are placed in their historical context and there is a perceptive understanding of historical processes and (where appropriate) comparison and contrast.
	There may be evaluation of different approaches to, and interpretations of, historical issues and events. This evaluation is integrated effectively into the answer to support and supplement the argument.
	Answers are well structured and clearly expressed, using evidence to support relevant, balanced and focused historical arguments.

From *History Guide* © International Baccalaureate Organization, 2007

1 WARS IN THE 20TH CENTURY

I see it only as a century of massacres and wars.

René Dumont

The Twentieth Century has been 'without doubt the most murderous century of which we have record by the scale, frequency and length of the warfare which filled it'.

From Eric Hobsbawm, *Age of Extremes: The Short Twentieth Century,* **1994**

At the end of the 19th century, many people were convinced that war could no longer be used as a 'tool of **diplomacy**', yet war would become the dominant theme of the 20th century. There were two 'world' wars, each of which killed millions of people; Niall Ferguson calls World War II (1939–45) 'the greatest man-made catastrophe of all time', costing the lives of more than 50 million people. Terrible as these wars were in terms of death toll, however, they are only two of many other conflicts that took place during the 20th century. In between the world wars and after 1945, there were numerous wars both between nations and within nations in which casualties were often high.

The changing nature of warfare in the 20th century not only dramatically increased the number of casualties, but also blurred the distinctions between combatant and non-combatant. At the beginning of the century, there were eight times as many military casualties in war as there were civilian casualties. By the 1990s, the situation had reversed.

The technological development of weapons has also brought the threat of the total destruction of humanity. Nuclear weapons have raised the destructive potential of any war; their use in 1945 and the clear dangers they posed to the future of mankind also affected the way that wars were fought in the second half of the century.

A nuclear bomb detonating. Nuclear weapons are the ultimate tools of total war.

Why is the study of war important?

As you can see from the map on p.6, and as we have suggested above, wars have played a pivotal role in the 20th century. World War I swept away empires and the 'old order', and set the stage for new social and political developments in Europe. World War II led to the emergence of the USA and USSR as **superpowers** and also to the decline of European powers such as Britain and France. These effects in turn led to the Cold War and the collapse of European empires, developments that dominated world politics after 1945 and shaped the world in which we live today.

What terms do we use to describe different types of war?

Total war

To access worksheet 1.1 on total war and the Geneva Conventions, please visit www. pearsonbacconline. com and follow the on-screen instructions.

'**Total war**' means that a country uses all its human, economic and military resources to fight the war and ensure complete victory over the enemy. In practical terms this means:

- Creating a large fighting force through the use of conscription
- Using civilians in the war effort, e.g. in industry and home defence
- Using all weapons available and developing new ones in order to ensure victory
- Government control of key aspects of the economy, so that it can be directed into the war effort
- Government control of the media in order to maintain civilian morale and also to ensure that the population sees the enemy as one that must be defeated at all costs
- The targeting of civilians as well as combatants in the quest for 'total' victory over the enemy's political, social and military structures.

World War II was 'total' for many civilians of Europe and Asia due to the intensive bombing of cities.

Limited war

In contrast to total war, '**limited war**', as the term suggests, is the idea of limiting or constraining the way in which war is conducted. This restraint can involve:

- Confining the geographical area in which fighting takes place
- Limiting the type of targets that can be attacked
- Limiting the weapons that can be used
- Limiting the degree of mobilization.

Limited war was a characteristic of many wars of the 19th century, reflecting both the limited aims involved in such conflicts and the fact that full mobilization of all resources was too difficult for the countries involved. After 1945, limited war became a necessity in order to prevent nuclear war – both the USA and the USSR had to impose restrictions on themselves in order to prevent the very real danger of a superpower confrontation involving nuclear weapons. Thus both the Korean War (1950–53) and the Vietnam War (1963–75) can be classed as 'limited' wars because they did not involve the USA using of all its military and economic resources (though, of course, for the Koreans and the Vietnamese these wars were total). Examples of limited war considered in this book are the Falklands War (1982) and the Gulf War (1990–91).

Civil wars

Civil wars are conflicts fought between two factions or regions of the same country, the warring sides clashing over ethnic, religious, political or **ideological** issues. An example is the Spanish Civil War (1936–39), fought between Republicans and Nationalists. Generally speaking, during a civil war the combatants aim to take control of the political and legal institutions of the state, although the violence is longer lasting than a ***coup d'état***. Usually, civil war combatants can be identified as either **incumbents** or **insurgents**. Often there is foreign involvement in civil wars, and depending on its role and impact, this could be viewed as broadening a civil war into an international conflict.

Guerrilla warfare

Guerrilla warfare (from the Spanish word for 'little war') was a key feature of 20th-century conflicts. It is described as 'unconventional warfare' because, rather than trying to attack an enemy head-on with conventional tactics, small groups of fighters use tactics such as ambush and small-unit raids against a larger and less mobile formal army. The forces of Chinese communist leader Mao Zedong, for example, used guerrilla tactics in the Chinese Civil War from the late 1920s through to 1949. This type of warfare became common after 1945 for several reasons:

- Many conflicts after 1945 involved peoples of Asia and Africa trying to free themselves from the **colonial** rule of powerful European countries. With only limited military resources, the insurgents have used guerrilla tactics as a way of attempting to achieve their goals. The use of guerrilla tactics has been promoted by the fact that many post-1945 conflicts have been fought in areas where the terrain has aided guerrilla fighting, e.g. jungles in Vietnam, or bush in Rhodesia and mountains in Afghanistan. In these conflicts the guerrilla fighters have often also had the support of the local population and good knowledge of the terrain. In contrast, combatants of the European countries often faced local hostility and mobility problems in places that lacked a developed infrastructure.
- The development of the **Cold War** after 1945 also encouraged guerrilla warfare; in a situation where all conflicts were seen in the context of a struggle against either **communism** or **capitalism**, unpopular governments were often supported by one or other of the superpowers, meaning that the local opposition often had no choice but to resort to guerrilla warfare. In fact, given that the dangers of direct confrontation in the Cold War were too great, the USSR and USA often fought war 'by proxy', sponsoring local insurgencies rather than fighting themselves.
- The spread of **Marxism** has also had an influence. The belief that the masses must rise up against established capitalist governments clearly supports the idea of guerrilla warfare, and indeed many successful guerrilla movements have been Marxist in orientation.

To access worksheet 1.2 on guerrilla warfare, please visit www.pearsonbacconline.com and follow the on-screen instructions.

- In the post-Cold War world, guerrilla warfare has become increasingly central, such as seen in al-Qaeda's war against the West, because **democratic** political systems are particularly vulnerable to guerrilla tactics.
- Technological developments have enabled insurgents to become more formidable warriors than was possible at the beginning of the 20th century, taking advantage of the global distribution of weapons such as shoulder-launched missiles and powerful **small arms**.
- The international coverage of the mass media now provides the kind of publicity that guerrilla fighters need in order to win support for their cause.

Mujahideen warriors in Afghanistan. In their wars against both the Soviets and the West, the *Mujahideen* have used the techniques of guerrilla warfare.

Key terms

When studying wars, historians not only use labels such as 'total' or 'limited', but they also divide both the causes and the effects of wars into different categories. Most wars will be caused by, and result in, a combination of the factors listed below.

Economic cause: This term refers to conflict over economic resources. For instance, a war could be fought over a country's need to secure foreign markets or raw materials. An example is the Gulf War of 1990–91, in which the Iraqi leader Saddam Hussein, looking to solve Iraq's drastic economic problems, invaded neighbouring Kuwait in an attempt to capture its oil reserves.

Economic effects: War can have a dramatic impact on the economic situation of a country, resulting in effects such as **inflation** or food rationing. The economic consequences of World War I for Germany, for example, were so severe that they contributed to the internal collapse of Germany in 1918.

Social cause: Wars are often caused by tensions between different social groups or classes in a country or region. Such tensions were a key element in the Spanish Civil War.

Social effects: The structures, customs and traditions of a society are frequently changed by war. For example, World War I brought about huge transformations in European society, including a shift in the status of women and the beginning of the collapse of the traditional ruling classes.

Political cause: A political cause refers to wars that begin through a clash between different political factions, such as occurred in the Spanish Civil War.

Political effects: Wars can change the structure of a government or nation, and result in a complete reconfiguration of how a country is run. For example, a key political result of World War I was the break-up of empires and the creation of new states.

Ideological cause: A fundamental clash of ideas between different groups about how government and society should be run is another leading cause of conflict. For example, at the root of the political clashes that caused the Spanish Civil War in 1936–39 were clear differences in ideology. The war was seen primarily as a clash between **fascism** and communism.

Ideological effects: War can also affect the ideological position of a country or of groups within a country. For example, World War I provided some of the conditions in which the communist revolution in Russia took place in 1917.

STUDENT STUDY SECTION

Questions

1   Look at the conflicts on the map (on p.6). Using the information above, decide into which category – total, limited, civil or guerrilla – each war would fit. (You may find that wars can fit into more than category.)

2   What other wars do you know of that are not shown on the map? What wars do you know about that are still being fought today?

3   Wars can be given many other labels. How would you explain the following definitions of wars?
- Revolutionary war
- Colonial war
- Ideological war
- Economic war
- Defensive war
- Religious war
- **Neo-colonial** war.

4   Consider the following developments of the 19th and 20th centuries. How has each one affected the conduct of war? Can you give examples of wars in which these developments have had an impact?
- The Industrial Revolution (which saw the rise of mass production and technological advances in manufacturing)
- The development of the railways
- The growth of the mass media
- The invention of the aeroplane
- The development of nuclear weapons
- **Globalization**
- Satellite technology
- The internet.

ToK Time

…the intensity of war often unleashes or accelerates numerous forces for change, transforming industry, society and government in ways that are fundamental and permanent. By weakening or destroying traditional structures, or by impelling internal reforms, wars may create conditions conducive to social change and political modernisation. From James Sheehan, *The Monopoly of Violence: Why Europeans Hate Going to War*, 2008

Can war ever be seen as a 'positive' force within and between societies? Discuss in pairs the above quotation and attempt to find examples of when and where war has brought about 'social change and political modernization'.

A century of conflict: this map shows only some of the wars fought in the 20th century.

13 2nd Indochina War 1960–75

14 Chinese Civil War 1928–37

15 Korean War 1950–53

10 Iran-Iraq War 1980–88

11 Gulf War 1990–91

12 Indo-Pakistan Wars 1947–49, 1965, 1971

7 Algerian War 1954–62

8 Nigerian Civil War 1966–70

9 Arab-Israeli Conflict 1960–Present

ToK Time
The statistics on casualties for these wars vary in different historical sources. Why might this be the case? What does this suggest about the use of statistics for the historian?

1 First World War 1914–18

2 Second World War 1939–45

3 Mexican Revolution 1910–20

4 Nicaraguan Revolution 1976–79

5 Falklands /Malvinas War 1982

6 Spanish Civil War 1936–39

2 THE CAUSES OF WORLD WAR I

As you read through this chapter, consider the following essay question:
- Why did a general European war break out in August 1914?

One of the most brutal and destructive wars in human history began in Europe in August 1914; it would last until November 1918. By the end of 1918, 60 declarations of war had been made between countries. Contemporaries and historians have argued ever since 1918 over what caused this catastrophe. This chapter looks at the long-term, short-term and immediate events that led the Great Powers of Europe, their empires and their allies into armed conflict.

Timeline of the causes of World War I – 1871–1914

1871	End of Franco-Prussian War / German Empire proclaimed
1873	The Three Emperors' League
1879	Dual Alliance
1881	The Three Emperors' Alliance
1882	Triple Alliance
1887	Reinsurance Treaty (Germany, Russia)
1888	Wilhelm II becomes German Emperor
1890	Bismarck resigns
	Reinsurance Treaty lapses
1892–94	Franco-Russian Alliance
1897	Austro-Russian Agreement
1898	Fashoda Incident
	German Naval Law
1900	Second German Naval Law
1902	Anglo-Japanese Alliance
1904	Russo-Japanese War
	Entente Cordiale (Britain, France)
1905	First Moroccan Crisis
1906	Algeciras Conference
1907	Anglo-Russian Entente; Triple Entente (Russia, France and Britain)
1908	Annexation of Bosnia by Austria-Hungary
1911	Second Moroccan Crisis
1912	First Balkan War
1913	Second Balkan War
1914	**28 Jun** Archduke Franz Ferdinand assassinated
	5 Jul German 'blank cheque' to Austria-Hungary
	23 Jul Austro-Hungarian ultimatum to Serbia
	30 Jul Russia orders mobilization
	1 Aug Germany declares war on Russia
	3 Aug Germany invades Belgium and declares war on France
	4 Aug Britain declares war on Germany

In this chapter, we begin looking at the causes of World War I with an earlier conflict that destabilized the balance of power in Europe before the dawn of the 20th century. This conflict is the Franco-Prussian War (1870–71), which created a unified Germany.

Franco-Prussian War (1870–71)

Map of the 39 states of the German Confederation.

After the Napoleonic Wars, which ended in 1815, there were 39 separate Germanic states in Europe; the two largest were Austria and Prussia. The Prussians, under the leadership of their Chancellor Otto von Bismarck, fought three wars with the objective both of consolidating these smaller states into a new German state, and of asserting themselves as the dominant Germanic state instead of Austria. The Prussians defeated Denmark and Austria in 1864 and finally France in 1871.

The final war in 1870–71 saw the well-equipped Prussian Army not only defeating, but also humiliating, France. In early September 1870, at Sedan, one French army was forced to surrender its 80,000 men. The core of the French Army, some 150,000 men, was encircled for two months at Metz and surrendered in October. The war continued for another three months. Paris, which had been under siege since mid September, finally fell in January 1871. Cut off from the rest of France, Paris had suffered horrendously, and there were some clear signs of the effectiveness of modern technology in supporting warfare; for example, in Prussia's use of railways to deliver men and material to the battlefield. Prussia won the military battles, and crippled Paris in an economic **blockade**.

The terms for peace were severe. France lost the territory of Alsace-Lorraine, had to pay an **indemnity** of 5,000 million marks and suffered Prussian occupation of parts of France until this sum had been paid. There was also a Prussian victory march through Paris. The King of Prussia was proclaimed the German Emperor in the Hall of Mirrors in the Palace of Versailles in January 1871. German unification (without Austria) was complete.

In France, political and **socio-economic** problems followed the humiliation of defeat. There was a desire for revenge in France that manifested itself in the political *revanche* movement.

From tomorrow, France will have only one thought: to reconstitute its forces, gather its energy, feed its sacred anger, raise its generation ... form an army of the whole people, work relentlessly to study the processes and talents of our enemies, to become again the great France, the France of 1792, the France of the idea and the sword... Then suddenly one day it will rise ... regain Lorraine, recapture Alsace.

The French poet Victor Hugo, 1871

Internationally, the war had far-reaching consequences. Germany was a new power in Europe, and France's position had been undermined. This situation shifted the balance of power in continental Europe. Germany now had the potential to be dominant. The Prussian Wars of Unification also offered important military lessons for the rest of Europe – the emphasis in modern warfare had to be on rapid mobilization and fast deployment. Modern armies had to be well trained and well equipped, and to a certain extent educated and probably conscripted. The General Staff of an army (the personnel distributing the orders of the top leadership down to the field officers) had to be competent, and able to plan and coordinate the use of railways in deploying millions of men and their equipment. Another lesson that seemed to come from the unification wars was that modern warfare would rely on movement, and be relatively short in duration.

STUDENT STUDY SECTION

Review questions

1 What was the impact of the Franco-Prussian War on France?

2 Why would the other European powers be worried about the unification of Germany?

What were the key characteristics of the Great European Powers, c. 1900?

The Great Powers in 1900.

Before reviewing the key developments in Europe that led up to World War I, it is important that you have a clear idea of the characteristics of the Great Powers of Europe by 1900.

Group activity

Using the information below on each of the European countries, complete the following table. This can be done as a group activity; each group researches a country and feeds back its information to the rest of the class.

	Germany	France	Britain	Austria-Hungary	Russia	Turkey
Political system						
Economic strength						
Socio-economic problems						
Foreign policy						
Key strengths/weaknesses						
Key aims/fears						

Germany

Germany was a **democratic monarchy**; its system was authoritarian, with power held by the Kaiser and the Chancellor. The power of the German parliament, the Reichstag, was limited. In the 30 years following the Franco-Prussian War, Germany became the strongest industrial power in Europe. By 1900, Germany had overtaken Britain in industrial output. However, although its economy was strong and effective, Germany had acute social problems. Rapid industrialization had produced a large working class in the expanding cities and a growing middle class. There were socio-economic tensions between these two groups and also between these groups and the authoritarian government. The great Prussian landowning classes, the Junkers, retained political dominance, promoting **militarism** and allegiance to the Kaiser; they were against reforms designed to move Germany towards becoming a more **liberal** democracy.

A growth in the German population, and pressure from capitalists to secure international markets and raw materials, led the German government to pursue the 19th-century European policy of developing and expanding an overseas empire. Yet, at least initially, the government was cautious in its approach, and attempted to cooperate with the other imperial powers – for example, at the Congress of Berlin in 1884, where the continent of Africa was carved up between the Europeans.

The key problem here was that although Germany wanted colonies, the globe had already been divided up by the other European powers. Britain's empire was territorially the largest. Germany's leaders were apparently undecided at the turn of the new century whether to attempt to work with Britain as an ally, or to compete with the British.

France

France was a democratic **republic** and offered extensive civil liberties. Its economy was agriculturally based, with most of the population living and working in the countryside. Nevertheless, France was a wealthy nation. It had a large empire, sizeable gold reserves and had made much overseas investment, particularly in Russia. Politically the nation was broadly divided between the '**pacifist**' **left wing** and the revanchist **right wing**. France was plagued by short-lived governments, which swung between the left to the right. This instability had a serious impact on foreign policy, as the right wing wanted to pursue

imperialist ambitions and the reclamation of Alsace-Lorraine, whereas the left were against these ambitions. France looked for an alliance with Russia to help 'contain' Germany.

Britain

Britain was a well-established **parliamentary democracy**, with a **monarchy** retaining limited powers, and had been the first European power to undergo an industrial revolution. It had built a vast overseas empire and established itself as the most powerful international trader of the 19th century. Britain had indeed been the number one economic power of the 1800s, but by 1900 it was to a certain extent in decline, both in terms of its international dominance of trade, and in its position as the primary economic power. Not only had the USA overtaken Britain in industrial production, but by 1900 Germany had too. Britain had similar socio-economic problems as Germany, with much working-class discontent. The long-standing political system, however, combined a degree of flexibility with coercion and therefore appeared better able to cope than Germany's autocratic fledgling democratic monarchy. The British government had learnt to be alert to public opinion and the power of the popular press.

The changing balance of power in Europe led to a corresponding change in the shape of British foreign policy. In the 19th century, Britain had followed a policy of 'Splendid Isolation', not wanting to be drawn into conflicts between other nations, as this could impact negatively on its international trade. By 1900, with competition from the USA and Germany, Britain was starting to review this policy and to look for allies. Britain's major military power was its navy. But in this strength lay Britain's weakness. Britain depended on the navy not only to defend itself against attack, but also to defend its sea-based trade and its vast empire. Resources were overstretched. It was paramount that the navy was invulnerable. Britain's traditional enemies and rivals had been the French and the Russians, and it remained particularly suspicious of Russia regarding its relationship to the overland Asian trade routes to India (see the Interesting Facts box on p.16). Britain's interests lay in maintaining its dominance of the seas, preserving the balance of power in Europe and defending the Indian trade routes.

Austria-Hungary

Austria-Hungary was a 'dual monarchy': an Emperor presided over the Austro-Hungarian Empire, with Austria and Hungary having their own parliaments. The system was heavily bureaucratic and inefficient.

There had been slow economic growth in this land-based empire. The key problem for the dual monarchy was the national rivalries within their European empire (see figures on next page). The 19th century had unleashed powerful **nationalist** forces and ambitions across Europe, leading to demands for national liberation from states within the Austro-Hungarian Empire. The empire lacked military strength, which had been highlighted in the brief war with Prussia in 1866. A key concern for the Habsburgs was the demise of the Ottoman Empire on their border. This process had strengthened the nationalist cause of many **Slavic** peoples, who now strived for independence from the Ottomans, and ultimately wanted to unite with their 'brothers' within the borders of the Habsburg Empire. The Austro-Hungarian regime, therefore, pursued a foreign policy of containment in the Balkans, and as the Ottoman decline left a vacuum of power, Austria-Hungary intended to fill it.

Austria-Hungary was a multi-national European empire in an age of nationalism. In general, the empire lacked cohesion economically, politically and socially. Its greatest

> **The Habsburgs**
> The Habsburgs were the rulers of the dual monarchy set up in 1867, Austria-Hungary, and the territories under Austrian and Hungarian control were known as the Habsburg Empire.

Franz Josef, Emperor of Austria, King of Hungary.

Tsar Nicholas II.

Ottoman Empire
The Turkish Empire came to be called the 'Ottoman' Empire after a 14th-century leader called Osman I. The Ottoman Empire was an Islamic empire led by a Sultan (the Arabic word for 'ruler'). The empire consisted of 29 provinces, and other states under the nominal authority of the Sultanate.

concern was the hostility and aggression of Serbia. The anxiety was accentuated by the support given to the Serb nationalists by Russia, who saw itself as the great defender of the 'Slav people'.

NATIONALITIES OF THE HABSBURG EMPIRE, 1910		
Austria	Hungary	Bosnia-Herzegovina
Germans 35.6%	Magyars 48%	Croats 21%
Czechs (inc Slovaks) 23%	Germans 9.8%	Serbs 42%
Poles 17.8%	Slovaks 9.4%	Muslims 34%
Ruthenians 12.6%	Romanians 14.1%	
Serbo-Croats 2.6%	Ruthenians 2.3%	
Romanians 1%	Croats 8.8%	
	Serbs 5.3%	

Russia

Russia was an autocratic 'divine monarchy', the Tsar being perceived by many as having been appointed by God. The state was again heavily bureaucratic and ineffective. There had been rapid industrialization at the end of the 19th century, yet the majority of people in Russia remained peasants, working the land with intensive labour processes long outdated in the modernized European states.

By 1900, discontent towards the regime was growing among the middle classes and among the new urban workers. This mood exploded into revolution in 1905 after Russia had been defeated in a disastrous war against Japan. Although this revolution did not achieve regime change, it led to a very limited degree of democracy being introduced. Working conditions, however, were not improved.

After its defeat in the Crimean War (1853–56) and then in the Russo-Japanese War (1904–05), Russia was no longer viewed as a 'great military power'. Russia's strength in 1900, and throughout the 20th century, was its huge resources of people. But again, this strength was also a weakness, as the Russian people were increasingly unhappy with their regime. Russia wanted to encourage Slav nationalism in the Balkans to establish its own influence in the region; however, it also wanted to prop up the ailing Ottoman Empire to prevent any expansion of Austria-Hungary.

Turkey

Turkey was the 'sick man of Europe'. The Ottoman Empire was in decline, and the power of its ruler – the Sultan – had been terminally undermined in most areas. The regime was corrupt and ineffective. Revolts by some national and Islamic groups within the empire could not be contained. Its weakness was exploited by the other European powers for commercial interest, and by 1900 foreign debt and political discontent meant the empire was near collapse. There were divisions between Turks, Slavs and other Europeans in the Turkish Empire, including between Christians and Muslims. European interference led to widespread Muslim resentment. The Sultan was overthrown in 1909 by the 'Young Turks', a group whose aim was to modernize Turkey, economically and politically.

The Eastern Question

The 'question' of what to do about the decaying Ottoman Empire preoccupied the other European Powers. As its decline would lead to a power vacuum in the territories it formerly ruled over, there was the potential for a conflict between the powers for the spoils. Most European powers agreed the best solution for the time being was to 'prop up' the Turkish regime, and try to persuade it to modernize. The Russians, on the other hand, preferred to promote self-government for the Balkan states, but Austria-Hungary was deeply opposed to this idea.

SUMMARY OF KEY CHARACTERISTICS OF THE MAJOR POWERS, c. 1900	
Great Britain	Parliamentary Monarchy / Trade / Industry / Maritime power / Empire
Germany	Authoritarian State / Military power / Industrial power
Russia	Autocratic Tsardom / Some industrialization / Foreign debt
France	Democratic Republic / Slow economic growth / Empire
Austria-Hungary	Dual Monarchy / Nationalities problems
Turkey	Sultanate / Decline of empire

Long-term causes of World War I

As we have seen, the creation of a new state in Europe – particularly one with the economic, military and imperial potential of Germany – created a certain amount of nervousness among other European countries. France, of course, was particularly hostile in its attitude towards Germany after the humiliation of the war in 1870 and the loss of Alsace-Lorraine. Nevertheless, Germany under its first ruler, Kaiser Wilhelm I, and its chancellor, Bismarck, did not pursue an aggressive foreign policy. Bismarck worked at creating a web of alliances that would protect Germany from future attack and would allow Germany to work on consolidating its position in Europe. These alliances can be seen below. Germany's main aim was to keep France isolated and stay allied with Russia to prevent the possibility of a two-front war.

Bismarck's web of alliances

The *Dreikaiserbund* or Three Emperors' League (1873)

The *Dreikaiserbund* joined Germany, Russia and Austria-Hungary into an alliance. Its terms were very vague, but it served Bismarck's purpose of keeping France isolated.

The Dual Alliance (1879)

Austria-Hungary and Russia came into conflict over events in the Balkans and the *Dreikaiserbund* collapsed. In its place, Bismarck made a separate treaty with the Austrians. This alliance was part of Bismarck's system to limit the possibility of war between the European powers, and was primarily defensive. Germany and Austria-Hungary agreed to assist one another if Russia attacked them. Each country also agreed to remain neutral if the other was attacked by another European country.

The Three Emperors' Alliance (1881)

Russia, feeling isolated in Europe, turned back to Germany, and Bismarck drew up a revised version of the *Drieskaiserbund*. Again, this offered Bismarck security. The terms of the alliance included an agreement that if either Russia, Germany or Austria were at war with another power, the others would remain neutral. The alliance also tried to resolve Austro-Russian disputes in the Balkans.

The Triple Alliance (1882)

This alliance was between Germany, Austria-Hungary and Italy. If any of the signatories were attacked by two or more powers, the others promised to lend assistance.

Two-front war
Military commanders usually want to avoid a two-front war, which means dividing their forces to meet an enemy in two different places. In the case of World War I, this would mean the German Army sending men, ammunition, supplies and communications to both the Western and Eastern Fronts, thus limiting their capacity to fight on either **front** (see later information on the Schlieffen Plan).

To access worksheet 2.1 on the Dual Alliance, please visit www.pearsonbacconline.com and follow the on-screen instructions.

The Reinsurance Treaty (1887)

The Three Emperors' Alliance fell to pieces due to Balkan problems in 1885. Thus, this separate treaty with Russia was drawn up in order to avoid any risk of a war on two fronts. Bismarck had to make new arrangements to ensure that Germany stayed friendly with Russia.

The New Course and *Weltpolitik*

In 1888, the young and ambitious Wilhelm II came to the throne in Germany, and Bismarck was replaced as Chancellor by Leo von Caprivi in 1890. Kaiser Wilhelm II and Caprivi took German foreign policy on a 'new course' that would overturn Bismarck's carefully nurtured system of alliances. The Reinsurance Treaty with Russia was allowed to lapse that year, creating the conditions for the Franco-Russian Alliance of 1894. Militarily, the alliance promised mutual assistance if either was attacked by Germany. It also agreed immediate mobilization in response to any member of the Triple Alliance mobilizing. There was also a political clause, which agreed mutual support in imperial disputes; the focus of this clause was essentially anti-British. Bismarck's system was destroyed. France was free of its isolation, and Germany now could face a war on two fronts.

Undeterred, however, German policy makers from the mid 1890s began to look beyond Europe and to follow a policy that they hoped would make Germany a colonial power, with an overseas empire and navy. Such a policy would also have the benefit of diverting the German population away from the social and political problems at home. This policy, known as **Weltpolitik** – which was supported by various patriotic groups such as the Pan-German League within Germany – was bound to have an impact on Germany's relations with other countries.

Wilhelm II.

Wilhelm II

Wilhelm was the son of Prince Frederick Wilhelm of Prussia and Victoria (who was the daughter of Queen Victoria). He was a keen advocate of all things military. He loved wearing, and having himself photographed in, his numerous uniforms, and he surrounded himself with the elite of German military society. Wilhelm acted very much as an autocratic monarch and also had a volatile and unpredictable personality. He was a strong opponent of **socialism** and vigorously believed in *Weltpolitik* – increasing the global strength of Germany through building up the German navy and colonial expansion.

STUDENT STUDY SECTION

Document analysis

I hope Europe will gradually come to realize the fundamental principle of my policy: leadership in the peaceful sense – a sort of Napoleonic supremacy… I am of the opinion that it is already a success that I, having come to govern at so early an age, stand at the head of German armed might yet have left my sword in its scabbard and have given up Bismarck's policy of externally causing disruption to replace it with a peaceful foreign situation such as we have not known for many years.

The Kaiser to Botho Graf zu Eulenburg, July 1892. Eulenburg was a close friend of Kaiser Wilhelm II and served as his Minister of the Interior until 1882.

Question

According to the Kaiser, what does he hope to achieve in foreign policy?

Imperialism

One of the main causes of tension between the European powers in 1880–1905 was colonial rivalries. Over the course of the 19th century, the Europeans had increased their domination of countries in Africa and the Far East and competed to build vast empires. This effort was initially driven by economic motives (cheap raw materials, new markets and low-cost labour forces). Over the course of the century, however, territorial acquisition increasingly occurred due to a mixture of the Social Darwinian belief that the spread of Western civilization was 'God's work' and also nationalistic competition with the other European powers (and to a certain extent the USA).

Germany's desire to make its influence felt outside Europe was to bring it into conflict with the more established colonial powers, particularly Britain. An example of this effect occurred in 1896, when the German Kaiser caused great offence in Britain over his response to the so-called Jameson Raid in December 1895. The Jameson Raid was a failed attempt by Britain to incite a rising against the Boer Republic of the Transvaal in southern Africa. It was led by a Dr Jameson, who was an administrator in the British South Africa Company, but led to the resignation of Cecil Rhodes, the governor of Cape Colony, when it became clear that he was also involved in the planning of this 'illegal' operation. Germany sent a telegram to the Boer leader, Stephanus Johannes Paulus Kruger, on 3 January 1896 congratulating him on his success in resisting the British attack:

> *I would like to express my sincere congratulations that you and your peoples have succeeded, without having to invoke the help of friendly powers, in restoring peace with your own resources in face of armed bands which have broken into your country as disturbers of the peace and have been able to preserve the independence of your country against attacks from outside.*

This telegram caused great offence in Britain. The coverage of the affair by the British press led to national outrage among the British public.

Social Darwinism

Social Darwinism was the application of some of Charles Darwin's theories of evolution to human societies. Herbert Spencer, an English philosopher, produced a very simplified version of Darwin's ideas that focused on the theory of 'survival of the fittest'. He suggested that countries were destined to evolve like species; through conflict the 'fittest' would triumph and the weakest die out. Peace was not an option – war *was* evolution. This theory gained influence in the latter half of the 19th century across European societies.

The emergence of the alliance system

Germany's policy of *Weltpolitik* brought it into conflict with Britain in other ways as well. In 1897, Admiral von Tirpitz was appointed as Secretary of State for the Navy. He shared the Kaiser's belief that Germany should mount a naval challenge to Britain, and within a year he had pushed a Naval Law through the Reichstag that provided for the building of 17 ships over the next seven years. This bill was followed by a second Naval Law in 1900.

Britain quickly responded to this threat to its naval supremacy. It was clear to many in Britain that the British position of 'Splendid Isolation' was no longer appropriate or useful. Britain had clashed with France in the Sudan over the territory around Fashoda and was a rival with Russia in the Far East over China. Now, with Germany challenging Britain, it seemed the right time to seek security through alliances. Thus in 1902, Britain made an alliance with Japan, which gave Britain an ally in the Far East and allowed the Royal Navy to bring back warships from this area. This alliance was followed by an **entente** with France. Although this entente was not a formal alliance, it settled the rivalry between the two nations over colonial issues and set a completely new direction for Anglo-French relations.

In 1907, Britain and Russia reached agreement over their relationship with Persia, Tibet and Afghanistan, again reducing British concern over security in India and the Far East. France had already secured Russia as an ally following Germany's failure to renew the Reinsurance Treaty of 1887. Now Russia, France and Britain joined together in the Triple Entente. German naval expansion had thus forced Britain into seeking an agreement with its former colonial rivals, leaving Germany concerned that it was becoming 'encircled'. Europe was now divided into two alliance systems, the Triple Entente and the Triple Alliance.

The naval race

A British dreadnought-class battleship.

The other effect of Germany's maritime challenge to Britain was to start a naval arms race. In 1906, Britain had launched a super-battleship, HMS *Dreadnought*. The battleship's name literally meant that this ship 'feared nothing', as its speed, range and firepower were far superior to those of any other existing battleship. The irony of the creation of this battleship was that it potentially nullified Britain's historical naval advantage over the other great powers. The dreadnought class made all the older battleships obsolete; this meant that in battleship terms Britain had taken the race back to zero and their traditional numerical advantage was lost. A competitor now could construct similar battleships and catch up with Britain. This situation triggered a 'naval scare' in the winter of 1908–09, as fears grew concerning Germany's rapidly expanding fleet. The British government responded by ordering the construction of eight battleships in 1909.

The naval race also caused a complete change of mood within the British population itself, as newspapers and popular fiction now portrayed Germany (rather than France or Russia) as the new enemy threatening Britain. As Norman Lowe observes, Britain's willingness to go to war in 1914 owed a lot to the tensions generated by the naval race.

EUROPEAN ECONOMIC AND MILITARY STRENGTH, 1900						
	France	Germany	Austria-Hungary	Britain	Russia	Italy
Population	38,641,333	56,367,176	45,015,000	41,605,323	132,960,000	32,450,000
Personnel in regular army	589,541	589,266	397,316	280,000	860,000	261,728
First-class battleships	13	14	0	38	13	9
Second-class battleships	10	0	6	11	10	5
Iron and steel production (tons p.a.)	3,250,000	13,790,000	2,580,000	13,860,000	5,015,000	5,000,000
Annual value of foreign trade (£)	460,408,000	545,205,000	151,599,000	877,448,917	141,799,000	132,970,000
Merchant fleet (net tonnage)	1,037,720	1,941,645	313,689	9,304,108	633,820	945,000

Table adapted from Purnell's *History of the Twentieth Century*, 1968

Study the statistics carefully for the different countries.

Questions

1 Which categories do you think are the most important for indicating the strength of a country in war?

2 Overall, which alliance system seems to be the strongest?

Discussion question

To what extent would you agree that Germany's position in 1900 was less secure than it had been in 1890?

Tirpitz's Risk Theory
Admiral von Tirpitz felt that if Germany could build enough ships so that it could be a threat to Britain, then Britain would decide that it had to avoid conflict with Germany. In fact, he believed that Britain would be inclined to seek accommodation with Germany and thus Germany would be able to pursue *Weltpolitik* without British interference. As you can see, however, the plan pushed Britain into making alliances and also into increasing and modernizing its own navy while turning government and public opinion against Germany.

The situation in the Balkans

The Balkans was a very unstable area that also contributed to the tensions that existed in Europe before 1914. As you have already read in the introductory section to this chapter, three different empires had interests here – Turkey, Austria-Hungary and Russia.

Turkey

Turkey had once ruled over the whole of the Balkans, but was now largely impotent. The Serbs, Greeks and Bulgars had already revolted and set up their own independent nation states and now Turkey was struggling to hold on to its remaining Balkan territories.

Austria-Hungary

The Austrians by 1900 were losing their grip on their multi-ethnic empire. Of the various ethnic groups in Austria-Hungary, the most forceful in their demands for independence were the southern Slavs – the Serbs, Croats and Slovenes – who were beginning to look to Serbia for support. They wanted to break away and form a South Slav kingdom with their neighbour, Serbia. Serbia was thus seen as a threat by Austria-Hungary.

Russia

Russia also had ambitions in the Balkans. First, the Russians sympathized with their fellow Slavs; indeed, Russia saw itself as the champion of the Slav people. Second, the Balkans was strategically important to Russia. The straits of Constantinople had to be kept open to Russian ships en route from the Mediterranean to the Black Sea. With ports in the north of Russia's vast empire iced over for six months of the year, continued access to warm-water ports was vital.

The fact that Turkey's power was so weak and could in fact collapse at any moment led the powers to talk of the 'Eastern question', i.e. what would happen in the Balkans if and when this situation arose. Clearly, both Austria-Hungary and Russia hoped to benefit from Turkey's declining power.

Growing tension in the Balkans after 1900

In June 1903, the pro-Austrian King Alexander of Serbia was murdered and replaced by the Russophile King Peter, who was determined to reduce Austro-Hungarian influence. This appointment caused great anxiety in Austria-Hungary, which already feared the influence of a strong Serbia on their multi-ethnic empire. A **tariff** war began in 1905–06, and the Serbs turned to France for arms and finance. Tension increased when the uncompromising Baron von Aehrenthal became Austria's foreign minister. He believed that an aggressive foreign policy would demonstrate that Austria was still a power to be reckoned with and would stamp out Serbian aspirations.

Short-term causes: the crisis years (1905–13)

Between the years 1905 and 1913, there were several crises which, though they did not lead to war, nevertheless increased tension between the two alliance blocs in Europe and also created greater instability in the Balkans.

The Moroccan Crisis (1905)

A pre-World War I German cartoon. The caption reads: 'The Franco-English Parliamentarian Alliance (Face and About-face)'.

1903   · JUGEND ·   Nr. 50

HURRRAAA FOR GREAT BRITAIN!   VIVE LA FRANCE

STERN

Die französisch-englische Parlamentarier-Verbrüderung
(Avers und Revers)

STUDENT STUDY SECTION

Cartoon analysis

What is the German view of the Entente Cordiale, according to this cartoonist?

Germany was worried by the new relationship between Britain and France and set out to break up the entente by attacking France in Morocco. Germany's plan was to expose the weakness of this new friendship. As part of the entente agreement, Britain supported a French takeover of Morocco in return for France recognizing Britain's position in Egypt. Morocco was one of the few remaining areas of Africa not controlled by a European power. The Germans thus announced that they would assist the Sultan of Morocco to maintain his independence and demanded an international conference to discuss the situation.

An atmosphere of crisis and the threat of war was cultivated by the Germans throughout 1905, until the French gave in and agreed to a conference at Algeciras, Spain, in 1906. Much to the surprise of Germany, the British decided to back the French and their demands for influence in Morocco. The Germans had little support at the conference, and after several weeks had to admit defeat. Their only gain was a guarantee of their commercial interests.

The results of the first Moroccan Crisis were a disaster for Germany:

- Germany had not gained notable concessions in North Africa, which was a failure for *Weltpolitik* and a blow for German pride.
- Germany had not undermined the Entente Cordiale – they had strengthened it. Military talks between France and Britain were initiated in January 1906. British foreign policy was now directed to support French interests.
- Several states had considered war as a possible outcome of the crisis, thus signalling an end to the relatively long period of peaceful relations in Europe.
- Germany was now seen as the key threat to British interests.

The Bosnian Crisis (1908)

Following the first Moroccan Crisis, the Anglo-Russian Entente of 1907 was signed, thus confirming to many Germans the idea of a conspiracy to encircle and contain them. This fear of encirclement forced Germany into a much closer relationship with its Triple Alliance partner, Austria-Hungary, a shift that was to have an impact in both the Bosnian Crisis of 1908 and the later Balkan Crisis of 1914.

In 1908, an internal crisis in the Ottoman Empire caused by the Young Turks revolution again raised the issue of the Eastern Question, and Austria-Hungary decided to act by annexing the two provinces of Bosnia and Herzegovina that Austria-Hungary had occupied since 1878, but which were still formally Turkish. The Austro-Hungarian annexation caused outrage in Serbia, which had hoped that these provinces would ultimately form part of a Greater Serbia and provide access to the sea. Russia's Foreign Minister, Alexander Petrovich Izvolsky, had earlier met with Aehrenthal and secretly given Russia's acceptance for this move on the understanding that Austria would support Russia's demands for a revision of the treaties governing the closure of the Bosporus and Dardanelles. However, Aehrenthal went ahead with the annexation before Izvolsky had managed to gain any international support for his plan. In fact, not only did he encounter hostile reactions in London and Paris, but the Russian Prime Minister, Pyotr Stolypin, and the Tsar were unenthusiastic about any agreement giving Austria control over fellow Slavs.

Relations between Austria-Hungary and Russia became very strained and there was talk of war. It was at this point, in January 1909, that Germany decided to stand 'shoulder to shoulder' with its ally. Germany reassured Austria-Hungary that it would mobilize in support if Austria-Hungary went to war with Serbia. By contrast, Russia had little support from Britain or France. The Russians – weakened by the 1904–05 war with Japan – had no alternative but to capitulate to the German 'ultimatum' and recognize Austro-Hungarian

Entente Cordiale

The Entente Cordiale marked the end of almost a thousand years of periodic conflict between Britain and France. It was a clear demonstration of the re-alignment between the old European powers in response to the perceived threat from the new European power, Germany. The most important of the three documents that made up the Entente Cordiale was an agreement over Egypt and Morocco. The British were to allow French influence over Morocco, while the French recognized British influence in Egypt. There was also a guarantee of free passage through the Suez Canal. The other documents recognized each others' rights in West and Central Africa, and in Thailand, Madagascar and the New Hebrides.

annexation of Bosnia. Serbia, facing the overwhelming military potential of Austria-Hungary and Germany, backed down.

The results of the crisis were important in raising tension in the region, and between the alliance blocs:

- Russia had suffered another international humiliation, following on from its defeat by Japan. It was unlikely that Russia could back down from another crisis situation and retain international influence and political stability at home. Russia now embarked on a massive rearmament programme.
- Serbia was enraged by the affair, and it led to an increase in nationalist feeling. The Austrian minister in Belgrade reported in 1909 that 'here all think of revenge, which is only to be carried out with the help of the Russians.'
- The alliance between Germany and Austria-Hungary appeared stronger than the commitments of the Triple Entente.
- It ended the era of cooperation in the Balkans between Russia and Austria-Hungary; the situation in the Balkans became much more unstable.
- Germany had opted to encourage Austro-Hungarian expansion rather than acting to restrain their approach to the region.

The Second Moroccan (Agadir) Crisis (1911)

In May 1911, France sent troops to Fez, Morocco, on the request of the Sultan to suppress a revolt that had broken out. The Germans saw this as the beginning of a French takeover of Morocco and sent a German gunboat, the *Panther,* to Agadir, a small port on Morocco's Atlantic coast, hoping to pressurize the French into giving them some compensation for such an action.

The Germans were too ambitious in their claims, demanding the whole of the French Congo. This assertiveness was popular with public opinion in Germany, but such 'gunboat diplomacy' as it was called by the British implied the threat of war. Britain, worried that the Germans might acquire Agadir as a naval base that would threaten its naval routes to Gibraltar, made its position clear. David Lloyd George (Britain's Chancellor of the Exchequer) gave a speech – called the Mansion House Speech – to warn Germany off. He said that Britain would not stand by and watch while 'her interests were affected'. This speech turned the Franco-German crisis into an Anglo-German confrontation. In November the crisis was finally resolved when Germany accepted far less compensation – two strips of territory in the French Congo.

The results of this crisis, again, increased tension between the European powers:

- German public opinion was hostile to the settlement and critical of their government's handling of the crisis, which was another failure for the policy of *Weltpolitik.*
- The entente between Britain and France was again strengthened. Naval negotiations between the two began in 1912, and Britain agreed a commitment to the defence of France by 1913.
- There was increased tension and hostility between Germany and Britain.

Thus, although imperial rivalries in themselves did not necessarily mean war (and in fact there had also been many agreements on colonial issues in the years before the war), nevertheless incidents such as those in Morocco helped to increase mutual suspicion and hostility.

Document analysis

Document A

L'INGORDO
TROP DUR

An Italian photo from the early 1900s shows the Kaiser attempting to eat the world. The caption roughly translates as 'The glutton finds this too hard.'

Document B

AGADIR

A German cartoon: 'The mailed fist of Agadir' c. 1912.

Document C

9 November 1905 – A leading member of the Reichstag was applauded when he declared:

Now we know where our enemy stands… The German people now knows when it seeks its place in the sun, when it seeks the place allotted to it by destiny … When the hour of decision comes we are prepared for sacrifices, both of blood and of treasure.

Quoted in Luigi Albertini, *The Origins of the War of 1914*, Volume 1, 2005

Document D

Cartoon in *Punch* magazine, 2 August 1911.

Questions

1   What are the messages of Documents A, B and C regarding the aims and methods of Germany in its quest for colonies?

2   What similarities are there between the messages of Documents B and C?

3   What do you think the caption of Document D, a 1911 cartoon, could have been?

Student review questions

1   Why had Germany interfered in Morocco in 1905 and 1911?

2   For what reasons did Germany strengthen its alliance with Austria-Hungary?

3   Why were the results of the Moroccan crises disappointing for Germany?

4   To what extent was German policy 'miscalculated'?

5   Explain why the Balkans situation was more dangerous as a result of the annexation of Bosnia-Herzegovina.

First Balkan War (1912)

In 1912, encouraged by the Russians, the Balkan states of Serbia, Greece and Montenegro formed a Balkan alliance. Their key objective was to force Turkey from the Balkans by taking Macedonia and dividing it up between themselves. Turkey was already weakened by a war with Italy over Tripolitania the year before and they were almost completely driven out of the Balkans in seven weeks. Austria was horrified; it could not accept a strengthened Serbia and Austrian generals called for war. There was a danger, however, that Russia would support its ally, Serbia, and that events could spiral into a wider European war.

Sir Edward Grey, the British Foreign Secretary, was anxious to stop the war spreading, and so called a peace conference in London. As a result of this conference, the former Turkish lands were divided up between the Balkan states. Yet Austria-Hungary succeeded in containing Serbia by getting the conference to agree to the creation of Albania, which was placed between Serbia and the Adriatic Sea. This agreement caused more resentment between Serbia and Austria-Hungary.

The Second Balkan War (1913)

Due to the disagreement over the spoils of the First Balkan War, *another* war broke out in the Balkans in July 1913. Bulgaria now went to war against Serbia and Greece, over territory Serbia had occupied. The Bulgarians felt that there were too many Bulgarians living in areas given to Serbia and Greece, namely Macedonia and Salonika.

The Austro-Hungarian Foreign Minister, Count Leopold Berchtold, did not approach this situation with the same caution that he had displayed towards the First Balkan War. He asked for German assistance, as he believed that the Russians would come in to support the Serbs this time. The German government, however, urged Austrian restraint.

The Serbs, Greeks and, ultimately, Turkey (which had joined in the fight in an attempt to redress some of its losses from the previous year's fighting) defeated Bulgaria. At the Treaty of Bucharest signed in August 1913, Bulgaria lost nearly all the lands it had won in the first war to Greece and Serbia. The war also had far-reaching consequences for Europe. Although a general war between the European powers had again been prevented, the essential causes of tension were exacerbated:

- Serbia was again successful. This fact encouraged the already strong nationalist feeing within Serbia.
- Serbia had doubled in size as a result of the two Balkan wars.
- Serbia had proved itself militarily, and had an army of 200,000 men.
- Serbia's victories were diplomatic successes for Russia, and encouraged Russia to stand by its ally.
- Austria-Hungary was now convinced that it needed to crush Serbia.
- By association, the outcome of the two wars was a diplomatic defeat for Germany, which now drew ever closer to Austria-Hungary.

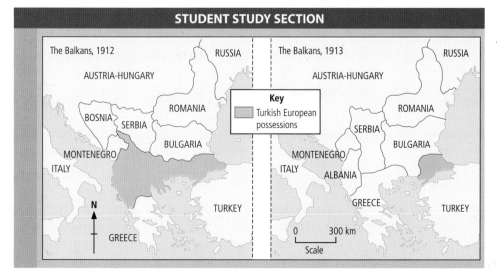

STUDENT STUDY SECTION

The Balkans, 1912–13.

Questions

1 Explain the position/feelings of each of the following states following the Second Balkan War:
   • Austria-Hungary
   • Serbia
   • Bulgaria
   • Turkey

2 For what reasons had the Balkan Wars of 1912 and 1913 not escalated into a general European War?

The international situation by 1913

The crises of 1905–13 had seen a marked deterioration in international relations. There was increasing division between the two alliance systems and an increase in the general armaments race, alongside the naval race that already existed between Germany and Britain. Nationalist fervour (see below) was rising in European countries. Each crisis had passed without a major European war, but every subsequent crisis exacerbated the tension and made a future conflict more likely. War was by no means inevitable at this stage, though. Clearly if there was to be another crisis, careful handling of the situation by the Great Powers would be vital.

Other developments, 1900–13

Alongside the international crises, other developments were occurring in European countries. These developments were fed and encouraged by the actual events that you have already read about.

The will to make war

Literature, the press and education did much to prepare the public of Europe for war by portraying it as something that would be short and heroic. Nationalism had also become a more aggressive force in many of the major states, and this trend was encouraged by the popular press, which exaggerated international incidents to inflame public opinion, and by right-wing pressure groups such as the Pan-German League and Action Française.

…the reactions of ordinary people in the crisis of 1914 were the result of the history they had learnt at school, the stories about the national past which they had been told as children and an instinctive sense of loyalty and solidarity with their neighbours and workmates. In each country, children were taught the duties of patriotism and the glory of past national achievements… In each country children were being taught to take pride in their historical tradition and to respect what were regarded as characteristic national virtues … [The] reactions in 1914 … and the patriotic language with which the war was greeted reflected the sentiments of a national tradition absorbed over many years.

From James Joll, *The Origins of the First World War*, 1992

The arms race and militarism

The naval arms race was actually part of a more general arms race. Between 1870 and 1914, military spending by the European powers increased by 300 per cent. The increase in the European population made it possible to have large **standing armies**, and **conscription** was introduced in all continental countries after 1871. In addition, there was a massive increase in armaments. Although there were some attempts to stop the arms build-up – for instance, at conferences at The Hague in 1899 and 1907 – no limits on arms production were agreed upon, although some agreements were made on restricting war practices.

Spending on armaments 1872–1912

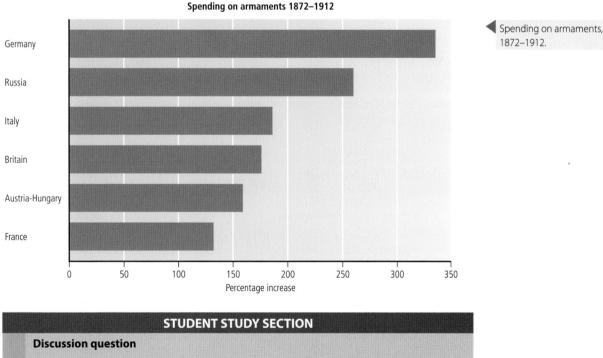

Spending on armaments, 1872–1912.

War plans

Every European power made detailed plans regarding what to do should war break out. One of the most important effects of the alliance systems is that they reduced the flexibility of the Great Powers' response to crises, and this issue can be seen most clearly in the German war plan. This plan was drawn up by German field marshal Count Alfred von Schlieffen and was intended to deal with the implications of the Triple Entente and the difficulty of fighting a two-front war. Knowing that it would take Russia six weeks to mobilize, Schlieffen worked out a plan that would involve crushing France first. He calculated that Germany could invade France through Belgium, Holland and Luxembourg (thereby bypassing the French defences along the German–French border) and then move down to encircle Paris. With Paris captured, troops could be moved swiftly to meet the Russian troops along the Eastern Front.

In 1911, Schlieffen's successor, Helmuth von Moltke, modified the plan by reducing the amount of neutral territory that Germany would pass through and by changing the deployment of troops (see map below). However, it still remained inflexible, and contained miscalculations regarding the impact of marching though Belgium, the amount of time Russia would take to mobilize, and Britain's effectiveness in coming to the aid of France.

All other countries had war plans as well:

- France's Plan 17 involved a high-speed mobilization of the majority of its forces and a swift attack to capture Alsace and Lorraine before crossing the Rhine into Germany.
- Russia had a plan to attack Austria-Hungary and Germany.
- Austria-Hungary had two plans – Plan R and Plan B. The plans differed in the amount of troops allocated to fighting Russia and Serbia.

Pre-World War I war plans. ▶

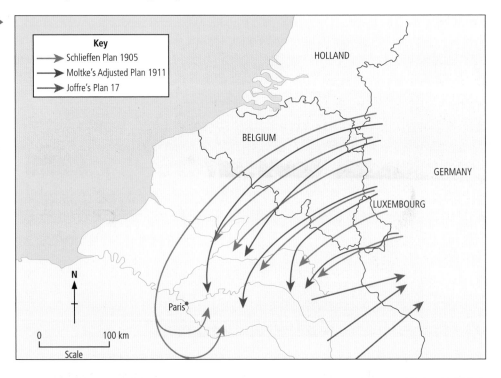

Key
→ Schlieffen Plan 1905
→ Moltke's Adjusted Plan 1911
→ Joffre's Plan 17

HOLLAND

BELGIUM

GERMANY

LUXEMBOURG

N

Paris

0   100 km
Scale

To access worksheet 2.2 on the causes of World War I, please visit www. pearsonbacconline. com and follow the on-screen instructions.

STUDENT STUDY SECTION

Document analysis

All the great powers had vast conscript armies. These armies of course were not maintained in peace time. They were brought together by mobilisation… All mobilisation plans depended on the railways. At that time the automobile was hardly used, and railways demand timetables.

All the mobilisation plans had been timed to the minute, months or even years before and they would not be changed… [A change] in one direction would ruin them in every other direction. Any attempt for instance by the Austrians to mobilise against Serbia would mean that they could not then mobilise as well against Russia because two lots of trains would be running against each other… Any alteration in the mobilisation plan meant not a delay for 24 hours but for at least six months before the next lot of timetables were ready.

From A.J.P. Taylor, *How Wars Begin*, 1979

The immediate causes of the war: July Crisis (1914)

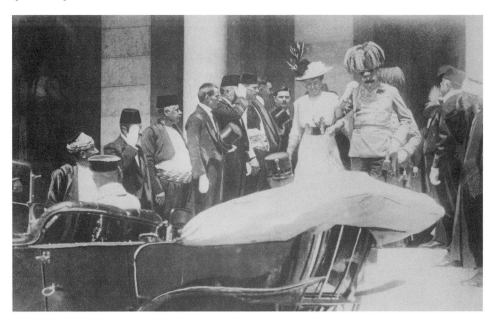

The Archduke Franz Ferdinand and his wife Sophie.

To access worksheet 2.3 on the assassination of Franz Ferdinand, please visit www.pearsonbacconline.com and follow the on-screen instructions.

The first few months of 1914 were a relatively calm period between the European states. There was even optimism that should another conflict erupt in the Balkans this would, for a third time in as many years, be contained locally. The event that broke the calm was the shooting dead of the heir to the Austro-Hungarian throne, and his wife, on 28 June 1914. Archduke Franz Ferdinand was on an official visit to Sarajevo, the capital of Bosnia, with his wife when a 19-year-old terrorist shot them both at point blank range. The assassin was Gavrilo Princip. He had been working with a small group of terrorists, armed by the Serbian Black Hand movement. Their aim in the assassination is not entirely clear, but their objective was the unification of all Slavs from the Austro-Hungarian Empire into a Greater Serbia. The Archduke was clearly symbolic of the Austro-Hungarian regime. It was unclear to what degree the Serbian government was involved with the group – the head of the Black Hand was a colonel in the Serbian General Staff.

The Austrian government saw its chance to crush Serbia, but initially hesitated. They knew that an attack on Serbia would bring in the Russians, so they needed assurances from their

King Peter of Serbia.

ally Germany that they would support them. On 5 July 1914, the Kaiser and his chancellor, Theobald von Bethmann-Hollweg, issued Austria a 'blank cheque'. The blank cheque was the German guarantee of unconditional support. Thus, the Germans were not exercising their power to restrain Austria-Hungary, as they had the previous year.

STUDENT STUDY SECTION

Document analysis

The Kaiser's 'blank cheque' to Austria

The following is a report of a famous conversation between Wilhelm II and the Austrian ambassador in Berlin, Count Szogyeny, in which the Kaiser seemed to promise his support for Austria-Hungary under any conditions.

Berlin 5 July 1914   *tel.237 Strictly Confidential*

…the Kaiser authorized me to inform our gracious majesty that we might in this case, as in all others, rely upon Germany's full support … he did not doubt in the least that Herr von Bethmann Hollweg would agree with him. Especially as far as our action against Serbia was concerned. But it was his [Kaiser Wilhelm's] opinion that this action must not be delayed. Russia's attitude will no doubt be hostile, but to this he has for years been prepared, and should a war between Austria-Hungary and Russia be unavoidable, we might be convinced that Germany, our old faithful ally, would stand at our side. Russia at the present time was in no way prepared for war, and would think twice before it appealed to arms … if we had really recognized the necessity of warlike action against Serbia, he [Kaiser Wilhelm] would regret it if we did not make use of the present moment, which is all in our favour…

From Immanuel Geiss (ed.), *July 1914: The Outbreak of the First World War – Selected Documents*, 1967

Question

How useful is this document for historians studying the immediate causes of the Great War?

Had the Austro-Hungarian response, and its bombardment of Sarajavo, been immediate, it might have averted the escalation of events that followed. Despite the blank cheque, however, their response to the crisis took nearly a whole month to manifest itself. Berchtold wanted an **ultimatum** sent to the Serb government, but he also intended that the demands of the ultimatum be so severe that the Serb sovereign government could never agree to them. The drawing up of the ultimatum took until mid July, and this delay meant they could no longer present their response as a shock reaction to the assassination; rather, they would appear far more calculating.

Then there was a further delay. The French President was in Russia until 23 July and the Austrians did not want the Russians to be able to liaise directly with their ally France concerning the demands. So finally, on 23 July, the ultimatum was sent, and a response from Serbia was required within 48 hours.

The Russians were shocked when they reviewed the terms on 24 July. Yet the Serb response was conciliatory, and most European powers thought that this might end the crisis. Such was not to be the case. Although the Kaiser suggested that the Serb response removed the 'cause for war', the Austro-Hungarians claimed it was too late to change their minds – they declared war on Serbia and bombarded Belgrade.

The Russians, determined to take a firm stance this time in the Balkans, ordered general mobilization on 30 July. Thus, the Third Balkan War had begun – Serbia and Russia against Austria-Hungary. Germany then declared war on Russia and began mobilization on 1 August. Due to the demands of the Schlieffen Plan, Germany sent an ultimatum to France demanding guarantees of French neutrality. When France responded by declaring they would follow their 'own interests', Germany declared war on France on 3 August.

Germany's plan to take out France swiftly meant that its forces were to march through Belgium to avoid France's heavily fortified border defences. Britain, choosing to uphold an old treaty agreement with Belgium from 1839, threatened to defend Belgium if Germany did not respect its neutrality. When there was no response from Germany, Britain declared war on 4 August 1914.

The European powers, with their vast empires, were at war. The Great War had begun.

STUDENT STUDY SECTION

Review activity

Create your own timeline of World War I. You should divide the timeline into long-term, short-term and immediate causes.

Alternatively, list all the factors (people, events, underlying forces) that you think contributed to the outbreak of war and try to create a flow diagram or a mind map to show how these factors are linked and how they led to the outbreak of a general war in 1914.

IBLP link

At the beginning of this book, on p.x, you have a copy of the IB Learner Profile, which outlines the key attributes promoted by the IB to 'develop internationally minded people who, recognizing their common humanity and shared guardianship of the planet, help to create a better and more peaceful world.' IB learners should attempt to live the IBLP. Consider the approach and decisions made by the European governments and statesmen and attempt to identify when they were acting like IB learners, and when they were not. Try to give specific examples, e.g. which of the leaders and statesmen was 'knowledgeable' in their decision-making?

In pairs reflect on the ways in which the process of crisis management, and the final descent into a general European war, might have been different if the leaders of the Great Powers had been IB learners.

What was the contribution of each of the European Powers during the July Crisis to the outbreak of war?

Germany

The Kaiser had encouraged the Austro-Hungarians to seize the opportunity to attack Serbia in the 5 July blank cheque. However, Germany may have been predicting another Balkans war, not the spread of war generally across Europe. Even as late as 18 July 1914, many in Germany's government believed that a united front of Germany and Austria-Hungary, together with a swift response, would keep the Russians from involving themselves. The Kaiser went off on a cruise, and on his return declared that the Serb response to the Austro-Hungarian ultimatum removed the rationale for a war.

Nevertheless, Germany was risking drawing the powers into a general war. What was the motive?

- It had to support its ally, Austria-Hungary
- It had to prevent itself and Austria-Hungary being crushed by the entente powers
- Russia's military modernizations were increasing the country's potential for mobilization, and this could undermine the Schlieffen Plan
- German generals, e.g. von Moltke, believed that it was a favourable time for Germany to go to war with its enemies

German Chancellor Bethmann-Hollweg.

- War would provide a good distraction, and unifying effect, to overcome rising domestic problems in Germany
- War could improve the popularity of the Kaiser.

Once the Russians ordered mobilization, the Schlieffen Plan meant that Germany would have to draw in the French.

…it seems very unlikely that the Russians positively desired a major war. Mobilization for them meant preparation for a possible war. The Germans, however, interpreted mobilization as the virtual equivalent to a declaration of war, and Germany's Schlieffen Plan meant that the German army would have to attack and defeat France before moving eastwards to combat Russian forces.

From Robert Pearce and John Lowe, *Rivalry and Accord: International Relations, 1870–1914*, 2001

Thus Germany's responsiblity for the beginning of war was:
- Urging Austria-Hungary on with the 'blank cheque'
- Declaring war on Russia on 1 August
- Violating Belgian neutrality
- Invading France
- Bringing Britain into the conflict.

Austria-Hungary

It is clear that Austria-Hungary was determined to respond to the Sarajevo incident, seeing it as an opportunity 'to eliminate Serbia as a political factor in the Balkans'.

The contribution of Austria-Hungary to the outbreak of war was that it:
- Exaggerated the potential threat of Serbia and was determined to make war
- Delayed responding to the assassination, which contributed to the development of the July Crisis
- Declared war on Serbia on 28 July, only five days after the delivery of the ultimatum (which in any case had a time limit of only 48 hours)
- Refused to halt its military actions even though negotiations with Russia were scheduled for 30 July.

Russia

The Russian Foreign Minister saw in the ultimatum to Serbia a 'European War'. Sergei Sazonov was determined to take a firm stand, as he believed that the Germans had seen weakness in Russia's previous responses to Balkan crises. Although the Tsar was in favour of partial mobilization, his generals ordered general mobilization on 30 July.

The contribution of Russia to the beginning of the war was that it:
- Did not try to restrain Serb nationalism, even though it was likely to lead to instability in the Balkans
- Supported Serbia, which deepened the conflict and possibly caused Serbia to reject the ultimatum
- Mobilized, thus triggering a general European war.

France

France's government was hesitant about getting involved in a war, and, after the ignominious defeat of 1871, it did not want to provoke a general war. France's ally Russia mobilized without consulting the French, and then the Germans declared war on France on 3 August. France had not decided to go to war; it was swept into it.

The responsibility of France was that it gave Russia assurances of support before the July Crisis.

Britain

Britain was divided over whether to fight Germany or not. The Foreign Secretary, Edward Grey, wanted to, and there has been criticism of his and Britain's ambiguous position in the July Crisis. Some historians argue that Britain should have made it clear to Germany that it would stand 'shoulder to shoulder' with the French, and this might have deterred the Germans from pursuing the Schlieffen Plan. Yet Grey himself did not have a mandate to make his position clear, due to the mixed opinions of parliament.

The violation of the neutrality of Belgium led to some popular demands for war with Germany, and gave the British government grounds, based on the treaty of 1839, to declare war. The responsibility of Britain for the start of the war was that it should have made its position clearer during the July Crisis.

John Lowe also makes the following point:

...the most serious charge against Britain, however, is that her naval talks with Russia in 1914 convinced the German chancellor that the ring of encirclement around her was now complete. Grey's false denial of these secret talks also destroyed his credibility as a mediator in German eyes in the July crisis.

From Robert Pearce and John Lowe, *Rivalry and Accord: International Relations 1870–1914*, 2001

Historiography: the causes of the Great War

STUDENT STUDY SECTION

THE TRIUMPH OF "CULTURE."

'The Triumph of Culture', a cartoon from *Punch*.

Cartoon analysis

What is the message of this cartoon, which was published on 26 August 1914, following Germany's invasion of Belgium?

Responsibility for causing World War I was placed on the Central Powers by the Versailles settlement in 1919. In the war guilt clause of the Treaty of Versailles with Germany (Article 231), Germany had to accept responsibility as one of the aggressors. (This is discussed in more detail in Chapter 4.) While the Treaty of Versailles was being drawn up by the victorious powers, the German Foreign Office was already preparing documents from their archives attempting to prove that *all* belligerent states were to blame. To this end, between 1922 and 1927 the Germans produced 40 volumes of documents backing up this claim.

Other governments felt the need to respond by producing their own volumes of archives. Britain published 11 volumes between 1926 and 1938, France its own version of events in 1936, Austria produced 8 volumes in 1930 and the Soviet Union brought out justificatory publications in 1931 and 1934. Germany's argument gained international sympathy in the 1920s and 1930s. There was a growing sentiment that the war had been caused by the failure of international relations rather than the specific actions of one country. Lloyd George, writing in his memoirs in the 1930s, explained that 'the nations slithered over the brink into the boiling cauldron of war.'

S.B. Fay and H.E. Barnes were two American historians who, to some extent, supported the **revisionist** arguments put forward by Germany regarding the causes of World War I. Barnes argued in his 1927 book, *The Genesis of the War*, that Serbia, France and Russia were directly responsible for causing the war, that Austro-Hungarian responsibility was far less, and that least responsible were Germany and Britain. He supported this view by arguing that the Franco-Russian alliance became offensive from 1912, and their joint plans intended to manipulate any crisis in the Balkans to provoke a European war. Both countries decided that Serbia would be central to their war plans and early in 1914 officers in the Serbian General Staff plotted the assassination of Franz Ferdinand. The Russian and French motives for starting a European war were to attain their key objectives: the seizure of the Dardanelles Straits and the return of Alsace-Lorraine, which could only be realized through war.

An Italian historian, Luigi Albertini, wrote a thorough and coherent response to the revisionist argument in the 1940s. Albertini's argument focused on the responsibility of Austria-Hungary and Germany in the immediate term: Austria for the ultimatum to Serbia, and Germany for its 'naivety' in demanding a localized war. Overall, Germany was in his view fundamentally to blame, as it was clear that Britain could not have remained neutral in a war raging on the continent.

Fritz Fischer

In 1961, historian Fritz Fischer published *Germany's Aims in the First World War*; this was later translated into English. Fischer's argument focused responsibility back on Germany. He discovered a document called the 'September Programme' written by the German Chancellor, Bethmann-Hollweg. This memorandum, which was dated 9 September 1914 (after war had started), set out Germany's aims for domination of Europe (see Chapter 3 for more discussion of this aspiration). Fischer claimed that the document proved that the ruling elite had always had expansionist aims and that a war would allow them to fulfil these. War would also consolidate their power at home and deal with the threat of socialism. Fischer went on to argue in another book that the War Council of 1912 proved that Germany planned to launch a continental war in 1914. At this War Council, von Moltke had commented that 'in my opinion war is inevitable and the sooner the better.'

Fischer's argument is persuasive, as he links longer-term policies from 1897 to short-term and immediate actions taken in the July Crisis. In short, he is able to explain why war began.

Given the tenseness of the world situation in 1914 – a condition for which Germany's world policy, which had already led to three dangerous crises [those of 1905, 1908 and 1911], was in no small measure responsible – any limited or local war in Europe directly involving one great power must inevitably carry with it the imminent danger of a general war. As Germany willed and coveted the Austro-Serbian war and, in her confidence in her military superiority, deliberately faced the risk of a conflict with Russia and France, her leaders must bear a substantial share of the historical responsibility for the outbreak of a general war in 1914.

From Fritz Fischer, *Germany's Aims in the First World War*, 1967

Fischer's arguments have been criticized in the following ways:

- Fischer argues 'backwards' from the German 'September war aims'. There is limited evidence to prove Germany had specific expansionist aims prior to September 1914.
- The December War Council is also limited evidence; its importance is debatable as the imperial Chancellor was not present.
- Fischer holds the domestic crisis in Germany as central to why war was triggered in 1914. However, Bethmann-Hollweg dismissed war as a solution to the rise of socialism.
- It could be argued that German policy lacked coherency in the decade before 1914.
- Fischer focuses too much on Germany; this priority leads to an emphasis on German actions and he neglects the role played by other powers.

After Fischer

Since Fischer's theses on German guilt, historians have continued to debate the degree of German responsibility. Conservative German historians such as Gerhard Ritter rejected Fischer's view in the 1960s, although Immanuel Geiss defended Fischer by publishing a book of German documents undermining the arguments of the revisionists of the 1920s. However, the majority of historians around the world now agree that Germany played a pivotal role in the events that led to war through their policy of *Weltpolitik* and their role in the July Crisis, though this was not necessarily as part of any set 'plan' as Fischer had argued. 'It has been widely asserted that German policy held the key to the situation in the summer of 1914 and that it was the German desire to profit diplomatically and militarily from the crisis which widened the crisis from an Eastern European one to a continental and world war' (Ruth Henig, *The Origins of the First World War*, 1993).

Other historians have stressed different issues in explaining the outbreak of war, however.

John Keegan

Military historian John Keegan focuses on the events of the July Crisis. He suggests that although there were long-term and short-term tensions in Europe, war was in fact not inevitable. In fact, war was unlikely due to the interdependence and cooperation necessary for the European economy, plus royal, intellectual and religious links between the nations.

The key to Keegan's theory is the lack of communication during the July Crisis. He highlights the fact that the Kaiser had 50 people advising him – mostly independent and jealous of one another: 'The Kaiser … in the crisis of 1914 … found that he did not understand the machinery he was supposed to control, panicked and let a piece of paper determine events.' Keegan suggests that had Austria-Hungary acted immediately, the war might have been limited to a local affair. It was Austria-Hungary's reluctance to act alone, and its alliance with Germany, that led to the escalation.

No country used the communications available at the time, such as radio. Information was arriving fitfully, and was always 'incomplete'. The crisis that followed the expiration of the ultimatum to Serbia was not one that the European powers had expected and the key problem was that each nation failed to communicate its aims during the crisis:

- Austria-Hungary had wanted to punish Serbia, but lacked the courage to act alone. They did not want a general European war.
- Germany had wanted a diplomatic success that would leave its Austro-Hungarian ally stronger in European eyes. It did not want a general European war.
- Russia did not want a general European war, but had not calculated that support for Serbia would edge the danger of war closer.
- France had not mobilized, but was increasingly worried that Germany would mobilize against it.
- Britain only awoke to the real danger of the crisis on Saturday 25 July, and still hoped on Thursday 30 July that Russia would tolerate the punishment of Serbia. It would not, however, leave France in danger.

None of the European powers had communicated their objectives clearly in the July Crisis. Therefore, for Keegan it was the events of 31 July that were the turning point. The news of Russia's general mobilization and the German ultimatum to Russia and France made the issue one of peace or war. The Great Powers could step back from the brink, but a withdrawal would not be compatible with the status of each as a Great Power. The Serbs, a cause of the crisis in the first place, had been forgotten.

James Joll

Joll attempts to link impersonal forces – factors beyond the specific control or influence of an individual leader, regime or government – to personal or man-made forces. He suggests an atmosphere of intense tension was created by impersonal forces in the long and short terms, and personal decisions made in the July Crisis led to war. Joll explains the outbreak of war in terms of the decisions taken by the political leaders in 1914, but argues that these decisions were shaped by the impersonal factors, which meant that the leaders had only limited options open to them in the final days of the crisis.

Personal Forces	vs	Impersonal Forces
expansionist aims		capitalism
war plans		international anarchy
calculated decisions		alliances

Marxist historians have focused on the role of capitalism and imperialism as the key causes of World War I, but a limitation with focusing on impersonal factors is that they do not seem to explain why the war broke out when it did. Joll's argument links the impersonal factors to the personal decision-making taking place during the July Crisis, and thus, apparently, overcomes this problem.

Niall Ferguson

In *The Pity of War* (2006), Niall Ferguson suggests that Germany was moving away from a militaristic outlook prior to World War I, and highlights the increasing influence of the Social Democrat Party there. The German Social Democrat Party was founded as a socialist party, with a radical agenda for Germany. By 1912 they had gained the most votes in the Reichstag and their influence increasingly alarmed the Kaiser's regime. Ferguson sees Britain as heavily implicated in the causes of war, particularly Sir Edward Grey. Britain misinterpreted German ambitions and decided to act to impede German expansionism. Ferguson does not see war as inevitable in 1914, despite the forces of militarism, imperialism and secret diplomacy.

Review activity

Draw up a grid summarizing the views of the key historians that you have read about in this chapter. Also include the views of the historians in the Student Study Section below.

Document analysis

Study the sources below. As you read, decide what factor each historian is stressing as the key cause for war.

Document A

The First World War was not inevitable. Although it is essential to understand the underlying factors that formed the background to the July Crisis, it is equally essential to see how the immediate circumstances of the crisis fit into this background in a particular, and perhaps unique, way. Europe was not a powder keg waiting to explode; one crisis did not lead necessarily to another in an escalating series of confrontations that made war more and more difficult to avoid. Europe had successfully weathered a number of storms in the recent past; the alliances were not rigidly fixed; the war plans were always being revised and need not necessarily come into play. It is difficult to imagine a crisis in the Far East, in North Africa or in the Mediterranean that would have unleashed the series of events that arose from the assassination in Sarajevo. The First World War was, in the final analysis, fought for the future of the near east; whoever won this struggle would, it was believed, be in a position to dominate all of Europe. Germany and her ally made the bid for control; Russia and her allies resolved to stop them.

From Gordon Martel, *The Origins of the First World War*, 1987

Document B

[For Germany]…war seemed to offer … a solution to both domestic and foreign antagonisms. And if that war could be made appealing to all sections of the population – as a war against Tsarist Russia most certainly would be, even to ardent socialists – then so much the better. There can be no doubt that German leaders were prepared for war in 1914 and exploited the crisis of June–July 1914 to bring it about… Just as the Germans sought to increase their power, so Britain and France sought to contain it, by military means if necessary. In this sense it could be argued that both powers fought to try to restore the balance of power to Europe.

Countries went to war because they believed that they could achieve more through war than by diplomatic negotiation and that if they stood aside their status as great powers would be gravely affected…

From Ruth Henig, *The Origins of the First World War*, 1993

Document C

It used to be held that the system of alliances was in itself sufficient explanation for the outbreak of war, that the very existence of two camps made war inevitable sooner or later. But this approach has, for two reasons, an over-simple appreciation of the individual alliances. In the first place, the primary purpose of the alliances was defensive… Second, the way that war actually broke out bore little relation to treaty obligations…

There were, however, two ways in which the alliances did affect international relations and contribute to the growth of tension in Europe in the decade before 1914. First, they provided the links across which crises could spread from peripheral areas like North Africa and the Balkans to the major powers themselves. Normally, the dangers were seen and the connections cut; hence the Moroccan crises of 1906 and 1911 were allowed to fizzle out. But, as the sequence of events after Sarajevo showed only too clearly, the means existed whereby a local conflict could be transformed into a continental war. Second, the alliances had a direct bearing on the arms race and the development of military schedules.

From Stephen J. Lee, *Aspects of European History 1789–1980*, 1988

Question

1   Read Documents A, B and C. Briefly summarize the points made in each source. Compare and contrast these arguments with those of the historians discussed on pp.32–34.

Essay writing guidelines.

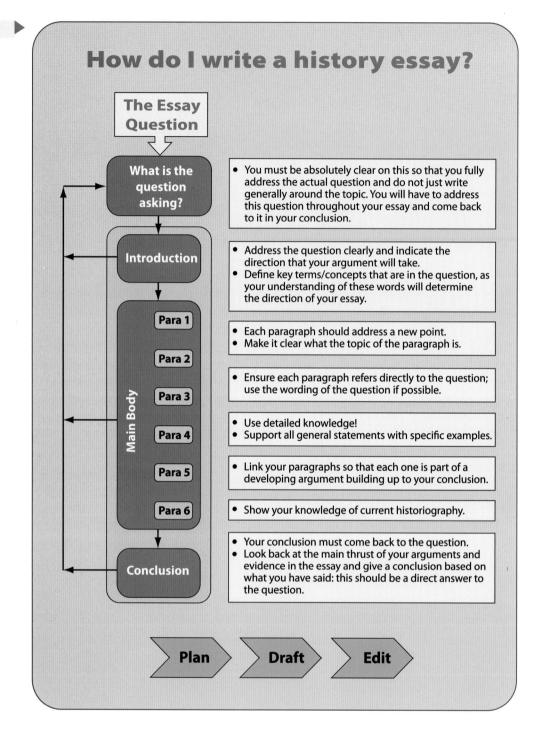

How do I write a history essay?

The Essay Question

What is the question asking?
- You must be absolutely clear on this so that you fully address the actual question and do not just write generally around the topic. You will have to address this question throughout your essay and come back to it in your conclusion.

Introduction
- Address the question clearly and indicate the direction that your argument will take.
- Define key terms/concepts that are in the question, as your understanding of these words will determine the direction of your essay.

Main Body

Para 1
- Each paragraph should address a new point.
- Make it clear what the topic of the paragraph is.

Para 2

Para 3
- Ensure each paragraph refers directly to the question; use the wording of the question if possible.

Para 4
- Use detailed knowledge!
- Support all general statements with specific examples.

Para 5
- Link your paragraphs so that each one is part of a developing argument building up to your conclusion.

Para 6
- Show your knowledge of current historiography.

Conclusion
- Your conclusion must come back to the question.
- Look back at the main thrust of your arguments and evidence in the essay and give a conclusion based on what you have said: this should be a direct answer to the question.

Plan > **Draft** > **Edit**

Essay Frame: The causes of World War I

Question

To what extent was Germany to blame for causing World War I?

Below is an essay frame to help you structure your answer. As you are writing your answer, keep referring back to the 'How do I write a history essay?' diagram. Check that you have covered all the pointers in the yellow boxes.

Introduction: Set the question into context. The Treaty of Versailles included the War Guilt Clause, Article 231, which laid the responsibility for causing World War I with Germany and its allies. Some historians, however, have argued that no one country can be held responsible for the outbreak of war in August 1914. Set down your line of argument. Attempt to keep your argument straightforward, i.e. do not attempt to cover several different lines of argument in a timed essay, as your arguments will lack depth and development.

Part 1: Always deal with the issue addressed in the question first. This means looking first at how Germany can be blamed. Make sure you consider:

- Long-term events causing tension, e.g. *Weltpolitik* and its impact on international relations
- Germany's role in the events leading up to war, e.g. the War Council of 1912
- July Crisis – the blank cheque, Schlieffen Plan, response to Russian mobilization.

Part 2: Here you need to give an alternative argument, e.g. the fact that all powers bear some responsibility. You cannot talk about all the different issues, so choose two or three to explain how they led to increasing tensions that shaped the way that the powers reacted in the July Crisis. Factors you could discuss include nationalism, colonial rivalries, the arms race and alliance systems.

Conclusion: Make sure that you come back to the actual question. Based on the weight of evidence on each side of the argument, conclude whether Germany should be held responsible for causing World War I.

Essay questions

Now plan out the following essay questions in pairs. Use the essay plan above as a guide.

1 How far do you agree that World War I was caused by colonial rivalries?

2 Was the outbreak of a general war in 1914 inevitable after the assassination of Archduke Franz Ferdinand? © IBO 1996

● **Examiner's hint**

You have read the views of several different historians on the causes of World War I. Try to include some of these views in your essay. Only use historians, however, where they are useful for backing up your arguments.

ToK Time

Consider the methodologies used by historians in attempting to find 'historical truth' (see Chapter 16 for a review of historians' methodologies). Why do historians reach different conclusions on what caused World War I? What are the strengths and limitations in the historians' methodologies?

WORLD WAR I AND TOTAL WAR

As you read through this chapter, consider the following essay questions:
- In what ways can World War I be considered a total war?
- Why were the Central Powers defeated in World War I?
- Why did World War I last so long?

Breakdown of events in World War I – 1914–18

	General	Western Front	Eastern Front	War at Sea	War in the Air	Africa and Asia
1914	Assassination of Archduke Franz Ferdinand Outbreak of general war Japan enters war Turkey enters war	Schlieffen Plan – German invasion of Belgium First Battle of Marne First Battle of Ypres Christmas 'truce'	Austrian invasion of Serbia Russian invasion of Germany Battles of Tannenberg and Masurian Lakes Austrian invasion of Russia	British blockade Battles of Heligoland, Falkland Islands and Coronel	Bombardment of British towns by Zeppelins	Conquest of German Togoland and possessions in the Pacific
1915	Italy joins the war on side of Allies Bulgaria joins on side of Central Powers	Battle of Neuve Chapelle Second battle of Ypres (gas used) Battle of Loos Battles on the Isonzo between Italy and Austria	Defeat of Serbia Gallipoli campaign Defeat of Russia in Galicia	U-boat warfare *Lusitania* sunk	Zeppelin raids on Britain	Conquest of German SW Africa
1916	Portugal and Romania join on the side of the Allies	Battle of Verdun Battle of the Somme	End of Gallipoli campaign Brusilov's breakthrough	Battle of Jutland	Machine guns are by now standard fittings on fighters	Arab revolt in Turkey Surrender of German Cameroon
1917	USA and Greece join war on side of Allies	Nivelle offensive French mutinies Battles of Vimy Ridge and Arras Third Battle of Ypres (Passchendaele) Battle of Cambrai Italians driven back at Caporetto	Russian Revolution – Tsar abdicates Russian armistice	Unrestricted U-boat warfare British convoy system established	Air superiority shifts from the Germans to the Allies	British capture of Baghdad Allenby's campaign
1918	US troops arrive in Europe Abdication of Kaiser	Ludendorff Offensive Allied counter-offensive Armistice signed	Treaty of Brest-Litovsk Surrender of Bulgaria, Turkey and Austria	Naval mutiny in Germany	British attack on Zeebrugge	Surrender of Turkey

War fever gripped the populations of Europe; many felt the war to be just and necessary and all felt that the war would be short and that soldiers would be home by Christmas. Unfortunately, the quick and glorious victories that were expected did not take place. The war was to last for four long years, during which time the fighting took place on several 'fronts'. The most important of these fronts is known as the Western Front, and this stretched 320km from the English Channel to the Swiss Alps. Fighting also took place on Germany's Eastern Front involving both Austria-Hungary and Russia, and both sides continued to hope that they would be able to break through on one of the other 'diversionary' fronts that existed in the Balkans, in Italy and in the Middle East.

Overview of the war: Western Front

Following the declarations of war in July and August 1914, governments made their opening moves: Austria-Hungary opened fire on Serbia, Russia mobilized its troops, Britain prepared its British Expeditionary Force (the BEF) and Germany put its Schlieffen Plan into action.

The failure of the Schlieffen Plan

The wars of German unification had convinced strategists at the beginning of the 20th century that future wars would be short and that rapid mobilization and a strong opening attack would be the key elements necessary for victory. Von Schlieffen's war plan for Germany followed these assumptions. Dealing with Germany's nightmare scenario of a two-front war, he decided to use the bulk of German forces to win a speedy victory over France, after which they could be transferred to the east to deal with the Tsar's armies. Specifically, his plan required the German armies to sweep through into northern France via neutral Belgium and then advance to the west of Paris, finally swinging back eastwards to defeat the main French forces, which would still be defending the German border. German troops would then be free to move to the Eastern Front to confront the Russian Army which, given the size of the army and the country, would only just have mobilized.

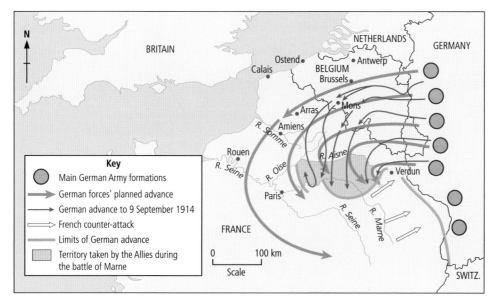

Map showing the failure of the Schlieffen Plan, 1914.

There were several key reasons for the failure of the Schlieffen Plan:
- Belgian resistance was unexpectedly strong and it took the Germans more than two weeks to capture Brussels, the Belgian capital.

German war aims

German war aims in 1914 were very comprehensive. In the September Memorandum of 9 September, Bethmann-Hollweg promised 'security for the German Reich in west and east for all imaginable time', and this was to be done through a combination of territorial expansion and economic control. In Africa, for instance, French, Belgian and Portuguese colonies would be incorporated into a Central Africa economic region – *Mittelafrika*. In Europe, Germany would have indirect control over much of Europe through a customs union, which would include Austria-Hungary, Belgium, Denmark, France, the Netherlands and Poland. Parts of Belgium, France and Luxembourg would be directly annexed and Russia would have to provide some level of self-determination to nationalities such as the Poles. (Poland had been part of Russia since the 18th century.) Britain's economic supremacy would be weakened by Germany's naval command of key international routes, as well as by Germany's economic domination of Africa and Europe. Such comprehensive aims increased the determination of both sides to fight for total victory, and they made a compromise peace difficult to achieve.

- The attack on Belgium also brought Britain, who was a guarantor of Belgian neutrality through the 1839 Treaty of London, into the war.
- The German delay in getting through Belgium gave the British time to organize themselves and left the Channel ports free, enabling the BEF to land.
- The German forces marching to Paris were weakened by the deployment of some of their troops to the east (where Russia had mobilized faster than expected), and by the difficulties of maintaining supplies. Thus instead of approaching Paris from the west, the Germans swept down too early, making for Paris from the east of the city.
- In Paris, **reservists** were sent to meet the Germans via taxis in the famous 'taxis of the Marne'; the Germans, slowed down by exhaustion and a lack of food and ammunition, were halted by British and French troops at the battle of the Marne on 9 September.

The 'miracle of the Marne' marked the failure of the Schlieffen Plan and ensured that there would be no short war. Indeed, the battle of the Marne was followed by a 'race to the sea', as each side tried to outflank the other army in order to get behind them and cut them off. This race eventually resulted in the building of a continuous series of trenches stretching from the Alps to the Channel coast, and it was these trenches that determined the type of warfare that was to exist for the whole of the war along the Western Front. The failures of both the British and the Germans to break through at Ypres in November 1914, and then the failure of the French to break through at Artois and Champagne in December, meant that a stalemate situation was in place by the end of 1914.

1915: stalemate

In 1915, the stalemate continued on the Western Front. Several attempts were made to break this situation, but they all failed: the British tried at Neuve Chapelle and Loos, the French lost thousands of men in an unsuccessful offensive in Champagne, and the Germans were driven back from Ypres in April. It was at this second battle of Ypres that poison gas was first used by the Germans, and although it was initially effective in clearing the British trenches, the gas also prevented the Germans from making any progress, and the attack was halted.

Trench line of the Western Front, with key battles, 1915–17.

1916: Verdun and the Somme

The two key battles of 1916 were those at Verdun and the Somme – both failed to achieve their aims and both were horrific in terms of loss of life.

Verdun

In February 1916, the Germans launched a massive attack against an important French fortress town, Verdun. The German commander, Erich von Falkenhayn, set out his plans:

> *Just behind the French lines on the Western Front there are objectives which the French command must defend to the last man. If it so defends them the French army will be exhausted by its bloody losses in the inevitable combat, regardless of whether or not we win the objectives immediately. If, on the other hand, it lets them go, the damage to French morale will be enormous… The essential question is not to take Verdun … but to pin down the French, pull them towards the battlefield, and since they will have to defend it shoulder to shoulder, we shall bleed them white by virtue of our superiority in guns.*

To access worksheet 3.1 on the battle of Verdun, please visit www. pearsonbacconline.com and follow the on-screen instructions.

STUDENT STUDY SECTION

Review questions

1 What were Falkenhayn's objectives in attacking Verdun?

2 What does this reveal about the way in which war was now being fought on the Western Front?

Cartoon analysis

"Father, we must have a higher pile to see Verdun."

'We must have a higher pile to see Verdun.' A cartoon by Louis Raemakers, A Dutch cartoonist.

Question

What point is Raemakers making in this cartoon?

Attacks were followed by counter-attacks. General Philippe Pétain, the commander in charge of the French troops, held out but at a huge cost: 315,000 men. He voiced French determination in the phrase 'Ils ne passeront pas' (They shall not pass), and by April, French counter-attacks had caused huge losses for the Germans – 280,000 men – with nothing to show for it. Falkenhayn was sacked in August 1916, but his policy at Verdun ran on for another four months. The casualties eventually numbered more than 800,000. Overall, the battle broke all previous records for killing and destruction.

The battle of the Somme

ToK Time

Casualties are an inevitable element of waging a war. However, the battle of the Somme has been seen as resulting in unacceptably high casualty figures. Can high casualty rates in war be justified? What *is* a high casualty figure? Did the sheer number of men in the mass armies of World War I mean that high casualties were unavoidable?

The battle of the Somme was a series of attacks led mainly by the British under General Douglas Haig. They began on 1 July 1916 and lasted through to the following November. The aim of these attacks was to take the pressure off the French at Verdun, and ensure that the Germans were fully committed so that they could not send reinforcements to the Eastern Front against Russia. The first attack was preceded by the most intensive preliminary artillery bombardment ever made. The aim of this demonstration of firepower was to destroy the forward defences. It failed, however, and as a result the first attack by British soldiers ended in heavy casualties. A second major attack was made in September. This used tanks for the first time, but again, there was no breakthrough and by the end of this battle the Allies had made only limited advances varying between a few hundred metres and 4km, along a 50km front. Losses on both sides were appalling: British killed or wounded totalled 418,000, German casualties were 650,000 and French 194,000.

1917: the USA joins the war

In February 1917, the Germans withdrew behind the heavily fortified Hindenburg Line fortifications in north-eastern France, which could be more easily defended. During the rest of the year, the French and the British continued offensive actions, without any major breakthroughs, in the battle of Arras (9–15 April), the battle of the Aisne in the French Nivelle Offensive (16–20 April) and in the third battle of Ypres at Passchendaele (July–November). Failure in the Nivelle Offensive proved intolerable to many soldiers and the French government was faced with mutiny, resulting in the courts martial of 300–400 ringleaders. Only the battle of Cambrai (20 November–3 December) indicated that there could be an end to the stalemate, when British and Australian forces using tanks broke through German lines and achieved an advance of 8km. Yet the tank was still mechanically unreliable, and many broke down under the stresses of the advance. The British advance slowed and the Germans were able to counter-attack successfully, forcing the British out of many of the areas they had captured.

The Treaty of Brest-Litovsk

When Lenin took over Russia in October 1917, he was determined to end the war with Germany. However, the 'robber peace' that Russia was forced to sign was extremely harsh. Russia lost Poland, Estonia, Latvia and Lithuania, the Ukraine, Georgia and Finland. These losses included a third of Russia's farming land, a third of its population, two-thirds of its coal mines and half of its industry. In addition, Russia had to pay an indemnity of five billion gold roubles.

Yet the Allies had cause for optimism when the USA entered the war in 1917. America had suffered as a result of the German policy of unrestricted submarine warfare in the Atlantic from February 1917, which had involved attacks on American ships and the consequent loss of American lives. When the Zimmerman telegram was intercepted (see Interesting Facts box on opposite page) it was the final straw, and America declared war on Germany on 4 April. Nevertheless, it took time for US troops to arrive in Europe, and at the end of 1917 the situation on the Western Front still looked bleak; the French Army was recovering from the mutinies, and following the success of the **Bolshevik** revolution in Russia, an **armistice** was signed between the Bolsheviks and the Germans. This event led to Russian troops being withdrawn from the Eastern Front, which meant that the Germans could focus their attention on fighting in Western Europe.

US neutrality, unrestricted submarine warfare and the Zimmerman telegram

At the beginning of the war, the USA had maintained a policy of neutrality, and President Woodrow Wilson had even attempted to negotiate a peace, arguing for a 'peace without victory' in Europe. **Isolationism** – keeping America out of Europe's affairs – was also strongly supported by public opinion in the USA. Neutrality, however, was very difficult when the USA was trading with the combatants, particularly the Allies. Germany's response was to use submarines to attack American ships without warning – a situation that led to the sinking of the ocean liner *Lusitania* in 1915. Germany suspended its **U-boat** attacks, but resumed them in January 1917 (see p.54). Germany knew that this action might draw the USA into the war on the side of the Allies. Thus in January 1917, Arthur Zimmerman, Foreign Secretary of Germany, wrote a telegram to the German ambassador of Mexico, Heinrich von Eckhardt, instructing him to approach the Mexican government with a proposal for a military alliance; it offered US territory in return for Mexico joining the German cause. The Zimmerman telegram was intercepted and decoded by the British. Its publication in the US media caused public outrage that helped swing public opinion in favour of entering the war.

STUDENT ACTIVITY

Cartoon analysis

An American poster uses the image of the sinking *Lusitania* to encourage young men to enlist in the US Navy.

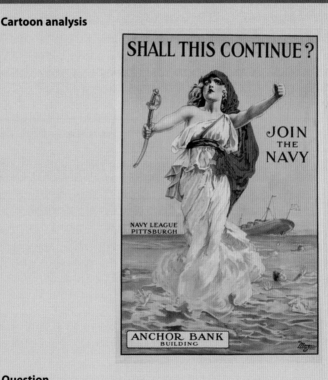

Question

What does this poster tell you about American attitudes to the sinking of the *Lusitania*, and about America's position of neutrality?

1918: victory for the Allies

With Germany on the verge of starvation as a result of the success of an Allied blockade, and under the threat of US troops arriving to join the Allies, the German commander Erich Ludendorff decided to risk everything on a quick victory in his 'Peace Offensive' (*Friedensturm*). Ludendorff's initial attacks were very successful; following the usual preliminary artillery bombardment came attacks of smaller bands of specially trained and lightly equipped 'storm troops' rather than the usual waves of **infantry**. Attacking along the entire frontline, the Germans broke the Allied lines in many places. In March 1918, 35

German divisions on the Somme made gains of about 65km against the British. In April, a breakthrough was made in Flanders, which threatened Allied control of the Channel ports, and in May, German troops once again reached the Marne River, so that they were only 80km from Paris.

Yet the Germans had overstretched themselves and they had no reserves to call on to replace the 800,000 casualties that they had sustained in the offensive. They made no further progress between May and August. Meanwhile, the Allied forces, now under the coordinated control of General Ferdinand Foch, and using planes and tanks, massed their growing forces around the salient that the German forces had created in their advance. The last German offensive in July met stiff opposition and was unable to make any progress. Instead, the French counter-attack made a breakthrough, forcing Ludendorff's units back to safer ground.

On 8 August – what Ludendorff called 'The Black Day' – the Allies achieved the furthest advance since the beginning of the war in 1914. By late September, they had reached the Hindenburg Line. By October, the Germans, by now suffering from low morale, hunger and indiscipline, were in full retreat. Germany was facing other problems – the impact of the blockade and the surrender of its allies. Back in September, Ludendorff had lost his nerve and urged the Kaiser to 'request an armistice without any hesitation'; only a 'quick end' could save the army from destruction. Thus on 11 November 1918, the Armistice came into effect, ending the fighting between the Allies and Germany.

STUDENT STUDY SECTION

Review questions

1   Why did a stalemate develop, and continue, on the Western Front?

2   Why did the Americans enter the war?

3   What factors contributed to the Germans agreeing to an Armistice in November 1918?

The Armistice

The Armistice was agreed at 5.00am on 11 November, to come into effect at 11.00am Paris time – thus 'the eleventh (hour) of the eleventh (day) of the eleventh (month)'. The terms contained the following major points:

- Termination of military hostilities within six hours after signature.
- Immediate removal of all German troops from France, Belgium, Luxembourg and Alsace-Lorraine.
- Removal of all German troops from territory on both sides of the Rhine, with ensuing occupation by Allied troops.
- Removal of all German troops from the Eastern Front, leaving German territory as it was on 1 August 1914.
- Renouncement of the Treaty of Brest-Litovsk with Russia and of the Treaty of Bucharest with Romania.
- Internment of the German fleet and surrender of other weapons.

The agreement was signed by the German delegation in Foch's railway siding in the forest of Compiègne (which Hitler subsequently used for the signing of the armistice that the French made with the Germans in 1940).

Map showing the different fronts on which fighting took place.

The Eastern Front

1914

The aim of the Schlieffen Plan had been for Germany to avoid fighting a war on two fronts. Yet not only did Germany fail to defeat France quickly, but the Russians mobilized their army much faster than Germany had predicted. On 17 August 1914, the Russians moved into East Prussia, forcing the Germans to divert troops from the Western Front. Although the Russians were initially successful against the Austrians, occupying the province of Galicia and helping to cause the failure of the Schlieffen Plan, they were defeated by the Germans both at Tannenberg in August and the Masurian Lakes in September. (Here was a pattern to be repeated several times – the Russians could defeat the Austrians but not the Germans, and the Germans had to keep coming to the aid of the Austrians.) These defeats boosted German self-confidence, forced Russia out of Germany and also resulted in the loss for Russia of huge amounts of equipment and ammunition. Russia's position worsened considerably when Turkey entered the war on the side of the Germany, as Turkey could cut Russia's main supply route through the Dardanelles.

1915

This year again saw the Russians defeated by the Germans, who captured Warsaw in August. A combined Austro-German offensive in the Carpathians in May also meant the loss of most of Russia's 1914 gains by late June. By the end of the year, the Russians had withdrawn some 450km with losses of a million dead and a further million taken prisoner. A Russian general reported to the Tsar; 'A third of the men have no rifles. These poor devils have to wait patiently until their comrades fall so they can pick up their weapons. The army is drowning in its own blood.' The Russians had to establish a new defensive line that extended from Riga on the Baltic Sea to Romania in the Balkans – a line that was soon to become 'six hundred miles of mud and horror'.

Russia was also starting to suffer from the effects of the Turkish blockade of the Dardanelles (see p.47).

British cartoon, September 1914.

● **Examiner's hint**
When analyzing any source, the date is a crucial piece of information that needs to be taken into consideration. Look at the sequence of events on the Eastern Front and the date of the cartoon to help you with Question 3.

STUDENT STUDY SECTION

"THE STEAM-ROLLER."
Austria. "I SAY, YOU KNOW, YOU'RE EXCEEDING THE SPEED LIMIT!"

Questions

1 How is Russia portrayed in this cartoon?
2 What is the message of the cartoon?
3 What reasons did the cartoonist have for giving this message?
4 How accurate was this message?

1916–17

The following year, 1916, saw the greatest Russian success of the war. Due to a determined effort on the home front, the Russian Army had better equipment than it had possessed in 1916, and on 4 June General Aleksei Brusilov, under pressure from France and Britain to divert German resources away from Verdun, launched a massive offensive over a wide front against the Austrians. Initially, this offensive was very successful, advancing 160km. By early August, however, with the Germans again coming to the support of the Austrians, the Brusilov Offensive came to a halt. It had cost the Russians a million lives.

The offensive had a devastating effect on both the Austro-Hungarian and the Russian empires. In Austria-Hungary the number of casualties – 340,000 with 400,000 more men taken prisoner – caused morale to reach rock-bottom. In Russia, the effect of a further million casualties combined with growing hardships at home to create yet more opposition to the ruling Romanov dynasty. The mounting pressure exploded in February 1917, when the Tsar was forced to abdicate. Although the new Provisional Government decided to maintain the war effort, the continued defeats of the Russian Army, and the ongoing economic crisis on the home front, helped increase support for the Bolshevik Party, who were successful in overthrowing the Provisional Government in October of the same year.

The new Bolshevik government then removed Russia from the war in December, ending Germany's need to fight a war on two fronts. The majority of German forces could now be used against the West.

The Balkan Front

Austria-Hungary failed to occupy Serbia in 1914, yet Bulgaria's entry on the side of the Central Powers allowed a successful joint Austro-German-Bulgarian offensive in October 1915. In August 1916, encouraged by the Russian successes, Romania joined the Allies, but was quickly overrun by the forces of Germany, Austria-Hungary, Turkey and Bulgaria. Allied attempts to relieve Romania by invading through Greece on the Salonika Front failed. It was not until 1918 that the Allies made advances against Bulgaria, leading to its surrender in September 1918.

The Italian Front

Italy joined the war in 1915 on the side of the Allies, having been promised by Britain and France (in the Treaty of London) possession of Austria's Italian-speaking provinces, as well as territory along the eastern shore of the Adriatic Sea. Italy's entry into the war opened up a front between Italy and Austria along the River Isonzo. However, fighting in the mountainous terrain was difficult and the Italians made little headway against the Austrians. In October 1917, a major Austrian offensive – the battle of Caporetto – was launched with German support. The Italians were forced to retreat more than 110km and the Central Powers' advance was halted only by the arrival of British and French reinforcements. Despite these failures, the Italian Front placed a heavy burden on Austria-Hungary, which in 1916 had to deploy half of its forces against the Italians.

Turkey and the Middle Eastern Fronts

Turkey joined Germany and Austria-Hungary in the war on 31 October 1914, mainly with the intention of halting Russian expansion around the Black Sea. The Allies attacked the Turkish Empire in three separate campaigns.

The Gallipoli campaign planned for British warships to sweep through the Dardanelles, attacking Constantinople and driving Turkey out of the war. This success would then open up a sea route to the Russian Front, so that the Allies could get supplies to Russia. It would also allow the Allies to march through the Balkans and attack Austria-Hungary, thus opening up a new front. The plan was an attractive alternative to the stalemate on the Western Front, seeming to offer the possibility of a quick and unexpected success. Lord Herbert Kitchener, the British Secretary of State for War, believed that it would be the plan that would win the war

The first stage of the campaign, a naval bombardment of the Turkish forts protecting the narrow Straits, was a failure. With British and French ships damaged by a combination of mines and shell fire from the forts, the Allied commanders decided that the risks were too great. They opted instead to launch a land invasion to capture the peninsula. Thus an Allied army, which included a large number of Australians and New Zealanders (Anzacs), landed on the Gallipoli peninsula on 25 April 1915. In the ensuing months, the campaign suffered from shortages, delays, lack of coordinated command and tactical errors. It was finally abandoned in November, having achieved none of its goals and having cost the Allies 250,000 men, dead, wounded or captured.

The second campaign against the Turks involved an operation to win control of oil supplies through an expedition to oil-rich Mesopotamia. The Turks, led and supported by German officers, resisted fiercely at first, but by the end of the war British forces were in control of Basra, Baghdad and Mosul.

The third campaign involved British, Anzac and Indian troops driving the Turks back through Palestine towards Turkey itself. The British were aided in this campaign by guerrilla warfare carried out by the Arabs, who had been promised independence from Turkey after the war. T.E. Lawrence, a British intelligence officer, became a military adviser to the Arabs. Known as 'Lawrence of Arabia', he led a guerrilla force in attacks on Turkish railways and supply lines. Under the leadership of General Edmund Allenby, the British and empire forces defeated the Turks at Megiddo in September 1918, and the Turks finally surrendered on 3 November.

War in the colonial territories

Most of the major powers fighting in the war had colonies, and so fighting also took place in other parts of the world. Britain's control of the seas, however, meant that attacks on overseas territories and colonies were all Allied attacks. Most colonies were manned by relatively small garrisons and their capture was not difficult, though it was not until 1917 that all German forces in Africa were overcome.

Britain, France and Germany also involved the people living in their colonies in the fighting; soldiers from India (one and a half million volunteers), Canada, Australia, New Zealand and South Africa contributed to the British war effort, for example. The French recruited some 600,000 combat troops and a further 200,000 labourers from North and West Africa. Many of these soldiers ended up facing not only the appalling conditions of the Western Front, but also racism from the European troops.

Indian troops: 57th Wilde's Rifles in action, October 1914.

In Asia, meanwhile, Japan joined the war on the side of the Allies and took the opportunity to attack and occupy Germany's islands in the Central Pacific and take over the heavily fortified German fortress at Kiaochow. A New Zealand force took over Samoa and an Australian battalion took New Guinea. By the end of the year, Germany had lost its Asiatic colonies, which Britain promised to their different conquerors.

STUDENT STUDY SECTION

IBLP link – Inquirer

Research the role of one of the colonial countries that contributed troops to the Allied war effort. This activity could include looking at the number of troops sent, casualties, impact on the home life of the country and impact on the colony's status and relationship with either Britain or France.

How was World War I fought?
War on land – the Western Front

Although fighting took place on several fronts throughout the four years of the war, the Western Front nevertheless remained the most important for several reasons:

- Because of its size and the length of time it remained an operational theatre of war. It was a continuous battlefield stretching for 320km from the North Sea to the French–Swiss border in the south. Across this line, the Allies and the Germans attacked each other continuously for four years without significantly breaking the position of the line.
- Because of the key role it played in the outcome of the Great War. Many of the other conflicts in the war were 'diversionary fronts', which were created to break the deadlock on the Western Front.
- Because the fighting on the Western Front was to have a significant impact on ideas about and attitudes towards war.

To access worksheet 3.2 on trench warfare, please visit www.pearsonbacconline.com and follow the on-screen instructions.

Why did trench warfare lead to a stalemate?

The feature of the Western Front that most affected the way the war was fought was the development of trench warfare. After the 'race to the sea', the conflict settled into static 'positional' warfare. The war of movement was over. In order to hold their positions, and keep out of the line of machine-gun and artillery fire, soldiers had to dig down into defensive positions; thus trenches were dug along the entire length of the front. As it became clear that these hastily dug ditches were to become permanent, they evolved into complex defensive systems on both sides, with the area between opposing trenches known as 'no-man's land'.

The Western Front, according to John Keegan:

…rapidly became a maze of duplicates and dead ends, in which soldiers, sometimes whole units rapidly lost their way. Guides who knew the trench geography were an essential accompaniment in unit reliefs, when one battalion took the place of another at the end of a front-line stint [tour of duty]. So, too were signboards pointing to the more enduring trenches and the ruined remains of human habitation; in the Ypres salient in the winter of 1914–15, there were still traces of the buildings the Tommies had named Tram Car Cottage, Battersea Farm, Beggar's Rest, Apple Villa, White Horse Cellars, Kansan Cross, Doll's House.

From John Keegan, *The First World War*, 1999

The diagram below shows the key features of this system:

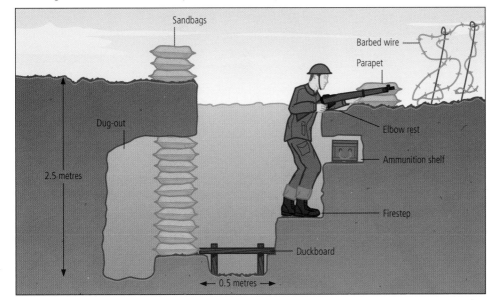

Cross section of a typical World War I trench system.

Trench warfare was deadlier for attackers than defenders; attackers suffed twice as many casualties during an assault on the enemy trench line. A major attack would begin with an artillery barrage, followed by the attacking troops going 'over the top' – climbing out of their trenches and attempting to reach and capture the enemy trenches on the other side of no-man's land. Soldiers had to walk or run into the direct firing line of the defenders, while mines and thick rolls of barbed wire slowed down their progress and made the chances of being hit by enemy machine-gun fire even more likely.

The nature of this type of warfare is described by John Keegan, who here looks at the battle of the Somme:

Descriptions of zero hour on 1 July abound, of the long lines of young men, burdened by the sixty pounds of equipment judged necessary to sustain them in a long struggle inside the German trenches, plodding off almost shoulder to shoulder; of their good cheer and certainty of success, of individual displays of bravado, as in the battalions which kicked a football ahead of the ranks; of bright sunshine breaking through the thin morning mist; of the illusion of an empty battlefield, denuded of opponents by the weight of bombardment and the explosion of twenty-one chambers, laboriously driven under the German front lines, as the attack began. Descriptions of what happened later abound also; of the discovery of the uncut wire, of the appearance of the German defenders, manning the parapet at the moment the British creeping barrage passed beyond, to fire frenziedly into the approaching ranks, of the opening of gaps in the attacking waves, of massacre in the wire entanglements, of the advance checked, halted and eventually stopped literally dead.

From John Keegan, *The First World War*, 1999

Because of the difficulties of attacking and taking the enemy's trenches, the Western Front became one of stalemate, with little change in the position of the front over the whole four years. Increasingly, the aim of battles became not so much to win territory held by the enemy, but to destroy or wear down the opposing army; it was a war of attrition intended to break the morale of the enemy and reduce their numbers.

Clearly the military education and mindset of the generals were inadequate to meet the demands of this new type of warfare. Similarly, the soldiers themselves were ill-prepared in their training to deal with the horrors in which they found themselves.

STUDENT STUDY SECTION

Research question

Find out more about:

- The Christmas truce
- Shell-shock
- Trench foot
- The work of miners tunnelling beneath the trenches
- Communication systems used in the trenches
- Conscientious objectors
- Those who were shot for 'cowardice'.

How did the development of weaponry lead to a change in tactics on the Western Front?

Both sides in the war utilized a wide range of weapons in order to try to break the deadlock. The infantry charge explained above remained the key battle tactic used throughout the war, and most weapons were applied or developed with the aim of making this strategy more effective.

Machine guns and grenades

The main weapon of the British soldier was a .303in, bolt-action Lee-Enfield rifle with a magazine that held ten rounds of ammunition; a bayonet could be attached to the end of the rifle for use in hand-to-hand fighting. Each side had similar types of rifle. The machine gun, however, was far more lethal against mass targets. Whereas an infantryman could fire 25 rounds a minute with a bolt-action rifle, he could fire 600 rounds a minute with a machine gun. The effects were devastating on attackers, as a German machine-gunner here recounts: '… the [British] officers walked in front. I noticed one of them walking calmly carrying a walking stick. When we started firing we just had to load and re-load. They went down in their hundreds. You didn't have to aim, we just fired into them.' Soldiers also used hand grenades – essentially small hand-thrown bombs. The British, for example, used the pineapple-shaped Mills bomb, while the Germans used stick-shaped grenades nicknamed 'potato-mashers'.

German soldiers carrying Model 24 stick grenades.

Another weapon innovation of World War I was the submachine gun, a lightweight hand-held automatic weapon that fired pistol-calibre ammunition. (By using low-power ammunition, the soldier could control the recoil better than if he was using high-power rifle ammunition.) The submachine gun was known as a 'trench sweeper', a weapon that could deliver heavy firepower at close-quarters during a trench assault.

Heavy artillery

British artillery position on the Western Front.

Although machine guns killed many thousands of people during World War I, nevertheless it was artillery that was the real killer. In World War I, artillery inflicted 70 per cent of all casualties. With the war being so static, the huge guns could take up permanent positions in strategically good locations, from where they could launch massive numbers of high-explosive shells. Commanders saw artillery as the key to overcoming the defences of the enemy and thus every major attack was preceded by a prolonged artillery barrage.

Yet the reality was that the artillery was not accurate or effective enough to destroy enemy trench systems completely – unless a shell fell directly into a trench, the occupants were relatively well protected behind their earthen walls. In the battle of the Somme, for example, the British fired more than 1.5 million shells in five days, but these failed to cut the barbed wire or destroy the German trenches. Even if the infantry made a breakthrough, the artillery was not mobile enough to be brought forward to protect the attackers. Another problem with the barrage was that it gave the enemy warning of the attack to come; when the barrage stopped that was the signal for the attack. The effect of the artillery on soldiers was nevertheless grim: brain damage, bleeding ears, shell-shock. It also churned up the land into a sea of mud and craters, which made attacking across no-man's land even more difficult.

Artillery tactics and **fire-control** technologies evolved over the course of the war to become more versatile, using techniques such as the 'creeping barrage' (a steadily advancing wall of fire) and 'artillery ambush' (a sudden storm of shells against a specific target). It also became possible to locate and attack enemy artillery more effectively; thus British guns could remain silent until the actual attack and then blanket the German guns with fire, bringing back the element of surprise.

Chemical warfare

The first poison gas attack was made at Ypres by the Germans in April 1915. Carried on the wind, the chlorine gas caused panic amongst the Allied soldiers and disabled 6.5km of trenches. More lethal gases were soon developed: phosgene gas, which was 18 times stronger than the chlorine gas, and the most feared of all, mustard gas, which burned, blinded or slowly killed the victims over several weeks. Gas, however, although a useful weapon for causing panic among troops, did not actually play any key role in breaking the stalemate. Its big disadvantage was that it was dependent on the wind for distribution and so it could blow back towards the side that was using it; this happened to the British at the battle of Loos in 1915. In addition, gas masks were quickly developed by scientists, making gas as a weapon much less effective.

British soldiers man a Vickers machine gun while wearing gas masks.

Tanks

The tank was another attempt to break the stalemate. Developed by the British and the French, 49 of them were first used at the battle of the Somme. The tank was able to advance ahead of the infantry, crushing barbed wire fences and attacking the enemy at the same time with machine-gun and cannon fire. Inside the tank, the crew was protected from small-arms fire by the outer metal armour. Yet the tank was not yet able to break the stalemate. It was slow and unreliable and many tanks broke down before they reached the German trenches. Their armour plating was also not strong enough to resist artillery, and the use of tanks at the Somme did not have any major effect other than causing initial panic amongst the Germans. The conditions for the tank operators were also appalling; the heat generated inside the tank was tremendous and fumes from the engine and guns nearly choked the men inside.

Larger numbers of tanks were used in the battle of Cambrai in 1917, but here initial successes were not sustained and breakthroughs were quickly reversed. 'As a result of the tank's limitations, there was little real agreement within the British Expeditionary Force on whether mechanical warfare truly offered a substitute for manpower. In that sense, tanks during the war remained what GHQ concluded in August 1918, a "mechanical contrivance" with potential usefulness only as an adjunct to combined infantry and artillery assault' (Ian Beckett, *The Great War 1914–1918*, 2001).

What impact did the technological advances during World War I have on the nature of the fighting?

As suggested above, none of the technological developments in weaponry or the variations in tactics were ultimately decisive during the fighting on the Western Front. Nevertheless, the developments that did take place during the course of war – in artillery, tanks, combat aircraft and aerial reconnaissance (see p.56 for more discussion of the air war) – did allow for a change of tactics by the final campaigns of 1918.

In 1914 the British soldier went to war dressed like a gamekeeper in a soft cap, armed only with rifle and bayonet. In 1918 he went into battle dressed like an industrial worker in a steel helmet, protected by a respirator against poison gas, armed with automatic weapons and mortars, supported by tanks and ground-attack aircraft, and preceded by a creeping artillery barrage of crushing intensity. Firepower replaced manpower as the instrument of victory. This represented a revolution in the conduct of war.

John Bourne in Charles Townshend (ed.), *The Oxford History of Modern War*, 2005

War at sea

What was the importance of naval warfare in World War I?

From the beginning of the war, it was clear that control of the seas was crucial to both sides. Britain needed to be able to transport men (including from places as far afield as Australia and Canada) and supplies to the battlefields of Europe and the Middle East. As an island, Britain's need for food and industrial supplies from other countries, particularly from the USA, was key to the country's survival. Thus Britain was also cautious in its use of its navies; it could not risk losing many ships to mines and submarines or in surface battles. As Winston Churchill (who served as First Lord of the Admiralty for part of the war) said, it would have been possible for Admiral Jellicoe, the commander of the British Fleet, to lose the war in an afternoon.

Germany did not need naval routes to supply and help its allies. However, Germany also needed food and other supplies from overseas. Thus control of trade routes was vital to both sides, both for their own needs and to stop supplies reaching the enemy.

ToK Time

The *Lusitania*, sunk by German U-boats on 7 May 1915, was a luxury liner built to convey its passengers between Britain and the United States. The Germans claimed they had evidence that the liner was transporting munitions as well as civilian passengers across the Atlantic. US President Woodrow Wilson had resisted public outrage, particularly in Britain, to respond to the attack with a declaration of war. This choice was seen by some as 'cowardice', and a shell that failed to explode was nicknamed a 'Wilson' in the British trenches.

At the time it was widely believed that the German claim about the ship was false, and was an attempt to justify the effects of unrestricted submarine warfare. In 2006, however, a dive team from Ireland claimed to have found munitions on board the sunken vessel. These included 15,000 rounds of rifle ammunition in the bow of the ship. These rounds were the same calibre as those used by the British in their rifles and machine guns on the Western Front.

Discuss as a class the implications of this new evidence. What does it suggest about our understanding of the past? Do we have more 'truth' about the past today than was possible at the time of the war? Does the 'truth', or our understanding of the past, change over time?

Britain was particularly successful in pursuing the latter objective. Royal Navy vessels went into action against German units stationed abroad, and destroyed one of the main German squadrons at the battle of the Falkland Islands in 1914. The Allies also started blockading German ports; British naval vessels enforced the right of search on neutral shipping to ensure that Germany and its allies were not getting supplies via other countries.

Mines and submarines

To access worksheet 3.3 on German submarine warfare, please visit www. pearsonbacconline.com and follow the on-screen instructions.

With their surviving warships vulnerable to the might of the Royal Navy, the Germans turned instead to submarine attacks and tried to enforce their own blockade of Britain using U-boats (*Unterseebooten* – meaning 'underwater boats') to sink merchant ships. Submarines, and also the use of sea mines, changed the conduct of naval warfare. Previously, naval actions had been carried out on the surface, often at close range. The development, however, of the torpedo and submarine made the large battleships vulnerable and almost defenceless, and the submarine campaign caused serious losses of Allied ships and cargoes. Yet it was also politically dangerous warfare. Some of the ships sunk belonged to neutral countries. The sinking of the *Lusitania* by torpedo attack and the loss of 1,000 lives, including 128 Americans, led to strong protests from the USA. Although the Germans scaled down their U-boat campaign in September 1915 in an attempt to keep America out of the war, the failure at Jutland (see below) to harm significantly the British Grand Fleet led to a decision to renew the campaign of unrestricted submarine warfare in February 1917. The Germans hoped that the underwater blockade would starve Britain and France into surrender before the USA could have any impact on the war. They were very nearly successful. In February 1917, Britain lost 464,000 tons of shipping. In April it lost 834,000 tons. Britain was soon down to only six weeks' worth of supplies of corn.

Sea minefields and major naval engagements around Britain and Western Europe.

Why was Britain able to survive the U-boat blockade?

The success rate of the U-boats was due to the fact that they were attacking unarmed merchant ships that were travelling alone or in small groups without any protection. Lloyd George supported the idea of a convoy system in which large numbers of merchant ships would sail together with a naval escort. Neither the Admiralty nor the shipping companies were enthusiastic about this idea, but they eventually agreed. It was the turning point. By October 1917, a total of 99 homeward-bound convoys had reached harbour safely and only 10 vessels had been lost. The last quarter of 1917 saw 235 ships lost compared to 413 ships in the second quarter of the year.

The convoy system did not eliminate the threat of the U-boats completely, but other factors now also came into play to help defeat the U-boat threat:

- As losses went down due to the convoy system, the total tonnage of Allied shipping increased due to the vast increases in output from American shipyards; thus the U-boat campaign was unable to achieve a reduction in the overall volume of Allied shipping.
- Weapons technology progressed so that surface vessels could locate and attack U-boats even when they were submerged. The hydrophone passive listening device enabled ships to 'listen' for U-boat engine noises, and depth charges were developed to attack submarines. By 1918, sonar had been developed and the French were also using echo ranging, both technologies that allowed U-boat detection. In 1918, the Germans lost 69 U-boats and, at this stage in the war, they were unable to replace them.
- Improved submarine nets were designed and deployed across the entrances to the English Channel, which forced the U-boats to go north around the top of Britain, thus seriously reducing their operational time in the war zone.

German poster of 1917: 'The U-boats are out!'

The battle of Jutland

Despite the expectations of a major confrontation between the main German and British fleets and the new dreadnoughts, such a clash did not occur until 1916 – mainly because both sides realized that they had too much to lose if they waged a head-on battle. Instead, the war at sea was dominated by submarines and mines, as explained above. Nevertheless, there was one major challenge to British supremacy of the sea at the battle of Jutland (31 May–1 June 1916).

The battle began when German admiral Reinhard Scheer tried to lure part of the British fleet out from its base, so that an attack could be made by numerically superior German forces. However, due to the fact that the British could decipher German radio signals, more British ships came out than anticipated, and so Scheer had to fight an engagement involving some 250 ships in total. After several hours of exchanging artillery fire, the Germans decided to sail back to port. Although the Germans could claim victory, having lost 11 ships to Britain's 14, the major result of this encounter was that the Germans had not destroyed the British fleet – Britain was left in control of the surface waters. The German High Seas Fleet stayed in Kiel for the rest of the war, and instead the Germans switched their focus to the submarine warfare outlined above. 'As one journalist famously remarked, the High Seas Fleet had succeeded only in assaulting its gaoler before returning to gaol' (Ian Beckett, *The Great War 1914–1918*, 2001).

The fact that Britain's navy enjoyed supremacy for the course of the war was central in allowing it to move 8.5 million troops across the British Empire, as well as troops and supplies from Britain across the Channel to France. Imports continued to reach Britain, and the Allies were able to establish and maintain the devastating blockade on Germany. Ultimately, they were also able to sustain the convoy system and transport American men and equipment to Europe for the final battles.

STUDENT STUDY SECTION

Discussion/review questions

To what extent can it be argued that German attempts to destroy British naval supremacy were a complete failure?

Document analysis

The new policy [of unrestricted submarine warfare] has swept every restriction aside. All vessels, irrespective of cargo and flag, have been sent to the bottom, without help and without mercy. Even hospital and relief ships, though provided with the Germans' safe conduct, were sunk with the same reckless lack of compassion and principle...

German submarine warfare is no longer directed against belligerents but against the whole world. All nations are involved in Germany's action. The challenge is to all mankind. Wanton, wholesale destruction has been effected against women and children while they have been engaged in pursuits which even in the darkest periods of modern history have been regarded as innocent and legitimate...

There is one choice I cannot make. I will not choose the path of submission, and suffer the most sacred rights of the nation and of the people to be ignored and violated.

With a profound sense of the solemn and even tragic character of the step I am taking, and of the grave responsibilities involved, but in unhesitating obedience to my constitutional duty, I advise Congress to declare that the recent course of the German government is nothing less than war against the United States, and the United States accept the status of a belligerent which has been thrust upon it, and will take immediate steps to put the country into a thorough state of defence, and to exert all the power and resource in bringing Germany to terms, and in ending the war...

Speech by President Woodrow Wilson to the joint houses of Congress, 2 April 1917

Questions

1   What is the overall message of this speech with regard to German actions in carrying out unrestricted submarine warfare?

2   What is the value of this speech to an historian studying the reasons for US entry into the war? What are the limitations of the speech?

War in the air

One of the major technological leaps in the Great War was the use of aircraft as military weapons. As the war progressed, the importance of aircraft became increasingly evident.

Airships, bombs and civilian targets

In the early stages of the war, it was the airship that had the most important role in the air. Certainly, military leaders saw them as more useful than aeroplanes because they were more reliable, could carry heavy loads and had a much greater range. The British used airships mainly for escorting ships and for spotting U-boats (they could then warn the escort ships by radio). The Germans, however, with their more advanced airship called the Zeppelin, soon realized the potential of the airship for carrying out bombing on civilian and industrial targets in Britain. At the start of the war, the Germans had a force of 30 Zeppelins, and although potentially an easy target – they contained 57,000 cubic metres of highly flammable hydrogen – they were initially reasonably safe because of the height at which they flew. Raids on London, the Midlands and the East Coast killed several hundred civilians. As British defences improved, however, Zeppelins became too vulnerable and were replaced with bomber aircraft, the most famous of which was the Gotha. This bomber caused nearly 3,000 casualties in raids against London and south-east England. The British responded with the development of their own bomber fleet as part of the Royal Flying Corps (RFC). The British aircraft also made bombing raids into enemy territory in the last year of the war. By February 1918, there were the first 'round the clock' raids, with British DH4 planes attacking the town of Trier by day and Handley-Page aircraft attacking at night. In March, there were raids on Mannheim, Mainz and Stuttgart during the day. Clearly the idea of attacking civilians from the air had already become a feature of 20th-century war by 1918.

Zeppelin airships were used for air raids against British towns and cities.

Aircraft – reconnaissance, dog-fights and ground attack

Aircraft were a relatively recent invention, and thus very primitive and unreliable at the start of the war. Yet they soon came to fulfil important functions over the battlefields. First, their speed and mobility meant that they could be used for detailed reconnaissance work over enemy trenches. Pilots were able to report on troop concentrations, artillery positions and enemy movements, in addition to directing the fire of their own artillery onto specific targets. Photographs of trench systems and artillery targets were taken from the air, and by 1918 photographic images could be taken as high as 4,500m. Messages could even be dropped from the aircraft. With the development of the aerial wireless, communication was also possible between aircraft and the ground.

The airmen in these reconnaissance planes soon began to experiment with improvised weapons to bring down rival reconnaissance flights. This innovation led to the emergence of aerial 'dog-fights'. At first pilots tried to attack each other with pistols and rifles, but by 1915 machine guns were fitted and synchronized so that they could shoot through the propeller of the airplane without striking the blades.

Dog-fights became a common sight over the trenches. Aircraft also became increasingly important for attacking enemy ground troops. For example, in 1918 ground-attack aircraft played their part in the Allied victory by dropping 1,563 bombs and firing 122,150 rounds of machine-gun ammunition in support of land offensives.

The growing awareness of the importance of air power meant that the aircraft evolved rapidly during the course of the war. The numbers of aircraft also grew; by 1918, there were more than 8,000 aircraft in operation on all sides. Control of the skies over the battlefield had become essential to victory. Politicians and commanders in all countries realized the potential importance of airpower – including the idea that bombing civilians could play a key role in undermining the enemy's morale. The end of World War I was still determined by what happened on the ground, but in both strategy and tactics, there were signs of what would come in the next war of 1939 to 1945.

The war in the air

The idea of honourable combat between fighter 'aces' caught people's imaginations during the war, and all countries had their own heroes. While the soldiers in the trenches remained anonymous, the names of the fighter aces became well known, such as Major 'Micky' Mannock in Britain, René Fonck in France and perhaps the most famous of all, Baron von Richthofen, or the 'Red Baron', from Germany, who headed his 'flying circus' squadron and shot down 80 planes. Governments soon realized the propaganda potential of glamorous war heroes and encouraged dramatic accounts of air combat, which were much better for morale than stories of the horrors of the trenches. However, the development of mass air actions with much greater numbers of aeroplanes led to the end of this 'romantic' individual action.

The 'Red Baron' – German fighter ace Baron Manfred von Richthofen.

The Sopwith Camel was one of the best fighter planes of World War I.

Strategy and tactics
A strategy is the overall plan of action. It involves looking at the 'bigger picture' and seeing how all the different battles and engagements are linked together. Strategy is different from tactics. Tactics are the actual ways in which a strategy is carried out, i.e. how a particular battle is conducted.

STUDENT STUDY SECTION

Review activities

Using what you have read in this chapter, copy and fill out the grids below and then answer the questions that follow.

	Western Front (land)	Eastern Front (land)	War in the air	War at sea
Key strategies/ tactics used				
Impact of tactics (consider casualties, land gained, strategic gains)				
Overall impact on outcome of the war				

Questions

1 Looking at the battles on both the Western and the Eastern Fronts, what differences can you see in how the war was fought and how it developed along these two fronts? (Refer to the map on p.45 and notice the amount of territory that changed hands on the Western and Eastern Fronts. Also compare casualty figures between the two fronts.)

2 Why do think that there were these differences?

3 What impact would the changing frontline in the east have had on the civilian populations of these areas?

4 What impact overall did the war at sea have on the outcome of World War I?

5 What was the impact of the war in the air?

6 Overall, which theatre of war was most important for the outcome of the war?

TECHNOLOGICAL DEVELOPMENTS			
	Technological developments	Impact on tactics	Impact on outcome of the war
War on land			
War at sea			
War in the air			

Questions

1 How important were technological developments in deciding the outcome of the war?

2 What do you consider to be the most important of the technological developments made?

3 How did these technological developments change the nature of warfare?

What were the reasons for Germany's defeat in World War I?

Looking back over this chapter, we can see several reasons for Germany's eventual defeat. These can be grouped into Germany's weaknesses and mistakes and the Allies' successes and strengths.

Germany's weaknesses/failures

Germany made several ambitious gambles that didn't pay off. It gambled on a quick victory with the Schlieffen Plan. Once that gamble had failed, there was no hope of a rapid conclusion to the war. The plan, with its march through Belgium, also resulted in Britain entering the war. The war that resulted on two fronts was the one that Germany had always dreaded and tried to avoid. Another gamble – that of Verdun, with its emphasis on wearing down the strength of France and Britain – also failed. The German high-risk strategy of unrestricted U-boat warfare not only failed, but also helped to bring the USA into the war, which was vital to boosting Allied resources in 1918. By August 1918, US troops were arriving at a rate of 300,000 a month

Germany also suffered from weak allies. As you have read, Germany constantly had to help out the Austrians and Bulgarians. With the defeat of Bulgaria and then the Serbs in September 1918, followed by the defeat of Austria by Italy and then the surrender of Turkey in October, it was only a matter of time before Germany had to surrender.

The failure of the Ludendorff Offensive was critical to overall German defeat. As historian Alexander Watson writes: 'Their [Ludendorff and Hindenburg's] desperate desire for peace derived not from any domestic considerations nor even the weakness of Germany's allies; it was due principally to the parlous state of their army. The war had been above all a contest of endurance and, during the course of 1918, the accumulated strain and the hopelessness of its situation had broken the army's will to continue fighting' (Watson, 'Stabbed at the Front', *History Today*, 2008). The Germans were ultimately unable to sustain their losses after the failure of the 1918 offensive. An epidemic of Spanish flu in 1918 made the situation much worse, and morale was very low in the German Army. When Ludendorff asked for an armistice in October 1918, he said it was because, 'No reliance can be put on the troops any longer. Since August 8, it has gone rapidly down hill. Continually units have proved themselves so unreliable that they have hurriedly had to be withdrawn from the front … the High Command and the German Army are finished.'

On top of military factors, the dire economic situation in Germany by 1918 played an important role in Germany's defeat. It meant that supplies were not reaching the German Army, and that the German population was ready for revolution. This situation was due partly due to the Allied blockade, which prevented imports reaching Germany, and also because the German government proved less efficient at organizing the country for war than the Allied countries. Germany spent 83 per cent of total public expenditure on military items, but just 2 per cent on the civilian sector. The figures in Britain were 62 per cent and 16 per cent respectively. Over the course of the conflict, there was a shift in resources away from the production of civilian goods in Germany. German agriculture was particularly hard hit by the war; production fell by 70 per cent in some areas. The economic situation, combined with the continual failures of the troops, meant that Germany was in a state of internal collapse by the end of 1918.

Even Russia's withdrawal from the war and the harsh terms of the Treaty of Brest-Litovsk did not help Germany. The lengthy deliberations over the treaty seriously disrupted planning for the German spring offensive that was to begin on 21 March 1918. The one million men who were needed in the west were also still in the east to enforce the treaty and to occupy the Ukraine. The chaos in Russia and the impact of the civil war on agriculture also meant that Germany was unable to get badly needed resources from Russia to help deal with shortages at home.

Allied strengths/successes

Ultimately, the Allies had greater men and resources and so the longer the war went on, the harder it was for the Germans to win. Germany could have beaten France on a one-to-one basis, just as Russia could have beaten Austria-Hungary, but all countries working together and helping each other out meant that the war would become one of attrition. This situation, in the long term, benefited the Allies (particularly once the USA had joined the war).

Maintaining control of the sea was decisive for the Allies. The blockade on Germany helped to cause dreadful food shortages, while Britain was still able to import food supplies both from its colonies and from the USA with the help of the convoy system. The British and French were also particularly successful in mobilizing their economies.

In the Allied counter-offensive of 1918, the Allies benefited from a greater coordination of effort and what Beckett calls a 'distinctly "modern" style of warfare' that took advantage of all of the technological and tactical developments that had taken place during the war – using tanks, artillery, aircraft and infantry in relatively close cooperation. The contribution of the USA to Allied victory in 1918 was also critical. US troops started arriving in France in June 1918. The two million soldiers eventually deployed brought a huge advantage to the Allied side in that they lacked the 'war weariness' of European soldiers now on the Western Front. America's massive economic resources were another key factor in the push for Allied victory. The USA made a substantial difference to the Allied fight, contributing money, weaponry and warships. Altogether America lent more than $7.7 billion to the Allies during the war. As Akira Iriye puts it in *The Globalising of America 1913–1945* (1993), 'American participation spelled the defeat of German ambitions.'

ToK Time

Before you go on to read about World War I and total war, it is important to consider whether or not there can be effective 'rules' when fighting a war. There had been attempts to limit warfare, and to draw up some rules of engagement, prior to the Great War, at The Hague in 1898 (see Chapter 1).

What rules of engagement *should* there be in war? Should chemical and biological warfare be forbidden? Should civilian targets be outlawed?

What rules of engagement *have* to be tolerated in warfare?

How far do ethics matter in wars? Are morality and warfare mutually exclusive ideas?

Discuss these ideas as a class. Write up the discussion in your ToK journal.

In what ways was World War I a total war?

The diagram below highlights the key elements of World War I as total war.

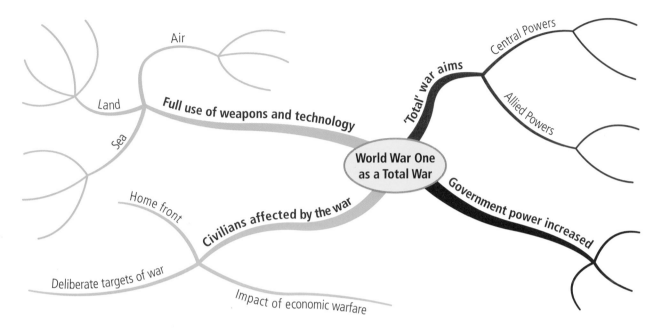

Air

Land

Sea

Full use of weapons and technology

'Total' war aims

Central Powers

Allied Powers

World War One as a Total War

Government power increased

Home front

Civilians affected by the war

Deliberate targets of war

Impact of economic warfare

Mind-map – World War I as a total war.

World War I is considered to be the first total war for several reasons:

- Both sides fought the war, not for limited aims but for total victory.
- Governments used all weaponry that they had at their disposal in order to win the war. They also developed new technologies and weaponry as the war progressed.
- It involved all people of the major countries – not only soldiers but also civilians. Civilians were deliberately targeted during the military conflict and they suffered from the economic warfare carried out by both sides. Women also played a major role in the war effort at home.
- In order to fight the kind of battles waged in World War I, and to weld the state into a united, efficient war-making machine, nations developed new ways of controlling the economy and their own populations. In the process of trying to do this, the countries of Europe experienced major changes in government as well as in established social and economic practices.

These points are discussed in more detail below.

The aims of the belligerents

The *aims* of the powers involved in the fighting were 'total' and made any negotiated peace very difficult to achieve. Germany's aims in the September Memorandum have already been discussed on p.40. However, all the Great Powers developed ambitious war aims that they were reluctant to give up. France was determined to regain Alsace-Lorraine and both France and Britain had committed themselves to crushing 'Prussian militarism'. **Propaganda** on both sides reinforced nationalist sentiment, justifying the war and demonizing the enemy. Governments would have had to do a serious turn around in terms of public opinion if they were to seek a compromise.

STUDENT STUDY SECTION

A GERMAN "PEACE."
(FOR THE INSTRUCTION OF OUR PACIFISTS.)

Cartoon analysis

What is the message of this British cartoon?

In 1917, there were several calls for peace, coming from such divergent sources as the Pope, Lenin (the new Bolshevik leader of Russia) and Lord Lansdowne, a British **Conservative** and former Viceroy of India and Foreign Secretary. Pope Benedict XV called for a return to the territorial status quo of 1914 and a renunciation of all financial demands. Lenin also called for a peace without annexations or financial demands. Lord Lansdowne made the point that the war was costing more in terms of human and economic resources than could ever be regained, even by victory.

Yet both sides continued to believe that they *could* win. As P.M.H. Bell writes, 'Only victory would do, and only victory could justify the sacrifices made in the war' (*Twentieth Century Europe*, 2006).

The use of weaponry

As you have read, both sides used the full arsenal of weapons at their disposal and also developed new technologies for land, sea and air warfare to try to break the deadlock and achieve total victory. This pursuit involved, in the case of gas, breaking international agreements; the Hague Convention of 1899 had prohibited the use of poisons as weapons.

The role of civilians

The impact of the fighting on civilians

As you have read earlier in this chapter, civilians were also affected by the actual fighting, and there were many casualties as a result of the new technologies available to both sides. Paris was shelled from a distance of 126km by the massive German gun known as 'Long Max', while first the Zeppelins, and later planes, made raids on Britain. British planes also inflicted severe damage on German factories and towns in the last year of the war.

On the Eastern Front, civilians were actually caught up in the battles. Because there was relatively little movement on the Western Front, civilians, after the initial battles, were able to keep away from the actual fighting and casualties only resulted due to inaccurate artillery fire. By contrast, the great advances and retreats that took place on the Eastern Front meant that civilians were involved in the violence, sometimes accidentally and sometimes deliberately. For example, Jews – viewed with suspicion by the Russian military – were actively attacked by advancing Russians. Other minorities also suffered: Germans, Gypsies, Hungarians and Turks were all deported from Russia's western provinces during the war. Ethnic violence also took place in the Balkans. As Niall Ferguson writes in *The War of the World*:

The Western Front had revealed a new level of industrialization of warfare – had seen the introduction of machines of death comparable in their lethal effectiveness with those Wells had imagined in The War of the Worlds. *But the Eastern Front had seen an equally important transformation of warfare. There the death throes of the old Central and East European empires had dissolved the old boundaries between combatant and civilian. This kind of war proved much easier to start than to stop.*

From Niall Ferguson, *The War of the World*, 2006

The lives of civilians in all countries were also affected by the huge losses of soldiers; all families and villages across Europe faced the consequences of the 'lost generation'. The enormous casualties in the early campaigns also led to the introduction of military conscription, in 1915 for France and 1916 for Britain.

Genocide

World War I also saw the 20th century's first **genocide**. Turkish propaganda at the time presented the Armenians as saboteurs and a pro-Russian 'fifth column'. Hundreds of thousands of Armenians died from starvation and thirst when the Ottoman Turks deported them en masse from eastern Anatolia to the Syrian desert and elsewhere in 1915–16. There is dispute over the number of Armenians killed. Armenians say 1.5 million, while the republic of Turkey estimates the total to be 300,000. According to the International Association of Genocide scholars, the total was 'more than a million'.

The impact of economic warfare on civilians

Both sides realized the advantages of cutting off supplies to their enemies. They tried to disrupt each other's trade routes, and prevent vital foods and raw materials getting through by laying minefields at sea or attacking merchant ships with submarines or warships. The British blockade had a devastating effect on Germany, causing desperate food shortages and contributing to Germany's defeat in 1918. The average daily calorie input for a civilian adult dropped from around 1,500 in 1915 to below 1,000 in the winter of 1916–17. Germany's use of submarine warfare also subjected British civilians to shortages, and Russia suffered from the blockade of the Dardanelles. Rationing was introduced in many countries.

Artwork by Käthe Kollwitz; 'The Children are Starving'.

Civilians as part of the war effort

The war saw the rapid growth of industry in all countries as governments tried to keep up with the production demands of total war. In Britain, France and Germany, these demands also meant women joining the workforce as more and more men left to fight in the war. However, in all countries there was resistance to employing women, and it was not until 1915 that serious recruitment of women into industries began. Even then, there was little enthusiasm from employers and trade unions for women entering the workforce, and in Britain there had to be negotiations to reach agreements on women entering 'men's jobs' in munitions and engineering, e.g. that such arrangements were only to be temporary and that the women would not be trained up as 'fully skilled tradesmen'. Women were supposed to receive equal wages to men for similar jobs, but rarely did; their wages remained low, though higher than traditional women's work. This situation was despite the fact that the work in munitions in particular was extremely dangerous, with risks of TNT poisoning and accidental explosions. By 1917, one in four war workers was female, leading Joseph Joffre to claim that 'if the women in the war factories stopped for 20 minutes, we should lose the war.'

Women working in a munitions factory.

The growth of government power

Other changes on the home fronts came with increased centralization of power in the hands of the governments of Britain, France and Germany. Citizens found themselves being subjected to much greater control from their governments as countries tried to ensure that maximum use was made of human and economic resources. In Britain, the government passed the Defence of the Realm Act (DORA) in 1914, which gave the government wide-ranging powers to police many aspects of people's daily lives, such as restricting the hours of pub opening, preventing the use of binoculars and limiting the lighting of bonfires. In France, a 'state of siege' was proclaimed by President Raymond Poincaré, who placed eight departments of government under the control of the commander-in-chief, Joffre, and subject to military law. This number was later increased to 33 departments. In Germany, executive power was given to the deputy commanding generals of Germany's 24 military districts. The Tsar in Russia, meanwhile, used the pro-war atmosphere in 1914 as an opportunity to reassert autocratic powers and rule without the Duma (Russian parliament).

Government control was exercised in several key areas:

Controlling manpower

To control manpower more effectively, conscription was introduced in most countries. In the UK it was introduced in 1916. This decision was taken not just because of the need for more men, but also because British industry could not afford to lose its skilled workers; so many miners had joined up, for example, that many had to be sent back in order to maintain the essential supplies of coal. The controlled direction of manpower was necessary to ensure that both industry and the armed forces were provided for; it has been estimated that it took three civilian workers to keep a soldier fighting in World War I. The government also took the lead in negotiating with the trade unions to get women to work in the munitions factories (see p.64).

Controlling production

To increase the efficiency of production, governments started to exercise more control over industry. In the UK, this involved nationalizing key industries such as coal mining and shipping and also regulating wages and prices to ensure that inflation did not get out of hand. In Germany, industrialist Walter Rathenau also tried to bring industry under the control of the War Boards to oversee production, but he was never as successful at achieving this as the British government, and faced frustrating interference from the German military.

In Britain, involvement in the workplace by the government extended to intervention in areas such as canteens and child care, and the setting up of various committees such as the Health of Munitions Workers Committee.

By 1918, the Ministry of Munitions owned more than 250 factories, administering a further 20,000 and the government employed 5 million workers. A huge experiment in 'state capitalism' was under way, and the significance of this was not lost on workers, employers, unions and Labour politicians. The change in attitude is aptly illustrated by Lloyd George's famous promise of 'habitations for the heroes who have won the war' the day after the armistice, and the subsequent establishment of the Ministry of Health.

From Ian Cawood and David McKinnon-Bell, *The First World War,* **2001**

Controlling morale

In order to motivate the home fronts and keep up morale, governments also spent a great deal of time and energy on wartime propaganda. At first, propaganda was used to emphasize the defensive nature of the war; each side produced propaganda to show that it was simply defending its soil and national pride. Later, propaganda became more important to justify the length of the war and to counter opposition to its continuation. Propaganda portrayed the enemy as an inhuman force that must be defeated at all costs. The British government also created a Ministry of Information, making propaganda a key element of its war policy.

Controlling the economy

In order to pay for the war, Britain increased direct taxation. It also abandoned its 19th-century policy of **free trade** by adopting tariffs on certain types of imported goods. All countries borrowed immense sums to pay for the war. The Russians, French and Italians borrowed heavily from the British and the Americans; the British also borrowed massive amounts from the USA. The governments of all combatants borrowed from their own people through 'war loans', which would be paid with interest after the war.

In Russia, borrowing led to rapid inflation as the amount of money in circulation increased; this contributed to the disastrous economic situation in Russia leading to revolution in 1917. In Germany, money for the war was raised almost entirely through loans and government **savings bonds**, which the government intended to repay when victory came. Only 6 per cent was raised by taxation as against 20 per cent in Britain. Germany planned to pay for the war through the imposition of severe treaties on its defeated enemies and did not plan for defeat. When defeat came, however, Germany was bankrupt and thousands of Germans lost their savings.

STUDENT STUDY SECTION

Essay plan

Why did World War I last so long?

Introduction

Don't forget to put the question into context here. Explain expectations that the war would be over quickly and why there was this expectation. You also need to identify the key points that you will be covering in your essay and give an outline of your main argument.

Main body of the essay

Below is a list of points that you could consider in this essay. Look back through this chapter, and in pairs discuss how each of these factors contributed to the length of the war. (You may want to make some of these points whole paragraphs in themselves, or combine two or more into one paragraph.)

- The two sides were of similar strength
- The trench systems on the Western Front
- The tactics of the commanders
- Technological developments
- Failure of the Schlieffen Plan
- Failure to gain command of the seas
- Failure at attempts to negotiate peace
- Failure of diversionary fronts.

Conclusion

State your overall argument based on what you have discussed in the main body of your essay.

Student Answer

The tactics of the generals were also a key reason why World War I lasted so long. World War I was a completely new type of war and one for which the generals had not been trained. It took a long time for the generals to adapt to trench warfare and the technological developments of the machine gun and artillery. Initially, for example, the French generals believed in 'élan' and forced their troops to wear red trousers even though this would cause huge casualties. Many generals, for example Haig and Falkenhayn, were and still are criticized for their tactics of 'attrition', resulting in hundreds of thousands of deaths at the battles of the Somme and Verdun. They believed the only way of breaking the stalemate was to wear down the enemy until you were the last man standing. However, this would take a very long time which is why the war would last for so long.

Annotate the above paragraph to indicate:

- The opening 'signpost' sentence (which should relate to the question and make it clear what the topic of the paragraph is going to be about)

● **Examiner's hint**
Constructing good paragraphs in your essay.

As indicated by the essay planning guideline on p.36, each of your paragraphs should follow a certain structure. The paragraph opposite, taken from a student answer to the essay question, makes a good attempt at doing this.

- An explanation as to why this topic is relevant to the question
- Evidence to support the argument
- The final sentence linking back to the question and restating the relevance of the paragraph.

How could you improve on this paragraph?

Also, plan and write this essay: Why did the Central Powers lose World War I?

Look back at the discussion on pp.59–60 for material on this subject. You may want to structure your essay along the same lines, i.e. failures of Germany and then strengths/successes of the Allies. Alternatively, you could divide the factors into the following sections:

- War on land
- War at sea
- Total war and how Germany organized its resources compared to the Allies
- Economic factors and the collapse of Germany. (Do you consider economic or military factors to be the most important reasons for the Central Powers losing the war?)

THE RESULTS OF WORLD WAR I

4

When the delegates of the 'victorious' powers met at Versailles near Paris in 1919 to attempt to create a peace settlement, they faced a Europe that was very different to that of 1914, and one that was in a state of turmoil and chaos. The old empires of Germany, Russia and Austria-Hungary had disappeared, and various successor states were struggling to replace them. A communist revolution had taken place in Russia and there appeared to be a real threat of revolution spreading across Europe. In addition, there had been terrible destruction, and the population of Europe now faced the problems of starvation, displacement and a lethal flu epidemic.

Against this difficult background, the leaders of France, Britain, the USA and Italy attempted to create a peace settlement. The fact that their peace settlement was to break down within 20 years has led many historians to view it as a disaster that contributed to the outbreak of World War II. More recently, however, historians have argued that the peacemakers did not fully comprehend the scale of the problems in 1919, therefore it is not surprising that they failed to create a lasting peace.

The impact of the war on Europe; the situation in 1919

The human cost of the war

The Tyne Cot cemetery at Passchendaele in Belgium.

The death toll for the armed forces in World War I was appalling. Around nine million soldiers were killed, which was about 15 per cent of all combatants. In addition, millions more were permanently disabled by the war; of British war veterans, for example, 41,000 lost a limb in the fighting. In Britain, it became common to talk of a 'lost generation'. Such was a particularly appropriate phrase for the situation in France, where 20 per cent of those between the ages of 20 and 40 in 1914 were killed.

Although civilians were not killed on the scale that they would be in World War II, populations had nevertheless become targets of war. In addition to the civilians killed directly in the war, millions more died from famine and disease at the end of the war and at least a further 20 million died worldwide in the Spanish flu epidemic in the winter of 1918–19.

Economic consequences

The economic impact of the war on Europe was devastating. The war cost Britain alone more than £34 billion. All powers had financed the war by borrowing money. By 1918, the USA had lent $2,000 million to Britain and France; U-boats had also sunk 40 per cent of British merchant shipping. Throughout the 1920s, Britain and France spent between one-third and one-half of their total public expenditure on debt charges and repayments. Britain never regained its pre-war international financial predominance, and lost several overseas markets.

The physical effects of the war also had an impact on the economic situation of Europe. Wherever fighting had taken place, land and industry had been destroyed. France suffered particularly badly, with farm land (2 million hectares), factories and railway lines along the Western Front totally ruined. Belgium, Poland, Italy and Serbia were also badly affected. Roads and railway lines needed to be reconstructed, hospitals and houses had to be rebuilt and arable land made productive again by the removal of unexploded shells. Consequently, there was a dramatic decline in manufacturing output. Combined with the loss of trade and foreign investments, it is clear that Europe faced an acute economic crisis in 1919.

Political consequences

The victorious governments of Britain and France did not suffer any major political changes as a result of the war. However, there were huge changes in Central Europe, where the map was completely redrawn. Before 1914, Central Europe had been dominated by multi-national, monarchical regimes. By the end of the war, these regimes had all collapsed. As Niall Ferguson writes, 'the war led to a triumph of republicanism undreamt of even in the 1790s' (*The Pity of War*, 2006).

Germany

Even before the war ended on 11 November 1918, revolution had broken out in Germany against the old regime. Sailors in northern Germany mutinied and took over the town of Kiel. This action triggered other revolts, with socialists leading uprisings of workers and soldiers in other German ports and cities. In Bavaria, an independent socialist republic was declared. On 9 November 1918, the Kaiser abdicated his throne and fled to Holland. The following day, the socialist leader Friedrich Ebert became the new leader of the Republic of Germany.

Russia

As discussed in the previous chapter, Russia experienced two revolutions in 1917. The first overthrew the Tsarist regime and replaced it briefly with a Provisional Government that planned to hold free elections. This government, however, was overthrown in the second revolution of 1917, in which the communist Bolsheviks seized power and sought to

The Spanish flu

Spanish flu was a flu pandemic that hit the world in 1918, causing millions of deaths. It first appeared in the United States, but spread to nearly every part of the world. It is estimated that anywhere from 20 to 100 million people died worldwide, at least more than double the number killed in World War I. It was called the Spanish flu primarily because the pandemic received such great press attention when it moved from France to Spain in November 1918. Spain was not involved in the war and had not imposed wartime censorship.

establish a dictatorship. In turn this, and the peace of Brest-Litovsk that took Russia out of the war, helped to cause a civil war that lasted until the end of 1920.

The Habsburg Empire

With the defeat of Austria-Hungary, the Habsburg Empire disintegrated and the monarchy collapsed. The last Emperor, Karl I, was forced to abdicate in November 1918 and a republic was declared. Austria and Hungary split into two separate states and the various other nationalities in the empire declared themselves independent.

Turkey

The collapse of the Sultanate finally came in 1922, and it was replaced by the rule of Mustapha Kemal, who established an authoritarian regime.

The collapse of these empires left a huge area of Central and Eastern Europe in turmoil. In addition, the success of the Bolsheviks in Russia encouraged growth of socialist politics in post-war Europe. Many of the ruling classes were afraid that revolution would spread across the continent, particularly given the weak economic state of all countries.

Impact of the war outside of Europe: the situation in 1919

America

In stark comparison to the economic situation in Europe, the USA emerged from the war as the world's leading economy. Throughout the war, American industry and trade had prospered as US food, raw materials and munitions were sent to Europe to help with the war effort. In addition, the USA had taken over European overseas markets during the war, and many American industries had become more successful than their European competitors. The USA had, for example, replaced Germany as the world's leading producer of fertilizers, dyes and chemical products. The war also led to US advances in technology – the USA was now world leader in areas such as mechanization and the development of plastics.

Wilson hoped that America would now play a larger role in international affairs and worked hard at the peace conference to create an alternative world order in which international problems would be solved through collective security (see next chapter). However, the majority of Americans had never wanted to be involved in World War I, and once it ended they were keen to return to concerns nearer to home: the Spanish flu epidemic, the fear of communism (exacerbated by a series of industrial strikes) and racial tension, which exploded into riots in 25 cities across the USA. There was also a concern that America might be dragged into other European disputes.

Japan and China

Japan also did well economically out of the war. As in the case of America, new markets and new demands for Japanese goods brought economic growth and prosperity, with exports nearly tripling during the war years. World War I also presented Japan with opportunities for territorial expansion; under the guise of the Anglo-Japanese alliance, it was able to seize German holdings in Shandong and German-held islands in the Pacific, as well as presenting the Chinese with a list of 21 demands that aimed for political and economic domination of China. At the end of the war, Japan hoped to be able to hold on to these gains.

China, which had finally entered the war on the Allied side in 1917, was also entitled to send delegates to the Versailles Conference. Their hopes were entirely opposed to those of the

Japanese: they wanted to resume political and economic control over Shandong and they wanted a release from the Japanese demands.

Problems facing the peacemakers in 1919

The Versailles peace conference was dominated by the political leaders of three of the five victorious powers: David Lloyd George (Prime Minster of the UK), Georges Clemenceau (Prime Minster of France) and Woodrow Wilson (President of the USA). Japan was only interested in what was decided about the Pacific, and played little part. Vittorio Orlando, Prime Minster of Italy, played only a minor role in discussions and in fact walked out of the conference when he failed to get the territorial gains that Italy had hoped for.

The first problem faced by the peacemakers at Versailles was the political and social instability in Europe, which necessitated that they act speedily to reach a peace settlement. One Allied observer noted that 'there was a veritable race between peace and anarchy'. Other political issues, however, combined to make a satisfactory treaty difficult to achieve:

- The different aims of the peacemakers
- The nature of the Armistice settlement and the mood of the German population
- The popular sentiment in the Allied countries.

The aims of the peacemakers

In a speech to Congress on 8 January 1918, Woodrow Wilson stated US war aims in his Fourteen Points, which can be summarized as follows:

1. Abolition of secret diplomacy
2. Free navigation at sea for all nations in war and peace
3. Free trade between countries
4. Disarmament by all countries
5. Colonies to have a say in their own future
6. German troops to leave Russia
7. Restoration of independence for Belgium
8. France to regain Alsace and Lorraine
9. Frontier between Austria and Italy to be adjusted along the lines of nationality
10. Self-determination for the peoples of Austria-Hungary
11. Serbia to have access to the sea
12. Self-determination for the people in the Turkish Empire and permanent opening of the Dardanelles
13. Poland to become an independent state with access to the sea
14. A **League of Nations** to be set up in order to preserve the peace.

A photo of the 'Big 3': Georges Clemenceau (Prime Minster of France), David Lloyd George (Prime Minster of the UK) and Woodrow Wilson (President of the USA).

STUDENT STUDY SECTION

Discussion questions

Look at Wilson's points. What would you consider to be his overall aims for the post-war world?

Which of these points would you consider as:

- ones that could be easily achieved?
- ones that would be difficult to achieve in Europe?

Are there issues not covered by Wilson's Fourteen Points which other countries might want to see addressed? Give reasons for your decisions.

As you can see from his points above, Wilson was an **idealist** whose aim was to build a better and more peaceful world. Although he believed that Germany should be punished, he hoped that these points would allow for a new political and international world order. Self-determination – giving the different ethnic groups within the old empires of Europe the chance to set up their own countries – would, in Wilson's mind, end the frustrations that had contributed to the outbreak of World War I. In addition, open diplomacy, world disarmament, economic integration and a League of Nations would stop secret alliances, and force countries to work together to prevent a tragedy such as World War I happening again.

Wilson also believed that the USA should take the lead in this new world order. In 1916, he had proclaimed that the object of the war should be 'to make the world safe for democracy'; unlike the ostensibly more selfish aims of the Allied powers, the USA would take the lead in promoting the ideas of democracy and self-determination.

Wilson's idealist views were not shared by Clemenceau and Lloyd George. Clemenceau (who commented that even God had only needed Ten Points) wanted a harsh settlement to ensure that Germany could not threaten France again. The way to achieve this would be to combine heavy economic and territorial **sanctions** with disarmament policies. Reparations for France were necessary not only to pay for the terrible losses inflicted upon their country, but also to keep Germany weak. Clemenceau was also keen to retain wartime links with Britain and America, and was ready to make concessions in order to achieve this aim.

Lloyd George was in favour of a less severe settlement. He wanted Germany to lose its navy and colonies so that it could not threaten the British Empire. Yet he also wanted Germany to be able to recover quickly, so that it could start trading again with Britain and so that it could be a bulwark against the spread of communism from the new Bolshevik Russia. He was also aware that 'injustice and arrogance displayed in the hour of triumph will never be forgotten or forgiven.' He was under pressure from public opinion at home, however, to make Germany accountable for the death and suffering that had taken place (see below).

The aims of Japan and Italy were to maximize their wartime gains. The Italian Prime Minster, Vittorio Orlando, wanted the Allies to keep their promises in the Treaty of London (see p.47) and also demanded the port of Fiume in the Adriatic. Japan, which had already seized the German islands in the Pacific, wanted recognition of these gains. Japan also wanted the inclusion of a racial equality clause in the Covenant of the League of Nations in the hope that this would protect Japanese immigrants in America.

STUDENT STUDY SECTION

Discussion question

How might the demands of France, Britain, Italy and Japan go against the spirit of Wilson's Fourteen Points?

The Armistice settlement and the mood of the German population

When the German government sued for an end to fighting, they did so in the belief that the Armistice would be based on Wilson's Fourteen Points. It offered an alternative to having to face the 'total' defeat that the nature of this war had indicated would happen. In reality, the Armistice terms were very tough, and were designed not only to remove Germany's ability to continue fighting, but also to serve as the basis for a more permanent weakening of Germany. The terms of the Armistice ordered Germany to evacuate all occupied territory including Alsace-Lorraine, and to withdraw beyond a 10km-wide neutral zone to the east of the Rhine. Allied troops would occupy the west bank of the Rhine. The Germans also lost all their submarines and much of their surface fleet and air force.

When the German Army returned home after the new government had signed the Armistice, they were still greeted as heroes. For the German population, however, the defeat came as a shock. The German Army had occupied parts of France and Belgium and had defeated Russia. The German people had been told that their army was on the verge of victory; the defeat did not seem to have been caused by any overwhelming Allied military victory, and certainly not by an invasion of Germany.

Several days after the Armistice had been signed, Field Marshal Paul von Hindenburg, a respected German commander, made the following comment: 'In spite of the superiority of the enemy in men and materials, we could have brought the struggle to a favourable conclusion if there had been proper cooperation between the politicians and the army. The German Army was stabbed in the back.'

Although the German Army was in disarray by November 1918, the idea that Germany had been 'stabbed in the back' soon took hold. The months before the Armistice was signed had seen Germany facing mutinies and strikes and attempts by some groups to set up a socialist government. Therefore the blame for defeat was put on 'internal' enemies – Jews, socialists, communists. Hitler would later refer to those who had agreed to an armistice in November 1918 as the 'November Criminals'.

Thus, at the start of the Versailles Conference, the German population believed that they had not been truly defeated; even their leaders still believed that Germany would play a part in the peace conference and that the final treaty, based on Wilson's principles, would not be too harsh. There was, therefore, a huge difference between the expectations of the Germans and the expectations of the Allies, who believed that Germany would accept the terms of the treaty as the defeated nation.

The popular mood in Britain, France, Italy and the USA

Lloyd George, Clemenceau and Orlando also faced pressure from the popular mood in their own countries, where the feeling was that revenge must be exacted from the Germans for the trauma of the last four years. Encouraged by the popular press, the populations of Britain and France in particular looked to the peacemakers at Versailles to 'hang the Kaiser' and 'squeeze the German lemon until the pips squeak'. The French having borne the brunt of the fighting, would be satisfied with nothing less than a punitive peace.

The press closely reported all the details of the Versailles Conference and helped put pressure on the delegates to create a settlement that would satisfy popular demands. Clemenceau and Lloyd George also knew that their political success depended on keeping their electorates happy, which meant obtaining a harsh settlement. Similarly, Orlando was under pressure from opinion at home to get a settlement that gave Italy the territorial and economic gains it desired and which would at last make Italy into a great power.

In America, however, the electorate had lost interest in the Versailles settlement and Wilson's aims for Europe. Mid-term elections held on 5 November 1918 saw Americans reject Wilson's appeal to voters to support him in his work in Europe. There were sweeping gains for his Republican opponents, who had been very critical of his foreign policy and his Fourteen Points. When he sailed for Europe in December 1918, he left behind a Republican dominated **House of Representatives** and **Senate** and a hostile Foreign Relations Committee. He thus could not be sure that any agreements reached at Versailles would be honoured by his own government.

To access worksheet 4.1 on the Paris Peace Conference, please visit www.pearsonbacconline.com and follow the on-screen instructions.

STUDENT STUDY SECTION

Role play

Before you read what the peacemakers decided at Versailles, consider in more detail the issues they faced. Now divide the class into four groups. Groups 1, 2 and 3 should take on the roles of France, Britain and America. Group 4 is Germany. Groups 1–3 need to look at the issues presented below, and decide their standpoint on each one (based on the views of their country as presented above). Each group will then have to make a presentation to the rest of the class based on their decisions.

Germany was not allowed to have any representative at the Versailles Conference. In this role play, however, Group 4 will be given the opportunity to respond to the presentations of the other groups. The German delegation should therefore consider the bullet points below, as well as how they feel that Germany should be treated on each of the issues.

Points that your delegates need to address:

- Look at the map below showing disputed territory around Germany. What decisions will you make concerning each of these areas?
- Germany's armed forces. Will you limit them? If so, how?
- Germany's colonies. Should Germany lose them? If so, why? What should happen to them?
- Should Germany pay reparations? What damages, losses or penalties are these reparations expected to cover?
- Will you make Germany guilty of starting the war? If so, why?
- What other restrictions, if any, would you place on Germany?

At the start of your country's presentation, you need to give a brief speech giving an overview of your country's views regarding the war and any peace settlement, the impact the war has had on your country, and your views on Germany's responsibility.

Key

1 Alsace-Lorraine
Important industrial area claimed by France

2 Saar
Coal-rich area claimed by France but with large German population

3 Eupen/Malmedy
Coal/iron-rich area claimed by Belgium

4 Rhineland
Populated by Germans, but claimed by France as a protective zone

5 Schleswig
German since 1860s, but claimed by Denmark and with mixed Danish and German population

6/7 West Prussia/Posen and Thorn
German-speaking areas claimed by Poles, who wanted access to the Baltic Sea

8 Danzig
German-speaking port city, claimed by Poland

9/10 Allenstein and Marienwerder/Upper Silesia
Mixed Polish and German populations

11 Memel
Clamed by Lithuanians, but predominantly ethnic German

Disputed territories at issue in the Treaty of Versailles.

The terms of the Treaty of Versailles

After six hectic weeks of negotiations, deals and compromises, the German government was presented with the terms of the peace treaty. None of the powers on the losing side had been allowed any representation during the discussions. For this reason, it became known as the ***diktat***. The signing ceremony took place in the Hall of the Mirrors at Versailles, where the Germans had proclaimed the German Empire 50 years earlier following the Franco-Prussian War. The 440 clauses of the peace treaty covered the following areas:

War guilt

The infamous Clause 231, or what later became known as the 'war guilt clause', lay at the heart of the treaty:

The Allied and Associated Governments affirm and Germany accepts the responsibility of Germany and her allies for causing all the loss and damage to which the Allied and Associated Governments and their nationals have been subjected as a consequence of the war imposed upon them by the aggression of Germany and her allies.

Article 231, Treaty of Versailles, 1919

This clause allowed moral justification for the other terms of the treaty that were imposed upon Germany.

Disarmament

It was generally accepted that the pre-1914 arms race in Europe had contributed to the outbreak of war. Thus the treaty addressed disarmament directly. Yet while Germany was obliged to disarm to the lowest point compatible with internal security, there was only a general reference to the idea of full international disarmament. Specifically, Germany was forbidden to have submarines, an air force, armoured cars or tanks. It was allowed to keep six battleships and an army of 100,000 men to provide internal security. (The German Navy sank its own fleet at Scapa Flow in Scotland in protest.) In addition, the west bank of the Rhine was demilitarized (i.e. stripped of German troops) and an Allied Army of Occupation was to be stationed in the area for 15 years. The French had actually wanted the Rhineland taken away from Germany altogether, but this was not acceptable to Britain and the USA. Finally, a compromise was reached. France agreed that Germany could keep the (demilitarized) Rhineland and in return America and Britain gave a guarantee that if France were ever attacked by Germany in the future, they would immediately come to its assistance.

Territorial changes

Wilson's Fourteen Points proposed respect for the principle of self-determination, and the collapse of large empires gave an opportunity to create states based on the different nationalities. This ambition was to prove very difficult to achieve and, unavoidably, some nationals were left in countries where they constituted minorities, such as Germans who lived in Czechoslovakia. The situation was made even more complex by the territorial demands of the different powers and of the economic arrangements related to the payment of reparations.

The following points were agreed upon:

- Alsace-Lorraine, which had been seized from France after the Franco-Prussian War in 1871, was returned to France.
- The Saarland was put under the administration of the League of Nations for 15 years, after which a **plebiscite** was to allow the inhabitants to decide whether they wanted to be

① **Alsace and Lorraine**
▸ handed back to France

② **Rhineland**
▸ demilitarized zone

③ **Saar**
▸ under League of Nations for 15 years

④ **Polish Corridor**
▸ gave Poland an outlet to the sea

⑤ **Danzig**
▸ free city under League of Nations

⑥ **East Prussia**
▸ separated from the rest of Germany

⑦ **Eupen-Malmedy**
▸ to Belgium

⑧ **Memel**
▸ to Lithuania

⑨ **Upper Silesia**
▸ to Poland

⑩ **Northern Schleswig**
▸ to Denmark

Key
New/successor states

Territorial changes resulting from the Versailles Treaty.

Recreating Poland

Poland had ceased to exist as a country at the end of the 18th century, when it had been partitioned between Russia, Prussia and Austria. The Polish people, however, had always maintained a strong national identity and Polish independence was proclaimed at the cessation of fighting in 1918, and supported by Point 13 of Wilson's Fourteen Points. The Polish frontiers in the west were fixed by the peacemakers in the Treaty of Versailles. Yet the borders in the east were fixed after the Poles fought a victorious battle with the Bolsheviks and forced the Russians back from Warsaw. The resulting Treaty of Riga in 1921 fixed the border in the east on what became known as the Curzon Line.

annexed to Germany or France. In the meantime, the coal extracted there was to go to France.

- Eupen, Moresnet and Malmedy were to become parts of Belgium after a plebiscite in 1920.
- Germany as a country was split in two. Parts of Upper Silesia, Poznan and West Prussia formed part of the new Poland, creating a 'Polish Corridor' between Germany and East Prussia and giving Poland access to the sea. The German port of Danzig became a free city under the **mandate** of the League of Nations.
- North Schleswig was given to Denmark after a plebiscite (South Schleswig remained German).
- All territory received by Germany from Russia under the Treaty of Brest-Litovsk was to be returned. Estonia, Latvia and Lithuania were made independent states in line with the principle of self-determination.
- The port of Memel was to be given to Lithuania in 1922.
- Union (**Anschluss**) between Germany and Austria was forbidden.
- Germany's African colonies were taken away because, the Allies argued, Germany had shown itself unfit to govern subject races. Those in Asia (including Shandong) were given to Japan, Australia and New Zealand and those in Africa to Britain, France, Belgium and South Africa. All were to become 'mandates', which meant that the new countries came under the supervision of the League of Nations.

Mandates

Germany's colonies were handed over to the League of Nations. Yet Article 22 of the Covenant of the League of Nations reflected a change in attitude towards colonies, requiring all nations to help underdeveloped countries whose peoples were 'not yet able to stand up for themselves'. The mandate system thus meant that nations who were given Germany's colonies had to ensure that they looked after the people in their care; they would also be answerable to the League of Nations for their actions. 'A' mandate countries – including Palestine, Iraq and Transjordan (given to Britain) and Syria and the Lebanon (given to France) – were to become independent in the near future. Colonies that were considered to be less developed and therefore not ready for immediate independence were 'B' mandates. These included the Cameroons, Togoland and Tanganyika, and were also given to Britain and France. Belgium also received a 'B' mandate – Rwanda-Urundi. 'C' mandate areas were considered to be very backward and were handed over to the powers that had originally conquered them in the war. Thus the North Pacific Islands went to Japan, New Guinea to Australia, South-West Africa to the Union of South Africa and Western Samoa to New Zealand.

Reparations

Germany's 'war guilt' provided justification for the Allied demands for reparations. The Allies wanted to make Germany pay for the material damage done to them during the war. They also proposed to charge Germany for the future costs of pensions to war widows and war wounded. There was much argument between the delegates at the conference on the whole issue of reparations. Although France has traditionally been blamed for pushing for a high reparations sum, and thus stopping a practical reparations deal, in fact more recent accounts of the negotiations at Versailles blame Britain for making the most extreme demands and preventing a settlement. In the end it was the Inter-Allied Reparations Commission that, in 1921, came up with the reparations sum of £6,600 million.

Punishment of war criminals

The Treaty of Versailles also called for the extradition and trial of the Kaiser and other 'war criminals'. However, the Dutch government refused to hand over the Kaiser and the Allied leaders found it difficult to identify and find the lesser war criminals. Eventually, a few German military commanders and submarine captains were tried by a German military court at Leipzig, and received fines or short terms of imprisonment. These were light sentences, but what is important about the whole process is that the concept of 'crimes against humanity' was given legal sanction for the first time.

STUDENT STUDY SECTION

Review questions

1 Consider the positions of the American, British and French delegations before the Versailles Conference. With which aspects of the treaty would each country be a) satisfied and b) dissatisfied?

2 Which clauses were likely to be most problematic to enforce?

3 Which aspects of the treaty were most likely to a) annoy Germany and b) damage Germany?

4 What would be the most likely response of a) Japan and b) China to the treaty?

What was the contemporary response to the Treaty of Versailles?

Read through the documents below and then address the questions in the following Student Study Section.

Document A

…the future life of Europe was not their concern: its means of livelihood was not their anxiety. Their preoccupations, good and bad alike, related to frontiers and nationalities, to the balance of power, to imperial aggrandisements, to the future enfeeblement of a strong and dangerous enemy, to revenge, and to the shifting by the victors of their unbearable financial burdens onto the shoulders of the defeated.

From John Mayard Keynes, *The Economic Consequences of the Peace*, 1919. Keynes was a British economist who worked at the Treasury during World War I and was a chief representative at negotiations prior to the Treaty of Versailles, although he resigned from the British delegation.

Document B

Now that we see [the terms] as a whole, we realise that they are much too stiff. The real crime is the reparations and indemnity chapter, which is immoral and senseless…There is not a single person among the younger people here who is not unhappy and disappointed with the terms. The only people who approve are the old fire-eaters… If I were the Germans, I shouldn't sign it for a moment.

From Harold Nicolson, Diary, 1919. Nicolson was a junior member of the British Foreign Office and was attending the Versailles Conference.

Document C

'Maybe we should let it stand up', a cartoon by David Low. ▶

Document D

The last time I had the opportunity of addressing the House upon this Treaty its main outlines had been settled. I ventured then to call it a 'stern but just Treaty'. I adhere to that description. The terms are in many respects, terrible terms to impose upon a country. Terrible were the deeds that it requites. Terrible were the consequences that were inflicted upon the world. Still more terrible would have been the consequences had they succeeded. What do these terms mean to Germany?

Take the territorial terms. In so far as territories have been taken away from Germany, it is a restoration. Alsace-Lorraine was forcibly taken from the land to which its population were deeply attached. Is it an injustice to restore them to their country? Schleswig-Holstein, the meanest of the Hohenzollern frauds; robbing a small, poor, helpless country, and then retaining that land against the wishes of the population for 50 to 60 years. I am glad the opportunity has come for restoring Schleswig-Holstein. Poland, torn to bits to feed the carnivorous greed of Russian, Austrian and Prussian autocracy. This Treaty has re-knit the torn flag of Poland.

Speech by Lloyd George to House of Commons, 1919

Document E

Today in the Hall of Mirrors of Versailles the disgraceful Treaty is being signed. Do not forget it! The German people will with unceasing labour press forward to reconquer the place among nations to which it is entitled. Then will come the vengeance for the same of 1919.

German newspaper, *Deutsche Zeitung*, 1919

Document F

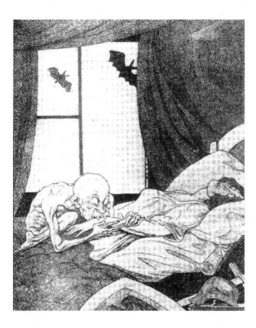

German cartoon entitled 'Clemenceau the Vampire'. From the conservative German newspaper *Kladderadatsch*, July 1919.

STUDENT STUDY SECTION

Document analysis

1 What are Lloyd George's justifications for the treaty in Document D?

2 What are the main criticisms of the treaty in Documents A, B, and C?

3 Compare and contrast the views expressed about the Treaty of Versailles in Documents A and D.

4 What were Germany's assessments of the treaty (Documents E and F)?

5 With reference to their origin and purpose, what are the value and limitations of using Documents D and E as evidence of attitudes to the Treaty of Versailles?

Criticisms of the Treaty of Versailles

As you can see from the sources above, there was already strong criticism of the Treaty of Versailles at the time that it was signed, not just from the Germans but also from among the Allies. These criticisms became stronger in the 1920s, forcefully expressed by contemporary observers like Harold Nicolson and Norman H. Davies, and economist J.M. Keynes. Many historians today also support these criticisms, which are summarized below.

The issue of war guilt

The 'war guilt' clause was particularly hated by the Germans, who felt that all countries should bear responsibility for the outbreak of war in 1914. It was especially harsh to put the whole guilt for the war on the new republic, which was already struggling for survival against the forces of the extreme right. This clause later helped Hitler to gain support, as he was able to play on the resentment and anger felt by the German population towards the war guilt clause, and also towards the fact that it was a *diktat*.

Disarmament clauses
These were hard for the Germans to accept. An army of 100,000 was small for a country of Germany's size. Germany was also very proud of its army. Germany's anger grew when, despite Wilson's call for disarmament in his Fourteen Points, efforts by the other European powers to disarm came to nothing in the 1920s and 1930s.

Reparations and loss of key resources
Keynes (see Document A above) led the criticisms of the treaty in the area of reparations. In *The Economic Consequences of the Peace*, he argued that 'the treaty ignores the economic solidarity of Europe and by aiming at the destruction of the economic life of Germany it threatens the health and prosperity of the Allies themselves.' Not only could Germany not pay the huge reparations bill, but by taking away Germany's coal and iron resources, it also meant that Germany's economy would be unable to recover. Keynes argued that the real problem of the settlement lay not in issues of boundaries 'but rather in questions of food, coal and commerce'. The fact that Germany was to face **hyper-inflation** in the early 1920s seems to provide evidence for his predictions.

Territorial changes to satisfy the issue of self-determination
On this issue, Germany was treated unfairly. Thus while the Danes were given the chance of a plebiscite in northern Schleswig, the Germans in the Sudetenland and Austria were not given any such choice. Many German-speaking peoples were now ruled by non-Germans. Historian W.H. Dawson claimed in 1933, in his book *Germany under the Treaty*, that Germany's borders 'are literally bleeding. From them oozes out the life-blood, physical, spiritual and material of large populations.'

Removal of colonies
Wilson's reason for removing regions like South-West Africa and Rwanda-Urundi from German administration was to remove them from the harsh nature of German rule. Yet this action was clearly hypocritical. States that received German colonies – South Africa and Belgium, for example – could not themselves claim to be model colonial rulers.

League of Nations
The failure of the peacemakers to invite Germany to join the League of Nations not only insulted Germany and added to its sense of grievance, but made it less likely that the League could be effective in promoting international cooperation.

STUDENT STUDY SECTION

The German Problem
The 'German problem' refers to the concern of other European powers regarding the huge potential that Germany had to dominate Europe. Given its geographical position and its economic and military potential, it was in a position to upset the balance of power and threaten other countries.

Question
Read again through the terms of the Treaty of Brest-Litovsk in the information box on p.42. Does this treaty change your views in any way concerning the harshness of the Versailles Treaty?

Alternative views of the Treaty of Versailles

Many historians take a different view of the Treaty of Versailles and its impact on the events of Europe after 1920. In fact, it is now argued by many that the treaty was in fact 'relatively lenient' (Niall Ferguson) and that, given the huge problems facing the peacemakers, it would have been difficult for them to have achieved a more satisfactory settlement. The key arguments of historians such as Sally Marks, Anthony Lentin, Alan Sharp and Ruth Henig can be summarized as follows.

Compared to the treaties that Germany had imposed on Russia and Romania earlier in 1918, the Treaty of Versailles was quite moderate. Germany's war aims were far-reaching and, as shown in the Treaty of Brest-Litovsk, indicate that Germany would have sought huge areas of land from the Allies if it had won. Thus, the Allies can be seen to have exercised considerable restraint. The treaty deprived Germany of about 13.5 per cent of its territory (much of this consisted of Alsace-Lorraine, which was returned to France), about 13 per cent of its economic productivity and just over 10 per cent of its population. In addition, it can be argued that France deserved to be compensated for the destruction of so much of its land and industry. German land had not been invaded and its farmland and industries therefore remained intact.

The treaty in fact left Germany in a relatively strong position in the centre of Europe. Germany remained a dominant power in a weakened Europe. Not only was it physically undamaged, it had gained strategic advantages. Russia remained weak and isolated at this time, and Central Europe was fragmented. The peacemakers had created several new states in accordance with the principle of self-determination (see below), and this was to create a power vacuum that would favour the expansion of Germany in the future. Anthony Lentin has pointed out the problem here of creating a treaty that failed to weaken Germany, but at the same time left it 'scourged, humiliated and resentful'.

The huge reparations bill was not responsible for the economic crisis that Germany faced in the early 1920s. In fact, the issue of banknotes by the German government was a major factor in causing hyper-inflation. In addition, many economic historians have argued that Germany could have paid the 7.2 per cent of its national income that the Reparations Schedule required in the years 1925–29, if it had reformed its financial system or raised its taxation to British levels. However, it chose not to pay the reparations as a way of protesting against the peace settlement.

Thus it can be argued that the treaty was reasonable, and not in itself responsible, for the chaos of post-war Germany. Why then is the view that the treaty was vindictive and unjust so prevalent, and why is it so often cited as a key factor in the cause of World War II? The first issue is that while the treaty was not in itself exceptionally unfair, the Germans thought it was and they directed all their efforts into persuading others of their case. German propaganda on this issue was very successful, and Britain and France were forced into several revisions of the treaty, while Germany evaded paying reparations or carrying out the disarmament clauses.

The second issue is that the USA and Britain lacked the will to enforce the terms of the treaty. The coalition that put the treaty together at Versailles soon collapsed. The USA refused to ratify the treaty, and Britain, content with colonial gains and with strategic and maritime security from Germany, now wished to distance itself from many of the treaty's territorial provisions. Liberal opinion in the USA and Britain was influenced not only by German propaganda, but also by Keynes's arguments for allowing Germany to recover economically.

France was the only country that still feared for its security and which wanted to enforce Versailles in full. This fact explains why France invaded the Ruhr in 1923 in order to secure reparation payments. It received no support for such actions, however, from the USA and Great Britain, who accused France of 'bullying' Germany. As the American historian, William R. Keylor, writes, 'it must in fairness be recorded that the Treaty of Versailles proved to be a failure less because of the inherent defects it contained than because it was never put into full effect' (*The Twentieth Century World and Beyond*, 2006).

The one feature of the Versailles settlement that guaranteed peace and the security of France was the occupation of the Rhineland. Yet the treaty stipulated that the troops should only be there for 15 years. In fact, the last Allied soldiers left in 1930, five years earlier than agreed and just as Germany was recovering its strength.

The settlement of Eastern and South-Eastern Europe

Four separate peace treaties were signed with Austria (Treaty of St Germain), Hungary (Treaty of Trianon), Bulgaria (Treaty of Neuilly) and Turkey (Treaty of Sèvres, revised by the Treaty of Lausanne). Following the format of the Treaty of Versailles, all four countries were to disarm, to pay reparations and to lose territory.

The Treaty of St Germain (1919)

By the time the delegates met at Versailles, the peoples of Austria-Hungary had already broken away from the empire and were setting up their own states in accordance with the principle of self-determination. The conference had no choice but to agree to this situation and suggest minor changes. Austria was separated from Hungary and reduced to a tiny land-locked state consisting of only 25 per cent of its pre-war area and 20 per cent of its pre-war population. It became a republic of seven million people, which many nicknamed 'the tadpole state' due to its shape and size. Other conditions of the Treaty of St Germain were:

- Austria lost Bohemia and Moravia – wealthy industrial provinces – to the new state of Czechoslovakia
- Austria lost Dalmatia, Bosnia and Herzegovina to a new state peopled by Serbs, Croats and Slovenes, a state that became known as Yugoslavia
- Poland gained Galicia
- Italy received the South Tyrol, Trentino and Istria.

In addition, *Anschluss* (union with Germany) was forbidden and Austrian armed forces were reduced to 30,000 men. Austria had to pay reparations to the Allies, and by 1922 Austria was virtually bankrupt and the League of Nations took over its financial affairs.

The Treaty of Trianon (1920)

Hungary had to recognize the independence of the new states of Czechoslovakia, Poland, Yugoslavia and Austria. In this treaty it lost 75 per cent of its pre-war territory and 66 per cent of its pre-war population:

- Slovakia and Ruthenia were given to Czechoslovakia
- Croatia and Slovenia were given to Yugoslavia
- Transylvania and the Banat of Temesvar were given to Romania.

In addition, the Hungarian Army was limited to 35,000 men and Hungary had to pay reparations.

Hungary complained bitterly that the newly formed Hungarian nation was much smaller than the Kingdom of Hungary that had been part of the Austro-Hungarian Empire, and that more than three million Magyars had been put under foreign rule.

The Treaty of Neuilly (1919)

In the Treaty of Neuilly, Bulgaria lost territory to Greece and Yugoslavia. Significantly, it lost its Aegean coastline and therefore access to the Mediterranean. However, it was the only defeated nation to receive territory, from Turkey.

The break-up of the Austro-Hungarian Empire.

To access worksheet 4.2 on the Treaty of Sèvres, please visit www.pearsonbacconline.com and follow the on-screen instructions.

The Treaty of Sèvres (1920)

The disintegration of the Ottoman Empire had been long expected and both Britain and France hoped to make some gains in the region. In the Treaty of Sèvres:

- Syria went to France as a mandate
- Palestine, Iraq, Transjordan and Cyprus went to Great Britain
- Eastern Thrace went to Greece
- Rhodes and the Dodecanese Islands went to Italy
- Smyrna was occupied by the Greeks for five years and then a plebiscite was held
- The Straits (exit from the Black Sea) were to become a **demilitarized zone** administered by the League of Nations, and Britain, France and Italy were to keep troops in Turkey.

The treaty was accepted by Sultan Muhammad VI. Yet there was fierce resentment to the terms. The nationalist leader Mustapha Kemal led a National Assembly at Ankara to pledge the unification of Muslim Turks and the rejection of Sèvres. Greece, ambitious for more land, attempted to take advantage of this internal disorder and declared war, but Kemal smashed their advance, captured and burned Smyrna and finally ejected all Greek soldiers and civilians from Asia. Kemal advanced on the Straits and for a while it looked as though he intended to attack the British soldiers at the town of Chanak. A compromise was agreed upon, however, which resulted in the Treaty of Sèvres being revised at Lausanne in Switzerland.

The Treaty of Sèvres and the Turkish Empire.

The Treaty of Lausanne (1923)

The provisions of the Treaty of Lausanne ran as follows:

- Turkey regained Eastern Thrace, Smyrna, some territory along the Syrian border and several Aegean islands
- Turkish sovereignty over the Straits was recognized, but the area remained demilitarized
- Foreign troops were withdrawn from Turkish territory
- Turkey no longer had to pay reparations or have its army reduced.

What were the criticisms of the peace settlements in Eastern and South-Eastern Europe?

It was very difficult to apply the principle of self-determination consistently and fairly. Because Czechoslovakia needed a mountainous, defensible border and because the new state lacked certain minerals and industry, it was given the ex-Austrian Sudetenland, which contained around three and a half million German speakers. The new Czechoslovakia set up on racial lines therefore contained five main racial groups: Czechs, Poles, Magyars, Ruthenians and German speakers. Racial problems were also rife in the new Yugoslavia, where there were at least a dozen nationalities within its borders. Thus the historian Alan Sharp writes that 'the 1919 minorities were probably more discontented than those of 1914' (*Modern History Review*, November 1991).

As well as ethnic strife, the new states were weak politically and economically. Both Hungary and Austria suffered economic collapse by 1922. The weakness of these new states was later to create a power vacuum in this part of Europe and thus the area became an easy target for German domination.

The treaties caused much bitterness:

- Hungary resented the loss of its territories, particularly Transylvania. Czechoslovakia, Romania and Yugoslavia later formed the Little Entente, with the aim of protecting one another from any Hungarian attempt to regain control over their territories.
- Turkey was extremely bitter about the settlement, and this bitterness led to a takeover by Kemal and the revision of the Treaty of Sèvres.
- Italy was also discontented. It referred to the settlement as 'the mutilated peace' because it had not received the Dalmatian coast, Fiume and certain colonies. In 1919, Gabriele D'Annunzio, a leader in Italy's fascist movement, occupied Fiume with a force of supporters in the name of Italian nationalists, and in 1924 the Yugoslavians gave Fiume to the Italians.

STUDENT STUDY SECTION

Discussion question

What do you think Alan Sharp means when he says that the peace settlement was a disappointment 'as much because of its virtues as its faults'.

What was the impact of the war and the peace treaties by the early 1920s?

Political issues

Although Western Europe was still familiar on the map in 1920, this was not the case in Eastern Europe, where no fewer than nine new or revived states came into existence: Finland, Estonia, Latvia, Lithuania, Poland, Czechoslovakia, Austria, Hungary and

Yugoslavia. Meanwhile, Russia's government was now a Bolshevik dictatorship that was encouraging revolution abroad. The frontiers of new states thus became the frontiers of the Europe from which Russia was excluded. Russia was not invited to the Versailles Conference and was not a member of the League of Nations until 1934.

The new Europe remained divided not only between the 'victors' and the 'defeated', but also between those who wanted to maintain the peace settlement and those who wanted to see it revised. Not only Germany, but also Hungary and Italy, were active in pursuing their aims of getting the treaties changed. Despite Wilson's hopes to the contrary, international 'blocs' developed, such as that formed by the Little Entente. The peacemakers had hoped for and encouraged democracy in the new states. Yet the people in Central Europe had only experience with autocracy, and governments were undermined by the rivalry between the different ethnic groups and by the economic problems that they faced.

Although Britain and France still had their empires and continued their same colonial policies, the war saw the start of the decline of these powers on the world stage. The role of America in the war had made it clear that Britain and France were going to find it hard to act on their own to deal with international disputes; the focus of power in the world had shifted away from Europe. Furthermore, the war encouraged movements for independence in French and British colonies in Asia and Africa. As P.M.H. Bell writes, 'Empires were wider than before, but in many places they were less secure' (*Twentieth Century Europe*, 2006).

Economic issues

As we have seen, the war caused severe economic disruption in Europe. Germany suffered particularly badly, but all countries of Europe faced rising prices; 'the impact of inflation on generations which had grown accustomed to stable prices and a reliable currency was enormous, and was as much psychological as economic. The lost landmark of a stable currency proved much harder to restore than the ruins of towns and villages' (P.M.H. Bell, *Twentieth Century Europe,* 2006). The middle classes of Europe were hit especially hard by inflation, which destroyed the wealth of many **bourgeois** families. In Germany, for example, the total collapse of the currency meant that the savings of middle-class families were made completely worthless.

In Eastern and South-Eastern Europe, the new fragmentation of the area hindered economic recovery. There was now serious disruption in what had been a free trade area of some 50 million inhabitants. From 1919, each country tried to build up its economy, which meant fierce competition and high tariffs. Attempts at economic cooperation foundered and any success was wrecked by the **Great Depression**. As noted, only America and Japan benefited economically from the war, and they went on to experience economic prosperity until the **Wall Street Crash** in 1929.

Social changes

The war also swept away the traditional structures in society. Across Europe, the **landed aristocracy**, which had been so prominent before 1914, lost much of its power and influence. In Russia, the revolution rid the country of its aristocracy completely. In the lands of the Austro-Hungarian Empire, estates were broken up; many governments, such as that of Yugoslavia, undertook land reform and distributed land out to the peasants. In Prussia, the land owners (*Junker*) kept their lands but lost much of their influence with the decline of the military and the collapse of the monarchy.

Other groups of people benefited from the war. Trade unions were considerably strengthened by the role that they played in negotiating with the governments during the war to improve pay and conditions for the valuable war workers. In both Britain and

Little Entente
This was a defensive alliance between Czechoslovakia, Yugoslavia and Romania. France supported the alliance by signing treaties with each member country. A key aim of the Little Entente was to prevent any kind of revision of the Versailles treaty by Germany of Hungary.

Self-determination outside Europe
Applying the principle of self-determination also proved problematic outside Europe. France and Britain were not interested in allowing this principle to operate in their colonies. Ho Chi Minh, a Vietnamese revolutionary, arrived at Versailles with a petition seeking support for the Vietnamese nationalist cause, but he was ignored. Claims from the Indian nationalist press that India's 'deeds and sacrifices justified its claim to an equality within the British Empire' were also unacceptable. Wilson also ignored a memorandum from the black American leader, W.E.B. Dubois, which suggested that Africa be reconstructed 'in accordance with the wishes of the Negro race'.

France, standards of health and welfare also rose during the war, thus improving the lives of the poorest citizens. Measures were introduced to improve the health of children. In Britain, social legislation continued after the war with the Housing Act of 1918, which subsidized the building of houses, and the Unemployment Insurance Acts of 1920 and 1921, which increased benefits for unemployed workers and their families.

After the war, women gained rights in society to which they had previously been denied. Such changes were reflected in a growing female confidence and changes in fashion and behaviour. In Britain and America the so-called 'flappers' wore plain, short dresses, had short hair, smoked cigarettes and drank cocktails. This kind of behaviour would have been considered unacceptable before the war. In Britain, some professions also opened up to women after the war; they could now train to become architects and lawyers and were allowed to serve on a jury.

The end of the war also saw women getting the vote in a number of countries; Russia in 1917, Austria and Britain in 1918, Czechoslovakia, Germany, the Netherlands, Poland and Sweden in 1919 and America and Belgium in 1920. The role that women played in the war effort was a contributory factor to this shift in some countries, though it was not the only factor. In Britain, for instance, the pre-war work of the suffrage movements in raising awareness of women's rights issues was also important. Yet the new employment opportunities that women had experienced during the war did not continue after the war, with most women giving up their work and returning to their more traditional roles in the home.

STUDENT STUDY SECTION

Research activity

Task 1
Research one country in which women received the vote after the war. How important was the effect of the war in bringing about this change? What other factors contributed to this? Did the lives of women in this country change in any other respect?

Task 2
Research the impact of World War I on the nationalist movement in India.

Essay Planning

Question
To what extent can the treaty settlements at the end of World War I be considered 'harsh and short-sighted'?

Introduction: Here you need to explain 'treaty settlements' as one of the key terms in the title. Notice that this will involve all of the treaties, not just the Versailles Treaty. Also, set out your main arguments and make clear the direction that you will take in your essay.

1st section: (May be two or more paragraphs.) Always start with the argument presented in the title, i.e. that the settlements were 'harsh and short-sighted'. You will need to deal with 'harsh' and 'short-sighted' separately. Give evidence to support both judgements. You may want to deal with the Treaty of Versailles first and then consider the other treaties.

2nd section: Give the other side of the argument. Was the settlement really so harsh and short-sighted? What arguments have historians given against this view?

Conclusion: Based on what you have written, which is the most convincing verdict of the treaty?

Now have a go at these essay questions:

1   To what extent did the Treaty of Versailles reflect the original aims of the peacemakers?
2   Assess the social and economic effects of World War I.

● **Examiner's hint**
It is very easy with the second essay question at the bottom to be too vague or general in your answer. The problem with social, political and economic effects is that it is hard to make sweeping generalizations; they varied from country to country and not all were caused by the war only. You thus need to ensure that you give very specific examples from a range of countries (European and non-European) to support your arguments.

5

THE CAUSES OF WORLD WAR II IN EUROPE: THE FAILURE OF COLLECTIVE SECURITY

The causes of World War II are complex, and so we have divided the key themes into two chapters. In this chapter we will look at the failure of collective security in preventing the outbreak of war, along with the impact of the Great Depression in Europe in the 1930s. In the next chapter we will look more specifically at Hitler's policies as a cause of war, and how the European powers responded to the threat that Nazi Germany posed to Europe.

As you read through this chapter, consider the following essay questions:

- Why had collective security failed to keep the peace between 1920 and 1935?
- To what extent was the League of Nations 'doomed to fail'?

Timeline of events – 1919–39	
1919	Treaty of Versailles
	Treaty of St Germain
1920	Establishment of the League of Nations
1922	Treaty of Rapallo between Germany and the USSR
1923	French occupation of the Ruhr
1924	Introduction of the Dawes Plan
1925	Locarno Treaties
1926	Germany admitted to League of Nations
1928	Kellogg–Briand Pact signed
1929	Introduction of the Young Plan
	Wall Street Crash
1932	Lausanne Conference on reparation payments
1933	Hitler appointed Chancellor of Germany

The failure of 'collective security'

As we have seen, one of Wilson's Fourteen Points led to the creation of the League of Nations, an organization that sought to prevent another war breaking out between states. Akira Iriye writes:

It [the League of Nations Covenant] proposed an alternative to the conventional international order, which Wilson was convinced, had been sustained by force. This had created a dangerous arms race and imperialistic activities abroad. Now military power and expansionism were to be replaced by a rule of law in which 'world public opinion' rather than alliances and armaments would be the key to international order.

From Akira Iriye, *The Globalising of America 1913–1945*, 1993

In the 1920s and 1930s, the League faced many challenges. Although it was successful in some areas, the overall failure of European states to work collectively through the League in dealing with various international crises was a major cause of World War II.

Collective security and the League of Nations

The principle of collective security was the idea that peace could be preserved by countries acting together – collectively – to prevent one country attacking another. Collective security was to be made practically possible by the machinery of the League of Nations. When there was a dispute between countries they would refer the issue(s) to the League's Assembly. If that body could not find a resolution, the Council could then apply 'collective security', i.e. as a group impose moral pressure then economic sanctions, to force the country that was deemed to be in the wrong to comply with its decisions.

The Covenant of the League of Nations

The League met for the first time in Geneva in December 1920. Its key objective was to keep the peace and avoid future conflict by advising on and settling international disputes. It also aimed to promote disarmament, supervise the mandated territories and promote international good will and cooperation through its various organizations dedicated to social and economic development. The initial membership of the League was 32 Allied states and 12 neutral states; however, by 1926 all ex-enemy states had joined. The USSR was not admitted until 1934, and the USA never joined.

There were 26 articles in the League's Covenant (including amendments made in December 1924), which prescribed when and how the League was to operate.
- Articles 1–7 were concerned with the membership and organization of the League, its Assembly, Council and Secretariat.
- Articles 8–17 were concerned with the prevention of war.
- Articles 18–21 concerned treaty obligations and the League's expectations of its member states.
- Article 22 concerned the mandated territories.
- Article 23 concerned humanitarian issues such as labour conditions, the trafficking of women, children and drugs, health issues and the arms trade.
- Article 24 concerned the commissions.
- Article 25 promoted the Red Cross.
- Article 26 set down how amendments to the Covenant were made.

Dealing with international disputes

It was set down in the Covenant that member states should refer their disputes to one of the following:
- The Permanent Court of International Justice
- **Arbitration** (having a neutral person or group of people listening to and judging a dispute)
- An investigation or enquiry by the Council.

If member states failed to refer their dispute to the League, or failed to follow its recommendations, the League could then impose economic sanctions, the main tool for the League against aggressors. In the aftermath of World War I, in which the economic blockade of Germany had been effective, this economic weapon appeared to have the potential to be effective in forcing compliance with the League's decisions.

In theory, the League could call for military action as a last resort against an aggressor. Yet the League did not have its own armed forces, and in reality member states did not want to put their sovereign forces under international control. In addition, the Covenant was rather ambiguous as to when and how such armed forces should be used. France had wanted

The League of Nations in session, 1920.

an armed force, or League Army, but Britain had resisted this option. Thus in reality, the League lacked military teeth.

To access worksheet 5.1 on the Covenant of the League of Nations, please visit www.pearsonbacconline.com and follow the on-screen instructions.

STUDENT STUDY SECTION

Review activity

Look up the League of Nations Covenant on the internet, for example via the online resource link on this page. As you read through the document, consider:

1 What aspects of the Covenant made the League of Nations an organization likely to fulfil its aims of collective security?

2 What aspects of the Covenant weakened the League's ability to deliver collective security?

◀ Structure of the League of Nations.

STUDENT STUDY SECTION

Document analysis

Document A

[the League] depended on the goodwill of the nations to work, though it was the absence of goodwill that made it necessary.

From Hugh Brogan, *The Penguin History of the USA*, 2001

Document B

…successive British governments took care to confine any specific political or military commitments they might make to western Europe, although under article 10 of the League Covenant they had undertaken to 'preserve…against external aggression the territorial integrity and existing political independence of all members of the League'.

From Ruth Henig, *Versailles and After 1919–1933*, 1995

Document C

The allies had been so impressed by the effect of economic embargoes employed against Germany in the war that economic sanctions were chosen as the League's main weapon. The possibility of military sanctions was admitted, but their extent was left undefined, and they could only ever be applied if a member state agreed to put its own forces at the disposal of the League. In its 20 year life, the League never once sought to apply military sanctions.

From R.M. Rayner, *The Twenty Years' Truce*, 1943

Document D

Rival states can be frightened into friendship only by the shadow of some greater danger.

Comment by the British historian A.J.P. Taylor

Question

What potential problems or weaknesses of the League are identified in each of the Documents A–D?

Problems for the League of Nations in the 1920s
Changing membership of the League

The changing membership of the League reflected the shifting priorities of its leading members, as the more liberal governments of the 1920s became increasingly polarized following the Wall Street Crash and the ensuing Great Depression. As right-wing governments within the League became more aggressive, so the perceived threat from the USSR shifted to the Axis powers.

ACCESSIONS TO AND WITHDRAWALS FROM THE LEAGUE OF NATIONS, 1920–39		
Country	Date of entry	Date of departure
Austria	Dec 1920	Dec 1939*
Ethiopia	Sep 1923	
Ireland	Sep 1923	
Germany	Sep 1926	Oct 1933
Japan	Original member	Mar 1933
Italy	Original member	Dec 1937
Spain	Original member	May 1939
USSR	Sep 1934	Dec 1939*

*The Council resolved on 14 December 1939 that Austria and the USSR were no longer members.

Absence of major powers

The absence of major powers from the League of Nations had a decisive impact on the working and influence of the League; indeed, this is possibly the key reason for why the League ultimately failed to prevent another world war.

The most important absent major power was the USA. The League had been the idea of the Americans and had been championed by President Woodrow Wilson. The US Congress, however, was too concerned that the League would drag the Americans into more disputes and conflicts in Europe, hence the country withdrew into isolationism. The USA had played a pivotal role in bringing World War I to an end, but it did not want to play such a central role in the controversial Versailles settlement.

The absence of the USA seriously weakened the potential of the League to use 'collective security' against aggression, for several reasons. First, the most powerful economic country in the world would have given the League's economic sanctions real weight; the US absence undermined this one essential weapon. Second, without the USA the make-up of the permanent members was distinctly European (except for Japan), and lacked the appearance of a genuinely 'worldwide' organization. Third, it highlighted that the new organization might be sidelined in favour of old-style agreements and treaties, as this was clearly how the USA was going to secure its future relationships. Finally, these factors meant that the League was primarily led by European powers that were arguably in decline.

STUDENT STUDY SECTION

Document analysis

Document A

The defeat suffered by Wilsonism in the United States strikes at the very existence of the League of Nations. America's place will remain empty at Geneva, and the two countries that dominate, France and Great Britain, are divided on almost every one of the topics to be discussed.

Marcel Cachin, a French politician, speaking in 1920 about the USA's decision not to join the League of Nations. From T. McAleavy, *Modern World History*, 1996

Document B

British cartoon 'The Gap in the Bridge', first published in *Punch*, December 1919.

Questions

1 According to Document A, what are the most significant problems for the League of Nations caused by the absence of the major powers?

2 What are the views of the cartoonist in Document B concerning the US absence from the League of Nations?

Absence of the USSR

The USSR was excluded from the League of Nations. The newly established Bolshevik government was regarded as a 'pariah state'; indeed, Western powers had invaded Russia during the Russian Civil War (1918–21) to join the 'White' counter-revolutionary forces. As the Bolsheviks consolidated their position in the Soviet Union after winning the civil war, the old powers of Europe looked on with great concern. Afraid that the 'revolution of the proletariat' would spread, they felt that it was expedient to isolate the Soviets rather than to embrace them in a new organization designed to prevent conflict.

Yet the exclusion of Russia further weakened the standing of the League, as it could be perceived by the USSR as a 'club for capitalists' – an organization to protect and promote their interests and empires at the expense of the exploited masses. Indeed, Lenin viewed the League as 'a robbers' den to safeguard the unjust spoils of Versailles.'

Absence of Germany

Germany was initially excluded from the League. This exclusion again undermined the ideals of the League and, perhaps more importantly, suggested that the League was something of a 'victors' club' – the four permanent members of the Council were the victorious Allies. In addition, the exclusion tended to ignore the important fact that Germany remained a strong power at the conclusion of World War I. The assumptions that there had been a clear victory over Germany and that there was now scope for a re-ordering of European politics were flawed. Germany had been militarily defeated in the west, but not in the east. Its expansionist politics had not evaporated, nor had its economic power. It would therefore seem, particularly with hindsight, vital that Germany be included in the League so that it could work towards its aim of revising the Treaty of Versailles within the confines of the League's machinery. Indeed, following the wave of optimism and positive thinking that ensued after Locarno, Germany was admitted into the League in September 1926.

Weakness of Central European states

The Austro-Hungarian Empire had collapsed following World War I, and had been replaced by a number of smaller states based on the principle of nationality. However, as we saw in the previous chapter, many of these states struggled politically and economically to achieve stability. This meant that instead of another large European state there were now several much smaller states that would require more support from the League, particularly in terms of economic development and territorial security. These states could not offer the League much tangible support in return.

STUDENT STUDY SECTION
Review questions
1   To what extent was the League of Nations 'doomed to fail' due to the limitations of its Covenant and structure?
2   Why might the failure of the USA to join the League be viewed as critically important?
3   How might countries/regions around the world perceive the role of the League of Nations differently?
4   Research the work of the commissions shown in the diagram on p.89. How effective was the League of Nations in dealing with the humanitarian issues identified by the commissions?

Conference of Ambassadors
The Conference of Ambassadors was set up in January 1920 in Paris to ensure that the peace treaties were implemented. It consisted of the British, Italian and Japanese ambassadors.

How successful was the League of Nations in the 1920s?

Peacekeeping 1920–25

Throughout the 1920s, the League dealt with various disputes arising mainly from the territorial changes of the Versailles settlement. The League had both successes and failures in its handling of these disputes.

Aaland Islands, 1920 – These islands were populated mainly by Swedes, but following the collapse of the Russian empire, Finland claimed sovereignty over them. The conflict was taken to the League and Sweden accepted the League's decision to give the islands to Finland.

Vilna, 1920–23 – Both Poland and Lithuania wanted control of the town of Vilna. It had once been the capital of Lithuania, but its people were Polish. The League was unable to prevent the Poles from seizing and retaining it by force. Finally the Conference of Ambassadors awarded Vilna to Poland.

Upper Silesia, 1921 – Both Germany and newly formed Poland wanted control of the important industrial area of Upper Silesia. The League decided to split the area between the two.

Corfu, 1923 – Three Italian army officers were shot while working on a boundary dispute between Greece and Albania. Mussolini blamed Greece and ordered compensation. When the Greeks did not pay, Italian soldiers occupied Corfu. Greece appealed to the League, but the Italian government ignored the Council's ruling and left only when compensation had been paid.

Mosul, 1924 – The area of Mosul was claimed by both Turkey and Iraq. The League considered the problem and awarded the area to Iraq, a decision that was accepted.

Bulgaria, 1925 – Following a Greek invasion of Bulgaria, the League ordered both armies to stop fighting. An investigation by the League blamed Greece for starting the dispute and ordered it to pay damages. Greece accepted the blame and was ordered to pay compensation.

STUDENT STUDY SECTION

Review questions

Study the list of League peacekeeping operations during the 1920s, and for more information go to the online resources.

1 Which of the following disputes can be regarded as a success for the League and which disputes can be regarded as a failure?

2 Are there any common factors that help to explain the successes and failures?

3 What lessons could be drawn for the 1930s from the challenges that had faced the League in the 1920s?

P.M.H. Bell argues that even though the League did not solve all disputes successfully:

What was important was that the League had settled down as a valuable forum for the conduct of international affairs. Germany was admitted in 1926, and at once became a permanent member of the Council; so the League was no longer a 'League of victors'. By 1928 every European state was a member (except the USSR). Nearly every foreign minister made a point of attending its sessions. The League was still young, but there seemed a good chance that Europe had found a workable successor to the pre-1914 states system.

From P.M.H. Bell, *Twentieth Century Europe*, 2006

Attempts to strengthen the League

Two attempts were made, in 1923 and 1924, to strengthen the machinery of the League of Nations. These were both initiated by France. The first of these initiatives was the Draft Treaty of Mutual Assistance, which would have required all members of the League to come to the assistance of a victim of aggression. Next, the Geneva Protocol of 1924 would have made arbitration compulsory in all disputes. Both initiatives were rejected by Britain, its Dominions and the Scandinavian powers, who believed that members would not be willing or able to carry out the huge commitment that would result from such a role.

The League thus remained divided between those states that wanted a strong League to enforce the existing territorial agreements, and those that wanted to be more selective in dealing with aggression. This division also arose because of the difference in vulnerability of the various states. While France felt highly vulnerable, others were not so worried and were not prepared to take on what they saw as extra commitments. These differences were to be highlighted further by the Ruhr Crisis, which would deeply undermine the principle of collective security.

The Ruhr Crisis (1923)

A German cartoon from 1923. France is represented by the figure of the woman, and the text says 'Hands off the Ruhr!'

For France, future security lay in upholding the terms of the Treaty of Versailles. However, France had begun to feel that this security was being undermined within a year of its signing. The USA did not ratify the treaty and signed a separate peace with Germany. In Germany, the political situation seemed unlikely to produce a government keen to comply with its terms. Indeed, reparation payments, crucial for rebuilding the French economy, quickly became a problem. The Germans protested that they could not afford the payments. In October 1921, the Wiesbaden Accords were drawn up, by which France agreed to assist Germany with their reparations by taking a proportion in raw materials and industrial produce rather than cash. The following year, however, even these payments had fallen into arrears.

The French inclination to use force rather than diplomacy to resolve the issue was enhanced by the appointment of Raymond Poincaré as Prime Minister in January 1922. The issue was brought to a head and became a crisis when Germany asked for reparation payments to be suspended for four years. The French had had enough. They believed that this suspension could jeopardize the enforcement of the treaty as a whole. The French and the Belgians, with the support of Italy, moved troops into the Ruhr Valley in January 1923 to take in kind what they thought they were owed. The German government of Chancellor Wilhelm Cuno protested that this action went against the terms of the Versailles Treaty, and in addition instructed German workers to strike. The German government continued to pay the now-striking workers, but found it had to print more paper money to cover the bill.

The floundering German economy now collapsed, and as the government continued to print money inflation became hyper-inflation. The French retaliated to this 'passive resistance' by encouraging the unemployed in France and Belgium to work in the Ruhr industries. The descent into economic chaos, indicated by the statistics below, coupled with growing political separatist movements in Germany, led to the replacement of Cuno with Gustav Stresemann in August 1923.

To access worksheet 5.2 on the German economy of the 1930s, please visit www.pearsonbacconline.com and follow the on-screen instructions.

THE IMPACT OF THE RUHR CRISIS ON THE GERMAN ECONOMY	
Value of £ sterling to German mark	
Jan 1914	£1 = 20 marks
Jan 1922	£1 = 760 marks
Nov 1922	£1 = 50,000 marks
Nov 1923	£1 = 16,000,000,000 marks
Coal production in Ruhr	
1922	90 million tonnes
Feb 1923	2.5 million tonnes
Operating iron smelting furnaces	
1922	70
March 1923	3

Stresemann called for an end to the 'passive resistance' in the Ruhr, and in 1924 the crisis was ended by the Dawes Plan. The plan was named after a commission chaired by US economist Charles Dawes. He produced a report on German reparations in April 1924, which decided the following:

- Reparations were to be guaranteed by two mortgages, one on German railways and the second on German industries (supplemented by taxation on the German population)
- A US 'reparations agent' would reside in Germany to supervise repayments
- Repayments were to be reduced.

Although reparations were to be reduced, France nevertheless accepted the plan because it brought the Americans back into the picture, involving them in the collection of reparations. In fact, this became known as 'the golden age of reparations' (until 1929), as the Allies received more than they had done before. The Germans were unhappy, however, as there was no fixed date for completion of reparations. Britain and France were also concerned about the link between German payments and their own payments of war debts to USA, which they had not wanted.

The Dawes Plan devised a new system of reparation payments. Stresemann promised to comply with these payments, and French troops were withdrawn from the Ruhr by August 1925. Yet the crisis had thrown up serious problems with the integrity of the League of Nations. Instead of going to the League, France had taken matters into its own hands and attempted to seize payments with force. Indeed, attempts by Britain and Sweden to take the crisis to the League were blocked by the French. This action by a permanent member undermined the League's credibility, as it appeared that the powers would take independent action when it suited them.

Although the hostility of Britain (and the USA) to the invasion of the Ruhr could be seen as a clear condemnation of unilateral action, the overall impact of the invasion was bad for both the League and for international relations. Despite France's economic gains (it had been guaranteed 21 per cent of the Ruhr's production until December 1923, and then this rose to 27 per cent), the results of its actions dramatically increased the tension between France and Germany, making future cooperation all the more problematic. Politically, France had alarmed its former allies, and heightened the sense of patriotism within Germany. In France, Poincaré came under heavy criticism from both left- and right-wing groups. The left argued that this act of aggression had been committed only to benefit capitalist groups in France, and the right were frustrated by Poincaré's withdrawal from the Ruhr, seeing it as a missed opportunity to exert some real control over Germany's economy. There was even unofficial support from certain elements for the promotion of an independent Rhineland.

The Rapallo Treaty

In April 1922, the Germans and Russians signed the Rapallo Treaty. By this treaty, Germany and Russia introduced diplomatic relations and pledged their future cooperation. Germany fully recognized the Soviet government and both powers denounced reparations. In addition, the Rapallo Treaty provided for close economic cooperation. Arguably a more important consequence of this treaty was that military cooperation would now take place, allowing Germany to rearm and train secretly in Russia. Knowledge of the Rapallo Treaty also made Britain more determined to win over Germany rather than alienate the nation further, lest Germany became even friendlier with Russia.

STUDENT STUDY SECTION

Review questions

1   What were the reasons for the French occupation of the Ruhr, and how were their aims realized by this occupation?

2   What were the perspectives of other countries in this crisis?

3   How did France's actions undermine the concept of collective security?

Document analysis

The invasion of the Ruhr in 1923 had the most serious consequences. Within Germany, it weakened the position of the middle classes in society and diminished their support for the Weimar government. Extremist parties on the right and the left were given a boost, because of the alarm at the prospect of complete economic collapse and social disorder. Many historians argue that the invasion of the Ruhr paved the way for Hitler's subsequent rise to power. Both the British government and the British public were alienated by French policies… The French franc … came under pressure and the French government learned … direct action carried a high political cost… It has been suggested that France's failure to take military action to stop Hitler's remilitarization of the Rhineland in 1936 stemmed largely from the unhappy experience in the Ruhr in 1923.

From Ruth Henig, *Origins of the First World War*, 1993

Question

According to Ruth Henig, what was the impact of the Ruhr Invasion on a) Germany and b) France?

The Locarno era

Following the disastrous Ruhr adventure, the political situation in Europe was improved with the Dawes Plan and also the Locarno Pact of 1925, the Kellogg–Briand Pact of August 1928 and the Young Plan of 1929 (see below for details). However, it should be noted that these agreements took place outside the League of Nations.

The Locarno Conference and the 'Locarno spirit' (1925)

Although French forces left the Ruhr, there were allied troops in other Rhineland cities, as dictated by the terms of Versailles. Stresemann wanted to rid Germany of these 'occupying forces', and he was also keen to quell any movement in support of an independent Rhineland. At a conference in Locarno in Switzerland in February 1925, Stresemann proposed a voluntary German guarantee of its western borders. Significantly for the French and Belgians, this meant that Germany was resolved to give up its claims over Alsace-Lorraine, Malmedy and Eupen. In return, Germany had some reassurance that France would not invade again, and it removed any potential for an independent Rhineland. A series of treaties were signed. The major treaty guaranteed the boundaries between France, Belgium and Germany. Also present at Locarno were representatives of Italy, Czechoslovakia and Poland. Germany signed treaties with Poland and Czechoslovakia, agreeing to change the eastern borders with these countries by arbitration only. It was also agreed that Germany should be admitted into the League of Nations.

The Locarno Conference, 1925.

For many in post-war Europe, the Locarno agreement gave hope for future security. It suggested that former enemies could work together to resolve disputes, and to uphold the Versailles settlement. The new mood became known the 'Locarno spirit'. When Locarno was followed up with a series of agreements involving the USA, this 'spirit' seemed to be embracing even isolationist nations.

The Locarno Pact seemed to bode well for the future of collective security. However, although this agreement appeared to herald a new era of cooperation between the Western European powers (Britain had been in favour of the agreement, as it expunged French excuses for occupation), what the agreement did not guarantee were Germany's eastern borders, and the border with Italy. Italy, present at Locarno, had not managed to get similar agreements from Germany on its southern border. The treaties France had with Poland and Czechoslovakia were little comfort to those respective countries, as it would be strategically difficult to offer tangible support following Locarno. In addition, France had not changed its view of Germany. Rather, it had just changed its strategy for containing Germany. Instead of confronting the Germans with force, France was now attempting to bring Germany into international agreements that involved the guarantees of other powers. In addition, Locarno had undermined both the Treaty of Versailles and the League of Nations. Security for France had been sought outside the League, and only a component of the Versailles Treaty had been guaranteed.

The Young Plan (1929)

The Young Plan attempted to redress some of the problems that remained with the Dawes Plan. The plan:
- Further reduced the total sum to be repaid by Germany
- Set a date for completion of repayments – 1988
- Continued US involvement in reparation payments.

As part of the deal, Britain and France agreed to end their occupation of the Rhineland five years ahead of schedule.

As Keynes had noted in 1926, the foundations for both the Dawes and then the Young Plan, and thus both German and European recovery, was foreign money. Two-thirds of investment in Germany during the 1920s came from America. Keynes wrote in 1926 that the reparation arrangements were 'in the hands of the American capitalist'.

STUDENT STUDY SECTION

Review questions and document analysis

1 What potential problems with the Dawes and Young Plans are highlighted by Keynes?

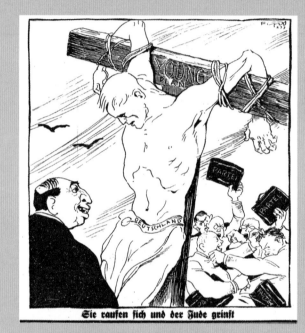

German cartoon, c. 1930, from *Der Stürmer*, a very anti-Semitic newpaper published by Julius Streicher as part of Nazi propaganda. The cross bears the words 'Young Plan', while German political parties can be seen fighting with each other in the background. The caption translates: 'They fight and the Jew grins.'

2 What views does the German cartoonist have towards the Young Plan?

Research question

Which countries face debilitating debt repayments today? How are these countries and economies supported? Is 'developing world' debt a 'developing problem'?

Kellogg–Briand Pact (August 1928)

The Kellogg–Briand Pact was initiated by American Secretary of State William Kellogg and the French Foreign Minister Aristide Briand. The pact renounced 'war as an instrument of national policy'; 62 of 64 invited states signed the agreement (Brazil and Argentina declined).

Perhaps the most dramatic expression of this era was the agreement signed in Paris in August 1928 in which the nations of the world solemnly stated 'in the names of their respective peoples that they condemn recourse to war for the solution of international controversies, and renounce it as an instrument of national policy in their relations with one another.' By declaring that Clausewitz's famous definition of war was illegal and guaranteeing that international disputes would be settled peacefully, this treaty … seemed to provide the legal foundation for a new international order.

From James Sheehan, *The Monopoly of Violence: Why Europeans Hate Going to War*, 2008

Contemporary views of the pact were often positive; it was seen as an important declaration by governments that they would pursue their objectives through peaceful means. The pact has been viewed as the high point of 'Locarno spirit' era. Unfortunately, this perspective would prove to be naive, as the encouraging elements of Europe's recovery were very fragile.

It could be argued that there was no major conflict in the 1920s because the main revisionist power, i.e. Germany, was still recovering from World War I. In addition, the 1920s were in the main a period of relative economic boom and prosperity, which decreased international tensions and encouraged cooperation. As P.M.H. Bell writes, 'Europe had survived, but was still on the sick list.'

STUDENT STUDY SECTION

Review questions

1   What had led to the mood of optimism in the 1920s?
2   Could the 'Locarno spirit' have survived? Why did it not last?
3   Why was there an improvement in relations between Britain, France and Germany in 1924–29? In what ways was the international situation more stable in 1929 than it had been in 1923?
4   What had the League of Nations achieved by 1929?

Why did collective security fail in the 1930s?

Although the concept of collective security had some degree of success in the 1920s, the League's failure to resolve key international crises in the 1930s meant that it had completely collapsed by 1939.

The Depression

The worldwide economic depression that followed the Wall Street Crash of October 1929 had far-reaching effects. The USA had become *the* globally dominant economic power, and this meant that the world's economy was ominously linked to its fortunes. The impact of the crisis on the economic, social and ultimately political landscape of the world ushered in a return to a world dominated by national self-interest and the dominance of military forces. The USA's national income fell by almost 50 per cent between 1929 and 1932, and its government struggled to cope with unemployment and popular discontent.

Poverty and despair have often fostered the rise of extremist groups, and the fragile liberal governments of the 1920s found resurgent nationalist and aggressive political groups very difficult to restrict. The delicate European stability that had been nurtured by the resources of American capitalism was particularly vulnerable to a major economic collapse in the USA. This was equally true of the recently democratic and liberal Japan.

Governments were blamed for the crisis. In France, a moderate government was replaced by a radical left-wing government in the May 1932 election. In Britain, iron and steel production fell by 50 per cent and politics shifted to right-wing parties (the British Labour Party lost seats in the 1931 elections). Germany had borrowed £9,000 million between 1924 and 1929. When the money stopped, its economy collapsed; German unemployment stood at 1.4 million in 1928 and rose to a staggering 12 million in 1932. The **Weimar** government and liberal democracy lost credibility and ended when Franz von Papen assumed the role of virtual dictator in May 1932. In Japan in 1931, 50 per cent of factories closed and silk prices fell by two-thirds. There ensued a radical shift to the right, linked to military factions. By 1932, following a series of assassinations, the era of liberal politics in Japan was over. In

The Weimar government
The Weimar government had been established at the end of World War I with the defeat of the German Empire. It replaced the imperial government with a constitution that was seen as one of the most modern in Europe. Universal suffrage was introduced and a lower house of parliament was to be elected every four years by a voting system of proportional representation. The President was to be elected every seven years and a guarantee of basic human rights was included in the constitution.

Belgium and Poland, the impact of the Depression led to new government initiatives that looked to improve their defences against a potentially expansionist Germany.

The Depression heightened the fears of the USSR's potential for fostering the spread of communist revolution into the impoverished working-class streets of European cities. Soviet propaganda claimed that the Depression demonstrated the inherent failings of capitalism, and its inevitable replacement with the communist system. Britain and France were also alarmed at the escalating nationalist and independence movements in their respective empires, and the corresponding costs of controlling these. With a pressurized domestic situation, it was particularly difficult to manage the growing forces of expansionism in both Europe and Asia. The democratic governments were thus increasingly forced to review their strategies for dealing with international tension. The League's key weapon of economic sanctions was now a weapon most countries would not want deployed as they attempted to protect their own trading interests. The USA pulled away further into isolationism. The British established **protectionism** for their trade within their empire in the Ottawa Agreements (1932). Although France and Italy took longer to be affected, as they were not as heavily dependent on international trade, they too had a downturn in their economies.

The responses to the Depression by the democratic states seemed to lead back to an old-style diplomacy, e.g. alliances and agreements outside the League. The strategy of appeasing countries in response to aggression became more realistic. Economic sanctions were not palatable and to take on aggressors by force was not, at least in the early 1930s when the Depression was tightening its grip, a viable option.

The Manchurian dispute

Japan was the only independent Asian power with its own empire – an empire that had expanded in 1920 when Japan took over the Mariana and Caroline Islands as mandates. Japan was also Asia's greatest industrial and trading power, and so was badly affected by world depression. Some sections of Japanese society believed that the key to Japan's future economic survival was to expand its empire. However, Asia was already dominated by the European colonial powers: Britain, France and the Netherlands. They would not tolerate any threat to their interests in the region. In addition, the USA was attempting to increase its influence in the Pacific and would be concerned with any 'aggressive' expansionism there.

In September 1931, the Japanese army in Manchuria, the Kwantung Army (responsible for protecting Japanese interests in the area), claimed that a bomb explosion near the town of Mukden was evidence of growing disorder, and used it as an excuse to conquer the province. In reality, the Japanese forces had planted the bomb, evidence of the Kwantung Army's desire to expand its influence in the territory.

In this incident, one key member of the League had attacked another member, China. China appealed to the League for assistance against an aggressor; here was exactly the type of incident that 'collective security' was designed to contain. The League of Nations took the following actions:

Japanese-controlled Manchuria, 1932.

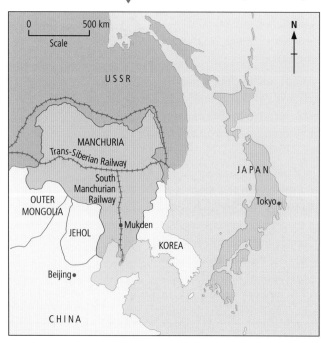

- It condemned Japan's actions and ordered the withdrawal of Japanese troops. The Japanese government agreed, but their army refused. This outcome exposed the lack of control the Japanese civilian government had over its military.
- It appointed a commission under Lord Lytton to investigate the crisis. The commission took more than a year to report, by which time the invasion and the occupation were complete. The commission found Japan guilty of forcibly seizing part of China's territory.
- It accepted the Lytton Report and instructed all of its members not to recognize the new Japanese state called Manchukuo. It invited Japan to hand Manchuria back to China.

In response, the Japanese said that they were leaving the League. They claimed that the condemnation of their actions in China was hypocrisy by powers such as Britain, which had a long legacy of using force to achieve its objectives in China. They may have had a point, but the new ideas embodied by the League represented a shift in international tolerance of this kind of empire-building.

STUDENT STUDY SECTION
Review questions
1 Explain Japan's motivation for attacking Manchuria.
2 What actions did the League of Nations take? What were the problems with these actions?

Why did the League fail to resolve the Manchurian Crisis?

There are several factors that contributed to the League's failure to resolve the crisis:
- The impact of the Great Depression caused the member states to be too preoccupied with their own troubled domestic situations. It also made them unwilling to apply economic sanctions. In any case, Japan's main trading links were with the USA, which was not a member of the League.
- Imposing any kind of military solution was problematic, as Manchuria was geographically remote and only Britain and the USA had the naval resources to confront Japan; again the USA was unwilling to do this. Britain was unwilling to act alone and also did not want to risk a naval conflict in the region, where they might well be outnumbered by the Japanese (following the Washington Conference – see p.107) and risk threatening their colonial interests.
- France and Italy were too occupied with events in Europe and were not prepared to agree to any kind of military or naval action against Japan. Again, as with Britain, France's colonial interests in the region made for a confused response. Japan was openly condemned, but privately the government sent a note suggesting that it was sympathetic to the 'difficulties' Japan was experiencing.

What was the impact of the Manchurian Crisis on the League of Nations?

The outcome of the Manchurian Crisis was a dire failure for the League. China had appealed to the League for help in the face of an aggressor, but had received no practical support, neither military nor in terms of economic sanctions. The moral high ground offered by the Lytton Report's verdict was little comfort. The whole affair had suggested that the League lacked the will to follow through with its philosophy of 'collective security'. The aggressor had 'got away with it'. Richard Overy points out that by leaving the League of

ToK Time

'In Manchuria today [there is] a collision between twentieth century international machinery and a nineteenth century point of view … [I] hope that the League's commission will be satisfied with no superficial approach to existing difficulties.' From a speech by the Honourable Vincent Massey, 14 January 1931, to the Empire Club of Canada. Published in *The Empire Club of Canada Speeches 1932*, Toronto, Canada.

What does the Honourable Vincent Massey mean by 'a nineteenth century point of view'? How was the 'twentieth century' view different? How far is our 21st-century view on empire-building different?

Nations, Japan had 'effectively removed the Far East from the system of collective security'. In Europe, meanwhile, Mussolini began planning his expansionist adventure into Abyssinia, encouraged by what had happened in Manchuria.

What was the impact of the Manchurian Crisis on the growth of Japanese militarism?

Traditionally, historians have seen the events in Manchuria as the starting point for the dominance of militarism within the Japanese government, which led ultimately to the Pacific war. Some historians, however, view the Manchurian Crisis as less significant to future events in Asia. In *The Manchurian Crisis and Japanese Society, 1931–33*, Sandra Wilson argues that the crisis had a more limited impact on Japanese thinking than has been suggested. Wilson argues that most Japanese regarded the end of fighting in Manchuria in 1933 as a return to normality, rather than the beginning of the militarization of Japanese society. Many people in Japanese society even believed that Japan would continue working cooperatively and diplomatically with Britain and the USA. She contends that the post-World War II idea of a 15-year war beginning in the Pacific in 1931 has affected *our* perception of the Manchurian incident.

To access worksheet 5.3 on the Manchurian Crisis, please visit www.pearsonbacconline.com and follow the on-screen instructions.

STUDENT STUDY SECTION

Document analysis

Questions

1 What is the cartoonist's message in each of the cartoons below?

2 How far do political cartoons reflect the public opinion of the time? Can cartoons 'shape' public opinion? (See discussion on David Low on p. 103.)

Document A

'Will the League stand up to Japan?', by David Low. The cartoon was first published in the *Evening Standard*, a British newspaper, in November 1931.

WILL THE LEAGUE STAND UP TO JAPAN ?

Document B

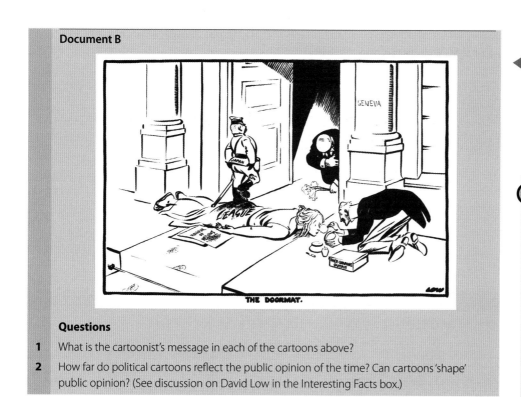

THE DOORMAT.

Questions

1 What is the cartoonist's message in each of the cartoons above?

2 How far do political cartoons reflect the public opinion of the time? Can cartoons 'shape' public opinion? (See discussion on David Low in the Interesting Facts box.)

The Abyssinian Crisis (1935)

In 1932, the Italian dictator Benito Mussolini began detailed planning for the annexation of Abyssinia (present-day Ethiopia and Eritrea). This move was not only an element of his long-term ambition of securing a North African Empire, but also a tactic to distract his people from the impact of the Depression.

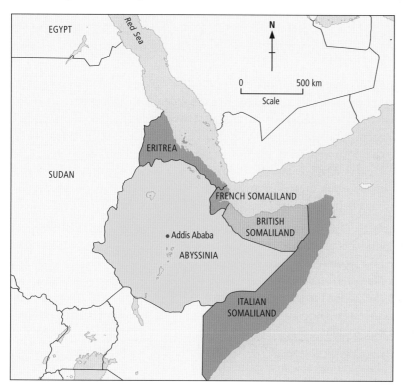

Abyssinia, 1934.

The conquest of Abyssinia would link together two Italian African territories – Eritrea and Italian Somaliland – and provide land for Italians to settle. At the Wal-Wal oasis, 80km inside the Abyssinian border with Italian Somaliland, Italian and Abyssinian forces clashed in December 1934. A full-scale invasion, however, did not begin until the following October, when Mussolini's forces were ready. He believed that the League would not respond, as Britain and France would not strongly object – Mussolini had been made aware by the French Foreign Minister Pierre Laval that he would be given a free hand in Abyssinia, and the British had wanted to reach an agreement in which Mussolini would have control over the territory without formally annexing it. Neither the French nor the British wanted to lose Italy as an ally against Nazi Germany. The Italians had already prevented Hitler from attempting *Anschluss* in 1934.

It was the brutality and ferocity of the Italian assault on Abyssinia, which began on 3 October 1935, that compromised Britain and France. When the 100,000-strong Italian army invaded, the Abyssinian Emperor, Haile Selassie, appealed to the League.

To access worksheet 5.4 on Haile Selassie, please visit www. pearsonbacconline.com and follow the on-screen instructions.

STUDENT STUDY SECTION

Research activity

Read the impassioned speech by Selassie, via the online resources link opposite. Identify the key points he makes to the League on why member states must act to defend Abyssinia. The British public (generally) supported action by the League, and public opinion was more important at this time, as a general election was pending in November. In France, the left-wing element also supported the League, whilst the right-wing was more sympathetic to Italy's cause.

Class discussion

What do you think were the different perspectives on the invasion? Consider the permanent members of the League, then consider the smaller nation members, and finally the views of non-members such as the USA. You may want to work in groups, each group taking a different country. You could take it in turns to be 'hot seated' to present to the rest of the class the perspective and recommendations of your country to the League. (Hot seating is where a student or teacher takes on the role of representing a country / person.)

The League's response came on 18 October. Italy's invasion was condemned and the League decided to employ an escalating programme of sanctions. Britain and France worked for a settlement outside the League in an attempt to avoid a breakdown in relations with Italy. France was hopeful of gaining Italian support for an anti-German alignment that might help to contain Nazi aggression. Britain was faced with possible Japanese aggression in the Far East and also had to consider the dangers of having Italy as an enemy, when Italy occupied an important strategic position in the Mediterranean Sea, a major sea route for Britain through to its imperial possessions.

In December, the British Foreign Minister Samuel Hoare and the French Foreign Minister Laval rekindled a plan that had already been considered by the League in September. The plan, called the Hoare–Laval Pact, was to allow Italian control of around two-thirds of Abyssinia. Mussolini could have accepted this idea, but it was never to be put on the table, as it was leaked to the French press. The pro-League British public was outraged and Hoare was forced to resign. The plan was shelved. Despite this strong public support, the League's sanctions were so diluted that they had little impact on the Italian war effort. No embargo was put on oil exports to Italy, and Britain refused to close the Suez Canal to Italian shipping. Mussolini was able to escalate his efforts until May 1936, when the Italians were in control of Abyssinia.

Cartoon analysis

A cartoon from *Punch*, a British satirical magazine, 1935.

THE AWFUL WARNING.

FRANCE AND ENGLAND
(*together ?*).

"WE DON'T WANT YOU TO FIGHT,
BUT, BY JINGO, IF YOU DO,
WE SHALL PROBABLY ISSUE A JOINT MEMORANDUM
SUGGESTING A MILD DISAPPROVAL OF YOU."

Questions

1 What is the message of this cartoon?
2 What evidence can be used to support the cartoonist's viewpoint of the handling of the crisis?

What were the effects of the Abyssinian Crisis on the League of Nations?

For the League, the Abyssinian Crisis was a disaster. A permanent member had again successfully ignored the League and had been victorious through violence and war. The League had proved itself ineffective in using 'collective security' to maintain peace. The crisis had revealed (as had already been seen in the Manchurian Crisis) that the leading League powers were not prepared to stand up to other major members of the League if their interests were not directly threatened. It was too dangerous to invoke a conflict with a power that – while upholding the idea of collective security – might adversely affect their own power and international position.

Italy, now isolated from its former allies, moved closer to Nazi Germany. The alliance between the British, French and Italians had collapsed. The League's ultimate weakness was exposed for Hitler to exploit, which he readily did with the militarization of the Rhineland in March 1936.

Many historians have viewed the Abyssinian Crisis as the 'final nail in the coffin' for the League of Nations. Thereafter, the League was simply symbolic of an ideal that had arisen out of the tragedy of World War I, an anomaly amidst old-style militaristic alliances and modern expansionist ideologies. The League of Nations could no longer exert any authority; collective security had failed.

The failure of disarmament

STUDENT STUDY SECTION

Document analysis

Document A

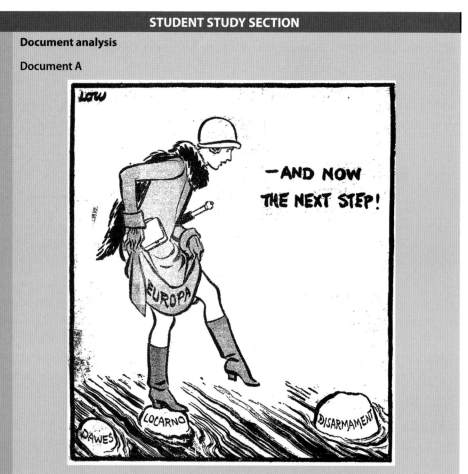

Document B

Article 8.1.

The members of the League recognize that the maintenance of peace requires the reduction of national armaments to the lowest point consistent with national safety and the enforcement by common action of international obligations…

4. After these plans shall have been adopted by the several governments, the limits therein fixed shall not be exceeded without the concurrence of the several governments.

5. The members of the League agree that the manufacture by private enterprise of munitions and implements of war is open to grave objections. The Council shall advise how the evils attendant upon such manufacture can be prevented…

6. The members of the League undertake to interchange full and frank information as to the scale of their armaments, their military, naval and air programmes and the conditions of such of their industries as are adaptable to warlike purposes.

Review/source questions

1. Read Document B. What were the key aims of the League of Nations with regard to disarmament?

2. What point is Low making about disarmament in his cartoon? Why do you think he had this opinion? What potential problems faced the League in the task of disarmament?

There were attempts to reduce weapons in the 1920s, though these were done outside the League of Nations rather than through it.

The Washington Conference (1921–22)

After World War I, Great Britain, the USA and Japan in particular continued to build up their navies. The cost of this military growth and the concern that the USA had regarding Japan's growing strength led America to call for the first post-war disarmament conference, held in Washington DC in 1921–22. The Five Power Treaty that was a result of this conference set naval tonnage to 525,000 tons for Britain and America, 300,000 for Japan and 175,000 for France and Italy (a ratio of 5:5:3 for America, Britain and Japan). The agreement would involve nations destroying battleships until their quota was reached. In addition, no new battleships were to be built for 10 years.

The Washington Conference also addressed other issues in the Far East. America and Canada wished to see Britain distance itself from the 1902 Alliance with Japan, and this was replaced with a Four Power Treaty involving the USA, Japan, Britain and France. It guaranteed the rights of all signatories to their possessions in Asia, and they also agreed to come to each other's defence in the case of an attack. A Nine Power Treaty affirmed the territorial integrity of China and endorsed the concept of an 'open door' through which all nations could trade with China on an equal basis.

The conference was successful in limiting naval armament and was seen as an example of how moves could be made towards disarmament in other areas as well. All countries gained something from the agreements. The fact that so few powers were involved helped make this disarmament conference a success. Nevertheless, the conference highlighted the growing isolation of France, which now had to accept the humiliating position of being on the same level as Italy. It also did not include Germany or Russia in the discussions and agreements.

The London Naval Conference (1930)

The London Naval Conference revised the agreement made at Washington. With the Great Depression now taking hold in Europe, the major powers were still keen to limit their defence spending. The 5:5:3 ratio for the USA, the UK and Japan was changed to 10:10:7. France and Italy refused to take part in this agreement, though they did agree to continue the ban on building capital ships for five years. Agreements were also reached on the size and numbers of cruisers, destroyers and submarines, and rules were made to control submarine warfare.

The London Naval Treaty (1936)

In 1935–36, the major powers met to re-negotiate the London Treaty of 1930. Yet the international situation had now changed dramatically. Japan no longer wished to limit its naval tonnage and be inferior to the USA and Britain, and so walked out of the conference. The Italians also left. Although Britain, America and France signed a treaty on cruiser tonnage, all disarmament agreements became meaningless given the rearmament programmes of Germany and Japan.

The Geneva Disarmament Conference (1932–34)

Between 1926 and 1932, preparations were made for a disarmament conference organized by the League of Nations. Even at the preparatory stage, there were disagreements over what types of armament limitations should take place and how agreements should be enforced. By the time that the actual conference took place in Geneva in 1932, delegates were faced not only with resolving these issues, but they were also faced with a German threat – if League members failed to bring about substantial disarmament, Germany would demand the right to rearm. By this time, Hitler's Nazi party was the largest party in Germany. Hitler's demands were forceful and they made France even more determined to resist pressure for it to disarm. Germany demanded 'equality of status', but this aspiration clashed with French security. If Germany was equal, France would not be secure; if France was secure, Germany could not be equal.

In October 1933, Hitler (now Chancellor of Germany), dramatically led the German delegation out of the conference, which finally ended in 1934 having failed to secure any of its goals.

Why did the League fail to achieve disarmament?

Supporters of the League of Nations were perhaps most disappointed with its failure to carry through its promises on disarmament. However, there were many factors that made its task in this area almost impossible.

- The economic instability of the 1930s following the Great Depression caused, as we have already seen, nations to concentrate on their own problems first rather than work for collective security. Competition for markets grew and with it the dangers of conflict over them. In this position, nations were unlikely to feel that they could reduce their armed forces; indeed, some countries used rearmament as a way of providing employment and thus helping their economies out of the Depression.
- The political instability of Europe, with the new communist regime in Russia, the fragility of new states in Central Europe and a discontented Germany, made many states reluctant to limit their arms. France in particular, neighbouring a potentially powerful Germany and lacking any real commitment of support from Great Britain and America, was unwilling to do anything that would increase its vulnerability. Similarly, Czechoslovakia and Poland were looking for increased security given their proximity to both Germany and Russia.
- Japan's invasion of Manchuria undermined the idea of collective security and meant that nations with interests in the Asia–Pacific region were unlikely to welcome disarmament suggestions.

STUDENT STUDY SECTION

Review exercise

You have read about many conferences/agreements that took place in the post-World War I era. To help remember the key points, look back over the chapter and summarize these conferences and agreements in a grid such as the one below.

	Participants	Terms/agreements	Significance for international situation
Washington Conference 1921–22			
Geneva Protocol 1921			
Rapallo Treaty 1923			
The Dawes Plan 1924			
The Locarno Conference 1925			
Kellogg–Briand Pact 1928			
The Young Plan 1929			

Essay planning

Question

Why did collective security fail to keep the peace between 1920 and 1935?

Introduction: You need to identify and explain key terms/concepts in the actual question. Here you need to explain the concept of 'collective security' and that the League of Nations had been established to facilitate this policy. You also need to show the examiner that you understand the relevance of the dates in the question. How did the situation regarding collective security change between these two dates? What is the relevance of 1935? Don't forget to set out your argument to show the direction that the essay will take.

Section 1: The main instrument for collective security was the League of Nations. In explaining why collective security failed, you need to outline the weaknesses of the League of Nations that were to undermine its ability to perform its task of keeping the peace.

Section 2: Collective security was undermined not just by the machinery of the League, but also by the continued willingness of countries to work outside the League to achieve peace: France in the Ruhr, the various agreements made in the 1920s, etc.

Section 3: The impact of the Great Depression needs to be examined here, as this had a big impact on the desire/ability of nations to work collectively for peace.

Section 4: Here analyze the specific events in the 1930s – Manchuria, Abyssinia and Disarmament Conference etc. – that showed the inability of the nations in the League to work together.

Opening sentences

As indicated by the essay-planning chart on p.36, the opening sentence of each paragraph in your essay is important for indicating the direction of your argument. Each 'topic sentence' should relate back to the question and set out the point that will be argued in that paragraph. A good topic sentence will also lead you into an analytical rather than a narrative approach.

Which of the following opening sentences to the essay above suggest an analytical approach linking to the question? Which suggest a more narrative approach or do not link to the question?

- There were several key events between 1920 and 1935 that created tension in Europe.
- The structure of the League meant that it would be difficult to follow through with the idea of collective security.
- The concept of collective security was damaged by France's unilateral actions in the Ruhr in 1923.
- The League of Nations was set up in 1919 with the aim of keeping peace.
- The Locarno conference took place in 1925.
- The Great Depression was triggered by the Wall Street Crash in America in 1929.
- The Manchurian Crisis undermined the credibility of the League and its will to follow through with its philosophy of collective security.
- In 1935, Mussolini invaded Abyssinia.
- The reaction of the League and of key powers such as Britain and France to the Abyssinian Crisis proved conclusively that collective security had failed.
- The League of Nations consisted of an Assembly, Council and Secretariat.
- Collective security was undermined by the impact of the Great Depression.

Essay question

To what extent was the League of Nations 'doomed to fail'?

Essay frame

Introduction: Again, you must always start by defining key words/terms in the question. Here you need to define 'doomed to fail', i.e. that the inherent problems with the League's structure, mandate and membership made it likely to fail. As this is a 'to what extent' question, you will need to present a counter-argument. State this clearly in your introduction; for example, that the League was not inherently flawed but failed due to the impact of the Great Depression and the actions of the powers themselves.

Section 1: Always start with the argument presented in the question itself, i.e. that it was 'doomed to fail', and give arguments to support this view, such as:

- Weaknesses in structure, mandate and membership
- Failures to keep the peace in the 1920s.

Section 2: Now address an alternative view – that the League was not doomed to fail. Look at:

- Strengths in structure, mandate and membership
- Evidence of success in peacekeeping in the 1920s
- The international impact of the Great Depression.

Conclusion: Based on the weight of evidence in the main body of the essay, refer back to the question directly and state whether the League was doomed to fail or not.

6 THE CAUSES OF WORLD WAR II IN EUROPE: HITLER'S WAR

A Nazi election poster from the 1930s. The text translates 'Break free now! Vote Hitler.'

As you read this chapter, consider the following essay question:
- To what extent was World War II 'Hitler's War'?

As you have read, there were problems with peacekeeping in the 1920s, and there were aggressive and expansionist states that were threatening peace (Japan in Manchuria and Italy in Abyssinia) in the 1930s. Yet according to some historians, and according to Britain's wartime leader, Winston Churchill, World War II was primarily caused by the ambitions and policies of Adolf Hitler – the conflict was 'Hitler's War'.

Timeline to the outbreak of war – 1933–39

1933	**Jan**	Hitler becomes Chancellor in Germany
	Feb	Hitler introduces programme of rearmament
	Oct	Hitler leaves Disarmament Conference / announces intention to withdraw Germany from League of Nations
1934	**Jan**	Germany signs Non-Aggression Pact with Poland
1935	**Jan**	Plebiscite in Saar; Germans there vote for return of territory to Germany
	Mar	Conscription re-introduced in Germany. Stresa agreements between Britain, France and Italy
	Jun	Anglo-German Naval Treaty
	Oct	Italian invasion of Abyssinia
1936	**Mar**	Germany remilitarizes the Rhineland
	Jun	Hitler sends military support to Franco's Nationalists in Spain
	Aug	Hitler's Four Year Plan drafted for war
	Nov	Anti-Comintern Pact with Japan; Rome–Berlin Axis signed
1937	**May**	Neville Chamberlain becomes Prime Minister in Britain
	Jul	Sino-Japanese War begins
	Nov	Hossbach Memorandum; war plans meeting
1938	**Mar**	*Anschluss* declared after German troops march into Austria
	Sep	Munich Crisis; Sudetenland Crisis
1939	**Mar**	Germany occupies rest of Czechoslovakia; Lithuania gives up port of Memel to Germany Anglo-French guarantee of Poland
	Apr	Introduction of conscription in Britain
	May	Pact of Steel signed between Germany and Italy
	Aug	Anglo-French military mission to Moscow; Nazi–Soviet Pact signed between Germany and the USSR; Anglo-Polish treaty signed
	Sep	Germany invades Poland; Britain and France declare war on Germany

In his account of the causes of World War II, *The Second World War: Volume One, The Gathering Storm*, 1948, Winston Churchill asserted that Hitler had a master plan for the domination of Europe, which Hitler had outlined in his book *Mein Kampf* ('My Struggle'; 1925–26). Churchill went on to suggest that the 'granite pillars' of his plan had been to reunite Germans in a Great German Empire and to conquer Eastern Europe by force. War was inevitable to attaining these goals, and Hitler pursued these ambitions by creating a militarized nation. In Churchill's analysis, the turning point was 1935 when Germany rearmed; from that point on war was the only way to stop Hitler.

As you read through this chapter, consider whether or not you agree with Churchill's perspective on events leading to war in Europe.

Hitler's foreign policy aims: 1919–33

Hitler had fought in World War I, and the war left its mark on the young Austrian. He had been temporarily blinded in a gas attack, and it was while he was recovering in hospital that he heard of Germany's surrender. It was then, Hitler has stated, that he decided to 'go into politics'.

With the defeat of Russia on the Eastern Front, and the terms of the Treaty of Brest-Litovsk in 1917, Germany had almost realized the domination of Eastern Europe (Poland and Lithuania became German territories). These gains, however, were lost when Germany was defeated on the Western Front. Nevertheless, as both the Russian and Austro-Hungarian Empires had fallen, Germany was left in a potentially dominant position in continental Europe, even after the peace settlements. If you look back to the terms of the Treaty of Versailles in Chapter 4, the perceived severity of the treaty meant that Germans, even democratic ones, wanted to reverse the settlement. Most could not accept the severe losses, particularly of territory to Poland. In addition, German commitment to making reparation payments was limited.

Nazi foreign policy was shaped by this historical context, but Adolf Hitler also had ambitions that went beyond redressing the outcome of World War I. In 1919, Hitler became the 55th member of a new political party, led by Anton Drexler, the Deutsche Arbeiterpartei (DAP; German Workers' Party), later renamed the Nationalsozialistische Deutsche Arbeiterpartei (NSDAP; National Socialist German Workers' Party) in 1920. By 1921, Hitler had become party leader. This 'Nazi' Party set down a 25-point programme, which included key objectives such as the union of all Germans, an end to the Treaty of Versailles, a strong state, the creation of a national army and the exclusion of Jews from German society. The programme is clear evidence that Hitler had long-term objectives that would cause tension, and potentially conflict, in Europe.

In November 1923, Hitler and his Nazis attempted to seize power in a *coup d'état* in Munich – known as the Munich Beer Hall Putsch (*putsch* is the German word for coup). The attempt failed, and Hitler was sent to prison for nine months. It was while serving his sentence in prison that Hitler wrote *Mein Kampf*. The book was a combination of autobiography and political philosophy – it covered racist and authoritarian theories and ideas for the direction of Nazi foreign policy. In this book, Hitler asserted the need for German racial purity and the absolute need to acquire 'living space' for the German population, known as **Lebensraum.**

Only an adequate large space on this earth assures a nation of freedom of existence… We must hold unflinchingly to our aim … to secure for the German people the land and soil to which they are entitled.

From Adolf Hitler, *Mein Kampf*, 1925

The historian Andreas Hillgruber suggested that the plans set down in *Mein Kampf* could be viewed as Hitler's *Stufenplan* or 'stage-by-stage plan'. The first stage would be the termination of the Treaty of Versailles, and the formation of an alliance with Britain and Italy. The second stage would be a war against France and her Eastern European allies; and the last stage would be a war with the USSR. Hitler, however, did not use the

Munich Beer Hall Putsch

The French invasion of the Ruhr had led to an intensified feeling of nationalism in Germany. A right-wing plot was drawn up late in 1923 by the Bavarian state commissioner, the local Reichswehr commander, the chief of the provincial police and Hitler's NSDAP to overthrow the Republic. On 8 November, Hitler burst into a political meeting in a Munich beer hall and, supported by units of his *Sturmabteilung* (SA) guard, declared that a putsch was taking place. However, as they were outnumbered on the streets the following day, Hitler attempted to get the local *Reichswehr* to join him. As they marched to the barracks, their path was blocked and 16 Nazis were killed. The rest ran away. After the attempted putsch, Ludendorff, a supporter of Hitler, and Hitler himself stood trial. Ludendorff was released, but Hitler was sentenced to five years in prison. He served only one.

term *Stufenplan* in his book. Indeed, *Mein Kampf*'s value as evidence of war planning by Hitler has been debated by historians. Statements like the quotation above were taken by many people as evidence of Hitler's clear intention for world domination. A.J.P. Taylor, by contrast, sees *Mein Kampf* as rather more irrelevant – just a work of wishful thinking by a then-failed revolutionary.

The Nazi Party did not do well in the German elections in 1928; Hitler retreated to Munich to dictate another book, *Zweites Buch*, known as the 'Secret Book' of 1928. This book provides historians with further evidence of Hitler's longer-term ambitions, and his more consistent foreign policy objectives. In the book, Hitler develops many of the foreign policy ideas he discussed in *Mein Kampf*, although he suggests that in the 1930s a final struggle would take place for world hegemony between the USA and the combined forces of a 'Greater Germany' and the British Empire. Hitler also wrote here about his admiration for Mussolini, and his anger towards the German Chancellor Gustav Stresemann, whose foreign policy ambition was to return Germany to its pre-1914 borders. Hitler saw this goal as far too limited. He restated his principal aim of attaining vast territories of *Lebensraum*, space to be taken from the USSR. The overthrow of Versailles was just the preamble to this objective.

Hitler's rise to power

As we saw in Chapter 5, there was a period of optimism in international relations in the 1920s. From Locarno in 1925, to the Kellogg–Briand Pact in 1928 and the commencement of the World Disarmament Conference in 1932, there had been a sense of international cooperation and accord, which was manifest in the new League of Nations organization. Indeed, Germany had signed or been involved with all these agreements. Yet the stability was fragile, and the weaknesses of the League to maintain peace by collective security had been tested and found wanting before Hitler came to power in Germany. The Great Depression undermined both the League's ability to resist aggressor states, and the willingness of member states to work together.

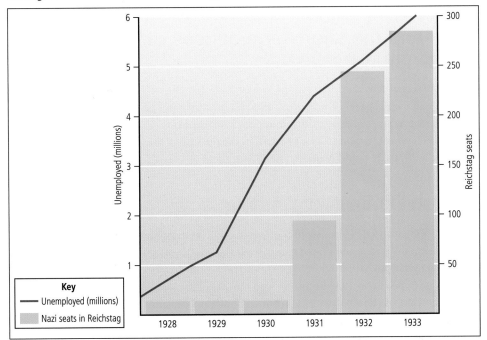

A graph showing unemployment in Germany and the seats won in the Reichstag by the Nazi Party, 1928–33.

The impact of the global economic crisis was particularly dramatic in Weimar Germany (see Chapter 4). The mass unemployment and despair that followed assisted Hitler's rise to power. Indeed, the Nazi Party's success at the polls directly correlated with the degree of unemployment in Germany (see graph); the more unemployed there were, the more successful the Nazis were in elections. In the end, Hitler was able to come to power legally; a group of conservative politicians, including the President, General von Hindenburg, concluded that Hitler would be useful to have on their side. They believed that they would be able to control him. Thus, Hitler became Chancellor of Germany, democratically, in January 1933. He was now able to pursue his long-term ambitions.

It could be argued that Hitler had to pursue certain aggressive foreign policy objectives, as such aims had brought him to power. His attack on the Treaty of Versailles and those who had signed it meant that many Germans believed he and the Nazis would restore Germany's international prestige through crushing the treaty. In addition, Hitler had been brought to power with the assistance of other right-wing parties in the Weimar Republic; much of this support was gained because of the Nazis' stated foreign policy ambitions.

Between 1933 and 1934, Hitler consolidated his control in Germany. He gained the tacit cooperation of the army and the industrialists, who both believed Hitler would bring in a massive programme of rearmament. The Nazi regime was **totalitarian,** and the rights of its citizens were subordinate to the state. Ultimately, this meant that the Nazis could gear domestic policy to meet the needs of its expansionist foreign policy. Military conscription and rearmament, meanwhile, could relieve mass unemployment.

To access worksheet 6.1 on Adolf Hitler, please visit www.pearsonbacconline.com and follow the on-screen instructions.

STUDENT STUDY SECTION

Review questions

1 From what you have read so far, what evidence is there that Hitler had a long-term plan that would lead to a general European war?

2 To what extent should a) German moderates and b) foreign governments have been aware of the potential danger of Hitler?

3 How far do you agree that the Nazis' popularity was due to the economic crisis in Germany?

Hitler and the short-term causes of World War II (1933–38)

As we have seen, there is evidence in the longer term that Hitler had a consistent ambition to control 'race and space' – the Nazis wanted racial purity and *Lebensraum*. These themes are consistent in his speeches, writing and policy statements throughout the 1920s, and then, once in power, appear to be consistent in the direction Hitler steered Germany through the 1930s. It would seem that neither of these objectives could be obtained *without* war.

Revising the Treaty of Versailles

Between 1933 and 1935, Hitler set about revising the Treaty of Versailles, a process that led to tension in Europe and placed pressure on the League of Nations. Hitler began by attacking reparations. Although repayment of reparations had been suspended before Hitler came to power, in 1933 he announced that the Nazis would not resume payments. The declaration was good propaganda, but was not a major cause of international friction, as most powers had already accepted this. What did increase tension was Hitler's intention to rearm Germany. As we have seen, Hitler manipulated the reluctance of France towards embracing general disarmament to justify Germany's withdrawal from the Disarmament Conference in 1933. German military spending in the year 1934–35 increased fivefold when compared to that of 1933–34. Historian Ted Townley writes in *Hitler and the Road to War*,

'For whatever final purpose, Hitler worked at this time to create a German economy that would provide total industrial backing for the German military.'

GERMAN MILITARY EXPENDITURE	
Fiscal period	Million marks
1933–34	750
1934–35	4,093
1935–36	5,492
1936–37	10,271
1937–38	10,963
1938–39	17,247

German armed forces in 1932 and 1939.

Hitler again showed his contempt for the Versailles settlement when he withdrew Germany from the League of Nations in 1933. Leaving the League, plus open rearmament, had put Germany on a new path. The Weimar Republic had attempted to work with the international community and the League to rehabilitate Germany. Hitler's new course, by contrast, alarmed the other powers, who were still suffering the effects of the Depression and therefore had limited means to respond.

Germany's rearmament can be seen as the fundamental first step in facilitating Hitler's expansionist foreign policy. Hitler's next step was to sign the ten-year 'Non-Aggression Pact' with Poland in January 1934. Although Germany resented Poland on account of the 'Polish corridor' separating Germany from East Prussia, Hitler had gone ahead with this agreement to secure his eastern border. Some historians, for example William Shirer in *The Rise and Fall of the Third Reich*, regard this agreement as evidence of Hitler's plan to dominate Europe. The terms of the pact not only secured Germany's eastern border with Poland, it also undermined the French alliance system in Eastern Europe – the Little Entente – as it directly countered the Franco-Polish Alliance of 1925. To some extent, it also gave the impression to the international community that Hitler's intentions were ultimately peaceful.

Hitler's attention then turned to Austria. One of Hitler's stated objectives was to unify Austria with Germany, a policy outlined at some length in *Mein Kampf*. However, unification was forbidden by the Treaty of Versailles, and any attempt to achieve this might lead to confrontation with the European powers. Yet there were pro-Nazi groups in Austria, and in 1934 they murdered the Austrian Chancellor Engelbert Dollfuss and attempted to seize power in a coup. Initially, Hitler saw the coup as an opportunity to obtain his goal of *Anschluss*, but was deterred when the Austrian government crushed the coup and Mussolini sent troops to the border with Austria to warn Germany off.

Some historians have focused on this episode as evidence of Hitler's 'improvisation' in foreign policy, and argue that it suggests he did not have a long-term plan. Others, however, argue that Hitler was not yet ready to pursue his expansionist ambitions. He was still developing the Nazi state within Germany.

Hitler was able to use the pro-German Saar plebiscite in 1935 as very positive propaganda. The Treaty of Versailles had set down that there would be self-determination in the Saar by a public vote or plebiscite. The plebiscite was held in 1935, and the result was overwhelming: 9–1 in favour of reuniting with Germany. With the Saar plebiscite acting as a boost to his 'popular mandate', Hitler announced he would introduce compulsory military service in Germany. This step, again, was a violation of the Treaty of Versailles. At the same time he announced the increase of his armaments programme. Hitler now declared the existence of an army of more than 500,000 men, and had admitted the existence of an air force. The other powers were deeply concerned, but continued to hope that a revision of Versailles would satisfy the more moderate elements of German society.

The European response

[handwritten margin note: Naval Agreement]

In a collective response to Hitler's attacks on the Treaty of Versailles, in particular German rearmament, Britain, France and Italy joined together in the 'Stresa Front' (named after the town in Italy in which the agreement was signed). The three powers failed to finalize an agreement on *how* the Stresa Front would stop Hitler, and within a month the Stresa Front was shown to be meaningless when Britain and Germany signed a Naval Agreement. The Anglo-German Naval Agreement of 1935 allowed for a much larger German Navy than was permitted by the Treaty of Versailles, and thus indicated British acceptance of German rearmament. The British had not consulted the French in signing the agreement and were pursuing self-interest, as the agreement was an attempt by Britain to limit German naval expansion. It was another passive victory for Hitler, as Britain had in effect condoned or at least accepted German naval rearmament. It also revealed that Hitler's aggression was successfully initimidating the other European powers.

Hitler was then able to manipulate the new international situation that had resulted from the Italian invasion of Abyssinia in October 1935. Abyssinia was a member of the League of Nations, and the invasion led to the breakdown of relations between Italy, Britain and France. Italy ultimately left the League and, with its humiliation at the hands of a key member state, the League was left impotent. Hitler's expansionist plans, with his rearmed Germany, could enter their next phase.

ToK Time

Consider the extent to which you are personally interested in politics. Are you interested in the politics of your own nation, or are you more interested in the politics of other nations? What political issues do think are important or engaging? Do you agree with the policies of mainstream political parties or do you hold more independent or radical views?

In pairs discuss why politics is important, and why young people often feel remote from current political parties. What are the topics that are most important to you, and what knowledge issues are there in attempting to find answers to political problems?

STUDENT STUDY SECTION

Review questions

1 Which of Hitler's aims, as set down in *Mein Kampf*, had he achieved by 1935?

2 Based on Hitler's stated long-term ambitions, what would his next objectives be?

3 How far do you agree that Germany was the *only* country causing tension in Europe in the first half of the 1930s?

Class discussion

Based on the evidence in this chapter and the previous chapter, to what extent do you agree that events in the 1920s and early 1930s made a general war in Europe likely?

German remilitarization of the Rhineland

Up until 1936, Hitler had been rather cautious. He had capitalized on the international understanding that his aims were to redress the 'wrongs' meted out to Germany at Versailles. Yet there had also been clear indications that his objectives were more extreme. In 1936 Hitler turned his attention to Germany's western border. Versailles had made the Rhineland a demilitarized zone to help secure the border between Germany and France. France deemed this provision as a key element in its security, and thus any attempt to remilitarize the area was potentially highly provocative. By this point, Hitler's army had grown, he had the backing of the more extreme nationalists in Germany, and he had the advantage of the divisions between the European 'defenders' of the settlement. Hitler bided his time until it was clear that Italy was going to be victorious in Abyssinia.

Nevertheless, some of Hitler's senior generals were concerned that France would take military action to defend the demilitarized zone; these included his commander-in-chief, Werner von Blomberg. Hitler assured them that he would pull out at the first sign of a French military response. The Germans sent 10,000 troops and 23,000 armed police into the Rhineland in March 1936. There was no response from the French or the British. In France, there was division over how to react, and no support from the British, who generally were against resistance. Some contemporaries, such as Winston Churchill, argued that this had been a crucial point at which Hitler could and should have been stopped. Not only was the German force relatively small, but stopping Germany at this point would have undermined Hitler's position both politically and militarily. Nevertheless, you will read later in this chapter that the reality of the situation for Britain and France was complicated. Hitler remilitarized the Rhineland, and moved on to his next objective.

Hitler's involvement in the Spanish Civil War

Hitler had entered the Rhineland while Mussolini was occupying international attention in Africa. When the League criticized Italian action in Abyssinia, however, Italy and Germany grew closer together. With the outbreak of a civil war in Spain in 1936 (see Chapter 12), both Germany and Italy sent support to Franco's forces. Germany's involvement in the Spanish Civil War was more limited than Italy's; for example, there were never more than 10,000 Germans fighting in Spain, whereas Italy had seven times that number. Hitler's motives for getting involved were not simply to benefit from another right-wing government in power in Europe, but also to test out Germany's new and improved armed forces. The nature of the German involvement in Spain is further evidence to support the argument that Hitler was preparing his forces for the realities of war in Europe. Infamously, at Guernica in northern Spain on 26 April 1937, the bombers of Hitler's Condor Legion tested out the effectiveness of civilian aerial bombing. It was an ominous indication of what was to come.

Rome–Berlin Axis and the Anti-Comintern Pact

A treaty of friendship between Germany and Italy was concluded in October 1936, and in November Mussolini first suggested the idea of a Rome–Berlin Axis around which the other European countries would revolve. Hitler broadened his alliance base when Germany signed the Anti-Comintern Pact with Japan in November 1936. In 1937 Italy joined the pact. The Nazi Foreign Minister, Joachim von Ribbentrop, believed Japan could be used as a force to counter Britain and Russia in Asia. The intention was that, by using Japan to apply pressure in Asia, Hitler would meet less resistance to his expansionist aims in Europe.

A photograph of the destroyed city of Guernica. Hitler's Condor Legion bombed the city in April 1937.

The Hossbach Memorandum

In August 1936 Hitler launched the 'Four Year Plan' designed to prepare the German economy for war by 1940. Then on 5 November 1937, he called a meeting in the Reich Chancellery in Berlin. This meeting was to result in the now infamous 'Hossbach Memorandum'. Present at the meeting were the key military men of Hitler's Germany. According to the minute-taker, Colonel Friedrich Hossbach, Hitler opened the meeting by suggesting that the subject for discussion was of the utmost importance, indeed too important for a wider discussion in the Reichstag. Hitler, Hossbach wrote, then went on to add that in the event of his death, the points he made at the meeting regarding Germany's long-term policy should be regarded as his 'last will and testament'. Hitler proceeded by stating that the key aim of German policy was to secure and preserve the racial community and to enlarge it. He then addressed the questions of when and how. Hitler suggested that after the period 1943–45, the international situation would not be favourable to German ambitions; the re-equipping and organization of the armed forces was nearly complete, and any delay could result in 'their obsolescence'. The meeting considered scenarios in which France would be less of a threat, e.g. domestic problems or a war with another nation, and the necessity of Germany seizing the initiative to take territory (e.g. Czechoslovakia and Austria). The second part of the conference focused on 'concrete questions of armament.'

This meeting has been seen by some historians as evidence of Hitler planning a general war, while others have questioned its importance. Many historians have agreed with the conclusions of Anthony P. Adamthwaite about the Hossbach Memorandum: '…there is no reason why the memorandum should not be accepted as a guide to Hitler's ideas on foreign policy. The Hossbach Memorandum confirms the continuity of Hitler's thinking: the primacy of force in world politics, conquest of living space in the east, anti-Bolshevism, hostility to France. Hitler's warlike intentions were now explicit' (Anthony Adamthwaite, *The Making of the Second World War*, 1989).

STUDENT STUDY SECTION

Review and research questions

1 What key aims does Hitler set down for German foreign policy during the Hossbach meeting?

2 Hitler did not seem interested in retaining the minutes of this meeting (none were taken). Is this significant?

3 Compare and contrast the nature and importance of the Hossbach meeting in November 1937 to the German War Council meeting in December 1912.

4 Read through a copy of the Hossbach Memorandum at The Avalon Project (see Internet links section at the back of this book). Would you identify any other points that suggest Hitler is planning for a general war?

The Hossbach Memorandum was used at the Nuremberg War Trials (a series of Allied war trials in 1945–46) as evidence of Nazi Germany's planning for war. However, A.J.P. Taylor has questioned its importance. Taylor points out that the memorandum is a copy of a copy, and even the original had been written from memory days after the conference. He suggests that historians have misunderstood what the meeting was really about; it was not, in his view, a war planning meeting at all. Its true purpose was an internal political device to get rid of Hitler's Minister for Economics, Hjalmar Schacht, who was opposed to the cost of proposed rearmament.

5 In pairs evaluate the value and limitations of the Hossbach document as evidence for historians looking at the causes of World War II.

For some historians, it is not the meeting itself that is the evidence of Hitler's war planning, but what happened as a result of the meeting. In *The Monopoly of Violence – Why Europeans Hate Going to War*, James Sheehan initially seems to agree with Taylor's view of the meeting, but he goes on to point out that the *purpose* of the meeting was to root out those high up in the military who would not support Hitler's foreign policy ambitions:

On November 5, 1937, Hitler summoned his foreign minister and the leaders of the army, navy and air force to the newly completed Chancellery for a discussion of his long-range objectives. The four-hour meeting, of which a summary prepared by Colonel Friedrich Hossbach, the Führer's adjutant, was not, as historians have sometimes claimed, a road map for war. But it did clearly formulate Hitler's central goal, which was 'to make secure and to preserve the racial community and enlarge it.' This, he insisted, was a question of space. Three of Hitler's listeners – the war minister, Field Marshal von Blomberg, the commander of the army, General von Fritsch and the foreign minister, Baron von Neurath – expressed some misgivings about these ambitions. Within a few months, they had all been replaced by more pliable subordinates.

From James Sheehan, *The Monopoly of Violence: Why Europeans Hate Going to War*, 2008

Anschluss

In March 1938, Hitler sent troops into Austria. Where he had been resisted in 1934, four years later he encountered no military resistance. Italy was now an ally, and Britain, under the leadership of Chamberlain, argued that the Versailles Treaty had been wrong to enforce a separation of Germany and Austria. Hitler had seized his opportunity when the Austrian Chancellor Kurt von Schuschnigg had called for a referendum over the issue of *Anschluss*. Hitler's excuse for sending in troops was to ensure the vote was conducted peacefully. With his forces in place, the vote was overwhelmingly in favour – 99.75 per cent. Hitler was now strengthened not only by the Austrian armed forces, but also by the country's rich deposits of gold and iron ore. Tension in Europe increased as Hitler prepared his next move.

The takeover of Czechoslovakia

Hitler's actions had clearly threatened peace in Europe. In pursuit of his long-term aims, it is apparent that he was methodically revising the terms of the Treaty of Versailles, so his next action was to regain the Sudetenland. The Czechoslovakian leader, Edvard Beneš, was fully aware of the imminent threat to his country, and appealed for help from Britain and France. France, bound by a treaty obligation, agreed to defend Czechoslovakia if it were invaded by Germany, although it was reluctant to do so. Britain then agreed to support the French. In May 1938, Hitler increased the tension by declaring that he would fight for the Sudetenland if he had to.

This was a bold threat from Hitler, as the Czechs had a modernized army, with state-of-the-art armaments. They also had guarantees of support from Britain, France and the USSR. However, central to their defences was the Sudetenland, a heavily fortified region containing key industries and railways. Hitler had initiated a crisis throughout Europe; there was a genuine fear that a war was coming.

On 15 September 1938, Chamberlain attempted to resolve the crisis by meeting with Hitler. At his initial meeting, it seemed as though Hitler wanted a compromise too – he moderated his demands, asking for only parts of the Sudetenland, and only those if a plebiscite showed that the people wanted to be part of Germany. However, at a second meeting on 22 September Hitler increased his demands; he now wanted *all* the Sudetenland. Britain

The Sudetenland
The Sudetenland was territory ceded to Czechoslovakia at the end of World War I. Its inhabitants were mainly ethnic Germans (three million of them) and the territory consisted of the border territories of Bohemia, Moravia and Silesia.

Map of Europe showing Hitler's gains up to August 1939.

responded by mobilizing its navy; war seemed imminent. A final meeting was held on 29 September. Britain, France and Italy decided to agree to Hitler's 'ultimatum', and give Germany the Sudetenland; this was known as the Munich Agreement. The three powers did not consult with Beneš and the Czechs, nor with the Soviets. Hitler had again achieved his objective by threatening force.

Although Chamberlain declared that the agreement meant 'peace in our time', he had at the same stroke authorized a massive increase in arms spending. Hitler's policies had led to a renewed arms race in Europe. On 15 March 1939, Germany marched in and occupied the rest of Czechoslovakia. The Munich Agreement was shattered. Hitler had taken over a sovereign territory, and the pursuit of his foreign policy objectives meant that war in Europe was inevitable.

STUDENT STUDY SECTION

Research activity

Research different newspaper reports on the Munich Agreement from the time. How was this crisis viewed?

'One People, One Nation, One Leader!' A poster of Hitler, 1938.

Hitler and the immediate causes of World War II (1939)

Hitler's actions put Europe on the brink of war. He was the aggressor; Britain and France had sought only peace. It was clear that Poland would be Hitler's next target. Britain and France had failed to respond to the occupation of Czechoslovakia, but now warned Germany that an attack on Poland would mean war. The policy of appeasement they had pursued throughout the 1930s was at an end. Britain and France attempted to back this threat up with an agreement with the USSR. During the summer of 1939, however, Stalin was also meeting with the German Foreign Minister, von Ribbentrop. On 24 August 1939, Germany pulled off one of the most controversial agreements in modern history, the Nazi–Soviet Pact. Essentially, the two ideological enemies agreed not to attack one another, and secretly they agreed to divide Poland between them. Although Hitler had signed an agreement with the country he intended to invade, this was a short-term strategic triumph as it would allow Germany to invade Poland without the risk of a two-front war, and gain a launch pad for the later goal of conquering the USSR.

Why did Germany sign an agreement with the USSR?	Why did the USSR sign an agreement with Germany?
Hitler wanted to avoid a war on two fronts. He did not believe that Britain and France would intervene to defend Poland once he had a pact with Stalin. The economic aid which the USSR would give Germany as a part of the pact would negate the impact of any Anglo-French blockade. Hitler still intended to invade the USSR at a later date – this agreement gave him time to deal with the West first.	The pact meant that the USSR would not have to get involved in a war in the West. This was important as it faced a threat in the East from Japan, and the Soviet Army had been weakened through Stalin's purges. It gave Stalin time to prepare for war, and there was always the hope that Germany and the West would weaken each other in the war and the USSR would be left as the strongest nation. As part of the deal, Stalin got half of Poland and the opportunity to take over Finland and the Baltic States. Germany was still the USSR's major trading partner.

STUDENT STUDY SECTION

Cartoon analysis

RENDEZVOUS

Question

What is the message of the Low cartoon of 1939?

'Rendezvous', a David Low cartoon, 20 September 1939. Hitler is addressing Stalin, 'The scum of the earth, I believe?' Stalin greets Hitler with 'The bloody assassin of the workers, I presume?'

The invasion of Poland

The most immediate cause of World War II was the conflict over the independence of Poland. If you refer back to Chapter 4, you will see how the Allied powers had created an independent Polish state that was given a land 'corridor' to the sea through territory that was formerly German. The important German port of Danzig was to be a 'free city' under League of Nations supervision, which meant the Poles could use it. Both sides knew that this solution would be a cause of future tension, and the Germans never accepted it. Soon after Hitler came to power, the National Socialists won a majority in the city's government.

Yet Poland was not only threatened by a resurgent Germany; the Soviets had also laid claim to the newly independent Polish territory. Poland had been given more territory in the east than it had before the peace settlements. In 1920, the Red Army (Soviet Army) had invaded in an attempt to crush this new state and consolidate their control in Eastern Europe. The Poles had rallied and managed to defeat the Red Army in the battle for Warsaw. This victory was key to the Poles' new sense of national identity, and it was important in their determination not to make concessions to either the Soviets or the Germans in 1939. In November 1938, Hitler had told his armed forces to prepare a plan for the forced seizure of Danzig, and by the beginning of 1939 Hitler was demanding the city's return. The Poles decided that they would have to meet German demands with force.

On 3 March 1939, Chamberlain announced that Britain and France would guarantee the independence of Poland. The British now saw the issue as being between German ambition to dominate Europe versus Polish determination to defend themselves. One month after the British guarantee was made, Hitler ordered preparations for the invasion of Poland. For the Poles, cooperating with the Soviets to deter the Germans seemed abhorrent. Fighting was seen as the only option, and by July 1939 the country was confident and prepared for engagement.

Once Hitler had secured his deal with Stalin on 24 August, he could unleash his attack on Poland. Germany ignored the Anglo-French threat, and invaded Poland on 1 September 1939. This time Britain and France had to keep their word, and declared war on Germany. Hitler had started a general war in Europe. It may not have been against the countries he had planned for, nor at the time he had expected, but it was Hitler's war.

Appeasement as a cause of World War II

As you read the next section, consider the following essay question:
• How important was the policy of appeasement as a cause of World War II?

Appeasement was the policy followed primarily by Britain in the 1930s in attempting to settle international disputes by satisfying grievances through compromise and negotiation. It has been argued that by pursuing such a policy, Britain and France encouraged Hitler's aggression. In consistently and continuously giving in to Hitler's demands, the Western democracies also further alienated the USSR and led Stalin to believe that the policy was designed to allow for German expansion in the East and to promote a conflict between the Nazis and the Soviet communists. In addition, appeasement also meant that Hitler gambled on that policy continuing in the case of Poland, and thus brought about a general European war when Britain and France changed their stance in 1939. Indeed, A.J.P. Taylor, in his 1961 book *The Origins of the Second World War*, disagreed with the view that World War II was Hitler's war; he suggests that it was at least as much due to the failures of the European statesmen.

Taylor and others have argued that although there is evidence of expansionist aims in Hitler's speeches and writing in the 1920s, this does not mean that he had a 'blueprint' plan of what he would do once in power in the 1930s. They argue that Hitler was not 'acting' to shape, but rather 'reacting' to, the actions of other European leaders. (Taylor dismisses the importance of *Mein Kampf*, suggesting it was written to pass the time in prison rather than as a coherent plan for a future regime.)

Taylor goes on to argue that Hitler's successful dismantling of the Treaty of Versailles was the fault of the other European leaders who failed to contain Germany. It was too late to stop Germany over Poland, and Hitler was not convinced that Britain and France would go to war, as this would go against their typical policy of appeasement. Ultimately Hitler, Taylor suggests, was not so different from previous German leaders.

There would seem to be a strong case against Britain's policy of appeasement. Appeasement had encouraged Hitler to be increasingly aggressive, and each victory had given him confidence and increased power. With each territorial acquisition, Hitler's Germany was better defended, and had more soldiers, workers, raw materials, weapons and industries. Many saw the betrayal of Czechoslovakia at Munich as one of the most dishonourable acts Britain had ever committed. Furthermore, this act was all for nothing, as Britain had not rearmed sufficiently to take on Germany in 1939. Appeasement had also led to the USSR signing an agreement with Hitler, thus unleashing World War II. The Nazi–Soviet Pact meant that Hitler did not have to fear a two-front war, and could continue to provoke the West over his claims to Polish territory. Indeed, Hitler's continued expansion would now only mean war to the west, as he had secured his eastern border.

STUDENT STUDY SECTION

Document analysis

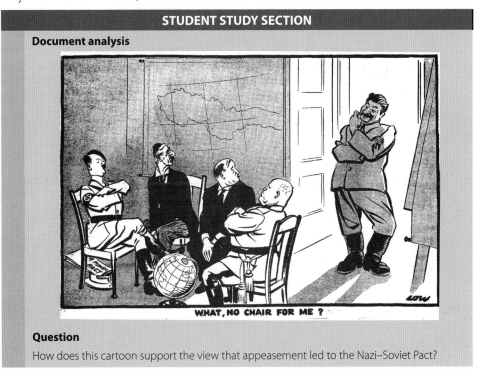

'What, no chair for me?' Cartoon by David Low, September 1938.

Question

How does this cartoon support the view that appeasement led to the Nazi–Soviet Pact?

Can appeasement as a policy in the 1930s therefore be justified at all?

Appeasement was viewed by many in the 1940s, and by many today, as a cowardly policy that facilitated the aggression of expansionist states. Much of the justification for hardline foreign policy initiatives since World War II has been based on the perceived damage caused by appeasing states that should have been resisted by force.

When British Cabinet minutes and government papers became available 30–40 years after the end of World War II, it became increasingly clear that the situation facing Chamberlain was complex. The reality of the British economy at the time meant that rearmament and the cost of then waging a drawn-out war with Germany would be very difficult. The memory of the horrors of World War I still haunted most Europeans, and there was little popular support to engage in another conflict of this scale. In a democracy, the people had to *want* war, or at least feel that war was literally unavoidable. This was also true of Britain's empire – in order to get the necessary material and human resources to fight a general war, Britain needed to convince its imperial domains of the 'just' and inescapable nature of war with Germany. Most of Hitler's demands, at least initially, were seen in the context of 'revising the Treaty of Versailles', a treaty that many British saw as being too harsh anyway. It was believed that once the unfairness of the treaty had been redressed, Hitler might be content. When Hitler broke the Munich Agreement, this showed the British public that there could be *no* negotiated peace with the regime in Germany.

Chamberlain and appeasement

The British Prime Minister, Neville Chamberlain, waves the peace of paper containing the Anglo-German agreement of 1938, assuring the British public that it represented 'peace for our time'.

Autarky
Autarky meant being self-sufficient. This was a key objective of both Hitler and Mussolini – both wanted economic autarky so that they could survive economically without any external assistance or trade. Ultimately this would enable them to have a degree of military autarky, so that their states could defend themselves without help from another country.

We have a clear conscience. We have done all that any country could do to establish peace, but a situation in which no word given by Germany's ruler could be trusted, and no people or country could feel themselves safe, had become intolerable… For it is evil things we shall be fighting against: brute force, bad faith, injustice, oppression, and persecution. And against them I am certain that right will prevail.

From Neville Chamberlain's speech to the British nation announcing war with Germany, 3 September 1939

Chamberlain's policy was grounded in the idea that Germany had three key issues that needed to be resolved – territorial grievances, economic problems and absence of raw materials. His solutions were to give territorial concessions, economic credits, and colonial concessions. Appeasement would then lead to the strengthening of the more moderate groups in Germany, and a move away from the pursuit of the policy of **autarky**. Britain would then benefit by being able to reduce arms spending, plus international markets would improve and manufacturers could sell to Germany.

To access worksheet 6.2 on appeasement, please visit www. pearsonbacconline.com and follow the on-screen instructions.

Chamberlain himself did not believe in peace at *any* price, and it has been argued that appeasement was buying time for Britain to rearm. After World War I, Britain had reduced its fighting forces, and was thus militarily unable to oppose Hitler in the mid 1930s. In 1936, the German government launched a Four Year Plan for rearmament. Between 1934 and 1939 the defence budget increased fourfold. Between 1938 and 1939 it doubled. During the crisis over Czechoslovakia, the British government ordered the digging of air raid shelters and distributed gas masks. Richard Overy argues that appeasement was pragmatic until 1939/40, when Britain's rearmament was at a stage that the nation could resist, if not defeat, Hitler.

Of course, the French also followed a policy of appeasement, although it can be argued that this was because they had little choice. The French could not act independently, and so they took their lead from Britain. However, their situation was also complex, as the case study of the remilitarization of the Rhineland suggests. Why, given the strategic importance of the Rhineland to the French and their concern that it be remilitarized, had they then not challenged the Germans when they sent in troops in 1936? The French government believed that the German Army might have forcibly resisted any French counter-force, and they might have received support from the population as they had done in the Ruhr in 1923. The French military were not ready for this kind of campaign; the focus of military planning from 1929 to 1934 had been the Maginot Line chain of border defences, and so the military could not give the government clear advice. In addition, the government in control was weak due to internal divisions, and some suggested that a military response would actually strengthen support for the Nazi regime.

Perhaps the key to understanding the policy of appeasement in the inter-war years is the fact that throughout the West there was genuine fear of communism. Hitler was seen by many, including leading politicians, as the 'lesser of two evils'. Indeed, it was hoped that Hitler's Germany would provide a strong bulwark against the spread of communism across Europe. In this case, the fear of one extreme ideology fostered another.

STUDENT STUDY SECTION

Class discussion questions

Read the following quotation and discuss the following questions:

Whatever the merits of Chamberlain's policy in 1938, it is well to remember that, in itself, appeasement is not necessarily a bad thing. In their efforts to resolve conflicts without resorting to violence, diplomats often must appease their opponents. It is also important to recognize that the alternative to appeasing Hitler in 1938 was fighting him. He was not bluffing, and the threat of war alone would not have stopped him...

From James Sheehan, *The Monopoly of Violence: Why Europeans Hate Going to War*, 2008

1 To what extent has the policy of appeasement had a negative impact on international relations since the 1930s?

2 Do you think that Chamberlain's policy was right?

Now organize a class debate on the motion: 'The policy of appeasement was the right policy for Britain in the 1930s.'

For the motion:

Look at the arguments mentioned above. Also consider the following:

Richard Overy argues that Chamberlain's policy was the right one for Britain at the time, and to a certain extent the policy paid off in that Britain forced Germany into a war sooner than it wanted and at a time when Britain stood a chance of *not* losing. Overy contends that Hitler's economic and military planning would have led to Germany being a military 'superpower' by the mid 1940s if they had continued without challenge.

Against the motion:

Churchill in the 1940s argued that World War II was an 'unnecessary war', as it would have been prevented by opposing Hitler before he rearmed.

ToK Time
How far do historians 'revise' their views of leaders and their actions with the benefit of hindsight? What are the knowledge issues involved in drawing conclusions about an historical leader? When we analyze current leaders, do we do this differently? Are there similar knowledge issues? Discuss this in pairs and write down your ideas in your ToK journal.

Reviewing the causes of war

As we have seen, each of the major European powers in some way made a contribution towards the outbreak of World War II. Below are some of the most important issues to consider when thinking about their responsibility:

Britain

- Signed the Anglo-German Naval Agreement, undermined the Stresa Front
- Did not attempt to use the League of Nations in response to the series of crises in the late 1930s – the League then became obsolete, and with it the possibility of 'collective security'
- Failed to encourage a firmer stance from France over the Rhineland
- Failed to support the Czechs at Munich
- Failed to work harder for an agreement with the USSR
- Committed itself to support Poland after it had pursued a policy of appeasement; so, it could be argued, Hitler did not believe that Britain would go to war over Poland
- The Polish guarantee made war inevitable.

France

- Committed itself to supporting states in Central Europe in the Little Entente, but did not follow up with military preparations to support them
- Like Britain, did not attempt to use the League of Nations in response to the series of crises in the late 1930s, undermining the principle of 'collective security'
- Failed to support the Czechs in 1938
- Followed a defensive strategy focused on the Maginot Line
- Did not work hard enough for an agreement with the USSR.

USSR

- Stalin had purged his armies in the 1930s and was militarily weakened; it was in the Soviet interest to work for a delay in a war with Germany
- Stalin believed that the Western powers' policy of appeasement was predominantly anti-communist
- As the USSR was not invited to the Munich Conference, and attempts to find an agreement in 1939 by Britain and France appeared half-hearted, Stalin saw that his interests were best served by an agreement with Germany
- The Nazi–Soviet Pact unleashed World War II by allowing Hitler to invade Poland
- The secret clauses in the agreement were cynical and expansionist; Stalin would recoup territories lost after World War I.

Italy

- Dealt a fatal blow to the possibility of collective security when it invaded Abyssinia and undermined the League of Nations. Italy then moved away from the Stresa Front towards Germany
- Italy encouraged the political polarization of Europe by intervening in the Spanish Civil War.

STUDENT STUDY SECTION

Review activity and exam preparation

Essay question

To what extent was World War II Hitler's war?

Introduction: Set up the debate, explaining the two sides of the argument. You should also state what your key argument will be in the essay.

Paragraph 1: Always address the issue given in the title first. Here you need to set out the arguments in favour of the 'Hitler's war' intepretation. Consider the evidence of long-term planning before he gets to power and then link this to the actions that Hitler takes after 1933. Bring in the views of historians mentioned in this chapter to support your views.

Paragraph 2: Now consider the other side of the argument. Make sure you have a clear opening sentence, e.g. 'However, it could be argued that World War II was not simply Hitler's war and that Britain and France must bear some responsibility…' Look at the role of appeasement in encouraging Hitler into actions that he might not have considered otherwise. Also, reflect on whether he was brought into a war for which he had not planned. Again, refer specifically to historians here in support of these arguments.

In his book *Churchill, Hitler and the Unnecessary War: How Britain Lost its Empire and the West Lost the World* (2008), Patrick Buchanan argues that the critical mistake was made by Britain when it gave Poland the guarantee that made war 'inevitable'. He goes on to suggest that by doing this, Britain unleashed the 'bloodiest war in all of history', lost their own empire and created the conditions for the ensuing Cold War.

Paragraph 3: An alternative argument is that it was Germany's war rather than just Hitler's war, and that there was in fact a great deal of continuity between World War I and World War II. This is a major argument of Fritz Fischer. Fischer suggested that there was continuity in the aims of German policy-makers in 1914 and Nazi leaders in the 1930s. This continuity was founded on the powerful industrial and landowning classes, which remained in authoritative positions. They had played a vital role in bringing Hitler to power in 1933. Both Wilhelmine and Nazi Germany wanted to establish control over Eastern Europe to provide economic benefits.

When comparing and contrasting the objectives of German foreign policy prior to both world wars, there are some vivid similarities: Wilhelmine Germany was pursuing an expansionist foreign policy before 1914, and attained this goal, temporarily, in Europe in the Treaty of Brest-Litovsk. The domination of Central and Eastern Europe, and the creation of an overseas empire, were objectives for both Kaiser Wilhelm and Hitler.

Conclusion: This should reflect the weighting that you have given the different sides of the argument in the body of your essay.

Essay question

To what extent did the unsatisfactory outcome of World War I lead to World War II?

This question could be argued using Marshal Foch's statement on the Versailles settlement: 'This is not a peace. It is an armistice for 20 years.' Points that you could develop for this essay include:

- German dissatisfaction with the Treaty of Versailles
- The 'German problem' (see Interesting Facts box on p.80)
- Italian dissatisfaction with the treaty
- How Britain's dissatisfaction with the treaty affected British policy towards Germany in the 1920s and 1930s
- The USA's retreat into isolationism and its impact on the League of Nations
- Weakness of Eastern European states after the break-up of the Russian and Austro-Hungarian empires.

Make sure that for each point you refer directly to the question and consider how it contributed to the outbreak of World War II.

Essay question

Why did World War II break out in 1939?

For this question, you can start with the thesis that it was Hitler's war. However, you also need to consider a range of other factors:

- The impact of the Versailles settlement and political instability in the 1920s and 1930s
- Weakness of the League of Nations
- The actions of Britain and France
- Effects of the Great Depression (very important!)
- Fear of communism.

Again, make sure you link each point to how it contributed to war in 1939.

● **Examiner's hint**
When revising for an exam, plan out as many essay questions as possible on one topic. This strategy means that you will have considered all the different 'angles' on a topic before sitting the exam.

You will also have to answer questions that compare the causes of both wars. Try planning out the following:

Compare and contrast the reasons for Germany's involvement in both world wars.

For this question, review Chapters 2 and 3. Consider the ambitions of Kaiser Wilhelm's Germany and compare and contrast these aims with those of Hitler's Germany. Refer to the first essay plan above on Fischer's ideas on this topic.

Essay question

To what extent should Germany be held responsible for causing both the First and the Second World Wars?

© IBO 1998

This is similar to the question above, except that you also have to look at alternative arguments for both wars, e.g. collective responsibility in World War I and the role of appeasement in World War II.

Historiography

This chapter has covered different perspectives on the reasons why war broke out in Europe in 1939. Review the key arguments presented in this chapter, and research the views of the historians listed in the grid below. Then list each historian's key ideas and evidence in the second column of the grid. (Draw out the grid separately if there is not enough room here.)

CONTEMPORARY AND HISTORIANS' VIEWPOINTS	
Contemporary / Historian	Summary of Key Ideas / Evidence
Winston Churchill	
A.J.P. Taylor	
Stephen Lee	
James Sheehan	
Richard Overy	
Fritz Fischer	
Patrick Buchanan	

● **Examiner's hint**

It is good to show knowledge of historical debate in your essay and to bring in direct reference to historians. However, these techniques alone will not get you a high grade! Avoid making your essay just a discussion about historians' views and avoid using historians' comments randomly. Historians' views or quotes should be used to support the evidence and arguments that you present as part of the argument in your essay.

THE CAUSES OF WORLD WAR II IN THE PACIFIC

On 7 December 1941, Japan attacked an American naval base, Pearl Harbor, in Hawaii. In response, the USA declared war on Japan:

> *Yesterday, December 7th 1941 – a date that will live in infamy – the United States of America was attacked by naval and air forces of the Empire of Japan. The United States was at peace with that nation… No matter how long it may take us to overcome this premeditated invasion, the American people in their righteous might will win through to absolute victory.*
>
> **Roosevelt's address to the nation, 8 December 1941**

As you read through this chapter, consider the following essay question:

To what extent was Japan responsible for the Pacific War?

Japan's responsibility for war in the Pacific: the historical debate

World War II ended up being two wars: the war in Europe and the war in Asia. In the previous chapter, we discussed Hitler's responsibility for causing the war in Europe and we will now consider Japan's role in causing the war in the Pacific.

Some historians, such as David Bergamini (*Japan's Imperial Conspiracy*, 1971), have argued that Japan had planned a war from the early 1930s, and the Emperor had been very much involved. Indeed, he argues that although Japan appeared willing to negotiate for peace, this was cynically part of its plan to keep the enemy off-guard. Many historians, therefore, suggest Japan planned the war and that it was a clear aggressor whose aim was to conquer Asia.

Other historians, however, suggest that Japan was pursuing a more traditional European-style imperialist policy in Asia, while others emphasize the 'co-prosperity sphere' and Japan's attempts to achieve their aims through diplomacy. This latter view suggests that Japan's actions led to war, not because it had planned for conflict, but as a result of taking too many risks. Initially, gambles paid off, so Japan continued to take them. There is a clear similarity here to the view that Hitler was a gambler who just could not stop. In this view, Japan had attempted to avoid a war with both Britain and the USA, but when negotiations broke down Japan 'stumbled' into war.

The counter-argument to Japanese responsibility can be seen in the Japanese declaration of war, which stated that the USA was to blame for the war in the Pacific. Some historians support a line of argument that suggests that Japan's aim was to 'liberate' Asia from Western domination. Some even compare Japan's actions to creating a sphere of influence not dissimilar to the USA's dominance of South America. Both argue that Japan had been continually provoked and mistreated by the West, and in particular the USA. Thus, Japan ultimately fought a *defensive* war that was triggered by American embargoes; Japan had to act when it did or it would be too late.

Unlike Hitler's Germany, the lack of a clear leader/leadership perhaps makes it more difficult for historians and students to decide on whether or not Japan had intended to cause the Pacific War. Although the head of state was Emperor Hirohito, he was not held

Flag of Imperial Japan.

responsible by the Allies in 1945 for causing the war. We will discuss his role at the end of this chapter.

A photo taken after Japanese bombing of Shanghai, 1937.

Timeline of events prior to the Pacific War – 1853–1941

1853		Commodore Perry first visits Japan
1902		Anglo-Japanese Alliance
1904		Russo-Japanese War breaks out
1915		The 'Twenty-One Demands' made on China
1919		Versailles Treaty confirms Japan's war gains
1921		Japan participates in the Washington Conference
1926		Hirohito becomes Emperor
1931		Kwantung Army invades Manchuria
1932		Proclamation of 'independent' Japanese puppet state of Manchukuo in Manchuria. Japanese and Chinese troops skirmish near Shanghai
1933		Tangku Truce establishes ceasefire line in north China. Japan withdraws from the League of Nations
1934		Japan abrogates the Washington Naval Treaty
1936		Japan rejects even the principle of nine-power consultation on China issues. Japanese government decides on fundamental objectives: maintenance of Japan's position on the Asian continent; resistance to Soviet ambitions; expansion into the South Seas. Japan enters into Anti-Comintern Pact with Germany
1937	**Jun**	Konoe Fumimaro becomes Prime Minister
	Jul	Marco Polo bridge incident near Beijing. Beijing conquered by Japan in July
	Aug	Japan captures Shanghai. Japanese drive Chinese nationalist troops from north China
1937	**Sep**	Konoe calls for 'spiritual mobilization' for a long war against China
	Dec	Japanese conquest of Nanjing results in perhaps 200,000 dead (the 'rape of Nanjing')
1939	**Jun**	Japanese Army blockades the British concession in Tientsin. USA notifies Japan that it will cancel the 1911 Treaty of Commerce and Navigation
1940	**Mar**	Japan sets up a puppet government in Nanjing. Japan demands that Britain and France stop providing aid to China.
	Jul–Sep	Burma Road closed
	Sep	Tripartite German–Italian–Japanese Axis alliance signed in Berlin; in response, Churchill reopens the Burma Road. France occupies northern Indochina. USA embargoes export of scrap iron
1941	**Mar**	Japan signs non-aggression treaty with Soviet Union
	Jun	Hitler attacks the Soviet Union
	Jul	Japan occupies southern Indochina. USA freezes Japanese assets
	Dec	Japan attacks Pearl Harbor, and the south-western Asia/Pacific region

As with Germany in Europe in the 1930s, Japanese aggression has been seen by many historians as the main cause of war in the Pacific. To analyze this line of argument, we need to look at the development and actions of Japanese foreign policy in the longer term.

Japan and the long-term causes of World War II in the Pacific

Background: Japanese relations with the West

From the mid 17th century Japan had been isolated from the outside world, a deliberate policy of Japan's rulers – the Shoguns – in response to the threat to their civilization posed by Christianity. The only exception was Dutch traders, but their activities were also severely restricted. For 200 years, the Japanese remained separate. Politically, economically and socially, Japan functioned as a **feudal** state until the arrival of the American, Commodore Matthew Perry, in 1853. He arrived from America determined to negotiate with the Japanese to open up to American requests for trade and refuelling stops.

Due to their isolationist mindset, the Japanese were duly awed by the impressive might of Perry's American gunboats. The government tried to buy time, and Perry agreed to return in one year – with more gunboats. Japan responded realistically; they could not take on the technologically advanced West, and attempting to do so would be suicide. Their much bigger neighbour, China, had attempted to resist Britain in the Opium Wars in the 19th century and had suffered a series of humiliating and unequal treaties. The Treaty of Kanagawa (1854), therefore, gave the USA what it had wanted, but more significantly it 'opened up' Japan to the outside world.

The ruling Shoguns could not recover from their inability to resist American force, and in 1867 power was officially handed back to the Japanese Emperor. From 1868 he became known as the Meiji or 'enlightened' Emperor, and his government set about modernizing Japan. In the ensuing period of reform, Japan became a limited democracy and stripped away its feudal system, including the rights of the ancient samurai classes. Japan rapidly industrialized and sent its young off to be educated abroad. A key reform was of its military, which was a priority for the new government. A new, modernized army was developed with the introduction of conscription in 1872 and the adoption of German military principles and methods. The Japanese followed the British in their construction of a new navy.

Japan proved the effectiveness of its modernization programme in victory over China in 1894–95. The results of their victory had far-reaching consequences. Japan became the first non-European nation to be considered by the West as a world power. It was also now an empire, dominating Korea. Imperial growth fostered the idea that an expansionist foreign policy could be successful if it was supported by a strong military. Only generals and admirals could be ministers for the army and navy from 1900, and this meant that the government had a military influence right from the beginning of the 20th century.

Japan's second victory was over Russia, which competed with Japanese interests in Manchuria. By the late 1890s, it was clear to Japan that Russia also intended to take over Korea. The Japanese needed a European ally to counter the Russian threat to their own foreign policy ambitions. As the British were at this time coming out of their own isolation, they were willing to consider an alliance with Japan, as this would suit their own policy of containing Russia. Britain also had already been heavily involved in the development of the Japanese Navy. In January 1902, the Anglo-Japanese Alliance was signed – it agreed that if either power was attacked by two other states, the other signatory would come to their ally's assistance; if only one power attacked a signatory, the other would remain neutral.

Sino-Japanese War (1894–95)
With a newly modernized army modelled on the Prussian military, and a new navy modelled on the British Royal Navy, Japan went to war with China in 1894. The Chinese were defeated, and forced to sign the Treaty of Shimonoseki in 1895. China had to recognize that Korea was an independent kingdom and cede Taiwan, the Pescadores and Liao-tung peninsula. However, the Russians, with the support of France and Germany, advised the Japanese to withdraw from Liao-tung, as the Russians wanted the ice-free harbour of Port Arthur. The main results of this war were the emergence of Japan as the key Asian power, the further collapse of China under the influence of the West and the frustration of Japan at having to relinquish territory to a Western power.

The alliance gave Japan a much stronger position in its rivalry with Russia. Russia was unimpressed with Japan's recent victory in China, and with her new alliance; in February 1904 both Russian and Japanese forces entered Korea. Admiral Togo Heichachiro destroyed the Russian fleet in the Tsushima Strait on 27 May 1905, and only 6,000 of 18,000 Russian sailors survived for just 116 Japanese sailors killed. The Russians were also convincingly defeated on the land, and they surrendered in March 1905.

The results of the war were far-reaching, as they encouraged Japanese nationalism and expansionism and triggered a revolution in Russia. The Russians were forced by the Treaty of Portsmouth to recognize Japan's 'paramount' political, military and economic interests in Korea. The indemnity demanded by the Japanese was refused by the Russians. The Russians simply refused to pay the Japanese for the cost of the war, even though this was a usual component of a treaty concluding a war. The Japanese had no way of enforcing payment from the Russians. In 1910, Japan made further gains by formally annexing Korea. In its actions, Japan had inspired the respect of the West, and the admiration of other Asian nations.

STUDENT STUDY SECTION

Review question

What characteristics did the new state of Japan show by 1905?

Japan and World War I

During the early 20th century, we can see a consistency in Japan's attempts to expand its influence and make territorial gains in the region, and this ambition would increasingly bring Japan into conflict with the Western powers. World War I gave Japan new opportunities to expand. Japan saw the potential benefit of joining the war on the entente side, and demanded German colonial possessions in China. This condition, they argued, was necessary to keep the peace in Asia. When the Germans ignored their demands, Japan declared war on them. In addition, while the Europeans were caught up in total war in Europe, Japan seized the initiative by making further gains in China. The government issued China with 'Twenty-One Demands' in January 1915. These demands would have given Japan the most influential political and economic position in China. International reaction to the demands was hostile. The USA was the most critical, and warned Japan that it would not tolerate any agreement that threatened US interests in the area. US–Japanese relations turned very sour.

After the USA joined the war in 1917, the Americans were determined that the Japanese would not gain more influence in China. The Japanese agreed to the Lansing–Ishii Agreement, which meant the gains they had made up to 1917 were recognized by the Americans, and assurances were given that no further expansion would be pursued at this time. The Chinese felt betrayed by America, which had been overtly sympathetic to their plight.

Japan again saw an opportunity to expand when the Bolsheviks seized power in Russia in October 1917. The Bolsheviks sued for a separate peace with Germany. Their former allies then launched a foreign invading force to support White forces (counter-revolutionary troops) in the ensuing civil war. It was agreed with the USA that Japan would send 7,500 troops to assist the White forces (which included the USA, Britain and France) in Siberia. However, Japan instead sent 70,000 men. The Bolshevik forces defeated the White generals, but although the USA, France and Britain withdrew their men in 1920, the Japanese stayed on. Nevertheless, they too were ultimately defeated, and had to withdraw in 1922. The Siberian expedition had failed, and was seen as a humiliation at home.

Japan and Versailles: a 'mutilated victory'

During the Versailles meetings, Japan, a victorious power, aimed to increase its gains, and demanded an annexation of the German Pacific territories and the inclusion of a racial equality clause in the Charter of the League of Nations (see Chapter 4). The USA, however, was sympathetic to the Chinese delegates' requests for the reversal of gains made by Japan during World War I. Nevertheless, the German concessions on Shandong remained in Japanese hands, which infuriated the Chinese and led to the demonstrations that became known as the May Fourth Movement.

Even though Japan felt that it had not gained what it deserved from Versailles, it did maintain its position in Shandong and it gained some of Germany's former colonies in the Pacific. Japan had also benefited economically from World War I: the lack of foreign trade resulted in Japan becoming more self-sufficient, and without the competition of the other powers in the region its economy boomed.

Yet Japan's influence over China was still causing concern to both the USA and Britain. In 1921, the Americans initiated the Washington Conference primarily to discuss tensions in China (see Chapter 6). As well as the USA, Britain, China and Japan, there were representatives from France, the Netherlands, Belgium, Italy and Portugal. As we have seen, three key agreements were signed: the Four Power Pact ended the alliance between Britain and Japan, and the Five Power Naval Treaty set the following ratios between each power's capital ship tonnage – 5:5:3:1.67:1.67 (USA: Britain: Japan: France: Italy). The final agreement was the Nine Power Pact, in which the signatories agreed to respect China's sovereignty. Both the Four Power and the Five Power agreements actually supported Japanese expansion in the region, the first by giving Japan security from Western attack, and the second by limiting US expansion – Japan could not afford to expand any more than the treaty allowed for, while the US could have expanded, but was prevented from doing so.

The tension between the USA and Japan was eased a little by the Washington agreements. In the 1920s, relations were relatively cordial, but this was due to the more 'peaceful' outlook of the liberal government in Japan, a situation that was to be short-lived.

The liberal 1920s: a peaceful Japan?

World War I had made Japan the industrial centre of the East. However, the profits from the war were not invested well, and much was spent on funding various Chinese warlords who did not pay back their debts. Japan's foreign debt therefore remained high. The crisis that hit the banking system led to the printing of extra money, which then led to a steep rise in the cost of living. In 1918, there were riots over rice availability in many cities. The riches from war production had stayed in the hands of the wealthy.

In the 1920s, Japan openly embraced Western culture; architecture, music, fashion and sport all reflected an enthusiasm for Western style. Hirohito became Emperor in 1926. His title was *Showa* ('Bright Peace'), and there was some degree of stability, with the government of Prime Minster Hara lasting from 1918 to 1921. This government introduced social and economic reforms, and the military was contained mainly due to a strong feeling of anti-militarism in the early 1920s. The army was also divided over foreign policy, but the military showed its continued power when it sent more troops to Siberia after the USA pulled out. Japan's government seemed to show its 'peaceful' intentions when Hara ensured that Japanese forces withdrew by 1922. Indeed, Hara's government led Japan into the League of Nations, and its membership of the Council meant that it was accepted as a leading power. But the regime fell into economic difficulties as the wartime boom ended in 1920. Fear of an increasingly strong left-wing movement grew when the Japanese Communist Party (JCP) was founded in 1920. The communists attempted to exert control over the trade unions, and in response the government clamped down on all 'communist suspects'.

Despite the power of the left, the undercurrent of right-wing nationalism remained, and surfaced in November 1921 when Hara was assassinated by a right-wing extremist. Korekiyo Takahashi took over. He failed to redress the economic crisis, and resigned in June 1922. After Korekiyo, until 1924, Japan was led by three ineffective governments. Kato Tomosaburo's government (1924–26) was built on constitutional principles, and Kato extended the **franchise** to all men over 25. Kato's attempts to cut costs meant that he came into conflict with the army as he took 2,000 officers off active duty. But Kato was not tolerant towards the left wing in Japan either. The Peace Preservation Law of 1925 meant that those with leftwing agendas could be imprisoned. Kato pursued a conciliatory policy with China, and did not attempt to take advantage of the internal chaos there, a policy with which the army did not agree.

Kato died in 1926 and was replaced by Wakatsuki Reijiro. He too had supported the Foreign Minister's 'Shidehura's policy' of cooperative relations with China. His attempts to address another economic crisis failed, and he was forced to resign a year later. Wakatsuki was replaced by General Tanaka Giichi and, under pressure from the army, a new more aggressive policy towards China was adopted. The Chinese nationalists under Jiang Jieshi (Chiang Kai-shek) had been quite successful in their campaign to unify China by defeating the warlords. This worried the Japanese, as there might be a threat to their interests in Manchuria. The Kwantung Army attempted to interfere in Chinese politics by assassinating their former Chinese ally in the area. They had acted without permission from the government. Tanaka attempted to get the General Staff to punish the offending members of the Kwantung Army, but they refused. It was clear that the army could ignore the government. Liberal parliamentary democracy was in decline, and the military was on the rise.

Osachi Hamaguchi became the new Prime Minister in 1929, but soon was caught up in the global economic disaster of the Great Depression. The demand for silk collapsed – this was Japan's key export. Millions became unemployed. The Prime Minister attempted to cut spending by limiting naval expansion, and cutting military salaries by 10 per cent. The military severely criticized the government, and in November 1930 another right-winger shot Hamaguchi, who died from his injuries in April 1931. Hamaguchi's death heralded Japan's descent into the 'dark valley' of the 1930s.

STUDENT STUDY SECTION

Review activity

What impact did the following have on political developments in Japan?
- Economic downturns
- Fear of communism
- Strength of the Japanese Army.

Japan and the short-term causes of the Pacific War: 'the dark valley'

As we have discussed in this chapter, Japan had a history of strong nationalism, which had reaped rewards during the Meiji period. The more liberal era during the 1920s was short-lived, as the army reasserted itself in the 1930s. As the military gained more and more influence, so Japan became increasingly aggressive. The increasing power of the military led Japan down the road to war. The attack on Manchuria in 1931 resulted from a plot devised by the Kwantung Army, not the Japanese government. Such unilateral action by the military alarmed the West, particularly the USA. Within Japan itself, the move was popular. The creation of Manchukuo had not been part of government policy, but it was accepted after the military success there. The army did not stop in Manchuria, but went on to Jehol. (Jehol was located to the north of the Great Wall, west of Manchuria and east of Mongolia.) Although the Western response to Japan's attack on Manchuria was cautious, relations between Japan and the Western democracies deteriorated in the 1930s for the following main reasons:

- The West was alarmed by the bombing of Shanghai in 1932
- In 1933, Japan left the League of Nations after the Council accepted the Lytton Report
- In 1934, Japan, unhappy at having to have an inferior navy to that of the USA, pulled out of the Washington Naval Treaty and refused to attend another conference.

Sino-Japanese War: no retreat

In May 1933, Japan signed a truce with Chinese nationalists, which led to relative peace until 1937. The military, however, were pressuring for expansion in northern China, and in 1936 a failed attempt at a coup in Tokyo nevertheless led indirectly to an increase in the power of the military. The failed military coup suggested that the government was not in control of its military and that maybe the military needed more involvement in national security.

The trigger for the war between Japan and China in 1937 was a clash between Japanese and Chinese forces at the Marco Polo bridge in Beijing. The Japanese government referred to the fighting as the 'China Incident', and many in the government suggested negotiating. Yet nationalism was running too high on both sides, and the fighting spread.

The war in China was to lead directly to the Pacific War. The Japanese had entered the war with no clear plan of how to end it, and a war on this scale required vast quantities of men and resources. It would be in the quest to acquire raw materials that the conflict with the USA was to intensify.

Marco Polo incident
On the night of 7/8 July 1937, Chinese soldiers, for reasons that remain unclear, fired at Japanese infantry soldiers on manoeuvres near the Marco Polo bridge, west of Beijing. This incident was used by the Japanese as an excuse to broaden their attack on mainland China, and within a few days they had ordered air, land and naval units into action against the Chinese. Their aim was to capture Beijing. Some historians view this incident in 1937 as the beginning of the Sino-Japanese War.

STUDENT STUDY SECTION

Research activity

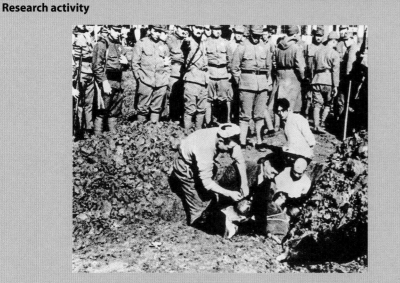

Japanese forces captured Shanghai in November 1937. They then moved up the Yangtze River and lay siege to Nanjing, the Chinese nationalists' capital. The Japanese finally took Nanjing in December, and then perpetrated what has become known as the 'Rape of Nanjing' or the 'Nanjing Massacre'. In pairs or small groups, research what happened in Nanjing.

Japanese soldiers prepare civilians for execution during the 'Rape of Nanjing'.

To access worksheet 7.1 on the Rape of Nanjing, please visit www. pearsonbacconline.com and follow the on-screen instructions.

With the tension increasing in Europe, Britain and France did not want to become enmeshed in a conflict in Asia in 1937. America was also unwilling to get involved. Indeed, the USA only verbally condemned Japan's aggression, and even when at the end of 1937 Japanese forces sank the American warship USS *Panay* during their attack on Nanjing, the Americans accepted a Japanese apology and compensation. (So too did the British when HMS *Ladybird* was attacked.) Nevertheless, the USA began to take a harder line in 1938, and in December started to give aid to China. In July 1939, the Americans cancelled the Commerce and Navigation Treaty with Japan.

From 1937, the war with China led to a complete takeover of the Japanese government by the military powers. Prince Konoe Fumimaro, Prime Minister from June 1937 to January 1939, had announced in November 1938 that Japan was aiming to create a 'New Order' in East Asia – 'cooperation' between China, Manchukuo and Japan. This idea developed into the Greater East Asia Co-Prosperity Sphere, which was based on the 'one state leading a group of states' model created by the Americans in Latin America. W.G. Beasley suggests that at a Japanese conference of ministers and military leaders in July 1940, it was agreed that Japan should 'establish herself' in Indochina, Thailand, Burma, Malaya and the Dutch East Indies. (As with the meeting recorded by Hossbach (see p.118), historians argue as to whether this meeting provides evidence of Japanese war planning.)

STUDENT STUDY SECTION

Review questions

1   To what extent was Japan pursuing nationalist and imperialist goals?

2   How far was militarism the driving force in Japan's foreign policy by 1940?

Document analysis

Document A

The army had prepared carefully for war against the Soviet Union, but had done no planning worthy of the name for a general war with China. Army leaders could not conceive of the Chinese putting up a good fight… How could China be brought to its knees? That was the major problem. Unable to get a negotiated settlement on favourable terms or win a final military success, Japanese leaders sought victory by expanding the conflict.

From Saburo Ienaga, *The Pacific War*, 1968

Document B

'Further and deeper', a cartoon by David Low in the *Evening Standard*, London, 19 January 1938.

FURTHER AND DEEPER.

Question

How far does Document A support the views expressed in Document B?

The immediate cause of the war

In June 1940, with Britain undermined by Hitler's swift victory over France, the Japanese forced the closure of the Burma Road, which was an important supply route for the Chinese. The Americans stepped up their attempts to stop Japan's war in China in September 1940, by banning the export of scrap iron to Japan. This measure had a severe impact on an already fragile economy. Economic growth in Japan in 1930 was 0.5 per cent and unemployment by 1934 was 6.8 per cent. Japan had to import the food and raw materials it needed to sustain its occupation of Chinese territories, e.g. oil and steel. It was heavily dependent on its trade with the USA for these goods.

In September, the Japanese signed the Tripartite Pact (see Interesting Facts box). In November, the Americans gave the Chinese nationalist leader, Jiang Jieshi, a massive loan to encourage and strengthen their ability to resist Japan. Within Japan, the Imperial Rule Assistance Association replaced political parties in 1940, and in October 1941 Prime Minister Konoe was replaced by General Hideki Tojo.

Japan's military was now divided over which specific territory should be targeted next – the USSR or the colonial territories of the Western powers in South-East Asia. When Nazi Germany invaded Russia in July 1941, Japan made its decision and attacked south, occupying southern Indochina. The USA, Britain and the Netherlands responded by imposing a total trade embargo. Here was a crisis for Japan – there was the danger that the country would run out of oil, and this would mean it could not continue to fight in China.

At this point the Japanese appeared willing to negotiate, but the American demand for Japan to withdraw from China was unacceptable to them. Japan decided it had to get the resources it needed by force.

Franklin D. Roosevelt immediately 'froze' all Japanese financial assets in the United States and declared a total embargo on trade of any kind with Japan… [Of] absolutely vital consequence was the fact that Japan imported more than 80 percent of its oil from the United States… To secure oil they would either have to accept American terms, which, in view of the sacrifices the Japanese people had borne to conquer China might well provoke revolution, or conquer Indonesian oil, which meant all-out war against the west.

From Robert Goldston, *The Road Between the Wars, 1918–1941*, 1978

On 2 December 1941, a Japanese fleet began its journey to Hawaii. Without warning, just before 8.00am on Sunday 7 December, Japan unleashed a two-hour attack on the key American Pacific naval base at Pearl Harbor. Japanese planes sank or disabled 19 ships, 150 planes were destroyed and 2,400 Americans died. Simultaneous attacks were made on the Philippines, Guam, Midway Island, Hong Kong and the Malay Peninsula. In response, the USA declared war on Japan the following day.

What was the impact of Japan's relationship with Germany?

Japan and Germany had some common interests, particularly in perceiving the USSR as an enemy, which led to the Anti-Comintern Pact of 1936. However, the Nazi–Soviet Pact of 1939 pushed Japan into real isolation. In addition, the pact was signed in August 1939, when the Japanese were clashing with Soviet forces near Manchuria.

Motivated by the staggering success of the German campaign in Europe (see next chapter), the Japanese signed the Tripartite Pact in September 1940 with Germany and Italy, which was primarily designed to deter the USA from becoming more involved in the wars in

Tripartite Pact
Also called the Three-Power Pact and the Axis Pact, it was signed by Germany, Italy and Japan in Berlin on 27 September 1940. The pact followed on from the Anti-Comintern Pact, and was intended to re-establish good relations between Japan and Germany following the Nazi–Soviet Pact of August 1939. The signatories agreed to establish a 'new order' and to promote mutual prosperity for the next ten years. They recognized each other's spheres of influence and agreed to come to the assistance of one another if attacked.

To access worksheet 7.2 on the beginning of the Pacific War, please visit www.pearsonbacconline.com and follow the on-screen instructions.

Europe and Asia. Japan's policies were linked to the successes of their ally, Germany; Hitler's successes in Europe encouraged a broader expansionist policy in Japan.

On 11 December 1941, three days after the Japanese attack on Pearl Harbor, Hitler declared war on the USA. In conversation the following month, Hitler gave his view that America was 'a decayed country... That's why, in spite of everything, I like an Englishman a thousand times better than an American... Everything about the behaviour of American society reveals that it's half Judaized, and the other half negrified. How can one expect a state like that to hold together ... a country where everything is built on the dollar?'

What was the impact of Japan's relationship with the USSR?

Japan's relationship with Russia/the USSR had been tense, apart from the period 1907–17 when they were both in alliances with Britain. After the revolution and the creation of the USSR, Japan was threatened not only territorially by the Russians, but also ideologically. Some historians have suggested that Japan considered the USSR as their only real enemy, and military planning in 1937 focused on this threat. During the initial stage of the Sino-Japanese War, the Soviets were the predominant suppliers of aid to China, and there was fighting between Japanese and Soviet troops on the Manchurian border in 1939.

Japan's isolation ended with the increase in hostility between Germany and the USSR in early 1941. The Russians were now focused on the threat posed by Hitler, and Japan willingly signed its own version of the Neutrality Pact with the USSR in April 1941. With the launch of Operation *Barbarossa* (the German attack on the Soviet Union) in June 1941, the Russian threat to Japan ended. Japan attacked south instead of joining in the assault on the USSR, and it was not until the last week of the war, in August 1945, that the Soviets declared war on Japan.

To what extent was the USA responsible for the war in the Pacific?

Japan was the actor, China acted upon. And the US was the self-appointed referee who judged by subjective rules and called fouls without penalties, until just before end of the contest. This provoked the actor into a suicidal attempt to kill the referee.

The diplomat John Paton Davies describing the relationship between the USA, Japan and China

At the beginning of this chapter, we briefly explored the historical relationship between the USA and Japan, starting with the 'opening up' of Japan to trade and foreign influence in the middle of the 19th century. Relations between the two nations had at times been strained, but were also often cordial, with the Japanese embracing American culture and trading relations. The Americans were suspicious of Japan's alliance with Britain, however, and did not want an Asian competitor to their interests in the region. Following World War I, the USA set out to contain Japan, first by limiting their gains at Versailles and second by ending their relationship with Britain.

Japan was very offended when the National Origins Act was passed by the American Congress in May 1924. The act set quotas on immigration to the USA, and Japan was not set a quota – this meant that immigration from Japan to the USA was to cease. The Japanese had warned the Americans prior to passing the act that this would have a serious negative impact on relations, but the USA passed the policy anyway. The importance of these events was that they gave the Japanese military good propaganda – proof of discrimination against Japan.

As Japan's liberal government stumbled and failed at the beginning of the 1930s with the 'success' of the Kwantung Army in Manchuria, and as the war of expansion spread in China, the Americans responded by increasing their moral condemnation of Japan and increasing their supply of aid to China. As we have already seen, relations between the USA and Japan deteriorated further with the escalation of the Sino-Japanese War in 1937. In January 1941, President Roosevelt gave a speech, in which he made it clear to Americans that a war might be coming, and clarified broader objectives should a conflict occur.

We look forward to a world founded upon our four essential human freedoms. The first is freedom of speech and expression – everywhere in the world. The second is freedom of every person to worship God in his own way – everywhere in the world. The third is freedom from want … everywhere in the world. The fourth is freedom from fear … anywhere in the world.

From Roosevelt's message to Congress, 6 January 1941

The four values outlined in the speech were clearly opposed to those of the fascist and militaristic regimes. Hitler's invasion of the USSR in June 1941 resulted in Britain and the USA sending aid to the Soviets. For if the USSR fell to Germany, the Germans could then focus again on Western expansion. In August 1941, the Atlantic Charter was published as a result of a meeting between Churchill and Roosevelt, and it set down their joint vision for the post-war world. The Atlantic Charter included the commitment to uphold the four freedoms, ban aggression, disarm aggressor states, give self-determination to liberated states, create the **United Nations** (UN) and secure the freedom of the seas.

Roosevelt believed that these aims could only be achieved through war, but was concerned that the American public would not support a conflict. Churchill told the British cabinet that Roosevelt would look for an 'incident' to justify waging war. It seemed, at the time, that this would most likely occur in the Atlantic.

In September 1941, the Americans indeed claimed that one of their Atlantic ships, the *Greer*, carrying civilians and mail, was attacked. The *Greer* had actually been chasing a German U-boat. Roosevelt now ordered the sinking of U-boats on sight, and sent convoys to protect merchant ships. By November, although the USA claimed it was acting only 'defensively', it was in a state of undeclared war with Germany in the Atlantic.

It could be argued that Japan was a small state that suffered from over-population and a shortage of key raw materials. Thus, in order to safeguard its national power Japan took control of Manchuria for its rich natural resources, then expanded into China in 1937, and had taken control of the coast and half of the Chinese population by 1941. Yet Japan could not make the coalition forces of nationalist and communist Chinese surrender. The USA was supplying the Chinese to secure its own trading interests. In 1940, as we have seen, Japan had created the 'Greater East Asia Co-Prosperity' sphere. The new organization directly challenged American interests in the region. Japan again sought security from attack when it signed the Tripartite Pact with Germany and Italy in April 1940, and the Non-Aggression Pact with the USSR in April 1941. The USA had pursued a policy of 'biased neutrality', and this was stepped up a gear on 11 March 1941 when the **Lend-Lease** Bill was agreed by Congress. This provided $7 billion of arms and supplies to be used to support countries whose defence was perceived as vital for the security of the USA.

German successes over the European imperial powers meant Japan could potentially move into British, French and Dutch colonies, and also the American protectorate of the Philippines. In July 1941, Japan gave further demonstration of its territorial ambitions by taking over Indochina. Roosevelt was focused on policy in Europe; policy towards Japan was the responsibility of Secretary of State Cordell Hull. In 1941, Hull had two choices, to increase support to China (probably through more direct military involvement) or to impose economic sanctions on Japan.

The USA imposed sanctions, but they did not achieve their objective. As it had failed to get an agreement on its terms, the USA then forced Japan into a desperate corner – threatening their oil supplies when they had only two years' supply in reserve. Without oil, Japan would be forced into retreat. These sanctions undermined the more moderate government in Japan, leaving it open to the takeover by the military. Tojo became War Minister and Japan took a calculated risk by bombing Pearl Harbor, intending to take out the USA's naval power before the nation could gear up for war.

The Americans did know that war with Japan and an attack on US interests were imminent in December 1941, as they had intercepted Japanese codes. They did not know, however, where the attack would come (they assumed it would be in the Philippines). Right-wing American historians have suggested that Roosevelt knew about the plan to attack Pearl Harbor, but withheld the information because this attack would force the USA into the war.

STUDENT STUDY SECTION

Research question

What was the role of Australia in the outbreak of war in the Pacific?

War in the Pacific: historiography

Left-wing historians have called Japan's war the 'Fifteen Year War', as they argue that the war in the region started with the Manchurian Crisis of 1931. Responsibility is put on the 'militarist capitalist clique' who directed Japan into war. More right-wing or nationalist Japanese historians date the war as starting in December 1941 with the attack on Pearl Harbor and the invasion of South-East Asia. The *Dai Towa Senso* – Greater East Asia War – as they call it, is in line with the Japanese propaganda of World War II that argued Japan was liberating Asians from Western imperialism. Michiko Hasegawa (an associate professor of philosophy) argued that although Japan's intentions were just, the USA forced it into a war in 1941 by embargoing oil shipments, and Japan then had to fight with countries that it would have preferred to assist in friendship.

In the aftermath of the freezing order, Japan shifted its military away from preparations for an attack on the Soviet Union and for preparations for attacks in the southwestern Pacific – and on Pearl Harbor. Japan could not wage war on China (let alone the Soviet Union) without supplies of oil; the Japanese navy did not believe that it could secure and hold oil-rich Indonesia as long as the undamaged U.S. battle fleet remained in the Pacific.
Thus that Japan attacked Pearl Harbor in December 1941 appears to be the responsibility of Dean Acheson. Had he administered the asset-freezing order more liberally, and had the flow of oil to Japan continued, the end of 1941 would have seen the Japanese army attacking Vladivostok and toward Lake Baikal. There would have been no reinforcements from Siberia to defend Moscow against the German final fall offensive.

Extract from a review of Akira Iriye's *The Origins of the Second World War in Asia and in the Pacific* (1987) by Brad DeLong, Professor of Economics, University of California, Berkeley

---

Historians have criticized this view with several arguments: the long-term anti-Chinese feeling in Japan since the war of 1894; the generally inhumane treatment of all occupied territories; the expansionist views of Japan's nationalist leaders; the need for Japan to secure resources; Japan's imperialist outlook. However, Japanese revisionists argue that the West was simply racist and did not want competition to its own spheres of influence in the

Pacific and Asia. American historians argue that they were less anti-Japanese but rather sympathetic to the Chinese. Their pursuit of an 'open door policy' aimed to contain all powers from expanding, which the Japanese ignored.

The role of the Emperor in Japan's road to war

Once His Majesty reaches a decision to commence hostilities, we will all strive to repay our obligations to him, bring the Government and the military ever closer together, resolve that the nation united will go on to victory, make an all-out effort to achieve our war aims, and set His Majesty's mind at ease.

From a statement by Prime Minister Tojo to Emperor Hirohito at an Imperial Conference, 1 December 1941

At the end of World War II, the American demand for total surrender meant that there was no guarantee of the Emperor's exclusion from the Tokyo War crimes tribunal. General Douglas MacArthur, however, convinced the US government that Emperor Hirohito was needed to facilitate a stable Japan. Against the wishes of the Australian, New Zealand, Chinese and Dutch officials, Hirohito would not stand trial as a war criminal and he would not be held responsible for causing the war in the Pacific. In the two-year trial, 28 men were charged with war crimes and seven were hanged. The official view was that Hirohito had basically been a prisoner of the militarists – he had had no choice but to follow their policies. The military claimed to be following the Emperor's lead, but he had in fact been passive, without any real power.

Emperor Hirohito.

Yet the historian David Bergamini disagrees with the view that Hirohito should not be held responsible for the war in the Pacific:

Emperor Hirohito had stamped the orders sending troops into north China in 1937. It was later said that he did so unwillingly, yet he went on two months later to stamp orders for the dispatch of troops to central and south China as well ... He became so immersed in war planning that the prime minister at the time complained of his preoccupation. Finally his own uncle assumed command of the attack on Nanjing, the Chinese capital, and moved into a hotel in Nanjing, to look on while his troops murdered over 100,000 defenseless military and civilian prisoners there. It was the first act of genocide in World War II, but when the uncle returned to Tokyo, Hirohito went out of his way to confer decorations and honors upon him.

David Bergamini, *Japan's Imperial Conspiracy*, 1971

Bergamini also identified evidence of Hirohito's responsibility in the diary of Japan's wartime Army Chief of Staff, General Hajime Sugiyama, who committed suicide when the war ended:

...Hirohito [was] asking detailed questions about military and economic planning in the months before Pearl Harbor... Most surprising, the Sugiyama Memoranda stated that in January 1941, eleven months before the outbreak of war with the United States, Hirohito had personally ordered a secret evaluation to be made of the feasibility of a surprise attack on Pearl Harbor... The Sugiyama Memoranda revealed that Hirohito had participated in the Pearl Harbor planning a full six months before any of his official military advisors were informed of it. Evidence taken before the Allied judges of the International Military Tribunal for the far east, and verified by witnesses under oath and cross-examination, demonstrated conclusively that none of the 'militarists' who were supposed to have dragged Hirohito to war knew of the Pearl Harbor plan until August 1941. General Tojo, the arch 'militarist' who headed Japan's wartime Cabinet, was not told of the plan until November 1941.

David Bergamini, *Japan's Imperial Conspiracy*, 1971

STUDENT STUDY SECTION

Class discussion

1   How far can Hirohito be held responsible for the causes of war between Japan and the USA in 1941?

2   Compare and contrast his involvement with the role played by Hitler in causing war in Europe in 1939.

Review activity

War in the Pacific: Action and Reaction

Review the sections on US and Japanese responsibility for the war in the Pacific. In pairs, create a diagram of the key 'actions and reactions' of the two countries. Discuss the extent to which war in the Pacific was caused by the USA 'reacting' to the perceived aggressive action of Japan, and vice versa.

Essay questions

1   Why did Japan bomb Pearl Harbor in December 1941?

Two possible approaches to this question would be: a) Long-term causes versus short-term and immediate causes; b) Japanese action and aggression versus American action and provocation.

2   Compare and contrast the causes of two 20th-century wars, each chosen from a different region.

You could answer this question effectively by selecting the causes of World War I in Europe and the causes of World War II in the Pacific. Your essay would then identify the key similarities in the causes of each war and then consider the key differences in the causes of war in Europe in 1914 and in the Pacific in 1941.

WORLD WAR II AND TOTAL WAR

Consider the following essay questions while reading this chapter:
- In what ways can World War II be considered a total war?
- Why did the Axis powers lose World War II?

World War II was even more deadly than World War I. More soldiers and civilians were killed than in any war before it. The impact on civilians in particular in terms of death, destruction and displacement also made it more of a total war than that of 1914–18. It was also very different to previous wars in that it was a conflict of rapid movement, with major campaigns taking place not only in Central and Western Europe, but also in the Far East, North Africa and the USSR. This chapter is structured in the same way as Chapter 3. First we will give a brief overview of both the war in Europe and the war in the Pacific. The war will then be analyzed in terms of the nature of the fighting and the reasons why it can be considered a total war.

The war in Europe

Blitzkrieg – the invasion of Poland (September 1939)

In the early hours of 1 September 1939, Hitler's Panzers (tanks), supported by the *Luftwaffe* (air force), smashed over the border into Poland. They rapidly cut though Poland's defences, thus making a path for the advancing infantry. This rapid and devastating method of fighting was known as ***Blitzkrieg*** or 'lightning war'. Polish resistance was heroic, but ultimately futile. The USSR invaded from the east, as agreed by the Nazi–Soviet Pact, and on 29 September Poland was divided up between the two countries.

The Phoney War

After the defeat of Poland, very little happened in the next five months. Although Britain had declared war on Germany two days after the Polish invasion, it could not get troops to Poland in time to have any effect, and thus only watched as a great part of Eastern Europe fell into the hands of Hitler and Stalin. The Soviet Union took over Estonia, Latvia and Lithuania and then invaded Finland in what became known as the 'Winter War'.

Meanwhile, the French manned the Maginot Line and waited for the next German move. Chamberlain believed that this period of inactivity would bring Hitler to his knees and that Hitler had in fact 'missed the bus'.

The invasion of Denmark and Norway (April 1940)

Four days after Chamberlain's misguided comment, Hitler invaded Denmark and Norway. Control of Norway was important for the Germans, due to the need for German access to Swedish iron ore, which was vital to the German armaments industry. The invasions brought about the downfall of Chamberlain in Britain, and on 10 May a coalition government was established under Winston Churchill.

The Winter War

In the Winter War, the Soviet forces were vastly superior in numbers to those of the Finnish Army – 450,000 troops against only 180,000. However, the Red Army had recently been subjected to a political purge that had removed 50 per cent of its commanding officers. This weakening, along with the determination and high morale of the Finns, meant that the Finns were able to hold out until March 1940. Although victory did eventually come to the USSR, the fact that the Soviet losses were so large meant that it was also a humiliation for Stalin.

War in Europe		War in the Pacific	
1939			
1 Sep	Germany invades Poland		
3 Sep	Britain declares war on Germany		
1940			
9 Apr	Nazis invade Denmark and Norway		
10 May	Nazis invade France, Belgium, Luxembourg and the Netherlands		
26 May	Evacuation of Allied troops from Dunkirk begins		
10 Jun	Norway surrenders to the Nazis; Italy declares war on Britain and France.		
1 Jul	German U-boats attack merchant ships in the Atlantic		
10 Jul	Battle of Britain begins		
23 Jul	Soviets take Lithuania, Latvia and Estonia		
7 Sep	Blitz begins against Britain		
27 Sep	Tripartite (Axis) Pact signed by Germany, Italy and Japan		
28 Oct	Italy invades Greece		
1941		**1941**	
6 Apr	Nazis invade Greece and Yugoslavia	**26 Jul**	Roosevelt freezes Japanese assets in USA and suspends relations with Japan
2 Jun	Operation *Barbarossa* begins	**1 Aug**	USA announces an oil embargo against aggressor states
		7 Dec	Japanese bomb Pearl Harbor
		8 Dec	USA and Britain declare war on Japan
		11 Dec	Germany declares war on the USA
1942		**1942**	
13 Sep	Battle of Stalingrad begins	**4–7 Jun**	Battle of Midway
23 Oct–5 Nov	Battle of El Alamein	**August**	US Marines land in Guadalcanal
1943		**1943**	
2 Feb	Germans surrender at Stalingrad	**Jan**	Allied gains in the Pacific continue (island hopping)
16–20 Mar	Battle of Atlantic climaxes with 27 merchant ships sunk by German U-boats	**Oct**	Allies invade Philippines
13 May	German and Italian troops surrender in North Africa		
9/10 Jul	Allies land in Sicily		
27/28 Jul	Allied air raid causes a firestorm in Hamburg		
3 Sep	Allied invasion of mainland Italy		
1944		**1944**	
6 Jun	D-Day landings	**Jan–Feb**	US forces capture the Marshall Islands. British forces make advances in Burma
25 Aug	Liberation of Paris	**17 Apr**	Japanese begin last offensive in China
2 Oct	Warsaw Uprising ends as the Polish Home Army surrenders to the Germans	**15 Jun**	US forces invade Saipan
16–27 Dec	Battle of the Bulge	**Jul–Aug**	US forces recapture the Mariana Islands
		23–26 Oct	Japanese Navy suffers critical losses in the battle of Leyte Gulf
1945		**1945**	
17 Jan	Soviet troops capture Warsaw	**19 Feb**	US forces invade the island of Iwo Jima
13/14 Feb	Dresden is destroyed by a firestorm after Allied bombing raids	**3 Mar**	US and Filipino forces take Manila
16 Apr	Soviet troops begin their final attack on Berlin; Americans enter Nuremberg	**1 Apr**	US forces invade Okinawa
30 April	Adolf Hitler commits suicide	**6 Aug**	First atomic bomb dropped, on Hiroshima, Japan
2 May	German troops in Italy surrender	**8 Aug**	Soviets declare war on Japan and invade Manchuria
7 May	Unconditional surrender of all German troops	**9 Aug**	Second atom bomb dropped, on Nagaski
8 May	VE (Victory in Europe) Day	**14 Aug**	Japan surrenders

The invasion of Holland, Belgium and France (May–June 1940)

Also on 10 May, Hitler launched attacks on Holland and Belgium, and then, skirting around the tip of the Maginot Line, invaded France on 12 May. The reason that the Maginot Line defences did not continue along the frontier between France and Belgium was because Marshal Pétain believed that the Ardennes forest further north would be a strong enough barrier to stop Germany attacking from that direction. However, this is exactly where the Germans broke through.

Using *Blitzkrieg* tactics, Hitler's victories were swift, and within six days the Panzers had reached the English Channel. Only Dunkirk remained in British hands, and a third of a million troops were then rescued by the British navy and other private boats owned by fishermen. Although a great opportunity to boost British morale with talk of the 'Dunkirk spirit' (see newspaper opposite), the evacuation was in fact a serious blow for the Allies; they lost a large amount of arms and equipment and had been driven from the European mainland.

The Germans now swept southwards. Paris was captured on 14 June and the French government, now led by Pétain, requested Germany's terms for an armistice. The ceasefire agreement was signed at Compiègne on 21 June in the same railway coach that had been used for the 1918 Armistice. All of the country except south-eastern France was occupied and demilitarized, thus giving the Germans access to important submarine bases on the Atlantic coast. Unoccupied France was allowed its own government under Marshal Pétain, but in reality it had no real independence and actively collaborated with the Germans.

The German propaganda magazine *Signal* shows German troops on the beaches of Dunkirk, having ejected British forces from France.

Blitzkrieg offensive, 1939–40.

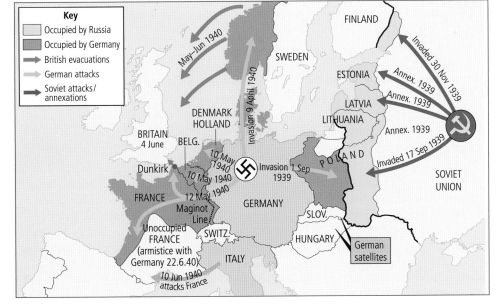

Hitler's Germany had achieved more in two months than the Kaiser's Germany had achieved in the whole of World War I. By the end of June 1940, Germany dominated Western, Central and Northern Europe. In addition, Italy had now entered the war as Hitler's ally and the USSR remained 'friends' with Germany in the east, under the terms of the Nazi–Soviet Pact. Franco in Spain did not actually join in the war, but remained closely associated with Germany and Italy.

Document analysis

Document A

We must conclude that it [the German attack into France] was a plan well executed and incompetently opposed. But there is no doubt that the French government was weak and showed little resolve. Moral authority and executive capacity both disappeared and military defeat turned into political collapse. Essentially Hitler's military successes were based on his preparedness to take the adventurous and unexpected course. He was fortunate that military thinking lagged behind military technology. Moreover whereas the Allies were cautious and conservative, Hitler was an impatient man who was psychologically predisposed to adopt daring and mobile strategies.

From Graham Darby, *Europe at War 1939–45*, 2003

Document B

…with good battlefield aviation supporting ground forces, and an effective system of radio communication, the German military made the most of their resources against an enemy whose cast of mind was defensive and whose communication and organization at the front proved woefully deficient. The British and French concept of a war of attrition and blockade, fought partly by bombing aircraft, never materialised. The two western states lost sight in the 1930s of the most basic element of warfare – the ability to fight effectively on the field of battle itself. Both sides possessed comparable resources (the Germans had in fact fewer and poorer-quality tanks) but German military leaders emphasised high standards of training and operational preparation and technical efficiency, the very virtues that brought victory in 1866 over Austria and in 1870 over France.

Richard Overy in Charles Townshend (ed.), *The Oxford History of Modern War*, 2005

Questions

1   According to Darby, what factors accounted for Hitler's success in taking over France?

2   In what ways does Overy agree with Darby? What are the differences between the two sources in their analysis of the German successes?

The Battle of Britain (1940)

Britain now stood alone against Germany. On 18 June 1940, Churchill correctly forecast the next stage of the war – 'The battle of France is over. I expect that the Battle of Britain is about to begin.' Hitler had in fact hoped for a peace agreement with Britain rather than an invasion. Yet Churchill was totally opposed to any negotiation with Hitler, and went on to inspire the British with his determination and memorable speeches:

The whole fury and might of the enemy must very soon be turned on us. Hitler knows that he will have to break us in this island or lose the war. If we can stand up to him, all Europe may be free, and the life of the world may move forward into broad sunlit uplands; but if we fail, then the whole world, including the United States, including all that we have known and cared for, will sink into the abyss of a new dark age made more sinister and perhaps more protracted by the lights of a perverted science. Let us therefore brace ourselves to our duties and so bear ourselves that if the British Empire and its Commonwealth last for a thousand years, men will still say 'This was their finest hour'.

From a speech delivered by Winston Churchill to the House of Commons, 18 June 1940

Hitler remained astonished that Britain should continue to resist. Although an amphibious invasion codenamed Operation *Sealion* was planned, it was given a low priority, as it was believed that the *Luftwaffe* would be able to destroy the Royal Air Force. With no air force to oppose it, the *Luftwaffe* would be able to dominate the Royal Navy in the English

Channel, leaving Britain totally exposed to German invasion and so willing to come to the negotiating table.

Thus the Battle of Britain began in July 1940, the *Luftwaffe* opening their offensive with a concentrated air attack on Britain's airfields in order to gain air supremacy. The *Luftwaffe* then started bombing London and other major cities in what became known as the 'Blitz', in an attempt to break British morale and destroy her major industries. When it became clear that Germany was unable to break the RAF or Britain's morale, Hitler postponed the invasion indefinitely; then in 1941 he turned his attention to his main priority, the conquest of the Soviet Union.

There are several reasons why Britain was able to survive:

- The numerical superiority of the *Luftwaffe* (about 1,200 bombers and 1,000 fighters to the RAF's 900 fighters) was offset by the fact that the German bombers were vulnerable once their shorter-range fighter escorts had turned for home, and they had limited range and a limited bomb load. The German Messerschmitt Bf-109 was an excellent fighter, but also had only enough fuel to stay in the air for about 10–20 minutes over Britain. Against this, the British Spitfires and Hurricanes were excellent fighters and could spend much longer in the air, being over their home airfields.
- Britain had a revolutionary new warning system – radar. This minimized the impact of the RAF's numerical inferiority as it allowed the RAF to locate the incoming enemy (the radar showed up enemy aircraft when they were about 120km away) and not have to waste aircraft in patrols looking for the German planes.
- Hitler's switch to bombing the cities instead of concentrating on the RAF airfields was a fatal error. By this changing of targets, the RAF was given time to recover and to rebuild airbases.

The Battle of Britain was the first time that Hitler had been stopped from achieving his aims. Britain's survival was going to be vital for keeping up the pressure on Germany, and ultimately to providing the launch pad for the allied invasion of Europe in 1944.

Foreign exiles

After the German conquests in mainland Europe, Britain also became the base for a number of European governments-in-exile. In 1940, the governments of Poland, Norway and the Netherlands were established in London. There were also other bodies representing Belgium, Luxembourg and Free France. Armed forces of these countries, e.g. Polish fighter pilots, also took part in the defence of Britain.

RAF pilots scramble to their fighters during the Battle of Britain, 1940.

The Mediterranean and the Balkans (1940–41)

The entry of Italy into the conflict in June 1940 spread the war to the Balkans, the Mediterranean and North Africa. In September 1940, Mussolini sent an army from the Italian colony of Libya to Egypt. Another Italian army invaded Greece from Albania in October. Both Italian offensives failed, however. The British pushed the Italians out of Egypt, defeating them at Beda Fomm in Libya. The British then sank half the Italian fleet in harbour at Taranto and occupied Crete. The Greeks forced the Italians back and invaded Albania.

Mussolini's failures brought Hitler into both North Africa and the Balkans. General Erwin Rommel and his Afrika Korps soldiers were sent to Tripoli, from where the British were driven out of Libya; by June 1942 the Germans had advanced close to El Alamein in Egypt. Meanwhile, in April 1941 Hitler's troops overran Yugoslavia and Greece. Within three weeks, the Greeks had surrendered and in May Crete was taken after a successful airborne attack. The British evacuated in May 1941.

These campaigns were significant because:
- They were severe setbacks for the Allies.
- British troops in North Africa were moved to the fighting in Greece, which weakened the British in North Africa at a time when Britain needed its strength to deal with the threat from Rommel.
- In going to assist Mussolini in Greece, Hitler's plan to attack the USSR was delayed by a crucial six weeks, which had an impact on the chances of the German Army reaching Moscow before the harsh Russian winter set in.

Operation *Barbarossa* (22 June 1941)

To access worksheet 8.1 on Operation *Barbarossa*, please visit www. pearsonbacconline.com and follow the on-screen instructions.

By attacking the Soviet Union, Hitler was fulfilling his aims for *Lebensraum* or living space for the German people. Clearly the natural resources of the USSR, including oil, were vast, and would be ideal for the expansion of the German race. Hitler's motives for invading the Soviet Union, however, were mainly ideological. Hitler was impatient to get on with destroying a country that was not only full of peoples inferior in his eyes, such as the Slavs, but also full of communists. During the 1930s, Hitler repeatedly expressed his belief that communism was one of the greatest threats to German society and culture, despite acknowledging that a temporary alliance with the Soviet Union could work in Germany's interests. Hitler's military endgame, therefore, always had the Soviet Union in its sights. Even in the early stages of the war, his attention was drawn to the East and to planning for the attack, and he was clearly frustrated by Britain's refusal to make peace, which thus delayed his plans for Russia. In the end, he decided to leave Britain undefeated, believing that it would not be in a strong enough position to open a second front and that the Soviet Union would easily be defeated. He was also anxious to launch an attack on the USSR to put a stop to Stalin's own territorial gains.

Plans for the invasion, codenamed Operation *Barbarossa*, were drawn up at the end of 1940. The plan envisaged a three-pronged attack: in the north towards Leningrad, in the centre towards Moscow and in the south through the agriculturally and industrially rich Ukraine.

The invasion started on 22 June 1941, and involved 121 divisions of the *Heer* (German Army) backed up by massive air support in a *Blitzkrieg* attack. Although the Soviets actually had greater numbers of men, tanks and aircraft, the Germans were able to take advantage of the element of surprise. The Soviets had ignored both the warnings of Churchill concerning the impending invasion and also their own intelligence, Stalin presumably believing that Hitler would honour the Nazi–Soviet Pact and continue to avoid a war on two fronts. The Soviets were also still re-equipping their army and air force following the humiliating war

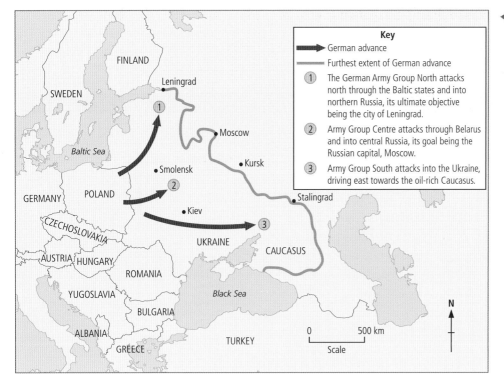

The German advance during Operation *Barbarossa*.

Key
- German advance
- Furthest extent of German advance
- (1) The German Army Group North attacks north through the Baltic states and into northern Russia, its ultimate objective being the city of Leningrad.
- (2) Army Group Centre attacks through Belarus and into central Russia, its goal being the Russian capital, Moscow.
- (3) Army Group South attacks into the Ukraine, driving east towards the oil-rich Caucasus.

with Finland, and the army was recovering from the impact of Stalin's purges, which had wiped out the cream of the Red Army's command.

In contrast to the Soviets' vulnerable position, the Germans attacked with the psychological advantage of knowing that their *Blitzkrieg* tactics had already been successful in conquering vast areas of Western Europe. Given this situation, the Germans were able to secure dramatic successes in the first months of the war. In the north, Leningrad was surrounded and besieged. In the south, Kiev was captured, and by mid October the German Army was within 80km of Moscow. The Soviets had lost some three million men in casualties and as prisoners of war. Yet the Germans failed to take Leningrad and Moscow. They were held back by the heavy rains of October, which turned the roads to mud, and then the severe Russian winter in which temperatures in some places fell as low as -38 degrees Celsius. The Germans, equipped only with their summer uniforms in the expectation that they would be victorious by the winter, suffered terribly. Thousands experienced frostbite and equipment froze and failed to function. For the first time, *Blitzkrieg* had failed to achieve its objectives; the great Soviet commander Marshal Georgy Zhukov launched a counter-offensive and Moscow was saved.

In June 1942, Hitler made a massive offensive towards southern Russia and the oilfields of the Caucasus. By August, the German attack had reached the city of Stalingrad and had occupied most of the city by the end of September. Yet the Russians refused to

Leningrad

The siege of Leningrad lasted from September 1941 to January 1944 and resulted in as many as 1.5 million dead, which is more than the total combined British and American casualties for the whole of the war. The inhabitants of Leningrad suffered from desperate food shortages and brought in supplies across an 'ice road' over Lake Lagoda. They were constantly bombarded by the Germans, but the city never fell.

An image of the terrible destruction at Stalingrad, 1942/43.

surrender, and in fact launched a counter-offensive, surrounding the Germans in a large **pincer movement**. Suffering from acute shortages of ammunition and food, and now overwhelmingly outnumbered, the Germans in Stalingrad had no choice but to surrender in early February 1943. Here was the turning point of the war on the Eastern Front.

STUDENT STUDY SECTION

Document analysis

Contrary to later accounts, Stalingrad was not the decisive event of the Second World War. It was far from being the largest battle on the Eastern Front. The 90,000 troops who were captured numbered only half as many as the British were to take at the end of the North African campaigns. And on the scale of military disasters it was no more significant than Timoshenko's recent disaster before Kharkhov. Yet, Stalingrad, in psychological terms, was immensely significant. It showed for the first time, that Hitler's Wehrmacht was fallible. It showed that Stalin's Red Army was not the shambolic giant with feet of clay that many experts had predicted. It sent shivers through Berlin, and gladdened the hearts of all Hitler's enemies. One cannot exaggerate its impact on the minds of Britons and Americans who at the time had no single solider fighting on European soil.

From Norman Davies, *Europe at War 1939–1945*, 2006

Question

According to Norman Davies, what was the significance of the Battle of Stalingrad?

In the summer of 1943, Hitler tried to launch another major attack. However, the Germans were again defeated, at the battle of Kursk, where a German tank army 17 divisions strong was destroyed. For the rest of 1943, the German Army was in retreat along nearly all the Eastern Front. By 1944, Leningrad was liberated and the Germans were pushed out of the Ukraine. In August, the Soviets reached Poland and Romania, and by January 1945 they were in East Prussia. They finally reached Berlin on 2 May.

Why were the Soviets able to defeat the German Army?

Despite the German successes, the Soviets ended up defeating the German Army. The Germans made several mistakes that contributed to their defeat:

- The Germans were not prepared for a long campaign and they suffered from lack of supplies and inadequate equipment to face their first harsh Russian winter.
- In 1941, Hitler took over the command of the army himself, which had a disastrous impact on the conduct of the war in the Soviet Union.
- During their invasion, the Germans carried out brutal attacks against the civilian population, which made Russian resistance much stronger (see below).
- The supply lines of the German armed forces became hopelessly overstretched.
- The German Army faced continual losses of aircraft and tanks that could not be replaced. Armoured divisions began the war with 328 tanks per division, whereas by the summer of 1943, they averaged only 73. The German Army increasingly fell back on the use of horses, concentrating their air and tank power in only a few divisions.

In contrast to the German situation, the Soviets underwent a programme of reform and modernization. Learning from the devastating invasion of 1941, and adapting to circumstances, the Soviet Army structure was reorganized to include a much greater reliance on tanks and artillery. The air force was also reformed; now fighter-bombers and ground-attack aircraft were put together to form a concentrated air striking force, centrally coordinated using radio communications so that it could give effective support to ground troops. The installation of radios in tanks and aircraft was indeed crucial for improving overall communications. Richard Overy argues that 'the revolution in Soviet communications was perhaps the most important single reform …[It] gave the Soviet commanders the ability to direct large and complex operations and to hold the battlefield together' (Overy, 'The Improbable Victory', *Modern History Review*, November1998).

Another important army reform involved Stalin withdrawing himself from military responsibility and allowing his commanders – such as Aleksandr Vasilevsky and Georgy Zhukov – much more freedom in how they conducted the war. Stalin also agreed to remove political influence over the army and restore the more traditional command structure, giving the troops back more confidence and pride.

Another key factor in the Soviet victory was the impact of patriotism. Spurred on by the atrocities committed by the Germans during their advance, which indicated what a German victory could mean, and fortified by the fact that Stalin did not abandon Moscow but remained with its civilians to resist the German attack, the Russian population united in a way not seen since the Revolution. Stalin, realizing that he could not call on the Soviets to mobilize in the name of communism, fed this patriotism by calling on them to save 'Mother Russia'. In addition, the Russian Orthodox Church, previously persecuted by the Soviet authorities, was reinstated to provide spiritual strength.

The Soviet Union lost three-quarters of its supplies of iron ore, coal and steel, one-third of its rail network and 40 per cent of its electricity generation in the German invasion. Yet it still managed to out-produce the Germans in guns and tanks and aircraft between 1942 and 1943. This was partly due to the fact that the Soviets moved huge quantities of industrial equipment east of the Ural mountains during the German invasion – 1,360 factories in 1942 alone. In addition, the centralized nature of the Soviet state enabled the Soviet leadership to create a successful war economy. Top priority was given to producing armaments, and all factories as well as all the labour camps (gulags) were set to work for the war effort. As in the army, political supervision was decreased in the critical years to allow the planners and managers in industry to work more effectively, even to take initiative.

The Allies also contributed to Soviet success. Weapons from the UK and USA only made up 4 per cent of the amount used by the Soviets, but there were other supplies in the form of food, raw materials and equipment that were crucial to the Soviet war effort. The Soviets also benefited from Lend-Lease agreements similar to those negotiated between Britain and the USA.

A Soviet propaganda poster. The text reads 'Soldier, save us!', imploring the Red Army to fight hard for its citizens.

STUDENT STUDY SECTION

Review questions

1   Why were the Germans so successful with *Blitzkrieg* in Europe?

2   Why did *Blitzkrieg* tactics fail in the Soviet Union?

3   Summarize in bullet points or in a spider diagram the reasons for the Soviet victory over the Nazis. Which factor or combination of factors stands out as the main reason for Soviet success?

The defeat of Nazi Germany

While Stalin was fighting a very bloody war in the Soviet Union, Britain – joined by America from December 1941 – was predominantly fighting an air and sea war. Although Stalin was desperate for Britain and America to open up a second front and thus divert the Germans away from the Soviet Union, this was not possible in 1942. Roosevelt agreed that defeating Nazi Germany quickly was a priority (even though it was the Japanese who had brought America into the war), but neither the USA nor Britain yet had the resources needed to launch a major invasion of mainland Europe.

El Alamein (1942)

Map showing war in the Mediterranean, 1942–43.

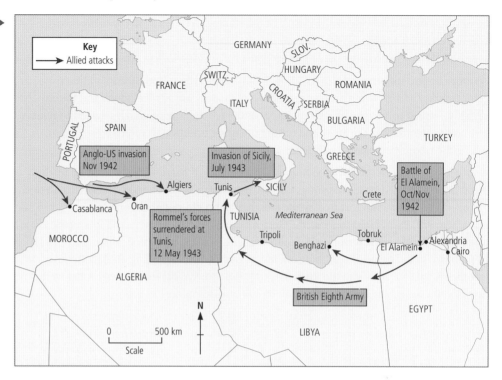

Instead, Britain decided to carry on the fighting in North Africa. Rommel's forces were finally defeated in October/November 1942 at El Alamein and were forced into retreat across Libya. Early in November, Anglo-American forces landed in French North Africa in Operation *Torch*, and by May 1943 the whole of northern Africa had been secured.

This campaign was important for the following reasons:

- It prevented Egypt and the Suez Canal from falling to Hitler
- It gave the Allies experience in large-scale seaborne offensives
- It provided a launching position for the next Allied target – Italy.

The fall of Italy (1943–45)

The southern offensive on 'fortress Europe' began on 10 July 1943, and within six weeks Sicily was in Allied hands. This event caused the downfall of Mussolini, who was dismissed by the Italian King. In October, Allied troops crossed to Salerno, Reggio and Taranto on the Italian mainland and captured Naples.

Mussolini's successor, Marshal Pietro Badoglio, signed an armistice and brought Italy into the war on the Allied side. The Germans, however, were determined to hold on to Italy. German divisions were diverted to Italy and the Allies had to fight their way slowly up the peninsula. Rome was not captured until June 1944 and northern Italy did not come under Allied control until April 1945. Despite the slow nature of the campaign, the Italian war had important consequences for the Allies:

- Fascism had ended in Italy, and Germany was deprived of its most important ally
- It tied down German divisions that were needed in Russia
- It meant that the Allies could not be accused by Stalin of leaving all of the fighting in Europe to the Soviet forces.

The war in Italy

While the price for the Allies of the Italian invasion was high, the Italians suffered not only in terms of casualties but also in the damage caused to the cultural heritage of their country. Beautiful buildings, such as the monastery at Monte Cassino, were destroyed as the Allies fought their way up the peninsula. In addition, the domestic economic situation was desperate and the government collapsed. Mussolini, ousted from government, was captured by partisans, shot and his body hung from a meat hook in a Milanese petrol station.

Operation *Overlord* (June 1944)

The invasion of France, codenamed Operation *Overlord*, began on 6 June 1944, a moment in history known as D-Day. The landings by 326,000 British, Canadian and American troops took place from sea and air on an 80km stretch of Normandy beaches. The invasion was a result of extremely complex preparations involving a huge amount of resources. Mulberry harbours – prefabricated, temporary habours – were built to provide anchorages for supply ships; oil pipelines were laid across the Channel; 4,000 ships supported the invasion; the whole assault was backed by massive airpower (12,000 aircraft in the sky on the first day of the invasion). Secrecy was also key to the success of the operation, and complex subterfuge plans were put into operation to convince the Germans (successfully) that the invasion would land at Calais rather than in Normandy.

Within a month, a million men had landed in Normandy. In the next few weeks, most of northern France was liberated, then Brussels and Antwerp were freed in the first week of September. However, German forces continued to resist and to enjoy successes. They defeated an Allied attempt to outflank the Siegfried Line at Arnhem in September 1944, and also temporarily regained ground in the Ardennes offensive (known in the West as the 'Battle of the Bulge') in December 1944–January 1945. Yet the losses in men and tanks sustained by the Germans in these battles could no longer be replaced, and the first months of 1945 saw the steady disintegration of the *Wehrmacht* (German armed forces). The Allies crossed the Rhine in March 1945. Germany was now being invaded on two fronts, and in Berlin on 30 April, Hitler killed himself. General Dwight D. Eisenhower, the supreme Allied commander in Europe, refused to race for Berlin to get there before the Soviets, and thus Stalin's forces were the first to arrive. On 7 May, the German government surrendered unconditionally to the combined Allied forces.

To access worksheet 8.2 on D-Day, please visit www.pearsonbacconline.com and follow the on-screen instructions.

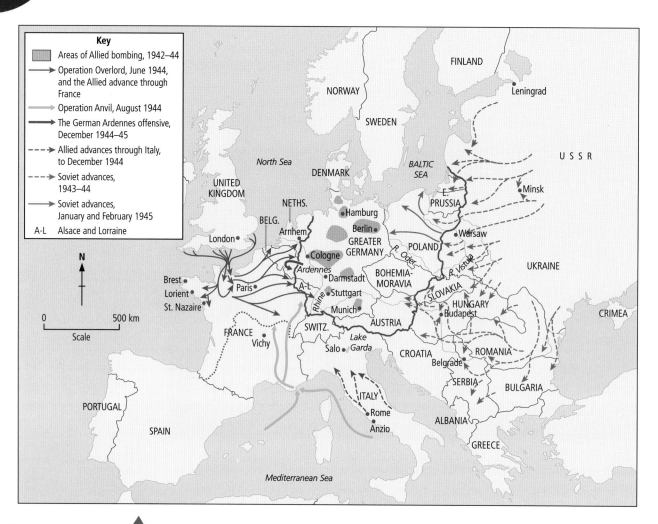

The collapse and defeat of Germany, 1944–45.

Why did the Allies defeat Hitler?

The weakness of the Axis powers

By not committing Germany's full military capacity to the invasion of Britain in 1941, Hitler allowed Britain to survive. Britain therefore kept the war going in the West, and also the Atlantic and Africa. The British resistance was to cause increasing problems for Germany, especially after 1942, as it had to divert resources away from the war in the East. Britain also acted as the launching pad for the bombing of Germany and Operation *Overlord*.

The invasion of the Soviet Union was to prove a huge mistake. It undid all the gains made by the Nazi–Soviet Pact and once again pushed Germany into a war on two fronts:

The effect of Operation Barbarossa was to commit Germany to war with a power which was three times her size in population, eighty times as large in area, and of much greater industrial capacity. It is hardly surprising that the major military setbacks experienced by the Wehrmacht occurred in Russia. These in turn, took the pressure off Britain and greatly assisted the latter's peripheral war effort in the Mediterranean and North Africa.

From Stephen Lee, *Aspects of European History, 1789–1980*, 1991

Declaring war on the USA, which Germany did on 11 September 1941, was also a major error, and showed a serious lack of judgement on Hitler's part. He was too dismissive of

America's capabilities and believed that the USA would remain in the Pacific fighting the Japanese. However, President Roosevelt made the defeat of Hitler his top priority, and US and British forces worked together to achieve this task. The USA's entry into the war allowed the Allies to invade Italy, carry out devastating bombing raids on Germany and open up the Second Front in 1944. Meanwhile, Hitler was unable to attack the USA directly and also did not face the same unity with his allies; Mussolini in fact was a constant drain on Hitler's resources.

Hitler's personal conduct of military operations was also disastrous. This can be seen most clearly in the USSR, where he did not prepare for a winter campaign and did not allow the forces at Stalingrad to conduct an orderly retreat or breakout from the Russian trap, with the result that it had to surrender in January 1943. Another serious mistake was to concentrate on producing V-rockets when Germany could have been developing jet aircraft, which might have restored German air superiority and weakened the Allied bombing campaign of 1944 and 1945.

Hitler's mistakes in the conduct of the war ensured that it went on much longer than he had expected. Germany increasingly suffered from material shortages as the war continued, particularly in rubber, cotton, nickel and, after mid 1944, oil. Although military production continued, and even increased right up until 1945, the emphasis on diversification of weapons (such as working on the V1 and V2 rockets) reduced the effectiveness of its efforts in this area. Women, for example, were not employed in munitions factories until late in the war. In addition, the German and Japanese military also resented and rejected interference and direction from civilians, which prevented any useful collaboration between civilian and military experts.

The strengths of the Allies

While Hitler faced increasing economic difficulties after 1942, the resources of the Allies grew stronger. As we have seen, the USSR's economy rapidly transformed to a wartime economy and, in the factories east of the Ural mountains, Russia was producing more armaments and better-quality armaments than Germany by 1943. The centralized state economy of the USSR proved more able than Hitler's Nazi state to produce what was needed to fight a prolonged war. Similarly, once the American economy geared up for wartime production, it also overtook the Axis powers in production of weapons. When the American war industry reached full capacity, it could turn out over 70,000 tanks and 120,000 aircraft a year.

Richard Overy points out, however, that greater economic resources and more armaments did not in themselves guarantee victory for the Allies. Key to Allied success was the fact that they 'turned their economic strength into effective fighting power' (Overy, *Why the Allies Won*, 2006). They learned from their mistakes of 1941 and took steps to increase the effectiveness of future combat forces. These steps involved:
- Improving the quality as well as the quantity of military forces and technology.
- Ensuring that there were excellent back-up services. In the Pacific theatre, there were 18 American support personnel for every one serviceman at the front, compared to a ratio of one to one in the Japanese forces. Stalin also paid close attention to the service of the Red Army. The chief of the Main Directorate of the Red Army Rear, General Khrulev, was responsible for the supply of the army and was treated equally with the military commanders. This was in contrast to the Axis powers, who put emphasis on operations and combat rather than on back-up organization and supplies. Men with the best organizational skills were fighting in the German Army rather than helping on the civilian front with planning.

V-rockets
The V-rockets were unmanned long-range missiles that Hitler used against Britain in 1944 and 1945, in what became known as the 'Second Blitz'. The V1 and V2 were to be weapons of revenge – the *Vergeltungswaffen*. These were the secret weapons that Hitler boasted about; the weapons that he previously hinted would win the war for Nazi Germany. The V1s carried an 850kg high-explosive warhead and travelled at 650km/h. Between 8,000 and 9,000 V1s were launched against southern England, primarily London. Yet although they caused initial shock, their impact was limited, as V1s could be shot out of the sky by anti-aircraft fire.
The V2 – the world's first **ballistic missile** – was far more dangerous. It carried a similar warhead, but travelled at such a speed that it could not be seen or heard until it exploded. These weapons spread considerable fear in London. About 1,000 V2s were fired at Britain before their launch sites were overrun by the advancing Allies. In total, they killed or wounded about 1,500 people.

- Setting up a large civilian apparatus to support the Allied forces, which allowed them to mobilize their economic, intellectual and organizational strengths for the purpose of waging war.

Strategic decisions made by the Allies were also vital for victory. First, the Allies made the decision to concentrate the mass of their attack on Germany; they realized that the defeat of this formidable military opponent was central to success. Thus 85 per cent of America's war effort was devoted to defeating Germany and only 15 per cent to the war with Japan. Second, the Allies poured massive amounts of money and effort into the **strategic bombing** campaign, and this had a serious effect on Germany's capacity to fight effectively at the front. Germany had to curtail its own bombing offensives and divert funds into an anti-aircraft strategy. Finally, the Allies had a tremendous will to win. Most people on the Allied side believed that this contest did not just involve the military forces, but concerned issues of life and death for whole communities and that it was a 'just' war worth fighting.

STUDENT STUDY SECTION

Review/essay question

Richard Overy argues that 'The war was won in 1945 not from German weaknesses but from Allied strengths.' How far do you agree with this statement?

War in the East: an overview

As we have seen, the USA was brought into the war by the Japanese attack on Pearl Harbor. The attack was brilliantly organized by Admiral Isoroku Yamamoto. There was no declaration of war. At 7.49am on 7 December, the first wave of Japanese planes, launched from nearby aircraft carriers, struck Pearl Harbor.

Roosevelt, calling the attack by Japan 'unprovoked and dastardly', asked Congress to declare war on Japan, which it duly did. Britain declared war on Japan the same day. They were followed by the Latin American states of Costa Rica, the Dominican Republic, Haiti, Honduras, Nicaragua, El Salvador, Cuba, Guatemala and Panama. On 11 December, Germany declared war on America, thus justifying those Americans like Roosevelt who believed that America should help Europe in the fight against Hitler. The conflict was now a world war.

Meanwhile, Japan caused devastation and shock throughout the Pacific. Within hours of the Pearl Harbor attack, Japanese forces attacked Wake, Guam, the Philippines, Malaya and Hong Kong. British naval defence depended on a new battleship, the *Prince of Wales*, and the old battlecruiser, the *Repulse*. Both were sunk by Japanese bombers on 10 December, leaving Singapore undefended. In mid December, the Japanese also invaded Burma.

Scene of the attack on Pearl Harbor, December 1941.

On 25 and 26 December, Hong Kong and 12,000 prisoners fell into Japanese hands. Japanese troops invaded the Dutch East Indies on 6 January 1942, and before the end of the month, British, Australian and Indian forces had retreated from the tip of the Malay peninsula to Singapore. This, too, was attacked and forced to surrender, along with 80,000 soldiers, one of the worst defeats in British history.

By mid 1942, the Japanese had successfully captured the Dutch East Indies, the Philippines and Burma. They now held a vast empire, which they labelled the Greater East Asia Co-Prosperity Sphere (see above, p.136).

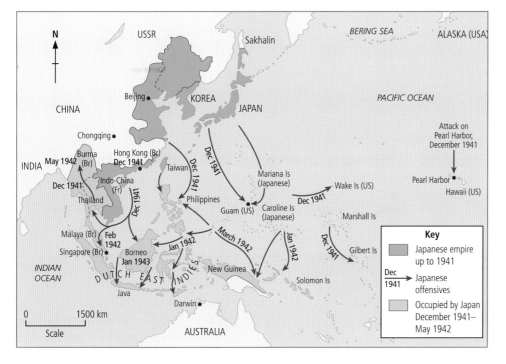

The battle of Midway (June 1942)

After these successes, however, the Japanese suffered two serious setbacks when they failed to capture Port Moresby on the south coast of New Guinea (which would have brought the north coast of Australia within reach of their bombers), or to take Midway Island in June 1942. The Japanese had hoped that an offensive against Midway Island would draw out the US Navy's vital aircraft carriers, which could then be destroyed and tip the naval balance in the Pacific in Japan's favour. However, partly due to the fact that the Americans had broken the Japanese codes and knew exactly when and where the attack was to be launched, the Americans were able to beat off the powerful Japanese naval force and to destroy three of the Japanese aircraft carriers (a fourth was sunk later in the day).

The American success at Midway proved to be a crucial turning point for the war in the Pacific:

Not only did the balance in the Pacific between fleet carriers now stand equal … the advantage the Japanese had lost could never be made good… Six fleet carriers would join the Japanese navy in 1942–4; America would launch fourteen, as well as nine light carrier and sixty-six escort carriers, creating a fleet against which Japan could not stand. It was now to be condemned to the defensive.

From John Keegan, *The Second World War*, 1997

Japanese retreat

Although a catastrophic defeat for Japan, the battle of Midway did not mean that Japan had lost any territory, and America had an extremely tough time in pushing back the Japanese occupation. Beginning in January 1942 with landings in the Solomon Islands, General Douglas MacArthur (Supreme Commander of Allied Forces in the Southwest Pacific Area) slowly began to recover the Pacific islands in a process nicknamed 'island hopping' or 'atoll hopping'. Superiority at sea and in the air enabled the Americans to conquer these stepping stones towards Japan.

In a two-pronged assault, Admiral Chester Nimitz (Commander-in-Chief, US Pacific Fleet) advanced through the Central Pacific, while MacArthur continued along a south-western

The Allied onslaught against Japan, 1943–45.

Key
- Japanese-held terrritories August 1945
- US/Australian advance
- Soviet forces
- Chinese Nationalist forces
- Chinese Communist forces
- British forces

Kamikaze

In fighting the Japanese, the Americans faced a formidable enemy. Japanese troops on the whole preferred death to surrender. Japanese warrior tradition prescribed surrender to be dishonourable, and thus many soldiers committed suicide rather than be captured. In fact, Japanese Army regulations laid down that their surrender was a crime punishable by death. Another horrific aspect of the fighting for the Americans was the *kamikaze* suicide tactics used by the Japanese, in which pilots would literally fly their bomb-laden aircraft into American ships. The 1,900 suicide missions between 6 April and 22 June sank 25 ships and scored 182 hits. Ironically, *kamikaze* attacks also damaged the Japanese Air Force by reducing the numbers of available aircraft.

route from New Guinea. In 1943, Nimitz's forces took the Gilbert Islands, then the Marshall Islands in February 1944, and began landing in the Marianas in June 1944 after the battle of the Philippine Sea. The US victories opened up the route to the occupied Philippines, and also Japan's sea route to oil supplies in the East Indies. In October 1944, the largest naval battle of all time, involving 282 warships and hundreds of aircraft, clashed in the battle of Leyte Gulf. Facing fanatical resistance from the Japanese, American forces now had to clear the Japanese out of the Philippines, and then the islands of Iwo Jima and Okinawa in 1945. Okinawa was the grimmest of all of these battles. The US Army divisions lost 4,675 dead and missing, and the US Marine Corps 2,938. The US Navy lost a further 4,900 dead, and 763 aircraft were destroyed and 38 ships sunk. The population of Okinawa suffered terribly, with perhaps as many as 160,000 dying in the fighting. The Japanese lost 16 ships and 7,800 aircraft – a thousand of these in *kamikaze* missions. Although the Americans took 7,400 prisoners, 110,000 other Japanese died refusing to surrender.

Meanwhile, the Allies had set up a new South-East Asia Command under Admiral Louis Mountbatten, whose objective was to clear the Japanese out of Burma and open the Burma Road to China. This objective was finally achieved in May 1945.

The atomic bomb and the Japanese surrender

With the Germans defeated in May 1945, it was possible for the Americans to focus all of their might on the defeat of Japan. The Soviets had also promised to bring their troops to the East to help with the final assault.

Japan was clearly on the verge of defeat. Not only were the American ground forces nearly at Japan itself, through their strategy of 'island hopping', but Japan had been consistently bombed since November 1944, with devastating effects on its cities. The new Japanese Prime Minster, Admiral Kantaro Suzuki, tried to get the Americans to agree to a peace that would preserve the position of the Emperor. However, the Allies would not accept anything other than 'unconditional surrender'. In addition, they were alarmed about the Soviets getting involved in a war that would ensure that Stalin received land in the East in return for his efforts, and they were also concerned about the number of casualties that the US Army would suffer in a land invasion.

These were some of the factors that influenced President Harry S Truman (the US President following the death of Roosevelt in April 1945) to use the new weapon possessed by the USA – the atomic bomb, or 'A-bomb'. The Americans and British had been secretly developing this weapon to use against Nazi Germany, in the Manhattan Project, but Germany had surrendered before it was ready.

The first A-bomb, 'Little Boy', was dropped over Hiroshima on 6 August 1945 with devastating effects, killing some 80,000 people and injuring 80,000 more. On 9 August, a second bomb was dropped, on the port of Nagasaki, and another 40,000 Japanese died. After this, the Japanese government surrendered. The war was finally over.

To access worksheet 8.3 on the atomic bomb, please visit www.pearsonbacconline.com and follow the on-screen instructions.

STUDENT STUDY SECTION

Review question

From what you have read, what arguments do you think Truman would have given for using the atomic bomb?

Document analysis

Document A

Based on detailed investigation of all the facts and supported by the testimony of the surviving Japanese leaders involved, it is the Survey's opinion that certainly prior to 31 December 1945 and in all probability prior to 1 November 1945, Japan would have surrendered even if the atomic bombs had not been dropped, even if Russia had not entered the war, and even if no invasion had been planned or contemplated.

From the report of the US Strategic Bombing Survey Group, July 1946, assigned to study the effects of air attacks on Japan

Document B

It is my opinion that the use of this barbarous weapon at Hiroshima and Nagasaki was of no material assistance in our war against Japan. The Japanese were already defeated and were ready to surrender because of the effective sea blockade and the successful bombing of conventional weapons. It was my reaction that the scientists and others wanted to make this test because of the vast sums that had been spent on the Project. Truman knew that and so did the other people involved… My own feeling was that in being the first to use it we had adopted the ethical standards common to barbarians in the dark ages. I was not taught to make war in that fashion.

Admiral William D. Leahy, Chief of Staff to the President of the United States, from his autobiography *I Was There* (1950)

Document C

Part of the appeal of the atomic bomb was that it allowed one plane … to achieve what had previously been achieved by hundreds. In more than 30,000 sorties between June 1944 and August 1945, only seventy-four B-29s were lost, a casualty rate of 0.24% … Yet seventy-four B-29s translates into nearly 900 highly trained men. Since 1940, the Allies had been applying the principle of maximum enemy casualties for minimum Allied casualties. The creation of the atomic bomb required a revolution in physics. But it did not require a revolution in the political economy of total war. Rather it was the logical culmination of the Allied way of war.

From Niall Ferguson, *The War of the World*, 2006

Document D

Most importantly, the bomb was part of an 'atomic diplomacy', in which the US tried to establish a post-war advantage over the Soviet Union (and, it may be argued, Britain) in Europe and Asia. In May 1945 Henry Stimson wrote that US economic power and the bomb were 'a royal straight flush and we mustn't be a fool about the way we play it'. Following this advice, Truman even delayed the

Potsdam Conference with Churchill and Stalin to await the first test of the new weapon. As soon as he received news of success, the president took a tough line over issues such as Germany and downplayed the prospect of Soviet entry into the war against Japan. Truman explained, 'I have an ace in the hole and another one showing. So, unless [Stalin] has three-of-a-kind or two pairs (and I know he has nothing), we are sitting all right.' Stimson admitted, on the day after the second bomb at Nagasaki, that the US wanted to end the war, 'before the Russians could put in any substantial claim to occupy and help rule [Manchuria and Japan].'

From Scott Lucas, 'Hiroshima and History', *Modern History Review,* 1996

Questions

1   Identify the key points being made in Documents A–D concerning the use of the atomic bomb.

2   Compare and contrast Documents A and B in their arguments against the use of the atomic bomb.

3   With reference to their origin and purpose, what are the value and limitations of Sources A and B for the historian?

Research and discussion

List the arguments for and against using the atomic bomb, as identified in the text above and in the documents. Research these arguments in more detail using websites. Now divide the class into two groups and organize a debate on the motion: 'This house believes that the dropping of the atomic bomb was necessary to save American and Japanese lives.'

Why were the Allies successful in defeating the Japanese?

The Allied victory in the Pacific and South-East Asia had several factors in common with the defeat of the Germans – the emphasis on effective back-up support for the military, and the involvement of the civilians in the military in planning and logistics, for example. As with Germany, these were areas that the Japananese had neglected. The post-war bombing survey of Japan noted the failure of the Japanese Air Force to provide 'adequate maintenance, logistic support, communications and control, or airfields and bases…'

Technologically, the Americans gradually overtook the Japanese in producing new fighting weapons. Although at a disadvantage at the beginning of the war, as in Europe, America learned from early mistakes and quickly pulled ahead, building up naval and air superiority, developing new planes and realizing the importance of aircraft carriers.

A critical factor behind the Allied victory lay in isolating Japan from its empire by destroying its merchant marine, navy and naval airpower. Japan had overstretched itself in the huge amount of territory it was trying to occupy. Denied use of the empire's manpower, equipment, food supplies and raw materials by US submarines, surface vessels and aircraft, the nation could not possibly survive. Japan being a small island with limited industrial power, the Japanese economy simply could not match the American capacity for rapid expansion. At the end of the war, the destruction of Japan's industries and cities by systematic bombing was also an important factor in Japan's ultimate defeat. By 1945, the national infrastructure was destroyed and industry was unable to produce the weapons it needed.

How was World War II fought?

The war on land

World War I not only had an impact on the causes of World War II, as you have read in the previous chapter, but it also had an impact on the way the war was fought. Germany had learnt from the 1918 Ludendorff offensive that in order to break through the enemy's ranks, concentrated attacks by stormtroopers, along with tactical air cover, were critical. In fact, strategists in Britain, France and Germany had all written about the need for rapid mobile attacks based on large numbers of tanks, but it was the German leadership that put these theories into practice. The result was *Blitzkrieg*. Now, instead of the defensive war of World War I, there was offensive war that consisted of surprise, speed and movement using tanks, armoured vehicles, mechanized transport and the aeroplane. An air strike took out the opposing air force and communications centres on the ground and parachutists were dropped behind enemy lines. The swift-moving tanks and motorized infantry – supported by air power – would then split the enemy lines, and allow rapid penetration into the unprotected territories beyond, with the aim of encircling the main enemy forces and destroying them. Thus a rapid, decisive victory was achieved.

Although many historians now doubt that *Blitzkrieg* was a coherent well thought-out strategy and believe that it was more of an improvised response, it was nevertheless well suited to Hitler's needs. He was not expecting a major war in 1939; his planning was for a widespread European war in 1943–45, and in 1939 the German economy was not yet ready for the demands of a long war. Thus *Blitzkrieg* allowed Hitler to achieve quick victories that were not too demanding in terms of casualties and resources. The speed and surprise elements of Germany's success prevented other countries from mobilizing fully for total war, and had a devastating impact on morale.

The successes and failures of *Blitzkrieg*

Up until 1941, *Blitzkrieg* in Europe was very successful. Although the German Army was not superior in terms of actual equipment, the surprise of a *Blitzkrieg* attack against an enemy that lacked the same levels of organization and morale allowed for dramatic German victories. Operation Barbarossa, however, showed the weakness of *Blitzkrieg*. Despite the massive advances in the first six months, the German Army was not sufficiently equipped to deal with such a large operation. The circumstances in which *Blitzkrieg* was effective – short wars in confined areas – did not exist in the USSR. With its huge areas of land and resources, the USSR was able to withstand the initial losses, reorganize its economy and military and fight back. By 1943, Germany had lost the key 'surprise' element of *Blitzkrieg* and its enemies had learnt from their initial mistakes of 1939–41. The Allies increasingly fought a war in the same attacking style as the Germans, with heavy use of tanks, mobile vehicles and, most importantly, air power. From 1944, the Allies had dominance of the skies on all fronts.

The war at sea

The battle for the Atlantic

For Britain, naval power was critical for maintaining the vital trade routes on which the British population depended for survival. It also allowed Britain to defend its empire and was essential to any army operation outside home waters. Thus, until 1944, Britain fought mainly a naval war. Yet even more so than in 1914–18 , sea warfare was no longer about battles between large fleets and huge battleships. German naval prestige suffered a blow after the scuttling of the *Graf Spee* in 1939 (the battleship was trapped by British warships in Montevideo harbour, Uruguay) and the sinking of the prestigious battleship *Bismarck* in the Atlantic in 1941. German capital warships were then removed from the Atlantic and as a result, there were no major surface engagements in the Mediterranean and Atlantic that compared to the battle of Jutland in World War I.

Sea warfare was now about controlling supply lines, and from 1940 to 1943 Britain and Germany fought to see who could dominate the Atlantic. Although the German U-boat

Enigma codes

The German military used the Enigma cipher machine during World War II to keep their communications secret. The Enigma machine is an electro-mechanical device that relied on a series of rotating 'wheels' or 'rotors' to scramble plain text messages into incoherent cipher text. The machine's variable elements could be set in many billions of combinations, each one generating a completely different cipher text message. The recipients of messages would know how the machine had been set up, so could type the cipher text back in; the machine would then unscramble the message. Without knowing the Enigma setting, the message would remain indecipherable.

The German authorities believed in the absolute security of the Enigma. However, with the help of Polish mathematicians who had managed to acquire a machine prior to the outbreak of World War II, British code breakers stationed at Bletchley Park managed to crack the Enigma code.

The U-boat war – annual loss of Allied shipping and U-boats as a percentage of total war losses.

fleet was small in 1939, it was developed quickly. Hitler needed the U-boats to keep Britain and the USA occupied while Germany was tied up in the Soviet Union. They were also a possible way of defeating Britain outright, and at first the German U-boats were very successful at harrying Britain's lifeline. In 1941, submarines sank 1,299 ships, and in 1942 1,662 ships were sunk with a total tonnage of almost 8 million tonnes. By 1943, Britain's survival was being seriously threatened by the losses of Allied shipping.

To combat the U-boats, the Allies had both to avoid them and attack them. Both strategies depended on precise knowledge of the position and movement of the U-boats. Fortunately for the Allies, mid 1943 saw the culmination of several factors that allowed them to do this, thereby eliminating the U-boat as a decisive threat:

- Britain was able to crack the Enigma codes (see Interesting Facts box). Also, in 1943 the codes of the Royal Navy were changed, after it was discovered that the Germans had been deciphering them all along. Thus from mid 1943, the Allies had an intelligence advantage.
- By May 1943, convoys were protected by various technical innovations. Included in these was the High-Frequency Direction Finder (HF/DF, known as 'Huff-Duff), which provided an accurate bearing towards any submarine that used its radio.
- Air power was used effectively to attack the U-boats. Long-range Liberator aircraft with short-wave radar and searchlights were able to pick out the U-boats on the surface at night. Small aircraft carrier escorts started accompanying the convoys to give protection when the Liberators were unavailable or out of range. In 1943, 149 out of the 237 German vessels sunk were victims of aircraft.

By the end of 1943, it was clear that the Allies had won the battle for the Atlantic. Richard Overy points to the importance of the British and American willingness to recognize and undertake a revolution in maritime strategy, something that the Germans were reluctant to do. After 1943, the Allies also managed to produce more ships than were being lost thanks to the dramatic increase in US shipbuilding.

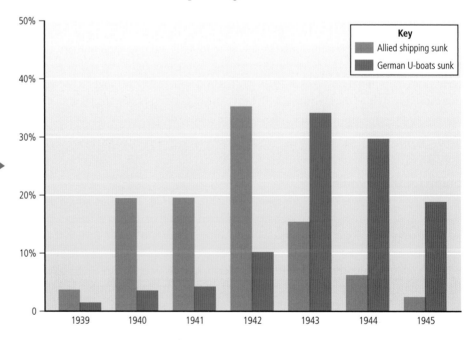

Key
- Allied shipping sunk
- German U-boats sunk

Naval war in the Pacific

The revolutionary effect of aircraft in sea warfare was demonstrated even more clearly in the war with Japan. Japan used air power highly effectively at the start of the war in the attack on Pearl Harbor and also against British and Dutch ships in the Pacific. Like Germany, Japan hoped to intercept Allied shipping to prevent any reinforcements reaching the Pacific. It also hoped to destroy the rest of the US fleet, as explained. However, the Americans had huge shipbuilding capability and also had realized – even before the Europeans – that aircraft were vital to naval combat. Thus the USA already had large aircraft carriers at the outbreak of war. American ships also had radar and access to Japanese codes. These factors were crucial in their success at the battles of Coral Sea and Midway in 1942. As explained on p.157, the loss of the Japanese carrier force in the battle of Midway put the Japanese into a position from which they could not recover, given their limited shipbuilding capacity. (In 1943 and 1944, Japanese shipyards produced seven aircraft carriers, whereas the American shipyards produced 90.)

What was the significance of the naval war for the outcome of World War II?

Naval warfare played a key role in both the course and the outcome of World War II. In Europe, the German U-boat campaign, as well as bringing the British close to subsistence levels of existence, delayed the opening of a second front, preventing the build-up of the American forces in Europe until after 1943. Taking routes to avoid the U-boats also made getting supplies to the USSR and the Allied armies in Africa much more difficult than it would normally have been.

The victory of the Allies in the battle for the Atlantic was vital, therefore, in allowing Britain and the USA to prepare for D-Day. John Keegan writes that 'Had it been lost … the course, perhaps the outcome, of the Second World War would have been entirely otherwise.' The victory of the Allies on the seas also allowed them to impose crippling sea blockades on Italy and Japan, which dramatically affected the industrial strength of these countries and prevented them from sending out reinforcements to other fronts.

The war in the air

Both the war on land and the war at sea were transformed by aircraft. Both sides used aircraft as a tactical support for armies on the ground. Radio communication was used to coordinate air support, with ground-attack aircraft attacking enemy strongpoints, supply lines, troops and vehicles. At sea, aircraft now were used to attack surface vessels and also submarines, as well as to protect convoys. In supply and reconnaissance, aircraft were also applied to great effect. Supplies were now dropped by aircraft (as were soldiers in several campaigns), and aircraft were essential in supplying partisan movements behind enemy lines. Camera technology was greatly improved throughout the course of the war, making photo-reconnaissance aircraft even more effective. Aircraft were used for identifying troop movements and also targets for bombing.

Strategic bombing

While aircraft played a *supportive* role, World War II also saw an even more radical and independent use for aircraft in strategic bombing. This type of bombing focused on destroying the military and industrial infrastructure of a country. It could also, however, be directed against civilians in an attempt to crush civilian morale. By focusing on the home front, strategic bombing blurred further the distinction between combatant and non-combatant, and its use in World War II remains highly controversial.

Strategic bombing in Europe

At the beginning of the war, the RAF was forbidden from indiscriminate bombing, and in fact both sides held back from being the first to attack cities directly in Western Europe. This policy changed when a *Luftwaffe* crew bombed East London in error, which was followed with a retaliatory raid by Churchill against Berlin. Hitler used the

Berlin attack as an excuse to launch a full-scale air assault against London and other British cities (the Blitz).

Apart from retaliation for the Blitz, the switch to **area bombing** by the British and Americans was also caused by the fact that precision attacks on German industrial targets in daylight led to high casualties, and localized night-time attacks were too inaccurate. In addition, strategic bombing allowed the Allies to show Stalin that they were playing their part in the war.

The key advocate of the bombing campaign in Britain was Sir Arthur 'Bomber' Harris, who was appointed Commander-in-Chief of Bomber Command at the beginning of 1942. Initially, bombing raids on Germany did not bring about the results that Bomber Command hoped for, and the high losses of RAF planes in 1942–43 were making the strategy unacceptable. The effects on parts of Germany were still horrific – 40,000 dying in Hamburg in a firestorm, for instance – but they did not lead to a collapse in civilian morale and German industrial production continued to rise into 1944. However, with the introduction of the P-51B Mustang in 1944, the bombing campaign became far more devastating. This plane was fitted with auxiliary fuel tanks so that it could accompany the bombers all the way to the target; it was thus able to take on the *Luftwaffe* fighters, causing huge losses in German planes and giving the bombers easier bomb runs. In February and March 1944, the Germans lost a total of 900 fighters, a situation from which they never recovered. By June 1944, the Allies had total air superiority.

With the *Luftwaffe* defeated, Bomber Command was able to bomb in daylight and to carry out 'precision' attacks on industrial targets such as the steel industry in the Ruhr. (The US Army Air Forces – USAAF – bombed almost exclusively in daylight. Previously the RAF largely bombed at night, while the USAAF took over in the day.) However, cities in eastern Germany such as Dresden, Leipzig and Chemnitz were also attacked in the spring of 1945. Joint Anglo-American attacks on Dresden in February 1945 created a firestorm that killed approximately 50,000 civilians.

The aftermath of the Allied air raids on Dresden, February 1945.

The Germans, who lacked a proper strategic bomber force, responded to the Allied attacks from 1944 with the V1, a pilotless flying bomb, and the V2 ballistic missile. These were targeted at London and did cause significant casualties. They could not be mass-produced, however, and were unreliable and inaccurate. They also came too late in the war to have any effect on the outcome. In fact, the rocket project did not help the German war effort, as it used up resources that would have been better spent on building more fighter planes.

Strategic bombing in the Pacific

Japan was also subjected to intense bombing. From November 1944, the USAAF, flying from the captured island bases of Saipan and Guam, began relentlessly hitting the Japanese mainland. Initially they carried out precision attacks on aircraft factories, but these gave way from March 1945 to area bombing using mainly incendiary munitions. The results were horrific for Japanese civilians living in houses made mainly of wood, bamboo and paper. In an attack on Tokyo on 9 March 1945, B-29s flying from Iwo Jima destroyed a quarter of the city – 1 million homes – and killed approximately 80,000 people. In fact, in the six months between April and August 1945, 21st Bomber Command under the direction of General Curtis LeMay devastated most of Japan's major cities. Terrified Japanese fled to the villages; absenteeism in the factories rose to 50 per cent. A combination of sea blockade and bombing devastated the economy and left Japan on the verge of defeat. However, the ultimate expression of strategic bombing came with the use of the two atomic bombs on Hiroshima and Nagasaki, after which Japan surrendered. Thus it was air power alone that caused the final collapse of Japan; no land invasion was necessary.

The debate about strategic bombing

There have been two major criticisms made against strategic bombing: that it was morally wrong and that it was ineffective. With regard to the first point, the justifications given by the Allies were that the Germans started it (Churchill quoted Hosea 8:7 saying 'now those who sow the wind are reaping the whirlwind'), that it was the only means that Britain had of hitting back at Germany, and that it would help end the war more quickly. It was thus a strategy of necessity. Yet critics at the time, and since 1945, maintained that the devastating effects on civilian populations did not justify such use of bombing.

With regard to its effectiveness, there is again much controversy. Some historians argue that the dramatic drop in German production in 1944–45 was due to the attacks of Bomber Command, while other historians argue that Germany's declining production figures were owed as much to the general attrition of the war as to the bombing. The sources below set out these arguments more fully.

STUDENT STUDY SECTION

Document analysis

Document A

There has always seemed something fundamentally implausible about the contention of bombing's critics that dropping almost 2.5 million tons of bombs on tautly stretched industrial systems and war-weary urban populations would not seriously weaken them. Germany and Japan had no special immunity. Japan's military economy was devoured in the flames; her population desperately longed for escape from bombing. German forces lost half of the weapons needed at the front, millions of workers absented themselves from work, and the economy gradually creaked almost to a halt. Bombing turned the whole of Germany, in Speer's words, into a 'gigantic front'. It was a front the Allies were determined to win; it absorbed huge resources on both sides. It was a battlefield in which only the infantry were missing. The final victory of the bombing in 1944 was, Speer concluded, 'the greatest lost battle on the German side…' For all the arguments over the morality or operational effectiveness of the bombing campaigns, the air offensive was one of the decisive elements in Allied victory.

From Richard Overy, *Why the Allies Won*, 2006

Document B

Harris later claimed that the bombers could have won the war on their own, had they been given the required resources. There is little evidence to suggest that area bombing (whatever we may say about its morality) contributed directly to the Allied victory. There was, for example, despite Harris' confident predictions, no general collapse in German morale. German productive capacity was reduced by about 9% in 1943 and about 17% in 1944. In mitigation, however, it is important to note three points. First, that in the dark days of 1940–41, after London and other cities had been blitzed and British forces had been expelled from Norway and France, the British felt they had to be doing something to hit back at the enemy; bombing was arguably of psychological importance. Second, that as the war dragged on, there was a need to placate Stalin, in the absence of a second ground front, to be seen to be carrying the war to the enemy, above all to deter the Soviets from signing a separate peace with Germany. Third, that area bombing operations against Germany, whatever their real effect on the ground, caused a substantial portion of German resources to be re-directed to home defence and reconstruction from other fronts; they also saved civilian lives in Britain by putting the Luftwaffe on the defensive.

From Peter Riddick, 'Strategic Bombing', in *Modern History Review*, 1994

Document C

'The pursuing eye', a cartoon by David Low in the *Evening Standard*, 29 November 1943.

THE PURSUING EYE

Questions

1   Identify the key points made in Document A and explain what they reveal about the impact of strategic bombing on the outcome of the war.

2   To what extent are the views expressed about strategic bombing in Document A supported by Document B?

3   What is the message of the cartoon? In what ways does this cartoon support the views of Richard Overy?

Review questions

What was the impact of a) the war at sea, and b) the war in the air, on the final outcome of the war? What technological developments in each of these areas had an impact on the nature of the fighting and the outcome?

World War II as a total war

STUDENT STUDY SECTION

Review question

Before reading this section, review the key features of total war by referring to p.2.
You may also want to copy out the spider diagram on p.61. and add to it as you read the following section.

World War II is considered to be more of a total war than World War I, for the following reasons:

- Learning from World War I, governments made every effort to ensure the fullest mobilization and most efficient utilization of the human and material resources of the state.
- Because World War I had shown that the productivity of the home front was the key to victory, so World War II saw the home front under direct attack in a way that had not occurred in the previous conflict.
- Governments used all weapons at their disposal and developed new ones during the course of the war, weapons that were capable of killing far greater numbers of civilians than ever before.
- In both the war in Europe and the war in the Far East, racial hatred led to the killing or relocation of vast numbers of civilians deemed to be untrustworthy or inferior.

The aims of the belligerents

As with World War I, the aims of the powers involved in the war were 'total'. Hitler's aims for Europe were clear; total domination and the takeover of the USSR to provide living space for the German peoples. They also involved the elimination of races considered inferior – Jews in particular – in all areas taken over by the Nazis. In combating these aims, the Allies could afford no compromise peace. They saw themselves as fighting for the freedom of Europe. The same was true in the Pacific, where the Japanese Co-Prosperity Sphere, with its aims of political, economic and racial domination, were considered unacceptable. Although Japan called for a negotiatied peace in 1945, this was rejected by the Allies, who demanded total surrender.

The racial aspect of the fighting, involving as it did whole populations, injected a greater intensity into the struggle and ensured a bitter fight to the finish. As with World War I, propaganda on both sides reinforced the need for unrestrained warfare, while also demonizing the enemy and making total victory the only goal.

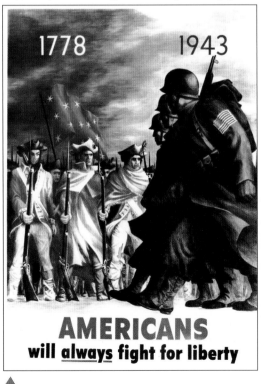

▲ A 1943 US poster makes an historical link between fighting the Nazis and Japanese, and the American revolution of the late 18th century.

▲ 'Bolshevism is treading on Europe.' A German poster distributed in Belgium in 1943.

The use of weaponry

As you have read, both sides used all weapons in their arsenals, and developed deadly new weapons during the course of the war in an attempt to win at all costs.

The future impact of wartime technological innovations

World War II saw major developments in military technology – radar, U-boat detection equipment, long-distance bombing, V1 and V2 rockets and, of course, the atomic bomb. Of these, radar was to have a huge impact in future air and sea navigation, the V2 weapons led indirectly to rockets for space exploration and nuclear missiles, while the jet engine would revolutionize air travel. The atomic bomb, as you will read later, would affect how the Cold War was to be fought. There were other developments, stimulated by wartime needs, that would have a big impact in peacetime. The large-scale production of the new sulphonamide drugs and of penicillin (which had been discovered in 1929) saved thousands of soldiers' lives and would save thousands of civilian lives after the war. The war also saw research into improved techniques for storing blood and plasma, and also plastic surgery for helping badly injured or burnt service personnel. Synthetic fibres such as nylon, which were used to make parachutes, would soon appear in all types of consumer products.

STUDENT STUDY SECTION

Review question

Go back over this chapter; add examples to your spider diagram of weaponry that show how both sides used every means possible to achieve victory.

The role of civilians

As we have seen, civilians were attacked in new ways during World War I and also suffered the effects of war in terms of rationing and deprivation. However, the large casualty figures were made up mainly of the men of the armed forces. In World War II these proportions changed profoundly. Whereas in World War I, civilians counted for only one-twentieth of the war dead, in World War II they counted for up to two-thirds of the deaths (see Chapter 9). This shift was because of the power of the new weaponry – the bombers, for example – and also because the new mobility of war brought the fighting to far greater numbers of people than had been the case in World War I.

STUDENT STUDY SECTION

Review question

Go back over this chapter; pull out examples of where civilians were either caught up in the fighting or deliberately targeted as a strategy for winning the war. Add to your spider diagram the examples and the impact on civilians.

Deportation and genocide

There was an ideological and racial aspect to World War II that meant that certain sections of populations were deliberately targeted, with the intent that they should be deported or even eliminated entirely. In Europe, this was particularly evident on the Eastern Front following the German invasion of Poland and the Soviet Union. Hitler believed that certain races – in particular Jews but also Slavs – were *Untermenschen* or subhuman. The space that was necessary for the Greater German Reich also meant that the existing populations in Poland and the USSR had to be destroyed or displaced. In one of the plans for German settlement drawn up by the Reich, it was estimated that 'the unwanted population would be closer to fifty or even fifty-seven million, assuming that 15 percent of Poles, 25 percent of Ruthanians and 35 percent of Ukrainians would need to be retained as agricultural labourers, the rest being deported to Siberia. The Russian population would wither away through the use of contraception, abortion and sterilization. The Jews would be exterminated' (Niall Ferguson, *War of the World*, 2006).

Many Poles and Russians were deported to the factories and mines of the Third Reich, where the work there ensured almost certain death for most of them. For the Jews, special SS squads called *Einsatzgruppen* accompanied the German Army as it invaded Poland and the USSR, and had the dedicated job to kill all Jews, communist officials and resisters they encountered. By the end of July 1941, the *Einsatzgruppen* had murdered around 63,000 men, women and children, 90 per cent of whom were Jews. Groups other than Jews were also at risk, such as the Gypsies and mental patients.

The method of killing such large numbers of people was, however, very time-consuming and costly – mass groups of people were generally herded into remote locations and shot. The Nazis came up with a new method to deliver their 'final solution' to the 'Jewish question' – the transportation of Jews from across Europe to concentration and extermination camps, where they could be eliminated either by poison gas or through overwork and starvation. The extermination camp at Auschwitz-Birkenau alone could kill 10,000 people a day.

The Soviet government also deported whole populations. It assumed that the minority peoples in the west were disloyal to the Soviet Union and thus the Germans on the Volga and the Tartars in the Crimea were deported. Estonians, Lithuanians and Poles were all dispersed to Siberia or other parts of the USSR.

A combination of lethal factors meant that the death tolls in Eastern Europe and the USSR during the war were terribly high. At least 20 million died in the Soviet Union (some estimates put the number much higher) and more than half of these were civilian deaths. Poland suffered the greatest proportional loss of life, with six million deaths out

Map showing the main extermination and concentration camps in German-occupied Europe by 1942.

Allied prisoners of the Japanese in the Pacific War, 1941–45.

of a population of 30 million. Three million of these were Jews and only 150,000 of these casualty figures represent deaths in military action. Overall an estimated one million Gypsies and six million Jewish civilians were killed by the Nazis in their racial extermination programme.

The Japanese also had ambitions linked to racial superiority. 'The Chinese people', wrote General Sakai Ryu, the Chief of Staff of the Japanese forces in North China in 1937, 'are bacteria infesting world civilization.' Such attitudes were commonplace, hence the genocidal Japanese treatment of the Chinese in 'the rape of Nanjing'. Such brutality continued during the takeover of South-East Asia following the attack on Pearl Harbor. Between 5,000 and 50,000 Chinese were massacred in Singapore in a series of 'purification-by-elimination' operations. Overall, 10 million Chinese died at the hands of the Japanese. Filipinos, Indonesians and Malays were also used as slave workers, resulting in thousands of deaths. Allied prisoners of war also suffered terribly from physical overwork, malnutrition and abuse.

Internment

German and Japanese civilians who found themselves living in Britain and America also suffered. It was assumed that their first loyalties would be to their country of origin. Thus Germans and Austrians in Britain were rounded up and put in internment camps. In America, more than 100,000 Japanese were relocated into camps, many losing their property or being forced to sell at very low prices. In 1988, the US Congress agreed on an apology for this policy and gave $20,000 compensation to all surviving internees.

STUDENT STUDY SECTION

Document analysis

As the Turks had treated the Armenians, as Stalin's henchmen were treating the kulaks, Poles and other 'enemies of the people', as the Nazis were soon to start treating the Jews, Gypsies and mentally ill, so the Japanese now thought of and treated the Chinese as sub-humans. This capacity to treat other human beings as members of an inferior and indeed malignant species – as mere vermin – was one of the crucial reasons why Twentieth Century conflict was so violent. Only make this mental leap, and warfare ceases to be a formalised encounter between uniformed armies. It becomes a war of annihilation, in which everyone on the other side – men, women, children, the elderly – can legitimately be killed.

From Niall Ferguson, *War of the World*, 2006

Questions

1 What point is Ferguson making about war in the 20th century?

2 What recent examples are there of where contempt for one race of people by another has led to violence?

Civilians as part of the war effort

As with World War I, civilians were mobilized in all countries to help with the war effort. This effort was, however, on a much vaster scale than in World War I. The major combatants mobilized between a half and two-thirds of their industrial workforce, and devoted up to three-quarters of their national product to waging war. This meant that, apart from in the USA, the vital resources of the country were directed to the war effort and the populations were therefore forced to live on a restricted range of rationed food and household goods.

The number of people required to both fight and to work in the factories to produce the necessary amount of war materials was vast, and countries used different methods to get the workforce that they required.

Britain

In Britain, military conscription was introduced from the beginning of the conflict (unlike in World War I), but it was carefully controlled to ensure that key workers were left in the important industries, such as coal mining. Industrial conscription was also introduced for women, and thus women played an even bigger role in British industry, agriculture and administration in World War II than in World War I.

Germany

In Germany, there was little change to the economy at the beginning of the war, as the early victories did not put much strain on the home front. When Albert Speer, the Minister of Armaments and War Production, tried to organize the deployment of human resources more effectively from 1942 onwards, he found little support. The regional and police authorities were reluctant to accept national schemes that affected their regions, and having women in the workplace went against Hitler's idea that women should focus on *Kinder, Kirche, Küche* ('Children, Church, Kitchen'). Hitler also insisted that consumer goods production remain a priority, and so workers in non-essential industries could not be transferred.

Soviet Union

In the Soviet Union, the already centralized nature of the state allowed civilians to be mobilized effectively from the beginning. Coercion also played a key role. Workers were forced to move to those areas of the Soviet Union in which they were most needed, hours of work increased, and crash training programmes were developed to make up for the shortage of skilled labour. Slacking or absenteeism could be punished by labour camps or death.

Women made up most of the workforce, but also volunteered to serve in the armed forces. They joined the Red Army or the Red Air Force; the latter had three regiments (two bomber and one fighter) consisting entirely of women. They also played a vital role in the Red Cross and Red Crescent organizations, and in civil defence and fire-watching operations. Richard Overy calls the civilians of Russia the 'real heroes' of the Soviet Union's economic revival after the Nazi invasion, due to the appalling conditions in which many of them worked, suffering under long hours, poor nutrition and political scrutiny.

America

In America, women also played a key role in war industries, doing semi-skilled jobs such as crane operators, tool makers, shell loaders, aircraft makers and lumberjacks. An estimated 350,000 women also joined uniformed groups such as the Women's Army Auxiliary Corps, the Marine Corps Women's Reserve and the Navy Nurse Corps.

Japan

As in Germany, the Japanese government was reluctant to use women in the workforce, preferring to use conscript students rather than women. Though more than two and a half million extra women did enter the workforce between 1940 and 1945, a much larger number did not.

A poster of 'Rosie the Riveter', a fictional female worker used by the US government in a propaganda poster campaign to encourage women to join the war effort.

Resistance fighters

In all countries occupied by the Nazis, there were civilians who joined resistance groups. Also called partisans, they gathered intelligence for the Allies, used sabotage and murder against the occupiers, helped rescue shot-down Allied pilots or took Jews into safety. Their work was vital for the Allies, but extremely dangerous, as can be seen by the contents of this poster that was put up on the walls of the French city of Nantes in 1941: 'Cowardly criminals in the pay of England and Moscow have killed, by shooting in the back, the Field Commander of Nantes on the morning of 20 October 1941. In expiation for this crime I have already ordered that fifty hostages be shot … fifty more hostages will be shot if the guilty parties are not arrested by midnight 23 October 1941. I offer an award totalling 15 million francs to those citizens who contribute to the discovery of the guilty parties.'

STUDENT STUDY SECTION

Research activity

Research one resistance group from one of the following occupied countries: Denmark, France, Belgium, Norway, Holland. Find out how it was organized, its activities and to what extent it had an impact on the final defeat of the Germans.

The growth of government power

Britain

As in World War I, the British government extended its powers to cope with organizing its human and economic resources. Churchill formed a **coalition government** and exercised supreme political and military power. However, Ernest Bevin was able to get on with his job as Minister of Labour and National Service much more effectively than Albert Speer was able to perform a similar role under Hitler.

Mines, shipping and railways again came under state control. Rationing was introduced and, as we have seen, conscription for both men and women. Bevin also intervened extensively in the health and welfare of the nation, improving health care, setting up nurseries to look after children of working mothers, and making sure all factories employing more than 250 people had a canteen and a welfare officer. Bevin took the idea of national welfare still further by making special food rations and vitamin supplements available to young children and mothers, rationalizing the chaotic health system and ensuring that public transport became a public service rather than a private business. This programme was to lay the foundations for the legislation that set up the National Health Service and the Welfare State after World War II.

Germany

In Germany, a single-party state already existed. Yet German planning remained confused and decentralized. In 1942 Albert Speer was put in charge of the Central Planning Board and in 1944, Joseph Goebbels, the Propaganda Minister, was appointed Commissioner for Total Mobilization of Resources for War. Yet neither appointment overcame the problems of a system that was 'poorly co-ordinated, uncooperative and obstructive' (Overy, *Why the Allies Won*, 2006). Until 1943, Germany also focused on high quality and technical sophistication rather than trying to mass produce large quantities of standard weapons. It thus failed to produce weapons on a large enough scale and, as you have read, the Soviet Union, although having a smaller industrial base, greatly out-produced the German empire throughout the war.

Soviet Union

In the Soviet Union, the centralized all-powerful state already existed. Its survival after 1941 was due to careful planning and mass production, as well as the efforts of the Soviet people. The USSR was turned into Stalin's 'single war camp', where war production was the only priority. A single national war plan was drawn up in 1943 and the planners were given the powers for getting their objectives completed. Unlike in Germany, Soviet planners concentrated on large numbers of weapons to be produced as simply and quickly as possible.

USA

In the USA, the government also took control of industrial production. The War Production Board, which was established in January 1942, changed production priorities to the needs of the military. Thus car factories now produced tanks and planes. The War Commission recruited workers for where they were needed most and new industries were created, particularly for the production of synthetic materials. However, the USA mainly relied on American business, with its expertise in mass production and technical innovation, and it granted contracts out to the big industries to produce what was needed. Thus without changing the free-market nature of the American economy, the USA was able to expand its manufacturing capacity immensely, ending the war as the most powerful economy in the world.

Japan

Even before the attack on Pearl Harbor, the military government in Japan had strengthened its powers. In 1940, all the main political parties went into 'voluntary' dissolution, and in their place a monolithic party of national unity, the Imperial Rule Assistance Association, was set up. Trade unions were also closed down, being replaced with the Great Japan Patriotic Industrial Association, which included employers and workers. As in Germany, however, it was difficult for the government to maintain tight control of war production due to the independent positions of the *Zaibatsu* (big companies) and the rivalries between the army and the navy.

Propaganda

Propaganda remained a key weapon of all governments in attempting to win support for the war effort. Germany and the USSR already had propaganda machines in constant action, and these played a key role in convincing their populations of the justification of their actions. Goebbels stoked the German fear of communism in the East, and Stalin cleverly dubbed the war as the 'Great Patriotic War', in which defence of the 'motherland' rather than of the brutal communist state was to be the driving motivation of the people.

The Western democracies faced a problem in 1939 in that pacifism in Britain, and isolationism in the USA, were the main attitudes to a new war. The change in public opinion, however, came not so much from propaganda as the actions of the Axis powers. After the war scare in 1938, public opinion in Britain hardened and generally the British were ready for war by 1939 and determined to fight, though lacking the enthusiastic response of the soldiers of 1914. In America, it was the attack on Pearl Harbor and the German declaration of war that changed attitudes.

Propaganda nevertheless remained important to the governments of both countries, and was controlled by special offices – Churchill, for example, established the Political Warfare Executive. In America, the Office of War Information was set up to help Americans understand that the purpose of the war was to defend the national belief in freedom and liberty. Propaganda and censorship were used to help maintain morale, encourage civilians to be more thrifty, get women to work and, of course, to stress the evil nature of the enemy regime against which they were fighting.

To access worksheet 8.4 on propaganda and total war, please visit www.pearsonbacconline.com and follow the on-screen instructions.

STUDENT STUDY SECTION

Student activity

Look at the propaganda posters shown in this chapter. For each poster explain the message and how the message has been conveyed.

Research activity

Research the propaganda methods of Goebbels in Nazi Germany. What different types of propaganda were used? Give examples of each type. Which were the most effective?

Propaganda was also used directly in the fight against the Nazis. The radio was the most important weapon in this war. The BBC's news broadcasts came to be seen as reliable reports and were listened to in occupied countries to maintain morale and also to inform resistance movements.

British and American propaganda against the Japanese was very different to that used against the Germans. Whereas the propaganda against Germany stressed that the Nazis specifically were the evil enemy, not the whole German population, with Japan the attack was of an openly racial nature and aimed at all Japanese, not just the leaders. The attitude towards the Japanese was that they were primitive, uncivilized and very much inferior, also that they were treacherous and barbaric. The *Daily Mail* newspaper in Britain referred to a Japan that is 'dominated by a fanatical belief in the superiority of the Japanese race and its mission to spread the paternal rule of the divine Emperor … the natural outcome of a primitive tribalism which has persisted beneath the veneer of different cultures borrowed from other countries'. In cartoons they were portrayed as apes.

What is the message of this cartoon from the *Daily Mail*, 18 February 1942 (three days after the fall of British Singapore to the Japanese)?

Planning for essay writing on World War I and World War II

When going over the key features of World War II, it is helpful to compare them to World War I both to enhance your understanding and also to help prepare for comparative essays. The introduction to this chapter identified some differences between the two wars. From what you have now read, brainstorm further differences. You may want to copy out and fill in the grid below to help you work out the differences between the conflicts.

	World War I	World War II	Conclusions on similarities/ differences
Aims and ideologies			
Scope and scale of fighting in the war (also casualties)			
Strategy and tactics on land			
War at sea			
War in the air			
Impact on civilians			
Power of governments			

● **Examiner's hint**

You can address the first part of the question in your introduction. (Go back to Chapter 1 to remind yourself of the characteristics of total war.) You will need to keep coming back to your definition of total war throughout your essay. If you completed the mind map exercise on total war on p.61, this can help you with your essay planning, and it should give you the examples you need to support your definition. Don't forget that you can give examples from both the European and the Asian/Pacific wars.

Turn to Chapter 15, where you will find comparative questions on the two world wars. Try planning these essays in pairs using the grid above as a guide. Also try the following question using World War II:

Question

What do you understand by 'total war'? Chose one example of a 20th-century war to support your explanation.

© IBO 1997

THE CONSEQUENCES OF WORLD WAR II

9

As you read through this chapter, consider the following essay questions:
- Why did the USA and the USSR emerge as superpowers following World War II, and what impact did this have on Europe up to 1949?
- What were the effects of the war on Asia?

The impact of the war in Europe

Human cost

No other war has recorded such a loss of life in so short a time. Some estimates put the number of dead at more than 50 million, with nearly 40 million of them in Europe. As you have read in the section on total war in the previous chapter, the impact on civilians in this war was huge. Perhaps as many as two-thirds of the war dead were civilians, the most extreme example of this situation being Poland, which lost a fifth of its population, almost all of them civilians. In fact, in Europe only Germany and the UK suffered military losses significantly greater than civilian losses. America's casualties, meanwhile, were almost exclusively military.

	Mobilized (thousands)	Military killed (thousands)	Civilians killed (thousands)
Germany	11,000	3,250	700
Italy	4,500	330	500
Japan	6,095	1,700	360
British Empire	8,720	452	80
France	6,000	250	360
Poland	1,000	120	5,300
USSR	12,500	9,500	21,500 (est.)
USA	14,900	407	Small number
China	8,000	1,500	7,800
Total from above countries	72,715	17,509	36,600

◀ Military and civilian death toll in World War II.

The horror for civilians did not end with the conclusion of hostilities. More than 20 million people had been displaced during the course of the war, not just as a result of the fighting, but also due to the actions of different countries in expelling and deporting whole groups of people. Stalin and Hitler alone were responsible for the forced removals of some 30 million people.

In addition, many people were forced to move from their homes once the war was over. In German-speaking areas in Hungary, Romania and Poland, Germans were driven from their homes and forced to move to Germany, which at this time was a bombed ruin. This also happened in German lands taken at the end of the war by Russia and Poland. In all, between 1945 and 1947, approximately 16 million Germans were expelled from the countries of Central and Eastern Europe, and many died as a result of this flight to Western Europe. Thus, although the war was over, the suffering continued for many.

Economic cost

World War II was also much more devastating economically than World War I. Whereas in World War I the fighting had been limited to a relatively small area on the Western Front, in World War II the fighting took place over nearly all of Europe. Aerial bombing was particularly destructive. Very few cities of any size were left unscathed, and the result was millions of dead and homeless people. In addition, transport and communications had been seriously disrupted, industry destroyed and farmland ruined.

The consequences of this was that Europe was prostrate in 1945, with the 'victors' of the war (apart from the USA) emerging from the conflict almost as devastated as the losers. Food production had fallen to half pre-war production levels and 150 million people were dependent on some sort of relief food distribution during 1945–46. Britain was bankrupted by the war, and the Soviet economy suffered badly, with much of western Russia devastated and 25 million homeless.

Political consequences

At the conclusion of the First World War it was borders that were invented and adjusted, while people were on the whole left in place. After 1945 what happened was rather the opposite: with one major exception boundaries stayed broadly intact and people were moved instead.

From Tony Judt, *Postwar: A History of Europe Since 1945*, 2005

Compared with the peace settlement at Versailles, the boundary changes after World War II were relatively slight with the exception of Poland, which saw its border being shifted westwards – it lost 179,000 sq. km of land in the east and gained 104,000 sq. km from German territories.

Map showing the new borders of Poland after World War II.

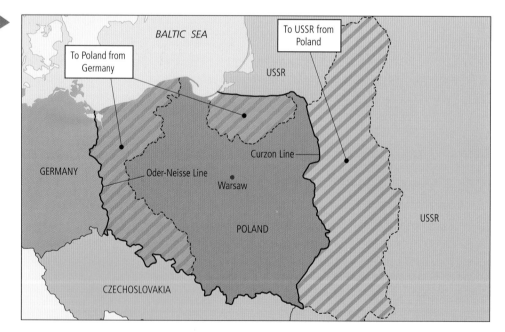

The new boundaries for Poland were decided at the Yalta Conference. There was no major treaty drawn up as there had been at Versailles in 1919, but the Allied leaders met twice in 1945 to make decisions about post-war Europe, first at Yalta in February, and then again at Potsdam in July.

Significantly, no treaty was signed concerning the future of Germany itself. Although it was agreed at the Yalta Conference in 1945 that Germany should be temporarily divided into

To access worksheet 9.1 on the Yalta Conference, please visit www. pearsonbacconline.com and follow the on-screen instructions.

four occupation zones, growing hostility between the Western Allies and the Soviet Union led to a permanent division of Germany by 1949. In addition, in all the countries that the Red Army had liberated – Poland, Hungary, Bulgaria and later Czechoslovakia – one-party regimes under Stalin's control had emerged by 1948, despite an agreement at Yalta that free elections would be allowed in all Eastern European states (see p.180).

Map showing when the Eastern European countries became communist after 1945.

STUDENT STUDY SECTION

Review question

Why was no peace treaty officially drawn up to end World War II?

The effects of the war on international relations
The USA and USSR emerge as superpowers

The most significant post-war development in international relations was the change in the balance of power. With some exceptions, such as Austria, the major powers before and after World War I were more or less the same. After World War II, however, the situation changed radically. American politician Dean Acheson wrote of the post-World War II situation: 'The whole world structure and order that we had inherited from the 19th century was gone.' The USSR and the USA emerged from World War II significantly more powerful than they had been before the war, while the 'old powers' of Britain and France emerged significantly weaker. Why was this?

Military reasons
- To defeat Germany, the USA had acquired the largest air force in the world, with almost 73,000 aircraft. By 1945, it also had 12 million men in the armed forces and more than 70,000 naval vessels. It also possessed the atomic bomb.
- To defeat Germany, the USSR had acquired the largest land army in the world.

- France and Britain's inability to defeat Germany had changed the balance of power. They had become 'second rank' powers. Without the USA and the USSR, there was no way that Britain could have defeated Germany on its own.
- The USSR now lacked any strong military neighbours. This made it a regional power.

Economic reasons

- The USA's economy was strengthened by the war. It was able to out-produce all the other powers put together.
- The USA was committed to more 'open' trade; its politicians and businessmen wanted to ensure liberal trade conditions and market competition prevailed. The USA was willing to play an active role in preventing the pre-war pattern of trade-blocs and tariffs re-emerging. The USA now took the lead in international collaboration through the **International Monetary Fund (IMF)** and **General Agreement on Tariffs and Trade (GATT).**
- The USA had the economic strength to prevent a return to instability in Europe.
- The small Eastern European countries that had been created by the Treaty of Versailles were not economically viable on their own; they needed the support of a stronger neighbour, and the USSR could replace Germany in this role.

Political reasons

- For the West, the ideals of democracy and international collaboration had triumphed over fascism. Thus the political system of the USA was the right path for the future.
- For the USSR, it was communism that had triumphed over fascism, and the Communist Party was given a new lease of life. Indeed, communism had widespread respect in Europe because of its part in resisting the Germans. Many of the earliest resistance movements in occupied Europe had been dominated by the communists, and immediately after war there were strong communist parties in several Western European states. Also, in Asia, communism filled the power vacuum left by the collapse of colonial empires.
- The USSR's huge losses and the role of the Red Army in defeating the Nazis gave Stalin a claim to a large role in forming the post-war world.
- The USSR had the political (as well as military) strength to prevent a return to instability in Eastern Europe. Communism could fill the political vacuum there.

STUDENT STUDY SECTION

Research activity

What actually is the definition of a 'superpower'? Who first used the term 'superpowers' and when? How far did the superpowers differ from the 'Great Powers' of pre-World War II Europe?

The impact of the superpowers

Given the new position of the USA and the USSR in 1945, and their relative strength compared to the weakened European countries, it is not surprising that they were to become the key players in setting up the post-war settlement of Europe. After 1945, at least until 1949, Europe continued to be at the heart of international relations, but now as the battleground between the USSR and the USA, as the two superpowers came into direct conflict over how the post-war settlement should be carried out. This tension developed into what became known as the 'Cold War'. The map of Europe after 1945 was determined by this growing conflict between the USSR and the USA, with a clear divide between Eastern and Western Europe. For the USA, this situation meant an end to isolationism and the beginning of a dominant role in world affairs.

The Cold War began where it had left off in 1941, with profound distrust of Soviet motives, and an ideological divide every bit as deep as that between liberalism and Nazism. Only two years after the end of the war the American Air Policy Commission reported to Truman that the essential 'incompatibility of East and West' called for the build-up of a 'devastating' force of bombers and missiles equipped with nuclear weapons capable of operation at a range of 5,000 miles. American strategists moved effortlessly from one Manichaean world to the next.

From Richard Overy, *Why the Allies Won,* 2006

Western Europe

One aspect of the developing Cold War was the intervention of the USA and the USSR in the economic recovery of Europe. With Western Europe's economic weakness translating into political weakness, the USA was forced to step in to provide economic aid. This took the form of the Marshall Plan in 1948; the USA was spurred into action to do this in order to prevent the weakened governments of France and Italy falling to communism. Thanks partly to the Marshall Plan, Western countries were able to implement necessary social changes and recover economically. In fact, in the 1950s and the 1960s, Western European countries enjoyed two decades of sustained economic growth.

With the elimination of fascism, Western Europe also saw the establishment of multi-party democracies, led for the most part by elder statesmen who had entered politics many decades before. Tony Judt explains this phenomenon:

The vogue between the wars had been for the new and the modern. Parliaments and democracies were seen by many – and not just Fascists and Communists – as decadent, stagnant, corrupt and in any case inadequate to the tasks of the modern state. War and occupation dispelled these illusions, for voters if not for intellectuals. In the cold light of peace, the dull compromises of constitutional democracy took on a new appeal. What most people longed for in 1945 was social progress and renewal, to be sure, combined with the reassurance of stable and familiar political forms. Where the First World War had a politically radicalising effect, its successor produced the opposite outcome; a deep longing for normality. Statesmen whose experience reached back beyond the troubled inter-war decades to the more settled and self-confident era before 1914 thus had a particular attraction… Whatever their party 'label', the elder statesmen of Europe were all, by 1945, sceptical, pragmatic practitioners of the art of the possible.

From Tony Judt, *Postwar: A History of Europe Since 1945,* 2005

STUDENT STUDY SECTION

Questions

1   How does Judt account for the political developments that took place in Europe after 1945?

2   According to Judt, what difference was there between the impact of World War I and World War II on political developments? Why do you think that there was this difference?

The 'social progress' that Judt mentions above took the form of new social legislation that revolutionized the role of the modern state and the expectations upon it. Every European country set up provision for a wide range of social services post-1945, though perhaps it was in Britain that the change in the role of the state was most marked. The election of 1945 swept out Churchill and the Conservative Party and returned the Labour Party led by Clement Attlee, which went on to establish the Welfare State, with care for the individual 'from the cradle to the grave'.

With Western and Eastern Europe divided economically, the traditional exchange between East and West was disrupted. On the other hand, the devastation of war and the communist

Marshall Plan

The Marshall Plan was an American economic aid programme for Europe. It was a response to the economic devastation of Europe after the war and the fact that the USA was aware that, without economic recovery, there was a danger that communist parties, already strong in France and Italy, would gain increasing support in Europe. The USSR refused to take part in the Plan, claiming that it was an attempt by the Americas to exercise 'dollar diplomacy' over Europe – establishing American economic domination. This helped to lead to the economic division of Europe as the USSR set up Comecon (see p.180).

threat led to a greater measure of economic cooperation in Western Europe than ever before, with the formation of the European Coal and Steel Community and ultimately the European Economic Community (**EEC**) in the 1950s.

Eastern Europe

Between 1944 and 1948, Stalin established control over Hungary, Czechoslovakia, East Germany, Romania and Poland. This involved:

- The establishment of one-party rule, including installation of national leaders dependent on the USSR.
- **Nationalization** of private enterprise.
- Establishment of Soviet-style Five Year Plans; heavy industry was encouraged and agriculture **collectivized**.

In addition, the USSR sought to integrate its economy with those of Eastern Europe to offset the weakness of industry and agriculture in the USSR. It established the Council for Mutual Economic Assistance (Comecon). Comecon was not a massive aid programme like the Marshall Plan, but more one of economic exploitation. Each **satellite state** had to produce what the USSR needed, e.g. Poland produced coal. The satellite states were not to cooperate economically with each other, however. This situation was one of exploitation for the satellite states, and it had disastrous effects on any attempts at economic modernization. There was not, therefore, the economic regeneration that Western Europe experienced. With no Marshall Plan, and with the priority of the USSR on heavy industry and the building of nuclear weapons, the citizens of both the Soviet Union and the satellite states suffered economic hardship in the next few decades.

This economic and political system was backed up by:

- Social and ideological controls, e.g. Cominform, secret police
- Censorship of all media
- Suppression of religious freedom
- Military presence of Soviet troops
- Political purges.

Conclusions on the effect of the war in Europe

By 1949, a remarkable symmetry had emerged in Europe, with the political, economic and military division of the continent. The Western bloc under the domination of the USA had a common political philosophy – democracy – and commitment by the USA, through the '**Truman Doctrine**', to its defence. The Western states were tied to the USA and to each other economically via Marshall Aid and the EEC, and by 1949 had a military alliance in the North Atlantic Treaty Organization (**NATO**). Similarly, the Soviet Bloc comprised communist states, members of a joint ideological organization called the Communist Information Bureau (Cominform); they supposedly had an organization for economic cooperation in Comecon and were 'protected' by Soviet forces (the Warsaw Pact, a communist version of NATO, was established in 1955).

STUDENT STUDY SECTION
Review questions
1   What was the effect of the war on the following: a) the international status of Britain and France; b) the international status of the USA and USSR?
2   Why did distrust start to develop between the USA and the USSR after 1945?
3   What impact did these changes have on international relations?

4 What were the key economic effects of the war? How did the economic situation of Europe change between 1945 and 1950?

5 What political, economic and social differences developed between Western European countries and Eastern European countries?

Discussion/essay question

Compare and contrast the differences in the impact of World War I on Europe from the impact of World War II on Europe.

IBLP link – Caring

Read the extract below, which is taken from George Marshall's speech that he gave at Harvard University on 5 June 1947 setting out the aims of and the conditions attached to Marshall Aid:

Its purpose should be the revival of a working economy in the world so as to permit the emergence of political and social conditions in which free institutions can exist. Such assistance, I am convinced, must not be on a piecemeal basis as various crises develop. Any assistance that this Government may render in the future should provide a cure rather than a mere palliative. Any government that is willing to assist in the task of recovery will find full co-operation I am sure, on the part of the United States Government. Any government which maneuvers to block the recovery of other countries cannot expect help from us. Furthermore, governments, political parties, or groups which seek to perpetuate human misery in order to profit therefrom politically or otherwise will encounter the opposition of the United States.

Could the response of the Americans to the economic situation in Western Europe be seen as 'caring' as defined in the IBLP?

The impact of World War II in Asia

The casualties of war and the extent of destruction were also huge in Asia; China had lost about 12 million people (some historians claim the toll was actually as high as 20 million), and Japan had lost more than two million people.

Japan

Japan was eliminated as a major power in Asia. It was occupied by the Americans under the leadership of General Douglas MacArthur, who was appointed Supreme Commander of the Allied Powers (SCAP). Unlike Germany, where the occupying forces assumed direct control due to the fact that the government had completely collapsed, SCAP was able to rule indirectly in a supervisory rule. With the Emperor endorsing the process, MacArthur presided over a set of dramatic reforms. These turned Japan into a democratic state. The military and secret police forces were dissolved; anyone who had played a part in 'Japanese aggression or militarism' was purged from political office and industry; a new constitution was introduced that stated 'the Japanese people forever renounce war as a sovereign right' and declared that 'land, sea and air forces, as well as other war potential, will never be maintained'. It also established protection for a wide range of human rights. The Emperor, however, remained; MacArthur believed that he would help maintain political stability and facilitate reform.

The Treaty of San Francisco

As we have seen, no peace treaty was signed with Germany at the end of the war. A peace treaty with Japan, however, was finally signed in 1951 – the Treaty of San Francisco. There were many problems in devising a treaty acceptable to everyone, especially with the development of the Cold War. The USSR raised many objections during the treaty meetings, seeing it as favouring Japan's relationship with America; the Soviets refused to sign it, along with Poland and Czechoslovakia. Neither the People's Republic of China on the mainland nor the Republic of China on Taiwan were invited to the peace conference; neither were North and South Korea. India and Burma refused to participate. The Philippines, though present, neither signed nor ratified the treaty until after it became effective, while Indonesia signed but never ratified it. In total, 49 of the participating 51 nations did sign the treaty.

Under the terms of this treaty, Japan:
- Renounced all claims to Taiwan, Sakhalin and the Kuriles
- Handed over the Pacific Islands of Micronesia (which had been given to Japan as a mandate after World War I) to be administered under a United Nations trusteeship
- Handed over the Ryuku and Bonin Islands to the USA (though Japan still had a claim on these islands)
- Accepted the judgments of the International Military Tribunal for the Far East and of other Allied war crimes courts both within and outside Japan, and agreed to carry out the sentences imposed thereby upon Japanese nationals imprisoned in Japan (see below).

The document further set guidelines for repatriation of and compensation to prisoners of war, and renounced future military aggression under the guidelines set by the UN Charter. The document nullified prior treaties and set out the framework for Japan's current status of retaining a military that is purely defensive in nature. No reparations were demanded, but Japan was to help rehabilitate countries that had suffered damage because of the Japanese occupation.

As with West Germany, Japan was to become allied to the Western powers, and was to become economically strong and politically stable. It also became an important military and strategic base for the USA in its fight against communism in Asia. On the same day that the San Francisco Treaty was signed, Japan and the USA also concluded a separate Security Treaty in which the USA promised to defend Japan until it could look after its own defence; this meant that the USA kept military bases in Japan.

STUDENT STUDY SECTION

Review question

What similarities and differences can you see between the Treaty of Versailles signed with Germany at the end of World War I, and the Treaty of San Francisco, signed with Japan at the end of World War II?

China

In China, fighting continued between the nationalist forces of Jiang Jieshi and the communist forces of Mao Zedong. The conflict led to the victory of Mao in 1949 and the establishment of a communist China. For the USA, this turn of events served to widen the fight against communism from Europe to Asia.

Decolonization: the decline of European influence in Asia

The weakness of Britain and France meant that they found it increasingly difficult to hold on to their empires in Asia (and Africa). Their position of superiority and invincibility had in any case been seriously weakened by defeats inflicted on them by Japan during the course of the war. Nationalist movements, such as that led by Ho Chi Minh in Vietnam, also grew in strength during their fight against the Japanese. Condemnation of imperialism by the USA and the UN also weakened the moral arguments for having an empire.

Thus although the Europeans tried to return, they found their old colonies unwilling to submit and, after bloody struggles, the Dutch recognized the independence of Indonesia and the French were defeated in Vietnam in 1954, and thus forced to give up Indochina. Meanwhile, Britain left India in 1947 and Burma and Ceylon in 1948. As with Europe, Asia was to become part of the Cold War as the USA and the USSR sought to increase their spheres of influence in this area.

Other effects of the war

The establishment of war tribunals

Tribunals were set up to try war criminals in both Europe and Asia. The Nuremberg Tribunal sat between November 1945 and October 1946. Such a trial was unique in history. Twenty-one leading Nazis were charged with war crimes and crimes against humanity. In Japan, General MacArthur carried out trials against war criminals and 28 of Japan's leaders were tried before an International Tribunal in Tokyo. Over a six-year period, 5,700 Japanese war criminals were tried before Allied tribunals and about 1,000 were executed.

The United Nations

World War II, like World War I, saw the emergence of an international organization, the United Nations, which again largely came about through US initiative. The UN was intended to be more effective in peacekeeping than the League of Nations had been, but with the onset of the Cold War and the possession of the veto in the Security Council by the USA and the USSR, the UN found itself marginalized in the superpower conflicts that dominated international politics after 1945.

The arms race

With the US invention of the atomic bomb, and its use on Japan in 1945, an arms race became central to the Cold War, with the main focus on the development and acquisition of nuclear weapons. Thus the world now existed under the threat of total destruction, though the horrendous implications of using these weapons also acted as a deterrent to the USA and the USSR fighting each other directly. Although the level of tension in 1946–50 was much greater than that after World War I, no direct war between the major powers resulted.

French Indochina
Ho Chi Minh, a communist who had led Vietnamese guerrillas against the Japanese, declared Vietnam to be an independent state after the Japanese had left in 1945. However, the French reoccupied their old colony of Indochina – which included Vietnam, Laos and Cambodia. The guerrilla fighting force of the Viet Minh thus fought the French, finally defeating them in an open battle at Dien Bien Phu in 1954. As a result, the French left Indochina.

Leading Nazis appear before the international court at the Nuremberg Trials.

To access worksheet 9.2 on the United Nations, please visit www.pearsonbacconline.com and follow the on-screen instructions.

STUDENT STUDY SECTION

Review questions

What was the impact of World War II on the following:
- The popularity and spread of communism?
- The defeated powers – Germany and Japan?

Working on your essay introductions

After having worked through this chapter, it should be possible now to attempt the essay set at the beginning: 'Why did the USA and the USSR emerge as superpowers following World War II?'

One of the key parts of an essay is the introduction. Refer back to the essay planning guidelines at the end of Chapter 2 and check what should be included in a good introduction. Then have a look at the introductions below and discuss which you think is the best one and why. Which bits of the introduction work well? How could each one be improved?

Introduction 1

A superpower is a country that has economic, political and military superiority over countries and therefore the ability to have worldwide influence. Both the USA and the USSR were able to fulfil these criteria after World War II. By 1945, they had overtaken France and Britain as the key players in international events and this essay will look at the military, political and economic reasons for this changed international situation.

Introduction 2

Following World War II, America and the USSR emerged as superpowers and went on to dominate world affairs for the next fifty years. The reasons for this lie in the events of World War II which I shall explain in this essay.

Introduction 3

The world that emerged after World War II was very different from that of 1939. The 'Great Powers' of France and Britain, who had been the key players in the 1919 settlement, were now weakened and were seen as second-rate powers. The USA and USSR had played the key roles in the defeat of Germany and now emerged as 'superpowers' in the post-war world, with military, political and economic influence outside their own borders. Why was this?

Review and research

Question

What was the impact of World War I and World War II on the roles and status of women?

Using the information in the last few chapters, copy out the following grid and complete it. Give specific examples where possible as to how the situation for women varied from country to country. You may want to research this topic further.

	Political situation	Economic situation	Social situation	Military situation
During World War I				
Change as a result of World War I				
During World War II				
Change as a result of World War II				

Refer to Chapter 15 to see examples of essay questions in which you could use this information.

LIMITED WAR CASE STUDY 1: THE MALVINAS/FALKLANDS WAR (1982)

The RFA *Sir Galahad* burns fiercely after being hit by multiple Argentine bombs on 8 June 1982 off Fitzroy, East Falkland. A total of 50 men were killed or missing in the incident.

Although there was no official declaration of war, Britain and Argentina went to war over the Falkland Islands/Malvinas in 1982. This conflict has been termed as one of the most 'unexpected wars' of the 20th century; 30,000 men fought over a remote group of islands with only 2,000 inhabitants. Both sides fought a *limited* war.

As you read through this chapter, consider the following essay questions:
- Why did war break out over the Malvinas/Falkland Islands in 1982?
- In what ways was this war a 'limited war', and why did Britain win the war?
- What were the key results of the Malvinas/Falklands war?

Timeline of events – 1828–1982

1828 First recorded Argentine settlement in Malvinas

1833 British take islands to prevent possible American seizure, and send Argentines back to mainland

1964 Falklands position is debated at the UN Committee on Decolonization

1977 In November, Argentine naval manoeuvres provoke British naval response

1979 Margaret Thatcher becomes Prime Minister in Britain

1981		In December, Leopoldo Galtieri takes power in Argentina in a military coup
1982	19 Mar	Argentines land at Leith Harbour, South Georgia, and raise an Argentine flag
	2 Apr	Beginning of Operation *Rosario*: Argentine forces invade Falklands
	3 Apr	UN Security Council Resolution 502 demands cessation of hostilities and withdrawal of all Argentine forces from Falklands. Britain announces Task Force to be sent to retake islands
	7 Apr	Britain declares Maritime Exclusion Zone (MEZ) of 200 nautical miles (321km) around Falklands
	19 Apr	Argentina rejects US Secretary of State Alexander Haig's peace proposal
	28 Apr	Britain establishes a Total Exclusion Zone (TEZ) around the Falkland Islands
	2 May	Submarine HMS *Conqueror* sinks battlecruiser *General Belgrano*, killing 323 Argentines
	4 May	British destroyer HMS *Sheffield* is sunk by an Exocet missile, with loss of 20 crew
	7 May	TEZ extended to within 19km of Argentine coastline. UN Secretary General announces peace initiative
	20 May	UN peace initiative breaks down, ending any real hope of diplomatic resolution
	21 May	British troops land at San Carlos Bay on East Falkland
	23 May	British frigate *Antelope* hit by Argentine bombs and later sinks
	23–24 May	Air attacks lead to heavy losses for Argentines
	25 May	HMS *Coventry* and *Atlantic Conveyor* sunk, the latter by an Exocet missile
	28 May	Battles for Darwin and Goose Green
	3 Jun	Bluff Cove and Fitzroy occupied by British troops. Versailles Summit opens. President Reagan presents five-point peace plan to British
	8 Jun	British landing craft *Sir Galahad* and *Sir Tristram* bombed
	11 Jun	Naval bombardment of Stanley; three islanders killed
	13–14 Jun	Second phase of attack on Port Stanley
	14 Jun	Brigadier-General Mario Menéndez surrenders all Argentine forces in East and West Falklands
	20 Jun	British forces declare end to hostilities
	12 Jul	Britain announces hostilities over the Falklands are regarded as ended. Argentina makes no statement
	22 Jul	TEZ lifted

Long-term causes of the Falklands War

The Falkland Islands as the British call them, or the Malvinas as they are known to the Argentines, are a group of 780 islands in the South Atlantic. The two main islands, West and East Falklands, are approximately 500km off the east coast of Argentina, and 13,000km from Britain. A war between Argentina and Britain was 'unexpected', as they had enjoyed close relations for many years. Indeed, Britain was Argentina's largest buyer of agricultural produce. In any case, Argentina did not pose a clear threat to Britain as it was relatively isolated, and it had not been to war since the 19th century. Britain was a nuclear power (Argentina was not) and a member of the UN Security Council and NATO. Neither country had any clear economic or strategic reasons to go to war over these remote islands, whose economy was primarily based on sheep farming (there were 60,000 sheep). In addition, the Falklands were a remnant of the old British Empire, which had been in steady decline since World War II.

Legacy of colonialism

The dispute over the Falklands/Malvinas began more than 150 years before the outbreak of the war itself. Britain had become an ally of Argentina in their long war of independence against Spain. After Argentina had declared itself independent in 1816, the British invested greatly in the country. Many British people went to live in Argentina, and relations between the two countries were good. However, there was one key area of tension – the Falklands. Argentina had laid claim to these islands in 1820, but Britain occupied and controlled them from 1833, and by 1885, there was a British community of around 1,800 people on the islands. In line with the broader expansion of the Empire, the British gave the Falklands colonial status in 1892. The Argentines continued to claim the islands were theirs.

Following World War II, the European empires began to collapse. Argentina pressurized the UN for the Malvinas to become an 'issue of decolonization' when it became a member state of the UN after the war. Their lobbying paid off. In 1964, the Falklands position was debated at the UN Committee on Decolonization. Argentine claims were based on historical papal records from the time of Spanish and Portuguese colonial rule, and they claimed that British colonial claims were illegitimate. Britain based its claim on its history of effective and continuous administration of the islands since 1833, and its determination to give the islanders self-determination as recognized in the UN Charter. Britain claimed that Argentine control would not end colonial rule, but *create* a colonial situation, as the islanders did not want to be ruled by Argentina. In 1965, the General Assembly of the UN passed Resolution 2065, which called for negotiations between Britain and Argentina. These discussions were still ongoing in February 1982.

In 1982, there were more British people living in Argentina than in the Falklands. To most commentators in the two decades leading up to the outbreak of war, the Falklands meant nothing to the British, but they meant everything to the Argentines. Indeed, the Argentine public had been taught in school as part of the core curriculum that the islands were rightfully theirs. In contrast, at the beginning of the crisis that led to war in 1982, John Nott, the Secretary for Defence in Britain, had to refer to a globe to see where they were. They had no economic or strategic value. There was only limited interest from the British in defending this territory, and in talks it was clear to the Argentines that the British wanted to hand them over. But there was one fundamental block to handing them over – the Falkland islanders wanted to remain British.

Short-term causes of the Falklands War

Economic issues

In the early 1980s, the military regime in Argentina had serious economic problems. It had cut **public sector** spending and tried to revive the **private sector**, but these measures had not worked and attempts to redress them made matters worse. There were similar economic problems in Margaret Thatcher's Britain. Some of the worst rioting in England in the 20th century raged through cities nine months before the outbreak of war, and unemployment had risen above three million for the first time since the Great Depression of the 1930s. Thus it could be argued that both regimes desired a foreign policy distraction from their domestic economic problems.

Political issues

General Leopoldo Galtieri had come to power in Argentina in a military coup in December 1981. In the late 1970s, the army had murdered thousands of people in what was know as the 'dirty war', and this period had been followed by a military coup in

Leopoldo Galtieri

Margaret Thatcher

1976. There followed a series of military **juntas**, and Galtieri's regime had continued the oppressive leadership of its predecessors. Many international observers believed Galtieri and his junta to be a 'fascist style dictatorship'. He was under pressure from the military for a political success to galvanize the regime and to bring about some degree of political stability.

Margaret Thatcher became Britain's first female Prime Minister in the general election of 1979. She lacked authority over her own Conservative Party, and before the outbreak of the Falklands War had been one of the most unpopular Prime Ministers in British history. She, like Galtieri, stood to benefit politically from a foreign policy victory. In addition, she relished her reputation as the 'Iron Lady', a name given to her by the Soviets. A crisis over British territory would be an opportunity for her to live up to this image.

Before Thatcher came to power, the British Foreign Office had decided that the islanders' interests lay in handing the islands over to the Argentines. To encourage agreement from the Falkland islanders themselves, Britain limited investment and agreed that the only flights to and from the island would be dependent on Argentina. The Falkland Islands Company, however, was controlled by the British company Coalite, and this company had political power. They were determined to prevent a handover. Their viewpoint gained more support during the 1970s when the 'dirty war' took hold of Argentina.

There had been deliberate neglect of the islands… What … was clear was they wanted me to win the confidence of the islanders so that they could sell them down the river to Argentina, because the Foreign Office regarded it as an anachronism.

Sir Rex Hunt, governor of the Falkland Islands at the time of the Argentine invasion in 1982

It has been argued that the war was caused by a breakdown in communication between the politicians and statesmen. Indeed, the British Foreign Secretary at the time, Lord Carrington, accepted responsibility for the crisis that led to war and resigned. Carrington believed that the war could have been averted if the political regimes in Britain and Argentina had not misread the situation. The British had thought Argentina was militarily posturing to toughen its position in negotiations. They had done this on and off for over 20 years. The Argentines did not think that Britain would go to war over the Malvinas, as the regime did not understand the dynamics of the democratic party political system, which would pretty much ensure a forceful response from Thatcher.

Military causes

The desire to reclaim the Malvinas was strong throughout Argentina, but it was most important to the military and in particular the Argentine Navy. The military-led junta that had seized power in November 1976 was determined to test Britain's commitment to the Falklands. In November 1977, they conducted provocative naval manoeuvres, but the British responded forcefully by sending a submarine and two frigates to the South Atlantic. This was sufficient to make the Argentines back down.

Significantly, British policy over the Falklands seemed confused; although talks had stalled, the British seemed to be giving signals that they would not be willing to protect the islands militarily. The results of a significant Defence Review in Britain had recommended the selling off of around one-third of the Royal Navy's surface fleet. There were even rumours that the Royal Marines, one of Britain's most elite forces, were to be abolished.

Immediate causes of the Falklands War

Military causes: the role of the navies

Both the British and Argentine navies could be held responsible for the immediate causes of the Falklands War. Indeed, Galtieri's coup had been supported by the commander-in-chief of the Argentine Navy, Admiral Jorge Anaya, allegedly on the premise that Galtieri would back naval plans to remove Britain from the Malvinas. Admiral Anaya applied pressure on Galtieri for an invasion. In Britain, it was the key representative from the Royal Navy, Sir Henry Leach, who suggested to Margaret Thatcher that Britain was capable of retaking the Falklands. However, he was not necessarily encouraging Thatcher to go to war, and it should be borne in mind that by this point Argentina had already invaded the islands.

In Britain, John Nott's defence cuts had fallen particularly heavily on the Royal Navy. A large surface fleet seemed to have become obsolete in the context of the Cold War. A war with the USSR would be fought for only a week, it was estimated, before nuclear weapons were used. In addition, as was later shown in the conflict, surface ships were vulnerable to air and submarine attacks. Thus in the deep recession of the early 1980s, Nott reasoned that expenditure on the navy could be cut.

The Argentine Navy had two plans to take back the Malvinas: the first was to set up an Argentine presence on South Georgia (an island approximately 1,400km from the Falklands), called Project Alpha, the second was for a full-scale invasion, Operation *Azul*. The invasion was scheduled for some time between the end of May and mid July, after the removal of HMS *Endurance*, as this would limit the British resistance. It is argued by Duncan Anderson, in *The Falklands War 1982*, that the British decision to withdraw the *Endurance* was a key factor in the Argentine junta's decision to attack the Falklands.

In December 1981, Project Alpha had begun; the Argentine Navy had landed 42 'workers' at Leith on the north-west coast of South Georgia. By March 1982 the British had become concerned at their presence, and their refusal to comply with entry procedures. The British then sent *Endurance* back to South Georgia, to remove the Argentines from Leith if necessary. Due to bad weather, the *Endurance* took four days to return, and during this time the British press had started rumours of an imminent war over the Falklands, and suggested that the *Endurance* would soon be joined by nuclear submarines.

Admiral Anaya convinced the Argentine junta that reports in the British media about nuclear submarines being sent to defend the islands were right, and that the invasion must start before the British could get forces to the region. A modified plan, *Rosario*, was drawn up, and on 28 March an invasion force headed for the Malvinas. This force comprised an ex-American tank landing ship, 20 US-built landing vehicles and 900 troops, and was supported by two destroyers and two frigates. To the north of this force was an aircraft carrier and the rest of the Argentine navy.

HMS *Endurance*
Endurance was a Class 1 Icebreaker, and its mission was to patrol and survey the Antarctic and South Atlantic. Its role was also to maintain a physical British presence in the area and to defend British interests.

The invasion

On 2 April 1982, the Argentines began their attack on the capital of the Falklands/Malvinas. Stanley became a battle-ground for a few hours until the defenders ran out of ammunition. Under a bombardment from the Argentines, and with Argentine troops being landed by helicopters, the local British commanders ordered their men to cease fire.

STUDENT STUDY SECTION

Review questions

1   How legitimate were a) the British and b) the Argentine claims to sovereignty over the Falklands/Malvinas?

2   What role did 'historical and cultural' factors play in the development of the crisis in 1982?

Failure of diplomacy

War was not inevitable at this point, even though British territory had been invaded. Indeed, the British analysis of the situation was that a war waged 13,000km from home, in difficult weather conditions, against a well-equipped and locally based adversary, would be incredibly challenging. It seemed that the best response was a diplomatic one.

Margaret Thatcher, however, was worried that the press and the public would be outraged by the Argentine aggression and would not be satisfied with anything less than a military response. This response could threaten her government, and in particular her position as Prime Minister. Although most of her advisers warned against a military campaign to retake the Falklands, the Chief of Defence was away, and in his place the First Sea Lord, Admiral Leach, persuaded Thatcher that it would be possible to win a war in the South Atlantic. In addition, he suggested that she had no other option; Britain's reputation and standing in the world were at stake.

Within hours of the Argentine landings in Stanley, the Ministry of Defence began to prepare British sailors, marines, soldiers and air personnel for war on the other side on the Atlantic. The British armed forces assembled a massive naval Task Force, which rapidly prepared for deployment to the South Atlantic. From this point on, military timetables rather than diplomatic meetings were guiding events. The new Foreign Secretary, Francis Pym, and the American Secretary of State, Alexander Haig, worked for a peaceful resolution.

Diplomatically, the British concentrated on isolating the Argentines and argued that they were in the wrong, as they were the 'aggressors'. The Foreign Office was able to apply years of experience to initiate a coherent international response, unlike the uncoordinated attempts by the Argentines. The British ambassador to the UN pushed through Security Council Resolution 502, which called for the immediate withdrawal of Argentine forces from the islands. On the same day, 3 April, the British got the French to agree to stop the export of Exocet anti-ship missiles, Super Etendard aircraft (which could be used for launching the Exocets) and engines for Pucara aircraft, which would impede Argentina's ability to wage war. Six days later, the EEC imposed a trade embargo.

The key diplomatic effort for both Argentina and Britain was to get the support of the USA. Galtieri's regime had gambled on some American support for Argentina, as he had a relatively close relationship with certain members of the US military. However, American support for Britain was almost inevitable due to the nature of the Cold War and the fact that Britain was a more important ally in the broader context.

The crisis intensifies

Although the crisis was intensifying, there was still hope that the mobilization and departure of the British Task Force would be a sufficient threat to Galtieri to force the Argentines to negotiate. The British carriers *Hermes* and *Invincible* set sail on 5 April, and these were followed by the departure of other ships, all of which were highly publicized in the media – the Task Force consisted of two aircraft carriers, five destroyers, 11 frigates, and three **nuclear submarines**. To a certain extent this show of force had the desired effect, and there was alarm in Argentina at the scale of the British preparations for war. The Argentines responded with a build-up of forces under the command of General Mario Menéndez, who had arrived in the Malvinas to take on the role of governor.

STUDENT STUDY SECTION

Review activity and document analysis

Document A

"I see! We're strong enough to blow the world to bits, but not strong enough to remove ten Argentinians salvaging bits of scrap ... "

'I see! We're strong enough to blow the world to bits, but not strong enough to remove ten Argentinians salvaging bits of scrap ... ' Cartoon by Michael Cummings, *Daily Express*, 31 March 1982. The missiles have the names of Soviet cities on them. The scroll reads: 'Falklands Crisis: Invasion by Argentine scrap dealers'.

Questions

1 What is Michael Cummings' message in the cartoon above?

2 British foreign policy was focused on a potential conflict with the USSR, conflict at home with the Irish Republican Army (IRA) in Northern Ireland, and instability in the Middle East. How far do you agree that the British apparent lack interest in the Falklands had led to the crisis?

Document B

In March 1976 there had been a coup in Argentina which paved the way for the most repressive dictatorship of the century in our country: a total of 10,000 disappeared, and that's a conservative estimate – it may have been about 30,000. This coup, like all the others in our country, at first had the support of the conservative classes. But that began to wane as the military government failed in everything and as the human rights abuses came to light.

To try and save face, they did something which they thought would generate popular support – they invaded the Falklands…

I spent many years studying the nationalistic content of educational textbooks and the doctrines which generated those texts. And it's very clear from those texts how we got the idea of the sovereignty of Argentina over the Falklands. The notion that right was on our side was absolutely irrefutable and nobody could reasonably doubt it, nobody could doubt the idea that the United States had to be on our side and that we would defeat Great Britain if the US didn't back her. Such naivety.

Argentine historian, Carlos Escudé, quoted on BBC website on the 25th anniversary of the Falklands War

Document C

Argentina wanted to occupy in order to negotiate, and the forces that were to accompany me were not meant to be more than 500 men. But we did not foresee a war.

Mario Benjamin Menéndez, commander of the occupying Argentine forces, and military governor of the islands, in an interview with a BBC correspondent, quoted on BBC website on the 25th anniversary of the Falklands War

Questions

1. Why did Argentina invade the Falklands/Malvinas in 1982 according to a) the Argentine historian Carlos Escudé, and b) General Mario Menéndez?

2. With reference to their origin and purpose, how useful is a) Document B and b) Document C for an historian analyzing Argentine motives behind the war?

Brinkmanship

Both sides in the crisis were engaged in a dangerous game of 'brinkmanship' or 'bluff'. The Argentine junta continued to believe that the British military response was a bluff until the end of April 1982, and the British too thought that Galtieri had gone too far with the posturing pursued by the Argentines for 25 years. Both ultimately believed that there would be a diplomatic resolution. On 24 April, the Argentine Foreign Minister Costa Méndez arrived in the United States to review a new peace proposal drawn up by Pym and Haig. Méndez rejected the plan. Peru, a supporter of Argentina, then took up the peace initiatives, but by this point the British Task Force had almost arrived in the Falklands.

The tension increased on 28 April when Britain announced a Total Exclusion Zone (TEZ) of 200 nautical miles (370 km) around the Falklands, which would come into effect as of 11.00am on 30 April. On 2 May, the British nuclear submarine HMS *Conqueror* sank the Argentine cruiser *General Belgrano* (see below for details). There could be no diplomatic solution now. Even though there was no declaration of war, Britain and Argentina were at war over the Falklands.

The route of the British Task Force to the Falklands, April 1982.

The British Exclusion Zone, with the position of the *General Belgrano* on her sinking, 2 May 1982.

Why did the search for peace fail?

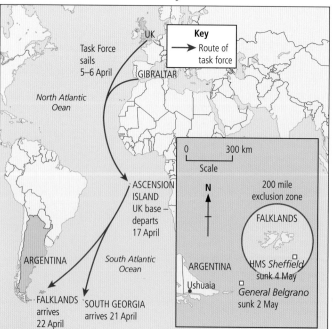

The Argentine government was not willing to negotiate for anything less than sovereignty, and the British position was similarly uncompromising. Argentina claimed the islands had been taken 'without a shot being fired' and the crowds that had gathered on the streets of Buenos Aires chanted 'Malvinas Argentina'. Argentina declared that they did not have to explain bringing about the end to the 'illegitimate British occupation of their islands'. At the UN, the Argentines defended the invasion as part of the decolonization process, saying they had 'just reclaimed their own land'.

Despite the shuttle diplomacy of Haig, and attempts by the UN to secure a diplomatic resolution to the crisis, neither side would retreat from its stated aim: to restore complete British/Argentine sovereignty to the islands. The UN could not send in a peacekeeping force until both sides had asked them to do so. The British government declared a broader aim as hostilities increased – the aim of upholding the principle that 'naked aggression by anybody should not be allowed to pay'. The Argentines dismissed this stance as an old-fashioned 'preservation of empire'. However, they had broken the international rule of law with their invasion of the Falklands/Malvinas, and this fact was recognized by the UN.

Course of the war

It was a 'clean' war, in which both sides sought to avoid civilian casualties and respected the rights of prisoners – indeed scrupulous respect for the rules of war meant that the British refused to interrogate captured Argentine officers about the very dirty war that they had conducted against civilians in their country... The war was fought by a small professional force, one of the many respects in which it differed from the Normandy landing.

Commander Sandy Woodward, commander of the British Task Force

The nature of the Falklands War was *limited* for a number of reasons. Britain had one of the largest navies in NATO and thus it was obviously capable of retaking the islands, but it was only willing to do so at a limited cost. The British government did not believe that the British people would support a war if there were high casualties.

At the outset, theoretically, the Argentines seemed to have many advantages over the British. They had much shorter communication and supply lines, an air force that could be operational from the mainland and time to build their defensive positions on the Falkland Islands before the British arrived. The British appeared to have some serious military obstacles. The first of these was actually getting their fleet to the South Atlantic and preventing a single attack taking out too many troops, as the fleet was vulnerable to anti-ship missiles. In addition, coordination was difficult between different elements of the Task Force and there was friction between navy, army and air force.

The Argentine war plan was to defend their position on the Falklands primarily by using their air force to cripple the Task Force before it could land troops on the islands. The British plan was first to gain control of the air and sea around the Falkland Islands, and then to make an amphibious landing of ground forces. Both sides knew that the only way to win back the Falklands was to win back the land. The British ships were in two groups. The group to the south was Commander Woodward's naval fleet, which was the advance force. This comprised two aircraft carriers and assorted warships. The objective of the first group was to gain air and sea superiority, and then the second group of ships would be able to land their troops for the land campaign.

The fighting focused on the two main islands – East and West Falkland – each only around 80km long. By the end of April 1982, the new Argentine governor and commander of the Malvinas was General Menéndez. He had 13,000 troops massed on the islands, with major concentrations on West Island, at Goose Green, and 10,000 in the hills to the west of Stanley on East Island. These hills would be Menéndez's last line of defence. Nevertheless, the Argentine plan was not to use these ground forces but to neutralize the Task Force at sea.

War in the air

The first battle of the Falklands War was in the air. The Argentine Air Force was well trained, with high-performance fighter-bombers, and these could be deployed from their bases on the mainland. Britain's first aim was to win air superiority, but it could only use the amount of aircraft they could take on their two aircraft carriers. This meant Britain had 34 planes to fight nearly 100 Argentine fighters. These planes also had the job of protecting

The Sea Harrier, the main fixed-wing carrier aircraft of the British during the Falklands War.

the fleet, and once they had control of the air they were to cover the amphibious landings. The British air force had to accomplish all this from the very restrictive confines of the aircraft carriers.

On 1 May 1982, the air battle began. Although the British were outnumbered, they had one key advantage in the new Sea Harrier planes. The Sea Harrier had not been combat tested, but it could take off and land vertically and operate from short runways. As the air battle developed, the Harriers demonstrated that they were both versatile and reliable. These jets were armed with the latest Sidewinder air-to-air heat-seeking missiles. On the first day alone, four Argentine planes were shot down by Sidewinders. It soon became clear that the British Harriers were destroying the Argentine Air Force. Using an effective combination of electronic warfare, Sea Harriers, surface-to-air missiles and anti-aircraft artillery, the British navy destroyed more than half of Argentina's 134 combat aircraft. The Harriers were the key to Britain's war. Argentina's Mirage planes were now cut off from the islands to enforce the exclusion zone in the air.

Yet the British fleet remained vulnerable, with the Argentines still able to fly from their mainland bases, and if the carriers were lost Britain would not be able to continue to fight. The Argentines used air attacks from the mainland on the British throughout the war.

War at sea

As the war continued in the air, the focus then shifted to the sea. The way the war at sea was fought was altered by the impact of new technology; battles would be fought using deadly missiles, including the ship-to-ship or air-launched Exocet missiles. The ability of the British to engage in the war at sea was limited by the fact that their nearest base, Ascension Island, was 5,300km away. It was vital for Britain that it protect its two aircraft carriers. If they were sunk, Britain's ability to wage an air war would collapse. In this way, the war could be lost in a day if the carriers were taken out.

On 1 May, Britain's main sea force was 160km north-east of the Falklands. To the north Argentine warships were approaching. This group included an aircraft carrier *Cinco de Mayo*, whose onboard aircraft would soon be in range of the British fleet. To the south of the islands there was another group of Argentine ships, including the cruiser the *General Belgrano* and two destroyers that were believed to be armed with Exocet missiles. These Exocets had the capability of sinking a British carrier. The Argentine ships seemed to be progressing against the British in a pincer movement, moving in from both the north and the south.

The *Belgrano* and its company were being tracked by the British submarine HMS *Conqueror*. The cruiser seemed to be pursuing a rather erratic course, and the British were concerned that if it went into shallow water the submarine would not be able to follow it, and then the Argentine group could move on towards a British carrier and destroy it. However, the *Belgrano* was just outside the TEZ, so was potentially not a legitimate target. Margaret Thatcher herself was consulted and she gave the order to attack. The *Belgrano* was torpedoed by the *Conqueror*, which put two torpedoes into the cruiser's stern – the *Belgrano* sank within 45 minutes, killing 368 of the Argentines on board. Immediately, the entire Argentine Navy turned and headed back home and remained there for the duration of the war. The Argentines feared repeated submarine attacks would destroy their fleet. Britain had won the war against Argentina's surface fleet.

STUDENT STUDY SECTION

Review activities

The sinking of the *Belgrano*, 1982.

The sinking of the *Belgrano* was a turning point. Up until then, few people had died, and most prisoners had been quickly returned via neutral countries. After the *Belgrano*, all other peace plans were doomed.

1   Discuss in small groups the following questions:

Certain Latin American and European nations supported the Argentine claim that the ship was not posing a threat to the Task Force, and Britain lost some international support. However, the attack on the *Belgrano* was popular in Britain. To what extent, in a limited war, is it more important to keep domestic opinion or international opinion on your side?

2   When was a diplomatic solution possible?

3   At what point did a war become inevitable?

To access worksheet 10.1 on the sinking of the *General Belgrano*, please visit www. pearsonbacconline.com and follow the on-screen instructions.

Even after the sinking of the *Belgrano*, the British government still claimed that they were not at war. They limited their description of the war to 'hostilities', and argued that the British had the right to self-defence through Article 51 of the UN Charter.

Argentina now waged its war at sea against the British from the air. They had recently purchased five air-launched Exocet missiles. These missiles could seek out and destroy ships from a range of more than 50km.

On 4 May, two Argentine strike aircraft, each loaded with an Exocet, left the mainland and headed for the British fleet. Commander Woodward had three destroyers armed with anti-aircraft missiles defending his ships. However, the anti-aircraft missiles were unreliable against low-level targets such as Exocets. HMS *Glasgow*'s radar picked up the approaching aircraft and sent out a warning to all other ships. The destroyer HMS *Sheffield* did not receive the full warning, as it was simultaneously sending its own message back to Britain.

An Exocet anti-ship missile.

HMS *Sheffield* on fire after being struck by an Exocet missile, 4 May 1982.

HMS Sheffield was hit by an Exocet, and it became the first British ship to be sunk through enemy action since World War II. Twenty men were killed and 26 were injured. The war was now claiming lives on both sides.

As the case of the *Sheffield* demonstrated, although the British had driven the Argentine Navy back home, the war at sea was far from over. Indeed, many British ships were lost supporting their land campaign as they came under attack from the air (see below).

War on the land

The war in the air had reached something of a stalemate. The South Atlantic winter was drawing in by mid May and this made flying the Sea Harriers almost impossible. British commanders made the decision that they would have to risk putting in ground forces without total air cover. This would make them very vulnerable to Argentine attacks. The land war would focus on the recapture of the capital, Stanley, so the British had to land on East Island. The Argentines had organized sound defences in the hills surrounding Stanley, and so the British decided to land troops some distance away at San Carlos Bay. The bay was not well defended and was out of range of the Argentine artillery. In addition, its surrounding hills would give protection from low-level air attack.

On 21 May, 3,000 troops began an amphibious landing. These troops were made up of Royal Marine Commandos and Paratroopers, and were led by Brigadier Julian Thompson. However, San Carlos was 80km from Stanley. To avoid having to march his men and equipment across harsh terrain in awful weather with all their kit, Thompson waited for the arrival of nine helicopters he could use as transport. The British troops dug in. The Argentines then began their air attack on the ground forces. All the supplies for Britain's land campaign were still being unloaded from ships under attack. For five hours, fighter-bombers bombed the fleet in San Carlos Bay while the landed troops watched on helplessly. Although the hills provided some protection for the troops on shore, they hindered the

British ships' fire-control radars. Five British warships were hit and one ship, HMS *Ardent*, was sinking by the end of the day. The Argentines continued their air bombardment the next day.

The British land campaign to retake the Falklands.

Although some Argentine planes were hit by anti-aircraft guns, this had little impact on the overall assault. The British ships were easy targets sitting in the bay, but they could not retreat, as it was vital for the land campaign that they unloaded their supplies. On 23 May, HMS *Antelope* was fatally hit. Eight British ships were damaged and two were sunk in a four-day battle. Menéndez and the Argentine forces celebrated this phase of their air campaign, which was seen as a victory. The Argentine air force then prepared another campaign against the British land forces.

The next Argentine air strike seriously threatened the British land campaign. A massive supply ship, the *Atlantic Conveyor*, began entering San Carlos Bay on 25 May carrying the helicopters the ground troops needed to get across East Island to Stanley. Two Argentine aircraft released Exocets, which locked on to two frigates in the British carrier group. These ships then fired up metal foil to confuse the missiles' radar and the Exocets steered away – but then picked up a new target, the *Atlantic Conveyor*. The missiles hit the ship and destroyed all of the helicopters on board. Without these helicopters, the British land force now had to march for four days to cover the 80km to the capital, each man carrying up to 55kg of kit.

The British split their troops into two groups. The main force of around 2,000 men marched east towards Stanley; the other force of around 500 marched south. This smaller group had been tasked to achieve a quick morale-boosting victory over the Argentines at the strategically important Goose Green. They needed to take the airstrip there, but the ground was flat and lacked any feature that could be used to protect the attackers. The plan

Soldiers of the 2nd Battalion, Parachute Regiment, stand at the 2 Para Memorial at Goose Green on the Falkland Islands. Seventeen members of the regiment were killed during the battle for Goose Green.

was to attack the airfield in the dark, and then take the Argentine settlement in daylight. The British troops had to attack a well-defended Argentine position on the high ground of Darwin Hill, which was defended by minefields in front and artillery from behind.

Under the cover of darkness the attack began, but one group of men became pinned down by machine-gun fire. There were more Argentines defending the position than the British had thought. The battle raged on until dawn, when the sun rose and lit up Goose Green. The British on low ground were now exposed to Argentine fire, and could advance no further.

STUDENT STUDY SECTION

Discussion question: war and the role of individuals

It is not only the decisions and speeches of political leaders that inspire their armed forces, it is also the actions of individuals on the battlefield.

Case Study: Colonel 'H' Jones, leading 2nd Battalion, The Parachute Regiment, at Goose Green, decided that he would 'lead from the front'. In an act of extreme bravery, heroism or madness (depending on your interpretation), he identified an Argentine position and proceeded to attack it. (It is unclear whether Colonel H had thought he could ultimately take the Argentine position alone, or whether he was attempting to encourage his men forward with him in attack.) He charged up the hill firing his sub-machine gun, but came under heavy fire and was shot dead.

To what extent are acts of this nature important in warfare?

The British were held a mile away from the airstrip, when their air support arrived. Two fighter-bombers dropped cluster bombs on Argentine positions as the ground troops edged forward. Both sides were exhausted. The British then attempted to bluff a victory from the Argentines. They sent a letter threatening them with a heavy bombardment if they did not surrender. The letter also said that the Argentines would be held responsible for any civilian casualties. The threat of being blamed for civilian casualties highlights the limited nature of the war – neither side wanted civilian blood on their hands. The Argentines surrendered. Britain had won the first battle of the land campaign, and in part this had been due to deception; 900 men surrendered to the smaller British force. The number of casualties at Goose Green was high for a limited battle in a limited war. About 70 soldiers had been killed, more than 50 Argentine and 17 British.

Although Goose Green was important, the key battle of the land war was the battle for Stanley. The British were now hit by a major setback. As the second group of 2,000 troops were nearing the capital, two ships with reinforcements, the *Sir Galahad* and the *Sir Tristram*, were hit by Argentine bombs. The 500 men aboard should have been disembarked under the cover of darkness, but due to a series of delays and communication failures, the men had been kept on board in broad daylight. After waiting on the ships for six hours, the soldiers were attacked by two Argentine fighters. Forty-nine British soldiers were killed and 115 were injured. The Argentines now had a victory in the land war, although not as significant as they suggested at the time; Menéndez claimed there had been 900 British troops killed.

Now led by Major-General Jeremy Moore, the British put 9,000 troops near the hills around Stanley. They again began their attack at night. The plan involved two phases. During the first night, troops would sweep from north to south in a three-pronged attack on Argentine positions. This movement would secure the outer ring of hills around Stanley. The largest and most important was Mount Longdon. The second night would see an assault on another ring of hills nearer Stanley; the key hill in this phase was Tumbledown. If this plan succeeded, the British would be within 3km of the capital.

The battle for Mount Longdon began on 11 June at 8.00pm and raged for seven hours. Although the British suffered high casualties due to getting trapped under fire in alleyways

---

Night-fighting

British forces were trained to fight as effectively at night as in daylight. This capability can be highly effective against defended targets, and when fighting in open terrain. The key is to stick to the set plan, and to maintain consistent and clear communication throughout the battle. Everyone needs to know where they are, and where the enemy is. But the strategy is dangerous and difficult. Attackers have to keep moving in the dark to prevent the defenders being able to target them.

of rock, their assault proved too forceful for the Argentines to push back. The Argentines became so desperate to repel the British that Menéndez ordered his artillery to fire on his own positions.

The British were now ready for the second phase of their plan. The 2nd Battalion of Scots Guards were tasked with one of the most difficult parts of the land campaign, the assault on Tumbledown, and they lacked experience. The Argentines had their elite 5th Marines there, heavily armed and dug into the caves and rocks of the mountain. There were 700 Argentines, outnumbering the British two-to-one, and they also had been trained to fight at night. After three hours of fighting, the British were in trouble, and their advance had been halted. However, 30 guardsmen then seized the initiative and climbed to higher ground so that they could fire down on Argentine positions. By the morning, the British were bombarding the remnants of the Argentine forces, and hundreds retreated towards Stanley.

The British surrounded Stanley, and on 14 June demanded the Argentine surrender. Menéndez agreed; discipline in his army had broken down and they had lost the will to fight.

STUDENT STUDY SECTION

IBLP link – Thinkers

There are mistakes, bad decisions and miscommunications during battle, or 'the fog [confusion] of war', as it is known. In pairs discuss whether leaders should be held responsible for mistakes made during the 'fog of war'. The following Case Study could be included in your discussion.

Case Study: On 8 June 1982, during the land campaign in the Malvinas/Falklands, the British Welsh Guards waited on unprotected ships, the *Sir Galahad* and the *Sir Tristram*, to be landed at Fitzroy Bay. They should have got off the ships at night, but there had been a number of delays. All the troops on board knew they needed to get off the ships as soon as daylight broke. After six hours, the Welsh Guards were finally preparing to disembark, but their luck ran out. The Argentine Air Force struck, causing the worst loss of British life in one strike since World War II.

War on the home front

The Falklands War inspired patriotism in Britain such as had not been seen for decades. Here flag-waving crowds see off the British Task Force as it heads out to the Falklands.

To access worksheet 10.2 on patriotism and the Falklands War, please visit www.pearsonbacconline.com and follow the on-screen instructions.

Due to the limited nature of the Falklands/Malvinas War, there was a correspondingly limited impact on the home front of each belligerent. There was no bombing of civilians in Argentina or blockade of Britain. There was no rationing or night-time air raids. Yet although Britain did not introduce conscription, the military regime in Argentina used conscripts in its army.

The war, nevertheless, had more of a social impact on Argentina than on Britain. For example, the Argentines had been enthusiastic consumers of Western pop and rock music, but once the war began radio stations were not permitted to play 'English language' music. There was also a demonstration outside the large Harrods store in Buenos Aires. The British in Argentina kept a low profile, and British schools abandoned their school uniforms so that their students could not be identified.

The media was censored in both Britain and Argentina during the Falklands War. In addition, there was the lack of effective satellite technology to get direct transmissions back to Britain. Generally, the British media managed to deliver a more accurate impression of what was going on than the Argentines – but both sides had a jingoistic popular press that used aggressive and often racist terminology to describe their enemy. In Britain, the BBC news presenter Jon Snow was attacked in the press and in parliament for using the term 'British' and not 'us' in his reports of the war. Although fighting a limited war, both countries ensured the press reflected the overall picture the government wanted shown to the general public.

STUDENT STUDY SECTION

Research activity

Go onto the internet, and research the British media coverage of the Falklands War, focusing particularly upon newspapers. Include the names of prominent British papers in your search strings, such as *The Sun*, the *Guardian*, the *Independent* and the *Times*. In small groups, compare and contrast the wartime headlines, looking at how the British media attempted to present the conflict, and also how they used language and imagery to shape public perceptions. An important example is *The Sun's* headline 'GOTCHA', relating to the sinking of the *General Belgrano*.

Role of the UN

The UN acted to limit the Falklands/Malvinas War, first by attempting to find a negotiated peace, and second by preventing the escalation and spread of the conflict. The UN had passed a resolution condemning the Argentine invasion and requesting the removal of their forces. Thus, although the UN had condemned Argentina, it did not resolve to take action – it was up to Britain to act. Initially, at least, the UN resolution gave Britain the moral high ground, and Britain received support from the Security Council, on which it had a permanent seat. As the war continued, however, and particularly after the sinking of the *Belgrano*, the British strategy of keeping Argentina isolated and 'in the wrong' began to fail. Indeed, on 4 June a Security Council ceasefire resolution was supported by nine countries, including China and the USSR, with four countries abstaining. Britain was forced to use its veto, and was supported by the USA. Yet almost immediately, Jeanne Kirkpatrick, the US ambassador to the UN, announced that if it were possible she would change the American vote from a no to an abstention. It was perhaps fortunate for Britain that they had been able to stall the UN's ceasefire resolutions until the land war was underway.

Role of the USA

Both sides recognized that the support of the USA was vital to their cause. Although the USA had developed an apparent 'special relationship' with Galtieri, he had not seen the bigger picture. Attempting to maintain its influence in Latin American was only a minor part of US foreign policy and this involvement was not key to its Cold War strategy against the USSR. The American decision to support the British was significant in the course of the war; logistical support was given through Ascension Island in the mid Atlantic, and

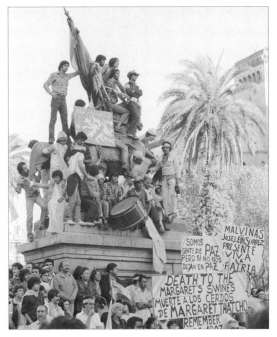

without this the war would have been protracted and subject to risk by the onset of the southern winter. The British Task Force stopped en route at Ascension Island, an island that was about halfway between Britain and the Falklands. The Americans had developed the island into a major military base during World War II. This stopping point was vital for the organization of British forces. In order to wage war effectively, Britain had to set up a 13,000km supply chain using the Royal Navy and RAF. The Americans also supplied the British with 12.5 million gallons of aviation fuel. This allowed the RAF to make 2,500 flights that transported 30,000 tons of equipment and thousands of personnel. The Americans also supplied the British with missiles during the war.

In attaining American support and using its position in the Security Council at the UN, Britain's Foreign Office won the diplomatic battle of the war.

STUDENT STUDY SECTION

Cartoon analysis

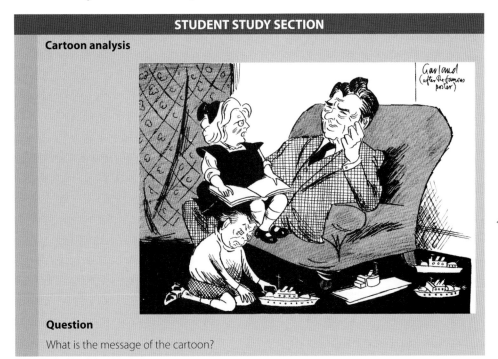

Cartoon by Nicholas Garland, 25 April 1982, in the *Sunday Telegraph*. 'Daddy, what will you do in the Great War?' (The British Prime Minister, Margaret Thatcher, is sitting on American President Ronald Reagan's knee. The British Foreign Secretary is playing with ships.)

Question

What is the message of the cartoon?

Why did Britain win the Falklands/Malvinas war?

It was the very best sort of war: fought at a distance against a second-class enemy and with no fear of retaliation on the homeland. And our servicemen were all regulars. It was a bit like the Boer War but without the Boers.

Julian Critchley (Conservative MP), quoted in Richard Vinen, *Thatcher's Britain*, 2009

British advantages

- The British were better trained and prepared for the conditions on the Falklands. British Royal Marine Commandos, for example, were trained for cold weather and amphibious warfare, whereas the Argentines were not skilled in this kind of warfare. The British Marines, Paratroopers and other infantry were total professionals, and had good prior information about the Falkland Islands.
- The USA was a useful ally. Although President Reagan was initially hesitant, Casper Weinberger, the US Secretary of Defense, supported the British. The key factor in US support was allowing Britain access to the base in Ascension Island.
- France was also an important ally. President Mitterand wanted a strong alliance against the USSR and did not want Britain in trouble. Mitterand blocked further sales of Exocet missiles to Argentina, and hindered sales to Peru that might have gone on to Argentina. French pilots went to Scotland to assist British pilots, helping them to practise dog-fights against Mirage and Super Etendard jets. France pressured other Europeans to support anti-Argentine sanctions. In addition, France was important in influencing other countries to support Britain in the UN.
- The British were able to use their position on the Security Council of the UN in their favour, and the USSR did not veto the motion in the UN condemning Argentine actions, which was the basic justification for British action.
- The British won the war of attrition, and caused many more Argentine losses (dead, wounded and prisoners), a ratio of nearly 14 to 1.
- The British forces maintained high morale.
- The British benefited from luck at certain times. For example, during the final days of the land campaign, Menéndez did not realize that the British guns were down to their last rounds of ammunition, and many of the British soldiers had not received any rations for 72 hours.

Argentine disadvantages

To access worksheet 10.3 on the Argentine surrender, please visit www.pearsonbacconline.com and follow the on-screen instructions.

The British … agreed that officers could keep their hand guns as a symbol of command. Finally the agreement was signed which included the words 'unconditional surrender' and I asked for the word 'unconditional' to be removed. Signing was very difficult for me; and I did it.

General Menéndez in an interview with a BBC correspondent

- The Argentine soldiers were generally not as well trained and lacked confidence.
- The Argentines lost the sympathy of the USA. Galtieri did not respond actively to American attempts to make a peace plan, which alienated the USA.
- Argentine forces were divided. The **non-commissioned officers (NCOs)** were socially removed from the conscripts they commanded, and the conscripts themselves served in the army for only one year. Many had received little or no training when the war began, and most had come from the tropical provinces of Argentina and were not prepared for the conditions in the Malvinas.

- Bad planning. The Argentines kept their best troops at home in case of an attack from Chile. They also over-reinforced their garrison in the Malvinas, which meant their troops ran low on food and supplies.
- Flawed strategies. The Argentines attacked warships instead of the weaker British logistical vessels. For example, if they had sunk the supply ships the British would have struggled to wage their land campaign.
- Weaponry failings. Many Argentine bombs failed to detonate, and this reduced British losses.
- The leadership. Argentine leaders made bad decisions at critical times in the fighting.
- Bad timing. The Argentines would have had a better chance of winning the war if the invasion had occurred *after* the Nott defence cuts.
- Lack of allies. Brazil, Peru, Ecuador and Bolivia all supported the Argentine claims to the islands, but none endorsed the invasion, and all said they wanted to see a peaceful resolution.

STUDENT STUDY SECTION

Review questions

Review the course of the war, and fill in your own copy of this grid:

	British	Argentines
Aims		
Scope and scale of fighting in the war (also casualties)		
Strategy and tactics on land		
War at sea		
War in the air		
Impact on civilians		
Nature of government		

1 Which was more significant in the outcome of the Falklands/Malvinas War: war in the air, war at sea or war on the land?

2 What was the impact of foreign influence in the Falklands/Malvinas War?

3 Why did the Falklands/Malvinas War remain a limited war?

4 The British commander of the land campaign claimed that the British had 'literally killed the Argentine will to fight'. How far do you agree with this assertion?

Research activity

Briefly research relations between Argentina and Chile prior to the Malvinas War. In pairs, then research the role played by Chile in supporting the British during the conflict. It should be noted that the Chilean involvement in the war remains a source of tension between Argentina and Chile today.

Results of the Falklands War

The Falklands/Malvinas War lasted for just two and a half months. Nearly a thousand people died, almost 700 Argentines, 252 British and three Falkland islanders. The war ended without a peace treaty.

Although a brief and limited war, the conflict in the Falklands/Malvinas was significant for a number of reasons. It challenged the idea that weaker nations would not challenge stronger nations, particularly if the strong nations were nuclear powers. It was an example of how leaders in the latter half of the 20th century had not learnt from those at the beginning of the century, i.e. that it was a bad idea to seek war as a distraction from domestic issues. In addition, as with other wars during the century, the Falklands/Malvinas War highlighted the dangers of miscalculating the response of other countries, governments or leaders. Finally, for both Britain and Argentina, cultural and historical perspectives had been important in causing the war.

Results for Argentina

The political results of defeat in the war were swift in Argentina. Galtieri was removed from power within three days of the surrender and soon after military rule was over. The authority of the army over Argentina had ended; crowds gathered in Buenos Aires shouting 'cowards' at the soldiers sent to disperse them. Under pressure from public opinion, the regime lifted bans on political parties, which finally resulted in a peaceful period of democracy. In October 1983, democratic elections brought to power Raoul Alfonsin of the Radical Party. In 1985, Galtieri and nine of his colleagues were put on trial for crimes committed during their rule, and sentenced to long terms in prison.

In terms of Argentine foreign policy, diplomacy would now be the tool used to regain the Malvinas. Some Argentine commentators, including the historian Carlos Escudé, believed 'that if Argentina had any chance at all of recovering the islands diplomatically before 1982, then after the invasion, the chances practically disappeared'. Argentina restored diplomatic relations with Britain. In September 1985, the two countries signed an agreement to promote the search for gas and oil supplies in the south-west Atlantic, which would avoid another potential issue of conflict and pave the way for future cooperation. In 1998, President Carlos Menem visited the UK on the first official visit by a leader since the 1960s.

In the longer term, the struggle for the Malvinas continued. Argentine President Nestor Kirchner, speaking on the 25th anniversary of the end of the conflict, asserted that Britain won a 'colonial victory' in the Falklands War that was unacceptable in the eyes of the world. He went on to pledge that the islands would be returned by 'peaceful means'.

The Argentines wanted to put the war behind them, and close this chapter in their history, particularly after the conviction of Galtieri's junta. However, many of those who had fought in the Malvinas could not forget the conflict. Indeed, it has been estimated that more ex-servicemen have since died from committing suicide than died in the war itself.

Results for Britain

I cannot agree...that those men risked their lives in any way to have a United Nations trusteeship. They risked their lives to defend British sovereign territory, the British way of life and the rights of British people to determine their own future... I do not intend to negotiate on the sovereignty of the islands in any way, except with those who live there. That is my fervent belief... We went to recapture what was ours.

Margaret Thatcher, 15 June 1982

The key political impact of the Falklands War in Britain was the strengthening of the leadership of Margaret Thatcher and the control of her Conservative Party in Britain. In the 1983 general election, the Conservatives were returned to power with a hugely increased majority. The 'wets' who had not wanted war were removed, and this in turn strengthened Thatcher's position. The Conservatives were to hold power for another 15 years.

There was a wave of nationalism, and a renewed sense of patriotism ran through Britain, as could be seen in the crowds gathered at Portsmouth to greet the returning Task Force. But although public approval for the armed forces radically increased after the war, in the longer term the effects of the war on the British armed forces was marginal. British defence policy continued to focus on tanks, nuclear weapons and war with the USSR. In addition, Britain also had to focus on its struggle at home with the IRA. Just after the Falklands victory, an IRA bomb exploded in London on 20 July 1982, killing two guardsmen and injuring 17 spectators. Another bomb exploded two hours later, killing six soldiers and injuring another 24.

The social impact of the war was a massive upsurge in national morale, and much was made in the media of the first 'crushing British victory' since 1945. The British economy also entered into a phase of recovery, leading to a period of growth and prosperity. Yet as was the case with the Argentine veterans, many returning British troops were suffering from undiagnosed **post-traumatic stress disorder** (PTSD). Some found it difficult or impossible to forget their experiences in the South Atlantic, which resulted in a high level of alcoholism and early death among their numbers.

Cartoon by Nicholas Garland, *Daily Telegraph*, 11 January 1983.

Nevertheless, the Falklands victory did not bring an end to the dispute with Argentina, and the British maintained a high military presence on the islands. In a message to mark the 25th anniversary of the liberation of the Falklands, the former Prime Minister, Baroness Thatcher, issued a rallying call to British troops in current war zones, saying that '[in] the struggle against evil … we can all today draw hope and strength' from the Falklands victory.

Results for the USSR

The Soviet Union's analysis of the Falklands/Malvinas War was that they had seriously underestimated the military capability of Britain. This had particular implications for Soviet security in Germany, and following the war the Warsaw Pact forces that faced the British across the Iron Curtain in northern Germany were reinforced.

Results for the USA

To a certain extent, Britain's success in the Falklands led the USA to review its reluctance to intervene militarily in other nations and regions after its disaster in Vietnam. In 1983, US Marines were sent to the Lebanon and US forces invaded Grenada.

Results for the Falkland islanders

For the Falkland islanders, their 19th-century way of life had been destroyed. The population increased due to the British maintaining a high military presence on the islands, one soldier to every two civilians. Their isolation also decreased due to more regular shipping services. A new industry grew up around battlefield tourism, and television was introduced. The islands also benefited from the exclusion zone in their waters, which gave them control over profitable fishing there.

Although the war should have brought the islanders an increased sense of security, the Argentine claims to the Malvinas have not ended. Indeed, after the war the British offered to return to Argentina their war dead, but the Argentine government refused. They asserted that the Malvinas were part of Argentina, and the bodies must remain there. Thus, for the islanders these graves are a constant reminder that the dispute continues, and that there was no concluding peace treaty to the Falklands War.

Results for the United Nations

The war also undermined the United Nations, as Peter Calvocoressi explains below:

The war for the Falklands was a setback for the UN as an organization and for those aspirations to world order which it embodied. For this setback the initial aggressors were overwhelmingly to blame, but the British government did not wholly escape the embarrassment of demonstrating that in a crisis a powerful state will not welcome UN diplomacy and will subordinate the rule of law and its treaty obligations under the Charter to its own assessment of national advantage and prestige. This was in 1982 no great surprise but it was not what the generation of 1945 hoped for.

Quoted in James Sheehan, *The Monopoly of Violence: Why Europeans Hate Going to War*, 2008

STUDENT STUDY SECTION

Essay skills review activity

The opening words – or 'stem' – of an essay question are important for telling you what exactly you should be aiming to do in your essay, and what the focus of your key arguments should be. Below are several different possible essays on the Falklands War. The opening key words or phrases have been italicized. In pairs, briefly discuss what each of the words/phrases is expecting you to do in the essay and how they might have an impact on how you structure the essay. Then have a go at creating essay plans for each of the essay titles.

- *Analyze* the causes of the Falklands War.
- *Assess* the results of the Falklands War.
- *Account* for why the Falklands War remained a limited war.
- *Evaluate* the contribution made by (a) sea power and (b) air power to the British victory in the Falklands War.
- *To what extent* was foreign support the reason for British victory in the Falklands War?
- *Examine* the impact of economic factors in causing the Falklands War.
- *How far* was 'misunderstanding' the cause of the Falklands War?
- *In what ways* can the Falklands War be seen as an 'unexpected war'?

LIMITED WAR CASE STUDY 2: THE GULF WAR (1990–91)

As you read through this chapter, reflect on the following questions:
- What were the causes of the Gulf War?
- In what ways was it a limited war?

On 2 August 1990, Iraqi tanks swept into Kuwait. The war that subsequently developed between a US-led coalition and Iraq was the first conflict to take place in the new international order following the end of the Cold War, and the first major conflict that the USA had undertaken since Vietnam.

The Gulf War was unique in several ways. For the first time ever, the UN had the support of both superpowers in authorizing force against a member country of the UN. Also for the first time, a coalition of more than 30 countries, more than 10 of them Arab, was mobilized against another Arab state. The US President, George Bush, declared that the war was about 'a big idea … a new world order' that would involve 'peaceful settlement of disputes, solidarity against aggression, reduced and controlled arsenals, and just treatment of all peoples.' However, this confrontation would change the whole future of the Middle East; the repercussions of the war were to lead to the US invasion of Iraq in 2003. It would also showcase the way in which wars would be fought at the beginning of the 21st century.

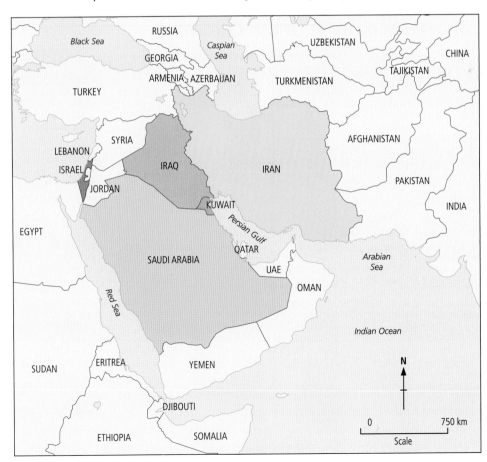

Map of the Middle East. The shaded areas indicate key regional players in the Iran–Iraq War (1980–88) and Gulf War (1990–91).

Timeline of the Gulf War – 1990–91

1990 **Feb** Saddam demands money from Kuwait and United Arab Emirates (UAE)

15 Jul Saddam starts moving Republican Guard to the border with Kuwait

25 Jul Saddam meets with US Ambassador April Glaspie and reasserts lack of intention to invade Kuwait

31 Jul Iraqi and Kuwaiti delegates meet in Jeddah – no agreement

2 Aug Iraq invades Kuwait. UN Resolution 660 condemns Iraq's invasion

6 Aug UN Resolution 661 imposes trade embargo on Iraq

7 Aug US troops and aircraft start deploying to Saudi Arabia (Operation *Desert Shield*)

29 Nov UN Resolution 678 authorizes member states to 'use all necessary means' to make Iraq comply with previous resolutions. Deadline of 15 Jan imposed

1991 **15 Jan** Deadline for Iraqi withdrawal passes; Iraq does not retreat

17 Jan Allied air bombardment of Iraq begins

18 Jan Iraqi ballistic missiles hit Israel

29 Jan–1 Feb Battle of Al-Khafji

24 Feb Land campaign starts

27 Feb Kuwait City liberated

28 Feb Coalition ceasefire

2 Mar UN Resolution 686 sets out terms for ceasefire

3 Mar Formal ceasefire agreed with Iraqi representatives

3 Apr UN Resolution 687 formally ends Gulf War; Iraq accepts conditions

Long-term causes of the Gulf War

The Gulf War was a direct result of the Iraqi leader, Saddam Hussein, launching an invasion of Kuwait in 1990. In order to understand why Iraq invaded Kuwait in 1990 and why this provoked an international reaction that led to war, it is necessary to look at the changing Middle Eastern situation during the 1980s.

The war between Iraq and Iran

In 1979, the secular, pro-American Shah of Iran had been overthrown. A popular revolution led to the Ayatollah Khomeini taking control and establishing an Islamic Republic. **Shi'ite Muslims** were now in control and, with their claim to Shi'ite spiritual leadership, they were therefore a threat to other states such as Iraq where, although the Shi'ites were in the majority, they were nevertheless ruled by the **Sunni Muslims**. The Iranian leadership hoped that the Shi'ites in Iraq would rise up against the nationalist and secularist ideology of the Ba'ath regime in Baghdad. There was a propaganda campaign against Saddam Hussein, and Iran also supported the Kurdish people in Iraq in their longstanding struggle against the Iraqi government. These provocations were the trigger for Saddam's invasion of Iran in 1980. Although Saddam Hussein intended a short war, which would teach Iran a quick but effective lesson, it dragged on for another eight years, ending in 1988.

Although Iraq proclaimed itself victorious in this war, the long conflict transformed Iraq from a rich and prosperous country to one that was physically damaged and crippled with debts, many of these owed to Kuwait and Saudi Arabia. In addition, Iraq faced a huge bill for repairing the war-damaged infrastructure. Western estimates put the cost of reconstruction at $230 billion. Although Iraq could rely on income from oil revenue, this was not as high as expected, due to the low prices of oil on the world market. And even if

Saddam Hussein, the leader of Iraq from 1979 to 2003.

> ### Saddam Hussein's regime in Iraq in the 1970s and 1980s
>
> Saddam Hussein was a leading member of the revolutionary Ba'ath Party, and he played a key role in the 1968 coup that brought the party to long-term power. The redistribution of land and wealth was part of the Ba'ath programme, along with a strong belief in the need to unify the Arab people. From the early 1970s, Saddam was an active member of the administration of Ahmed Hassan. During this time, he built up the security forces and put his own relatives into key positions. He also applied the socialist ideas of the Ba'ath Party by bringing all economic activity under the control of the government. This programme included nationalizing the foreign-owned oil company IBC. The increase of oil prices in the 1970s allowed the rapid economic and social development of Iraq at this time and the country began to prosper.
>
> In 1979 Hussein became Iraqi President. He immediately directed the deaths of dozens of government officials suspected of treason. He executed another 300 officers in 1982 for rebelling against his tactics in the war with Iran. Saddam also became notorious for using chemical weapons both in the war against Iran and in his own country against the Kurds. During a seven-month scorched-earth campaign in 1988, an estimated 50,000 to 100,000 Kurdish villagers were killed or disappeared, and hundreds of villages were razed.
>
> By 1987, Saddam's army was the fourth largest in the world. He had an arsenal of Scud missiles, a sophisticated nuclear weapons programme underway and deadly chemical and biological weapons in development.

every dollar of oil revenues had been spent on reconstruction, it would still have required two decades to repair the total damage.

Saddam Hussein also needed to rebuild Iraq's economy for political reasons. Inside Iraq, there had been opposition to the war. Moreover, the debts Iraq faced meant that Saddam could not follow through on promises to Iraqis of better living standards. With the end of the war, there was also huge potential for civil unrest with the planned demobilization of 1.5 million Iraqi soldiers, many of whom were Shi'a and therefore a potential threat to Hussein and his regime. On the other hand, keeping such a huge standing army could also be a threat to his own security, and Saddam survived at least one coup attempt after the Iran–Iraq War.

The relationship between Iraq and the West

Although Saddam's government was clearly a violent, repressive regime, the USA had supported him in the 1980s as a counterweight to the new anti-US regime in Iran led by Ayatollah Khomeini. In 1982, the Department of State removed Iraq from its list of terrorist countries, so that it could qualify for US aid and credits. Annual trade between the two countries was more than $3 billion by 1990, most of this providing Iraq with food, though also weapons through 'back door' routes. Turning a blind eye to Hussein's slaughter of thousands of Kurds with chemical weapons, other Western countries had also been happy to trade with Iraq. France provided Iraq with billions of francs' worth of weapons, including the technology to build a second nuclear reactor, and by 1990 Britain was Iraq's third largest trading partner. There was a belief in the USA and the West that Saddam Hussein could be turned away from militarism into a more moderate force in the Middle East. A National Security Directive issued by George Bush Snr stated that 'Normal relations between the United States and Iraq would serve our longer-term interest and promote stability in both the Gulf and the Middle East.' It instructed the USA to 'propose economic and political incentives for Iraq to moderate its behaviour and increase our influence with Iraq'. Therefore, even when Saddam Hussein's behaviour became more belligerent, there was no attempt to deter him.

The arguments in London, Paris, Bonn and Washington remained the same: Iraq's war with Iran was over and it was time for domestic reconstruction and thus good business opportunities. Saddam was undoubtedly ruthless but he was no longer a Soviet client and he had shown a potential for flexibility on the Arab–Israeli dispute. There was no international support for ostracizing the regime – therefore the only logical policy was to cultivate it to advantage, claiming that this could encourage Saddam to stick to a more moderate path. Meanwhile, they turned a blind eye to the intensive efforts being made by Iraqis to procure the most sensitive military technologies – especially from Europe.

From L. Freedman and E. Karsh, *The Gulf Conflict, 1990–1991*, 1995

The decline of Soviet influence

The Middle East had, since the 1950s, been a key area in the Cold War struggle for influence between the USA and the USSR, with both superpowers supporting '**client states**'. However, in the early 1990s the policies of the new Soviet leader, Mikhail Gorbachev, were leading to a waning of influence in this area. Soviet preoccupation with its domestic problems and the new climate of cooperation with the West meant that it was unwilling to maintain its commitments to its 'client' states. Thus Syria, Iraq, South Yemen and the Palestine Liberation Organization (PLO) could no longer get economic or military, or even diplomatic, support from the Soviet Union.

This situation inevitably led to the USA stepping into the vacuum as it sought to build support for a new peace initiative between Palestinians and Israelis. This US dominance was viewed with suspicion by many Arab states, including Iraq, who saw any increased US influence as benefiting Israel only. The power vacuum was also a situation which Saddam saw that he could exploit.

The Palestinian problem

In the 1980s there was growing unrest in the **Occupied Territories** of Israel. This unrest exploded into what became known as the *Intifada* ('uprising') in December 1987, a rebellion by Palestinians that included general strikes, boycotts on Israeli goods, barricades and stone-throwing by youths against the Israeli soldiers. Saddam committed $25 million to keep the *Intifada* going. Yet ultimately the *Intifada* helped push both the Israelis and PLO leader Yasser Arafat (who feared he was losing control of the Palestinian situation to the more extreme Hamas) to the negotiating table.

STUDENT STUDY SECTION

Review questions

1 What social, economic and political problems faced Saddam Hussein by 1990?

2 What a) concerns and b) opportunities faced Saddam Hussein as a result of the Soviet Union's waning influence in the Middle East?

3 What justifications did the West give for supporting Saddam Hussein's regime?

Short-term causes of the Gulf War

Western hopes of Iraq moving to a more moderate stance evaporated in 1990 when Saddam made a series of ruthless moves. There was already a growing concern in the West over Iraq's human rights record and also over the vast amounts of money that Iraq was spending on weapon systems. In March 1990 Farzad Bazoft, a journalist working for the British newspaper *The Observer*, was executed in Iraq on trumped-up charges of spying. British intelligence also intercepted items of technology from the West that appeared to be necessary for long-range missiles and **weapons of mass destruction** (WMD). These events now put pressure on the Western countries to halt arms sales. In April, meanwhile, Saddam made a threat to use chemical weapons against Israel. He also gave more financial aid to sustain the *Intifada* and, at an Arab summit meeting in Baghdad, claimed that the enemy of the Arab camp was now 'Greater Israel'.

Meanwhile, the relationship between Iraq and Kuwait was deteriorating fast. Some disagreements between the two countries went back a long way:

- There was a long-standing argument over the frontiers between the two countries. In the 1930s, the new state of Iraq had claimed that Kuwait, formerly a British protectorate, belonged to Iraq. It also laid claim to the islands of Bubijan and Warbah at the head of the Persian Gulf.
- There was unresolved disagreement over the right to exploit the Rumaila oilfield on the Iraq–Kuwait border.

As explained above, however, the real issue for Iraq in 1990 was its economic crisis, and in 1990, Iraq put increasing pressure on Kuwait to help it solve this crisis:

- At a summit meeting in Amman in February 1990, Saddam asked King Hussein of Jordan and President Mubarak of Egypt to inform Kuwait that Iraq not only wanted cancellation of wartime loans, but that he also needed additional funds of some $30 billion. Both requests were refused.
- Iraq also requested that Kuwait keep to **OPEC** quotas for oil output. More oil on the international market meant lower prices per barrel and thus less income for Iraq. Kuwait was the chief culprit in overproduction in a deliberate strategy to drive down the price of oil, so that more nations became dependent on OPEC oil. The long-term benefits of such a strategy were of no help to Saddam Hussein who, facing increasing political unrest at home, needed money immediately.

Iraq's invasion of Kuwait

In July 1990, the dispute with Kuwait became much more intense. Saddam Hussein started making accusations against Kuwait; that it had stolen more than $2 billion of oil from the Rumaila oilfield, which Iraq claimed as its own, and that the loans that Iraq had received during the Iran–Iraq War came from profits due to overproduction (see above). He said that Kuwait's unwillingness to cancel Iraq's war debts constituted 'military aggression' and that Kuwait was 'stabbing Iraq in the back with a poisoned dagger'. At the same time, Saddam backed up his verbal attacks on Kuwait with a military threat; large numbers of the elite Republican Guard divisions were moved towards the border with Kuwait.

Efforts were made to resolve the crisis peacefully:

- 27 July – OPEC put up the official oil price from $18 to $21 a barrel as requested by Iraq.
- After much persuasion by the Egyptian and Jordanian leaders, an Iraqi delegation led by Izzat Ibrahim (Saddam's deputy) met Kuwaiti representatives in Saudi Arabia on 31 July. However, little progress was made and the meeting was abandoned by Iraq, who claimed that Kuwait was acting 'against Iraq's basic interests'.

There was also a meeting between Saddam and the US ambassador to Iraq, April Glaspie. Rather than deterring Saddam from invading Iraq, it seems that Glaspie's conversation with Saddam gave the impression that the USA would take no action. She stated that 'We have no opinion on the Arab–Arab conflicts, like your border disagreement with Kuwait', although she did make it clear that differences should be solved by peaceful means. Saddam also received no warning from the USA, despite the fact that the Pentagon had detected Iraqi military divisions close to the Kuwaiti border.

Certainly Saddam Hussein seems to have believed that the world would not act against him when, on 2 August, he launched the Iraqi invasion of Kuwait with more than 100,000 soldiers and almost 2,000 tanks. Within 12 hours of the invasion, the bulk of the resistance had been extinguished and the Kuwaiti royal family had fled to Saudi Arabia. On 28 August, Kuwait was declared to be the 19th province of Iraq.

STUDENT STUDY SECTION

Review questions

1   How would the invasion of Kuwait solve the problems that you identified in the review questions on p.210?

2   What reasons would Saddam Hussein have had for believing that the USA would not take any action against him?

Document analysis

Document A

The invasion of Kuwait promised a cure to both the economic and military legacy of the Iran–Iraq war. Kuwait's oil wealth would enable the Iraqi regime to reconstruct the state and to pay its non-Arab creditors. It would keep the army busy and far away from the capital. The claims of victory over Iran would be replaced with a real victory for Kuwait. The invasion was also seen as way to project Iraqi hegemony not just over Kuwait but also over the Gulf as a whole. This would allow Iraq to dictate oil prices and quotas to serve its own interests, as it would control 21 per cent of OPEC's total production. And, ultimately, the extension of military and economic power would enable Iraq to claim the mantle of pan-Arab leadership as the region's most powerful country, especially as it was the only country which had never even signed so much as an armistice with Israel and the only Arab state left to embrace the PLO wholeheartedly.

From Antony Best et al., *International History of the Twentieth Century*, 2004

Document B

The move was a power grab, pure and simple. Kuwait was a timely acquisition for Iraq whose war with Iran had left it $70 billion in debt and with tremendous reconstruction costs. And even though the long war had weakened Saddam's military muscle, the little monarch would be no match for him. Not only could he now loot Kuwait's treasury, but by acquiring its enormous oil fields he would control 20 percent of the world's oil supply and thus exercise a stranglehold over the Western countries he hated. Even more important than the financial spoils would be his new economic power. He would make himself the new Gamal Abdel Nasser and become the hero of the Arab world. And if he could march into Saudi Arabia as well before anyone thought of stopping him, his domain would resemble that of his idol, Nebuchadnezzar.

From J.G. Stoessinger, *Why Nations Go to War*, 1998

Document C

The fault here, therefore, was in not warning Saddam away from the logic of this campaign. Saddam was well aware of the implications of America's post-cold-war pre-eminence, and sensitive to the possibility of its interference in his dispute with Kuwait. It is not at all clear whether a tougher stance by the Bush Administration would have sufficed to stop Saddam. However, since the campaign was essentially a means to ensure his political survival, it would have made no sense whatsoever if its hazards came to outweigh its political gains. Furthermore, even if Saddam, as many widely supposed, was 'only bluffing', then that was no reason for passivity. His threats and demands against Kuwait were still unacceptable. Extortion should not only become intolerable when the exorted refuses to comply and the threat is implemented. The importance of the principle of non-aggression could have been stated far more clearly than quiet comments about the inadvisability of solving disputes through force.

From L. Freedman and E. Karsh, *The Gulf Conflict, 1990–1991*, 1995

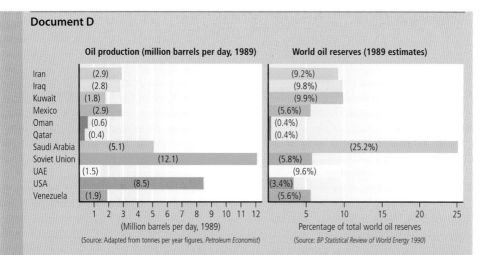
International reaction to Iraq's invasion of Kuwait

Saddam Hussein had miscalculated first on the USA's reaction to the invasion. Not only was this an act of aggression by one UN country against another, but the appropriation of Kuwait's oilfields meant that Iraq would now have an unacceptable level of influence in OPEC and the pricing of oil worldwide. There was also now the possibility of an attack on Saudi Arabia, which would place virtually all Arab oil under Iraq's control (see graph above) and cause economic and political instability in the region. As the USA relied on imports for about 50 per cent of its oil requirements, it could not afford to let one country, especially one with a leader such as Saddam Hussein, have such control. American allies in the West were also highly alarmed and ready to join the USA in confronting the Iraqi regime. Given the new international context with the ending of the Cold War, Saddam could not even rely on support from the USSR.

Saddam also badly miscalculated on the effect the invasion would have on Arab states. Many had believed that Saddam was only bluffing. The outrage that was felt by Arab states at the deception, and at the fact that one Arab state had invaded another, with all of the implications that this had for regional stability, set the stage for a coalition with the West.

The countdown to war

The UN Security Council quickly established a comprehensive set of sanctions against Iraq. These were supported by the Soviet Union, a clear indication of the new international order that was now emerging. Meanwhile, the USA had managed to persuade King Fahd of Saudi Arabia of the need for a US force in his country in order to protect Saudi Arabia from invasion. From 8 August, US troops started arriving in his country as part of Operation *Desert Shield*. Two days later, the Arab League passed a motion condemning Iraq's occupation of Kuwait and authorizing the dispatch of Arab forces to Saudi Arabia to join those of the USA.

Kuwait
The sheikdom of Kuwait, as you can see from the map on p.207, is much smaller than its neighbours. Its small population (two million before the invasion, of which fewer than a million were Kuwaitis), however, and its large oil resources meant that it was extremely rich. Its **GNP** was more than $26 billion in 1989. Kuwaiti City had become a capital city of great wealth and there were good health and education services. Yet there were also big divisions in society. The thousand or so members of the ruling al-Sabah family effectively ruled the country. In 1986 the Emir had disbanded the Kuwaiti parliament and in 1989 he rejected pleas to reinstate it. The bulk of Kuwaiti citizens themselves were divided into first- and second-class citizens. Half of the emirate's population were immigrants without citizenship or full civic rights. Nomadic Bedouin were denied rights because they could not prove fixed residence, as too were Palestinians and others, even if born in Kuwait.

Why was a peaceful settlement not possible?

To access worksheet 11.1 on UN resolutions against Iraq, please visit www.pearsonbacconline.com and follow the on-screen instructions.

It was hoped by many that negotiation combined with sanctions would achieve a solution to the crisis that would avoid war. Saddam did suggest on 12 August a peace plan that involved the USA leaving Saudi Arabia, Syrian troops leaving Lebanon and Israel withdrawing from the Occupied Territories. Yet his attempt to link the wider Palestinian issue with the invasion of Kuwait was highly problematic, and was more an attempt to play for time in the hope that the coalition would become divided and weakened.

Freedman and Karsh write that:

> *Saddam never himself acted as if a diplomatic solution based on a combination of withdrawal from Kuwait and a face-saver was readily available. He did not engage in an active search for an escape route. His response to the various formulas offered by anxious third parties and regional allies was generally dismissive. At no time did he ever spell out his conditions for withdrawal, other than to suggest that once all other problems in the Middle East had been dealt with the question of Iraq's new nineteenth province might also be addressed.*
>
> From L. Freedman and E. Karsh, *The Gulf Conflict, 1990–1991*, 1995

Thus, although several attempts at mediation were made, Saddam's determined intransigence on the issue of withdrawal from Kuwait made a peaceful solution increasingly unlikely. Meanwhile, international opinion was also hardened against Saddam by reports of Iraqi brutality in Kuwait and by Saddam's plans to use civilian hostages trapped in his country as human shields.

Although many in Bush's administration wanted to give sanctions more time to work, ultimately Bush could not allow this to happen. There was no guarantee that they would have enough impact on Saddam himself to get him to back down, and in any case the USA did not have the time to wait and see if this would happen. It had to keep the coalition together and keep the political and military pressure on Saddam, and this situation could not be maintained indefinitely. Nevertheless, sanctions did play an important role by giving a focal point for international unity before armed conflict, and imposing economic hardship on Iraq:

> *...an international coalition could be forged around them in a way that would not have been possible in a rush to armed force, and this was also the means by which the United Nations was drawn into its central role. Five months of the embargo undermined the ability of Iraq to sustain a long war.*
>
> From L. Freedman and E. Karsh, *The Gulf Conflict, 1990–1991*, 1995

STUDENT STUDY SECTION

Source analysis

Study the two extracts from Freedman and Karsh above.

What do they suggest were: a) Saddam's attitude to a diplomatic solution to the crisis; b) the importance of economic sanctions in the months before the war started?

IBLP link – Risk-taker

Although the IBLP promotes risk-taking, this can be misinterpreted by students; a risk-taker should 'approach unfamiliar situations and uncertainty with courage and forethought, and have the independence of spirit to explore new roles, ideas and strategies. They are brave and articulate in defending their beliefs.' Deciding to take military action to stop Saddam Hussein was a 'risk' – how far do you agree that this 'risk' was appropriate? In what other situations is taking risks appropriate, and also think of examples when it would not be appropriate.

Why did Saddam not respond to the military threat that faced him?

By 15 January 1991, the Allied forces had reached a figure of 555,000 men and women, and more were still arriving. Some 350,000 of these troops were American. The remainder belonged mainly to Arab and Western European forces.

The hope, other than negotiation and economic sanctions, was that Saddam would see the impossibility of taking on the might of the American war machine. Yet Saddam was overconfident, after the war with Iran, in his ability for survival. It is also possible that he believed right up to January 1991 that the Americans would not actually risk a war, and that the peace movement would grow in voice and undermine the solidarity of the coalition. He thus ended up miscalculating yet again on American actions.

The outbreak of war

On 29 November 1990, the UN Security Council had approved another resolution (its 12th of the crisis) authorizing the use, after 15 January 1991, of any necessary measures to secure the removal of Iraq from Kuwait and the restoration of its former rulers. This resolution provided the legitimate grounds for war and it was passed by 12 votes to two (Yemen and Cuba voting against and China abstaining). Operation *Desert Shield* now became Operation *Desert Storm*, which had the objective of militarily pushing Saddam's forces out of Kuwait. Last-minute mediation attempts all failed, and *Desert Storm* started on 16 January 1991.

STUDENT STUDY SECTION

Review question

For each of the following headings, write notes to explain the significance of each factor in contributing to the build-up of tensions and the eventual outbreak of war.

Long-term causes of the war
- Iran–Iraq War
- Decline of Soviet Influence
- Saddam's attempt to expand his influence in the region
- Western support for Saddam.

Short-term causes (events in 1990)
- Iraq's economic position by 1990
- US failure to give stronger signals concerning Saddam's actions
- Saddam's invasion of Kuwait.

Triggers for war
- Limited impact of sanctions
- Failure of negotiations
- The US need to keep the coalition together
- Saddam's miscalculations.

Class debate

Take the motion: 'This House believes that the Gulf conflict was a simple case of "blood for oil"' (see Interesting Facts box on p.219).

Divide the class into two teams. Each team should have three speakers. The rest of the team should also help in researching and writing the speeches. Follow the standard rules for a formal debate.

Overview of the war

A US F-14A Tomcat aircraft flies over an oil well still burning in the aftermath of Operation *Desert Storm* in 1991.

The *Desert Storm* campaign was carried out in two parts. First, there was a series of bombing attacks on Baghdad and on military targets. In more than 100,000 sorties during the course of the war, Iraq's military and industrial infrastructure was completely destroyed. Saddam responded with Scud ballistic missiles directed at Saudi and Israeli cities and by devastating Kuwait City and maltreating its citizens.

The second phase was the ground campaign against the Iraqi Army itself. This began on 24 February, and within four days the Iraqis had been driven out of Kuwait. Kuwait was liberated and Saddam Hussein accepted defeat.

The nature of the fighting

The coalition forces faced a formidable Iraqi Army. The overwhelming victory achieved in the war by the US and coalition forces was due partly to state-of-the-art American weaponry. The American military had been rebuilt throughout the 1980s, and the results of their new technology were clearly seen in *Desert Storm*. Four developments had particular impact: precision-guided munitions (PGMs), night-vision devices, space-based systems and **'stealth' technology**.

The war in the air

The technological superiority of US air power was clearly shown in the opening days of the war. The first night of operations over Iraq saw the longest bombing run in history, with B-52G bombers from Louisiana making a round trip of some 15 hours. Eighty-nine per cent of the missiles dropped by these bombers hit their targets.

The total weight of bombs dropped on Iraq was just below 90,000 tons, which is the same as only two months of bombing in the Vietnam War. However, due to the improved accuracy of the bombs – known as 'smart' bombs – air power was much more effective than in the Vietnam War.

In stark terms, a fighter-bomber of the 1990s armed with just two smart bombs possessed such a level of accuracy that it would have taken more than 100 B-17 bombers [a World War II-era bomber] to achieve the same results.

From Alastair Finlan, *The Gulf War 1991*, 2003

Yet it is also important to remember that although the Americans used 9,300 PGMs, in fact 90 per cent of all aerial munitions used were unguided munitions.

Thermal-imaging and laser designation systems were used to guide the bombs to their target – pilots launched bombs into the 'cone' created by a laser beam locked onto the target, in order to score a direct hit. As a result of the smart bombs, the coalition forces were able to take out the Iraqi air-defence system on the first night of operations, with devastating effects on the Iraqi ability to retaliate.

The coalition air force went on to bomb command and communication facilities (second phase) and then military targets throughout Iraq and Kuwait, before focusing on Scud missile launchers, weapons research facilities and naval forces (third phase). Night-vision devices also allowed coalition aircraft to use the cover of darkness for protection, while still being able to attack exact targets using the PGMs.

Fortunately for the coalition forces, Saddam's air force adopted a defensive position, and did not intervene. In fact, soon after the start of the war, the Iraqi Air Force began fleeing to Iran, possibly because Saddam wanted to maintain it intact for after the war. Air supremacy was thus achieved within days of the start of the campaign.

The impact of the bombing

The technology used by the Americans in the smart bombs allowed them to destroy more targets faster, contributing to the breakdown of the Iraqi command structure and making it difficult for Saddam to coordinate his forces and mount an effective defence. The Iraqi war machine was crippled, and bridges, roads and telecommunications equipment destroyed.

The bombing campaign also destroyed the Iraqi artillery units (see below), and made it difficult for Iraq to operate on the battlefield. The psychological impact on the Iraqi forces of this devastating air attack must also not be underestimated.

To access worksheet 11.2 on the Allied bombing campaign, please visit www.pearsonbacconline. com and follow the on-screen instructions.

STUDENT STUDY SECTION

Document analysis

The following comes from an interview with Lieutenant-General Charles Horner, who was the coalition air commander during the war. General Horner was interviewed by washingtonpost. com staff over a period of several months, ending in July 1998.

Question: Did the air war succeed at achieving strategic and tactical goals?

Gen. Horner: Bombing Baghdad had success and failures. First of all we did not have strategic and tactical goals, we had the goal of evicting the Iraqi Army out of Kuwait and other goals of keeping casualties down on both sides – getting as much of the weapons of mass destruction programs as possible and suppressing SCUD attacks on Israel. The precision attacks on the Iraqi command, control and communications targets in Baghdad were a huge success as far as a military strategy to gain control of the air. Remember, that was job number one – all else depended on that – gaining control of the air. We sure didn't succeed in our efforts to disrupt Iraqi leadership, not because we were unable to kill the needed targets, but because we were unaware of what targets we needed to destroy.

From http://www.washingtonpost.com/wp-srv/inatl/longterm/fogofwar/horner2.htm

Questions

1 According to General Horner, what were the aims of the air attack on Baghdad?

2 What were the successes of the air war?

3 What were the failures?

4 What are the value and limitations of using these interviews for the historian?

● **Examiner's hint**
When analyzing an interview for value and limitations, you need to consider:
● *Who* the people are and thus their knowledge/ involvement of the event in question. Do they know what they are talking about? Also, do they personally have anything to lose/gain by the handling and outcome of the war?
● The *date* of the interview – how long after the actual event did it take place? Is hindsight likely to affect their comments?
● The *purpose* for which the interview was given.

The land war

The technological developments mentioned above played a key role in the land war as well. The American M1A1 and the British Challenger tanks, unlike many Iraqi tanks, could move and fire at the same time. Tanks were fitted with precision munitions and sophisticated firing systems. The role of the GPS (Global Positioning System) was also essential for American forces finding their way through the desert, and the night-vision devices, such as night-vision goggles, allowed the coalition to fight around the clock.

Airpower continued to play a key role in the land campaign. During the 1980s, NATO had developed a new strategy for warfare called the AirLand Doctrine, which emphasized, among other things, close integration between the ground forces and a dedicated air campaign. Thus the fourth phase of air operations was as part of the ground war, which started on 24 February 1991. The air attack on the Iraqi forces significantly damaged the Iraqi fortifications and minefields behind the Kuwait–Saudi border, as well as killing many Iraqi troops. When the land attack came, it quickly succeeded in driving the Iraqi Army from Kuwait; it was a hundred-hour rout that shattered Saddam's prediction that this would be the 'Mother of all Battles'.

Map of coalition movement during Operation *Desert Storm*, 1991.

GPS and the Gulf War

The Global Positioning System (GPS) is a satellite-based navigation system made up of a network of 24 satellites placed into orbit by the US Department of Defense (DoD). GPS satellites broadcast signals from space that are used by GPS receivers to provide three-dimensional location (latitude, longitude, and altitude) plus the time. During the Iraq War, the DoD improved the performance of its GPS satellite navigation system to provide accuracy within 3m for precision guidance systems for munitions, aircraft and ground forces, thus allowing unprecedented accuracy of fire and navigation in battle.

The land war developed in the following stages:

- 24 February am: US Marines and Saudi task forces attacked in the east into Kuwait, while in the west French and US forces launched an attack against Salman airfield.
- 24 February pm: US Marines and Saudi forces broke through Iraqi defences in the east and made rapid progress. VII Corps (consisting of three US armoured divisions, one US infantry division and one British armoured division) attacked north into Iraq.
- 25–26 February: US Marines, Saudis and Egyptians closed on Kuwait City. The escape route out of Kuwait was cut off to the Iraqis. The coalition troops that had invaded first into Iraq now moved into Kuwait.
- 27 February: Remaining Iraqi forces were surrounded, including the elite Republican Guard. President Bush announces the liberation of Kuwait.
- Hostilities cease and Iraq accepts all UN resolutions.

The overall commander of the coalition forces was Norman Schwarzkopf. Thanks to changes made through the AirLand Doctrine, Schwarzkopf was able to command and control his different forces with far greater authority than had ever previously been allowed, and so achieve greater coordination between the land, sea and air units. As his forces consisted of both Western and Arab troops, he was assisted by the Saudi commander General Khaled bin-Sultan, who controlled the forces from the Arab states. Schwarzkopf was personally very visible during the course of the war, giving frequent press conferences, and was nicknamed 'Stormin' Norman'.

Norman Schwarzkopf, the commander of coalition forces during the Gulf War.

STUDENT STUDY SECTION

The role of technology

The general impact of technology upon the technique of modern warfare, as demonstrated in Desert Storm, was at least threefold. First, it increased the intensity of combat. Modern combat has become a round-the-clock proposition with no respite. Second, technology has made combat much more efficient. Precision munitions make it possible to do much more much faster, with fewer assets. The side benefit is less collateral damage – fewer unnecessary casualties and less unnecessary destruction. Third, the gap in capabilities between those who can exploit modern military technology and those who cannot is growing ever more significant. Precision munitions, 24-hour capability, space systems, stealth technology, and many other technologies provide the possessor with much more than marginal improvements in military capabilities. Properly used, they provide an overwhelming advantage.

From D.M. Snow and D.M. Drew, *Lexington to Desert Storm: War and Politics in the American Experience*, 1994

Question

According to this source, how have new technologies in fighting, as shown in the Gulf War, impacted on combat?

Research activity

Research the role of the following in the Gulf War:
- The Lockheed F-117A Nighthawk stealth attack aircraft
- AH-64 Apache helicopter
- F-111F Aardvark interceptor aircraft
- E-3A Airborne Warning and Control (AWAC) aircraft
- Patriot surface-to-air missiles
- Scud ballistic missiles
- Hawk surface-to-air missiles
- Tomahawk land attack missiles (TLAM)

The sea war

The bulk of the naval forces in the Gulf War were provided by the USA, which deployed six carrier battle groups in support of operations. A real problem for the US Navy was the small amount of sea space in the Gulf. Even more problematic was the threat of Iraqi mines, which were largely dealt with by the British Royal Navy (though two US ships were still holed by Iraqi mines).

The coalition navy had several roles in Operations *Desert Shield* and *Desert Storm*:
- Enforcing the UN embargo on Iraq.
- Supporting the air campaign. The US aircraft carriers carried some of the world's most advanced air defence fighters, such as the F-14 Tomcat. In addition, the new hi-tech Tomahawk land attack missiles (TLAMs) were fired from naval vessels at targets that were considered too dangerous for the coalition aircraft.
- Persuading Iraq that the land invasion of Kuwait would come from the sea.

Public opinion on the Gulf conflict

Although many Arab governments were hostile to Saddam's actions, there was a lot of support for Saddam Hussein amongst ordinary Arabs. Part of this was due to the lack of sympathy for Kuwait. The emirate was seen as arrogant, and its treatment of foreign workers (see Interesting Facts box on p.213) was also disliked. Iraqi propaganda during the war played on the fact that Arab soldiers were dying to save rich Kuwaiti leaders who were far from the battle zone. Similarly, in the West, a section of public opinion was sceptical about the moral reasons for the war, pointing to the fact that had Kuwait not had oil, Saddam would probably have got away with his actions. The slogan 'blood for oil' became a common cry for protesters against the war.

Media coverage of the Gulf War: censorship and propaganda

With the advent of news channels such as CNN in the USA, it was now possible to watch news on the Gulf War 24 hours a day. However, civilians around the world knew far less of what was actually happening in this war than they had in the Vietnam War. Partly as a result of the political impact that unrestricted reporting had in this earlier war, the military stringently managed the media in the Gulf War, providing the majority of images of bombs hitting targets and making sure that all press teams had an escort officer who could monitor what was filmed.

The media was also used by the Iraqis to their advantage, not only to illustrate the impact of US bombing on civilians, but also to show video tapes of captured US pilots forced to read prepared statements condemning the war. The Iraqi propaganda was controlled by the Information Minister Muhammed Saeed al-Sahaf, who claimed Iraqi victories thoughout the course of the war, regardless of what was actually happening. In addition, both sides used the radio to try to win over enemy troops.

Iraqi propaganda leaflet designed for American soldiers.

The Iraqi Navy put up very little resistance and many ships were destroyed in the act of trying to escape to Iran.

Reasons for Allied success

There are several reasons for the overwhelming success of the Allied coalition in the Gulf War:

The timing of the war. The US Army had been modernized in the 1980s in terms of weaponry, planning and organization, in readiness for an attack on the Soviet Union. The Cold War had only just ended, and so the US military was still at full strength. Had the conflict happened a few years later, it might well have lacked such resources. The Soviet Union at this point was also willing to work with the West, and the political unity amongst so many countries might have been difficult to achieve in following years.

The quality of military technology. As we have seen, technology was key in allowing such a rapid victory. US technological superiority – the ability to fight at night, the smart bombs, the intelligence provided by satellites, the state-of-the-art tanks and aircraft – put the coalition forces at a huge advantage.

Saddam's errors. Saddam miscalculated American will and capabilities. His military strategy was highly flawed. The failure of the Iraqi Air Force or ground troops to take an offensive action, for instance by attacking Saudi Arabia in the early phases of *Desert Shield*, was an enormous error. The Iraqis surrendered mobility by entrenching themselves to protect Kuwait. Saddam's prediction that the entrenchments would be difficult to take, and that the Iraqis would be able to force attrition warfare on the coalition with heavy casualties, proved mistaken. He also underestimated the importance of air warfare.

Throughout, Saddam was fighting not only a military battle, but a political one as well. He thus kept back key units so that they would be ready to fight to save his regime. His one clear strategy was that of firing Scud missiles at Israel, so that Israel would join the war and thus inflame Arab opinion, causing the collapse of the coalition. This strategy, however, failed to work.

STUDENT STUDY SECTION

Document analysis

DEAR SOLDIERS :
YOUR COMMANDERS HAVE SAID THAT THE WAR WILL TAKE FEW DAYS WERE THEY CORRECT ? AND CONVINCED YOU THAT LOSES WILL BE MINIMUM IN THE GROUND COMBAT, WE ASSURE THAT THEY WONT BE CORRECT

Question

What is the message of this propaganda leaflet, and why might Iraqis consider it to be particularly effective on American soldiers?

To access worksheet 11.3 on the language of war, please visit www. pearsonbacconline.com and follow the on-screen instructions.

Results of the Gulf War

Ultimately, the coalition forces stopped short of an invasion and takeover of Iraq. It can be argued that this was not in the original mandate of UN Resolution 678, and a push into Iraq would have split the coalition, particularly from the Arab countries. Given the fact that the USA was still very conscious of failure of Vietnam, it was also reluctant to get involved in what could have been a long drawn-out campaign.

Gulf War Syndrome

Despite initially low casualties, coalition veterans of the Gulf War have continued to die or suffer from mysterious illnesses since 1991. This has become known as Gulf War Syndrome. It is not clear what has caused this. Possible causes put forward have included the exposure to depleted uranium used in tank shells and large-calibre bullets, or a side-effect of the 'cocktail' of drugs given to soldiers to protect them from the possible dangers of biological and chemical warfare.

In military terms, the war was successful in achieving its aims as defined by the UN Security Council. Iraq had been defeated and forced to pull out of Kuwait. Kuwait's sovereignty was restored and the al-Sabah family was put back in power. However, as shown below, there was no real change in the Middle East as a result of this conflict. Saddam Hussein remained in power and the Arab states and international community remained divided as to how to deal with Iraq. The 'new world order' predicted by George Bush seemed very elusive, as new wars started in the wake of the collapse of the USSR and the disintegration of Yugoslavia.

Casualties

For the Allies, the casualties were very low considering the huge numbers deployed. The USA lost fewer than 150 killed in action, a dramatic difference from US casualty figures in the two previous major wars involving US troops. Korea had cost the US forces more than 30,000 dead, and in Vietnam they suffered just over 58,000 dead. Britain had lost 24 killed in action and the Arab countries (not including Kuwait) suffered 37 deaths. The greatest number of soldiers killed or seriously wounded (1,500 Americans and 700 British) came from illness and accidents, including incidents of **friendly fire** or 'blue on blue'.

The exact number of Iraqi deaths is unknown, though recent estimates suggest in the region of 20,000 (though some sources still put the figure as high as 200,000). There was much controversy over the number of civilian deaths in Iraq – reports range from 1,000 to 15,000. It is impossible to have a clear picture of civilian deaths because Iraq never released the correct figures.

In Kuwait, attacks on civilians continued after the ceasefire. This time it was due to reprisals of Kuwaiti citizens against those whom they considered were supporters of Saddam Hussein: Palestinians, Sudanese and Yemenis in particular.

Physical damage

The cost of the damage to Kuwait, with the damage to the oilfields and loss of foreign investments, was estimated at around $30 billion. In Iraq, the effects of the 40-day bombing campaign were huge: power, water and sanitation facilities were destroyed in Baghdad and other cities, along with roads, bridges and telephone exchanges. One UN official who toured the country after the war described Iraq as having been 'relegated to a pre-industrial age'.

Environmental damage

The environmental costs of the war were also huge. They were partly due to oil spillages. On 23 January, Iraq was accused of dumping 400 million gallons of crude oil into the Persian Gulf in order to stop US Marines coming ashore. This act was the largest oil spill in history, resulting in the deaths of thousands of seabirds and marine animals. (The Iraqis denied they had acted deliberately, claiming that the coalition bombers had damaged and destroyed oil tankers.)

Retreating Iraqis also set alight 600 oil wells in Kuwait. John Stoessinger describes the effects of the destruction:

Across the darkened landscape hundreds of orange fireballs roared like dragons, spewing poisonous vapors high into the air. From overcast skies dripped a greasy black rain polluting everything it touched. Black, choking smoke blotted out the sun. Oil-soaked workers turned in twelve-hour shifts, struggling with hand tools to control the burning flow. Some five million *gallons of oil a day, worth about $100 million, were going up in flames. Oil covered thousands of acres, killing plants and animals and threatening subsurface water. Hospitals reported a dramatic increase in respiratory cases. Antipollution masks were selling briskly for thirty dollars apiece in supermarkets. Breathing, said one Kuwaiti, was 'like taking the exhaust pipe of a diesel truck in your mouth and breathing that.'*

From J.G. Stoessinger, *Why Nations Go to War*, 1998

Political effects

For Iraq

It was widely believed that Saddam's humiliating defeat would trigger rebellions in Iraq by Baghdad's political and military elite, rebellions that would lead to his downfall. Indeed, there were risings, but by the Kurds in the north and Shia Muslims in the south. Saddam had enough strength and military hardware left to crush these rebellions brutally, which also caused a flood of refugees into Turkey and Iran. At first there was no international intervention, as the USA did not want to see a dismembered Iraq that would be unable to provide a counterweight to Iran. Yet eventually, international outrage at Saddam's bombings of his people caused the USA and Britain to declare 'no-fly zones' and set up a 'safe-haven' in the north for the Kurds.

In April, the UN Security Council passed Resolution 687, requiring Saddam to be completely open with all of his nuclear, chemical and biological weapons programmes. Until he did, tough economic sanctions, including a ban on Iraqi oil exports, would remain. Although no evidence that Saddam made WMDs after the war has emerged, nevertheless, the Allies at the time remained convinced of his capacity and will to do so, and UN inspection teams visited Iraq in an attempt to find evidence of the weapons.

Saddam Hussein remained in complete power until the 2003 Allied invasion of Iraq. The ordinary people of Iraq suffered the most from the Allied bombing, the loss of infrastructure and also from the sanctions that were imposed after the war. As a result of the sanctions, infant mortality trebled and life expectancy fell by 15–20 years, and the general health and nutrition of the nation declined significantly.

For the USA

Desert Storm seemed to highlight a new world unipolar order, in which the USA was to play the dominant role in dealing with world problems. Ultimately, the events of this war were to lead on to the Iraq War of 2003. After the attacks on the World Trade Center and the Pentagon on 9 September 2001, the USA under George Bush Jnr moved rapidly to complete Saddam Hussein's removal from power.

For the Middle East region

The USA became an even stronger force in the region, which in turn provoked Muslim radicals to become increasingly hostile towards America. There was not the move to democracy in states in the Middle East, as had been hoped by the West. The National Assembly was restored in Kuwait, but with its narrow, male-only franchise. Women finally got the vote in 2005.

The Palestinian peace process was given a new boost. This impetus was not because of any earlier effort by Saddam Hussein to create 'linkage', but because Yasser Arafat's credibility had been undermined owing to his friendship with Saddam, and because the USA was now the key player and could move forward on the peace process. The result was the Oslo Accords of 1993, the first face-to-face agreement between the Israeli government and a representative of the Palestinian people.

Document analysis

Document A

Thus the coalition achieved its immediate objective of expelling Iraq from Kuwait but at a terrible cost which could only breed resentment against the West among many people in the region, while the outcome did nothing to resolve other issues troubling the Middle East – notably the Palestinian question or relations with Iran. Nonetheless, in the USA the war created a patriotic consensus on America's role as global gendarme, with what consequences only time would tell. As President Bush exclaimed, 'By God, we've kicked the Vietnam syndrome once and for all'.

From T.E. Vadney, *The World Since 1945*, 1998

Document B

The failure to keep military objectives and political goals in harmony, however, helped ensure that the Gulf War did not lead to the hoped-for overthrow of Saddam Hussein. The American decision to end the offensive was taken in haste, in a war that was very high tempo, without an adequate consideration of how to translate the outcome of the campaign into a durable post-war settlement. This was linked to military factors, specifically the persistence of 'friction' and 'fog': a failure to distinguish victory from operational success helped ensure that the wrong decisions were taken. The civilian leadership permitted the decision to end the war to be governed by military considerations, specifically the expulsion of Iraqi forces from Kuwait: but the major goal, in fact, was political; the need to create a stable post-war situation in the Gulf, the military preconditions for such stability being ultimately a political judgement.

From Jeremy Black, *Introduction to Global Military History*, 2005

Document B

Before the 1991 war began, President George Bush had established limited objectives for a limited campaign. Through six weeks of combat he stuck to those goals with fixed determination. He resisted the temptation to march on Baghdad, certainly a decision that spared countless lives and incalculable political complications.

From Rick Atkinson, http://www.washingtonpost.com/wp-srv/inatl/longterm/fogofwar/intro.htm

Document D

'He who fights and runs away, lives to fight another day'. Cartoon from Nick Garland, in the *Daily Telegraph*, 8 March 1991.

Questions

1 According to Document A, what were the results of the war for a) the Middle East and b) the USA?

2 Compare and contrast Documents B and C in their assessment of Bush's decision to end the war without going into Iraq.

3 What is the message of Document D?

Gulf War as a limited war

Look back at Chapter 1 and the definition of limited war. How does the Gulf War meet the criteria of a limited war in terms of :

- Geography
- Weaponry
- Range of targets attacked
- Degree of mobilization?

Essay planning

'The Gulf War of 1991 was a very limited campaign that merely reinstated the status quo of the region' (from Alastair Finlan, *The Gulf War 1991*, 2003). How far do you agree with this statement?

Intro

There are two clear halves to this quotation, which both need to be addressed: the question of how far it was a 'limited' campaign, and the impact that it had on the region. Make sure in your introduction that you show that you understand these points. You also need to define key terms – 'limited campaign' and 'status quo'. Don't forget to set out what your key argument will be for each part of the quotation.

Section 1

Here you need to deal with why the Gulf War can be seen as a 'limited' campaign; use your answer to the limited war exercise above as a basis for your analysis here.

Section 2

Next deal with the question of 'status quo'; what stayed the same in the Middle East? Were there any changes that occurred in the region as a result of the war? Also look at the post-war situation in Iraq.

Conclusion

Come back to the original quotation and address both parts in your conclusion.

● **Examiner's hint**
When you have a quotation to deal with, make sure that you study it carefully. If it is a long quotation with more than one assertion in it, break it down into its different sections. Deal with each section separately and structure your essay accordingly. In your conclusion, however, come back to the whole quotation.

12

CIVIL WAR CASE STUDY 1: THE SPANISH CIVIL WAR (1936–39)

General Francisco Franco, the leader who took Nationalist forces to victory in the Spanish Civil War.

'A civil war is not a war but a sickness,' wrote Antoine de Saint-Exupéry. 'The enemy is within. One fights almost against oneself.' Yet Spain's tragedy in 1936 was even greater. It had become enmeshed in the international civil war, which started in earnest with the Bolshevik revolution.

From Antony Beevor, *The Battle for Spain: The Spanish Civil War 1936–1939*, 2006

The Spanish Civil War broke out in 1936 after more than a century of social, economic and political division. Half a million people died in this conflict between 1936 and 1939.

As you read through this chapter, consider the following essay questions:
- Why did a civil war break out in Spain in 1936?
- How significant was the impact of foreign involvement on the outcome of the Spanish Civil War?
- What were the key effects of the Spanish Civil War?

Timeline of events – 1820–1931	
1820	The Spanish Army, supported by liberals, overthrows the absolute monarchy and makes Spain a **constitutional monarchy** in a modernizing revolution
1821	Absolute monarchy is restored to Spain by French forces in an attempt to reinstate the old order
1833	In an attempt to prevent a female succession following the death of King Ferdinand, there is a revolt by 'Carlists'. The army intervenes to defeat the Carlists, who nevertheless remain a strong conservative force in Spanish politics (see Interesting Facts box)
1833–69	The army's influence in national politics increases during the 'rule of the Queens'
1869–70	Anarchist revolts take place against the state
1870–71	The monarchy is overthrown and the First Republic is established
1871	The army restores a constitutional monarchy
1875–1918	During this period the constitutional monarchy allows for democratic elections. The system is corrupt, however. Power remains in the hands of the wealthy oligarchs or 'caciques' Spanish nationalism suffers when Spain is defeated in 1898 in a war with the USA
1914–18	Spain remains neutral during World War I and experiences economic growth
1918–23	The economy falters and 12 different governments fail to redress the crisis. The regime reaches new lows in 1921, when the army, sent to crush a revolt led by Abd-el-Krim in Spanish Morocco, is massacred by Moors
1923–30	General Primo de Rivera takes control in a bloodless coup and rules for seven years, thus fatally undermining the legitimacy of the monarchy
1931	The King abdicates and the Second Republic is established

Carlism

Carlism is a political movement in Spain that looks to establish a separate line of the Bourbon family on the Spanish throne. This line is descended from Carlos V (1788–1855).

STUDENT STUDY SECTION

Review questions

Study the timeline above and then read the following quotation.

The notion that political problems could more naturally be solved by violence than by debate was firmly entrenched in a country in which for a thousand years civil war has been if not exactly the norm then certainly no rarity.

From Paul Preston, *The Spanish Civil War: Reaction, Revolution and Revenge*, 2006

1 Looking at the timeline above showing events in Spain in the 19th and early 20th centuries, what evidence is there for Preston's argument?

2 What factors were causing tensions in Spain during this time? (Economic, military, religious, political?)

3 What example of foreign intervention was there in Spain in the 19th century?

Long-term causes of the Spanish Civil War: political instability (1820–1931)

In the 19th century, Spain had struggled between periods of conservatism and liberalism. As you can see from the timeline above, there were several issues that caused tension and division in Spain in the century before the 1930s, fractures that were to become more acute in the decade before the civil war broke out.

Weakness of government

From 1871, Spain had been a constitutional monarchy. The King was head of state, and he appointed a Prime Minister who should have commanded a majority in the parliament (Cortes). Yet although the Cortes was elected by the male population, real power was held by the wealthy oligarchs, and political control shifted between their different cliques. There were two main parties, the Conservatives and the Liberals, but in fact there was no real difference between them. Elections were rigged or decided by corruption. There were no mass democratic political parties:

the consequence was, at a very superficial level, political stability, but beneath it tremendous social instability, because nothing ever really changed ... Elections changed virtually nothing. Only a relatively small proportion of the electorate had the right to vote, and since nothing changed ... the population was forced into apathy or violent opposition to the system.

From Paul Preston, *Modern History Review*, September 1991

The role of the Spanish Army

The army had a powerful political position in Spain due to its role in Spain's imperial past. It believed that it was the protector of the nation, and that this meant it had the right and duty to intervene in politics if a crisis occurred. It had intervened in this way several times, in 1820, 1871 and 1923. It did not, however, act to save the King in 1931, and this led to his exile. The army intervened again during the Second Republic and lastly in 1936. It was this last intervention that was to lead to civil war.

The army was unpopular with the people. It had a reputation for brutality, it was expensive and required heavy taxes to maintain. The army had also proved ineffective when it lost the Spanish Empire during the 19th century, and lost the war with America in 1898. It had also struggled to keep control of Morocco between 1906 and 1926.

The army was in need of reform. It was too big, and had too many officers. The upper and middle classes, however, defended their interests, as they dominated the officer corps. The army was generally conservative, but the 'Africanistas' – those who were experienced in the wars in Morocco – were the most traditional and nationalistic.

The role of the church

The Catholic Church was rich and powerful in Spain, and there had been disputes between church and state throughout the 19th century. The state had guaranteed the role of the church in education and in elements of the economy, and the church had used its wealth to gain considerable political and social influence. It used its power to support social, political and economic conservatism and was opposed to modernizing and liberal forces. The aristocracy was closely tied to the church; they made up the vast majority of senior clergy, and provided much of the funding for the church. This meant the church was inclined to defend the rights and status of the upper classes, which led to resentment amongst the poor. In many urban areas there were protests against the church, although it was more popular in the rural areas.

Economic causes

The plight of the agricultural workers was a key factor in the discontent that led to the civil war. Spain was mainly an agricultural economy, and agriculture was the main source of employment. Unfortunately, there were fundamental problems that made it inefficient. It did not provide sufficient food and work was only seasonal. There was the need for workers to migrate in search of work – most lived in abject poverty and the gap between rich and poor was vast. In the centre and south of Spain, land was owned in huge estates, the *latifundia*, by the 'Grandees' who dominated the political system. In the north, peasants owned small plots of land, but often these were too small to make an adequate living.

Rioting and disorder often broke out in the countryside. The Civil Guard were deployed to ruthlessly repress any disorder. With no support from the church, some looked to groups such as the **anarchists**, who argued for the redistribution of land. Yet many of the Catholic small landholders were very conservative and resistant to socialist or anarchist ideas. The conservatism was exploited by the Catholic Agrarian Federation, which provided support for farmers in return for their rejection of socialist ideas; these same farmers were later to support Franco and to fight on his side during the war.

Industrially there was also the need for modernization and reform. Apart from in the north, there had been little Spanish industrialization in the 19th century. Expansion was limited by endemic poverty. Workers in the towns, meanwhile, faced low wages, long hours, unregulated working conditions, poor housing and little in the way of welfare provision. This situation led to the growth of trade unionism. But the trade unions competed with each other (for example the CNT and UGT). The unions failed to achieve anything substantial, as the employers could always find alternative labour sources from the countryside. The workers' political parties had no real political power. With no legal means of improving their situation, violent uprising appealed to many as the means to effect change.

Spain's neutrality during World War I facilitated a short period of economic boom. With the increase of exports, however, there were also inflation and shortages, working-class living standards went down and working-class militancy increased. By the early 1920s, there were major economic problems, and this led to violent conflict between employers and employees particularly in industrial cities in Catalonia.

General Francisco Franco

General Franco was born Francisco Franco Bahamonde. He came from a military background, and had begun his career in the navy. However, as Spain's empire declined, the navy was cut down in size and Franco joined the army. He became a general after demonstrating sound leadership skills fighting in Morocco. Before the outbreak of the Spanish Civil War, Franco had been stationed on the Spanish mainland and was active in suppressing anarchists and anti-government forces in the early 1930s.

The Civil Guard

The Civil Guard was founded in 1844. Its purpose was to control the peasantry, maintain the status quo and stamp out any anti-monarchist, revolutionary sentiment. It was particularly active in the Basque provinces and was hated by the peasantry. It was later to play a role in supporting the conservative landowners in resisting the reforms of the Second Republic.

UGT and CNT

The Unión General de Trabajadores (UGT; General Union of Workers) was the socialist-led trade union, and the Confederación Nacional del Trabajo (CNT; National Confederation of Labour) was the anarchist trade union.

The role of the regions

A significant cause of tension was the ongoing struggle between the centralist state and Catalonia and the Basque provinces, which wanted decentralization and independence. The Catalans and the Basques had their own separate languages and cultures, and by the early 20th century they had their own industrialized economies and churches. Primo de Rivera took back the self-governing rights of Catalonia, and these separatist forces supported the Republican movement that overthrew Alfonso in 1931 (see below). (De Rivera was an experienced military official before becoming Prime Minister in 1923. He ruled Spain as a dictator until 1930.)

Political opposition

There were a number of groups opposed to the political status quo in Spain, and each would play a part in the political divisions that led to violent conflict in 1936. The liberal movement in Spain had achieved little in opposing conservative forces in the 19th century, although they remained a political force and supported the revolution that ousted the King in 1931. The Partido Socialista Obrero Español(PSOE; Spanish Socialist Party) had grown in urban areas in the late 19th century, but had minimal impact, whereas the UGT was more visible in organizing strikes and protests in the urban regions. In addition, following the Bolshevik revolution, a small Communist Party had emerged. The socialists, as with the liberals, played a significant role in the revolution of 1931, but the parties became divided over what reforms should take place. The more moderate socialists were led by Indalecio Prieto, and the radicals were led by Largo Caballero.

The anarchists were also a major political group in Spain; as previously suggested, this was mainly due to their demand for the redistribution of land, which was popular with the peasants. The anarchists argued for revolutionary methods and boycotted all democratic processes. Their trade union was the CNT, which like the UGT was active in organizing strikes and protests. In addition, there was a more extreme anarchist faction called the Federación Anarquista Ibérica (FAI; Spanish Anarchist Federation), which perpetrated bombings and assassinations.

The fall of the monarchy and the establishment of the Second Republic

King Alfonso XIII (1885–1931) was not a modernizer. The impact of military defeat in Morocco, and the post-World War I Depression, put pressure on the King, and after 12 unsuccessful governments during the period 1918–23 Alfonso did not resist the coup of General Primo de Rivera.

De Rivera tried to establish an authoritarian right-wing regime to redress Spain's problems, similar to the Italian fascist model. He started various infrastructure programmes for railways, roads and electrification, as well as irrigation schemes. Industrial production developed at three times the rate of output before 1923 and he ended the war in Morocco in 1925. Nevertheless, he ran up massive debts that put Spain into a dreadful situation when the Wall Street Crash came. He managed to alienate most of the powerful elements of society, including the landowners and the army. Thus De Rivera resigned in 1930, having not resolved Spain's economic problems, or brought about long-term political stability. It seemed that dictatorship as a solution to Spain's problems had failed. After municipal elections in April showed support for the San Sebastián Pact coalition of parties (republicans, liberals, socialists and Catalans), the King went into voluntary exile. This time neither the church nor the army intervened to save the King – there seemed nothing they could put in his place. A 'velvet revolution' had occurred and the Second Republic was established.

Review questions

1 Draw a mind map or spider diagram of the key issues dividing Spain by 1931.

2 Explain the events that led to the fall of King Alfonso in 1931.

3 Looking at the long-term issues in Spain and the political events of the 19th century, what problems was the Second Republic likely to face? Do you consider that war was inevitable by mid 1931?

Short-term causes of the Spanish Civil War: political polarization

Timeline of events – 1931–36

1931	Apr	Second Spanish Republic proclaimed
1933	Nov	Spanish right wins general election
1934	Oct	Asturias rising
1936	Feb	Popular Front government elected
	July	Army rising

Picture analysis

A symbolic representation of the Second Republic.

Question

What image is given here of the Second Republic? (Look carefully at all the symbolism in the painting.)

Between 1931 and 1936, Spain became politically polarized. You may have already decided in your answers to the review question 3 on p.230 that civil war in Spain was very likely given the long-term structural problems and clear divisions that already existed in the 19th century. Nevertheless, it is important to note the following: '…in 1931 when the Second Republic was established, no-one, except a tiny minority on the lunatic fringe on the extreme right or left, believed that Spain's problems could be solved only by war' (Paul Preston, *Modern History Review,* September 1991). The events of the Second Republic were thus central in bringing about a situation, only five years later, in which large numbers of people thought war was inevitable, if not desirable.

The Left Republic (April 1931–November 1933)

In the elections that followed Alfonso's departure, the centre-left won with the objective of modernizing Spain. The government declared a new constitution, stating that Spain was a 'democratic republic of workers of all classes'. Manuel Azaña became the President and leading figure in the new regime. However, the key issues causing tension in Spain before the 'velvet revolution' of 1931 continued to dominate the political, economic and social atmosphere under the new left-wing government.

Prime Minister Manuel Azaña.

Azaña addressed the issue of the church's power. His speeches were anticlerical, and an attempt was made to separate the church and state, and to limit church powers. The church was no longer in control of education, and the state payment of the clergy was to be stopped gradually over a two-year period. The power of the army was also attacked; the government attempted to reduce numbers by offering early retirement on full pay, an offer taken up by 50 per cent of officers. The military academy of Saragossa was closed (Franco had been its director). Yet this policy backfired to a certain extent, as not only was it expensive for the government, but it meant that the army was radicalized; those who remained in the army were the conservative and nationalist core, including the Africanistas.

The desperate economic problems that existed in Spain had been exacerbated by the Depression: agricultural prices were tumbling, wine and olive exports fell and land had gone out of cultivation. Peasant unemployment was rising. The effects were also being felt industrially; iron production fell by one-third and steel by almost one-half. Largo Caballero was Minister of Labour, and he initiated an extensive land redistribution programme, with compensation for landowners. In 1932, a law enabled the state to take over estates and to redistribute land to the peasants. Yet the government did not have the money for this change, and fewer than 7,000 families had benefited from the programme by 1933. The right saw this as a major threat to its interests, and an attempt to copy the Soviet system.

Civil unrest and violence continued under the Left Republic, and it dealt with its perpetrators brutally. The government introduced the Assault Guard in an attempt to produce a more left-wing military force. There were risings by both the right (General José Sanjurjo in 1932) against the reforms, and by the left (a good example was the Casas Viejos anarchist rising in 1933 – see below) against the slow pace of change. At this time, the risings were suppressed, as the majority of the army remained loyal.

As for the regional issues, Catalonia was given its own parliament, and some powers including law and order and dual control over education. Right-wing groups were angered by this change, as they saw it as a move towards independence for the regions and the break-up of Spain.

Each reform was perceived as an attack on one or more right-wing groups, i.e. the church, army, landowners or industrialists. A new right-wing party, the Confederación Española de

Derechas Autónomas (CEDA; Spanish Confederation of the Autonomous Right), was formed to defend church and landlords. CEDA was led by José María Gil-Robles and was modelled on the German Nazi Party. Indeed, the political divisions within Spain seemed to increase under the Second Republic. The right wing opposed the reforms, sometimes with violence.

Although some historians see the failure of land reform as central to the failure of the government during this period, historian Paul Preston has argued that the right wing was in any case never going to give the regime a chance. Azaña also did himself a disservice when in January 1933 government guards set fire to houses in the village of Casas Viejas near Cadiz in an attempt to 'smoke out' a group of anarchists. Twenty-five people were killed. This incident lost the left-wing Republic a lot of working-class support, and led even the socialists to withdraw support from Azaña, who resigned in 1933.

STUDENT STUDY SECTION

Review question

How did the actions of the Second Republic create more tension? In what way did they, in Paul Preston's words, 'ensure that Spain's underlying conflicts were transmitted into national politics'?

The Right Republic (November 1933–February 1936)

In the elections of 1933, the Republic swung to the right, with the right-wing and centrist parties benefiting from the disunity of the left. Although CEDA was the largest party, the President resisted giving Gil-Robles power. However, CEDA forced the government's hand in October 1934 by withdrawing support. Gil-Robles was made War Minister and two other CEDA party members were given cabinet posts.

The new government ruled for two years in what became known as the black years, because they embarked on systematically reversing the Left Republic's reforms. Church control was restored over education and the clergy were again to be paid by the state. Azaña's key economic reform – the land programme – was halted. Catalonia attempted to resist interference, and declared itself independent after CEDA joined the government. Its autonomy was suspended after the Asturian miners' uprising in 1934. This rebellion was put down by troops, including Moroccan forces. Threats from the left of a 'general strike' increased. Historians have argued that the violent suppression of this uprising increased the likelihood of a civil war in Spain. In addition, the right lost the support of the Basques, who now backed the left wing. Violence was widespread.

STUDENT STUDY SECTION

Research activity

Research the Asturian miners' uprising of 1934. In pairs, discuss the extent to which you agree that this was an 'attempted revolution'.

The political response to the Right Republic was divided. Caballero was more extreme in his speeches than the more moderate Prieto. He suggested that CEDA was the Spanish Nazi party and that the left should seek a Soviet-style solution for Spain. Thus, he articulated the parallels in Spanish politics to the broader European political landscape.

In response, Gil-Robles demanded a shift to a more authoritarian approach to control the communists in Spain. This response led to more cooperation between the left's factions: socialists, anarchists, syndicalists and now communists. Indeed, Prieto attempted to find some common ground between the left and centre groups to enable them to take on the right wing.

The destabilization of the Spanish electoral system

It is worth noting that the Spanish electoral system ensured that only a small swing in the number of votes cast had a huge effect on the parliamentary system. Thus, although there was only a minor shift of votes from the left to the right, there was a big change in parliamentary power. The same was to happen in 1936 when the Popular Front gained control. The instability created by the electoral system was a contributory factor to the breakdown of the Second Republic.

Prieto

Prieto, whose full name was Indalecio Prieto Tuero, was one of the leading figures of the Socialist Workers' Party (Partido Socialista Obrero Español, PSOE) in Spain. He was a prominent critic of de Rivera's government, and was appointed finance minister in Zamora's government in 1931.

The Popular Front (February–July 1936)

The right wing disintegrated as the economic and the political situation deteriorated, and in the elections of February 1936, the 'Popular Front', which was an anti-fascist pact made up of various left-wing groups including the socialists and the communists, was victorious. However, here was the same policy that was being advocated by Stalin in his 'Popular Front' policy from 1935. Thus, the Popular Front was for many in Spain a final attempt to uphold democracy and peace, but others associated it with Stalin and the more extreme communist supporters.

The manifesto promoted by Azaña, now returned to power as the President, was liberal and not radical. Nevertheless, the government wanted to restore the reforms of the 1931–33 regime, and political prisoners were released. But there was still no political consensus; Caballero's socialists did not join the government and the right would not accept the restoration of reforms.

The anarchists encouraged peasants to seize land, which led to an increase in violence in the countryside. They also openly recruited for their militias and organized bombings and assassinations. Open conflict between the anarchist FAI and fascist CEDA and Falange youth movements increased. The government again faced increasing disorder. In May, the CNT called a general strike, and there were several strikes throughout June. The right wing believed that Spain was in the early throes of a left-wing revolution.

Immediate causes of the Spanish Civil War

The victory of the left in the 1936 elections threw the right-wing CEDA into turmoil. Gil-Robles began to use his funds to support military plans for a coup. In fact, military officers began planning for a coup as soon as the Popular Front gained power. An extreme nationalist group of junior officers joined with the senior Africanista officers, including Mola and Franco. The catalyst for the coup was the murder of a popular CEDA leader on 13 July 1936.

Azaña knew that there were plans for a coup, and attempted to prevent it by moving key military figures to remote posts. However, they had already made their plans and set a date for the coup – 18 July 1936. The conspirators made contact with the fascist Falange and the monarchist 'Carlist' group. Spain was clearly polarized between groups inspired by the Soviets, who feared the fascists, and the right, which was inspired by Hitler and Mussolini and feared the communists.

When the details of the coup were discovered, the coup was initiated earlier, on 17 July, from Morocco. It spread to the mainland, and was successful in taking northern Spain and parts of Andalusia. Yet the rising failed in the main industrial areas, and the rebels did not take Madrid. Half the army had remained loyal to the Republic. Thus the coup overall was unsuccessful, and, had it remained a Spanish affair, it is quite possible that the Republicans would have won.

> **Falange**
> Falange (Phalanx) was founded by Primo de Rivera, the son of the former dictator, in 1933. By early 1936, it had 8,000 members (mainly students). They had a 'blue shirted uniform'. The Falange demanded a strong authoritarian leadership, but was also committed to radical social change.

STUDENT STUDY SECTION

Review questions

1 To what extent did economic issues lead to a civil war?

2 What was the impact of international events on the growing divisions in Spain?

Class debate

Divide the class into three groups. Each group needs to argue one of the following:
- The right wing was responsible for the Spanish Civil War
- The left wing was responsible for the Spanish Civil War
- Both left and right were equally responsible for the Spanish Civil War

Document analysis

Document A

When considering which side, the Right or Left can be held responsible for causing the Civil War, the debate often focuses on which side departed from democratic and legal means first. The Socialists are held responsible, by some, for refusing to join the Popular Front government which in turn concerned the Right; they thought this could be because the Socialists were now intent on revolution. The Right then planned the coup to prevent this.

In terms of which side resorted to violence first, it could be viewed as the Left in attempting to seize power in the Asturias Rising – but the right had attempted this earlier, in 1932 in the Sanjurjo Rising. In the end most historians agree that it was the right's coup that triggered the general conflict.

From Antony Beever, *The Battle for Spain: The Spanish Civil War 1936–1939*, 2006

Document B

Faced with the difficulties of modernising a backward economy and social structure in a country without strong democratic traditions, and against the background of the Depression, the Republic was facing insurmountable problems by 1936. Civil War may not have been inevitable but certainly did not come as a surprise.

From Patricia Knight, *The Spanish Civil War*, 1998

Question

Explain the key points made by Antony Beevor in Document A and Patricia Knight in Document B.

ToK Time

Discuss in small groups how the political and socio-economic situation of a contemporary observer influences his or her opinion of a crisis such as the Spanish Civil War. Write up the key points of your discussion in your ToK journal.

'Soft Construction with Boiled Beans (Premonition of Civil War)' (1936), by the Spanish Surrealist painter Salvador Dalí.

Research question

Salvador Dalí painted 'Soft Construction with Boiled Beans (Premonition of Civil War)' in 1936. In pairs, research Dalí's motives in painting this picture and what the images in the picture represent with regard to Spain and war.

The course of the Spanish Civil War

With the assistance of Nazi Germany, General Franco airlifted 24,000 experienced troops of the Army of Africa to Spain. It was the fact that Hitler responded to Franco's pleas for help, that kept Franco's efforts alive. Once on the Spanish mainland, he used a policy of terror as his forces moved towards Madrid in August. Franco's success was complemented by the achievements of General Emilio Mola, who took territory in the north (see map).

The army coup had aimed to crush the 'left revolution', but had instead politicized and radicalized many Spaniards towards the left. The supporters of the Republican regime of 1936 became known as the 'Loyalists', and those that supported the rebels called themselves 'Nationalists'. Divisions could generally be drawn by class: the workers supporting the Republic and the middle and upper classes the Nationalists. The Nationalists also had the support of much of the church. However, alliances could also be accidental, depending on where they were when the war developed. The peasants of the north and central Spain tended to be Nationalists, while the landless labourers of the south followed the Republicans. The Basques and Catalans supported the Republic, as it had backed their autonomous ambitions.

Although the Nationalists made gains in the first weeks of the war, the Republic retained some advantages. It remained in control of most major cities and key industrial areas, it had Spain's gold reserves, and important elements of the military – most of the air force and navy – remained loyal. Yet as you can see from the timeline and the maps below, the Nationalists were able to make steady progress in pushing back the Republic.

'Death of a Loyalist', photograph by Robert Capa, 5 September 1936.

Timeline of the Spanish Civil War – 1936–39

Republican- and Nationalist-held territory, July 1936.

1936	Jul	Franco's forces airlifted from Morocco to southern Spain
	Aug	Britain and France begin policy of non-intervention
	4 Sep	Largo Caballerro forms new Republican government
	13 Sep	San Sebastián taken by Nationalists
	Oct	Republic incorporates militias into new Popular Army
	1 Oct	Franco becomes head of Nationalist government and supreme military commander
	29 Oct	Soviet intervention begins; German and Italian planes bomb Madrid
	6 Nov	Republican government leaves Madrid for Valencia
	23 Nov	Nationalists abandon attempt to take Madrid
1937	Feb	Nationalist offensive to cut the links between Madrid and Valencia fails at the battle of Jarama. Russian tanks and planes play a crucial role in the battle
	8 Feb	Fall of Málaga to the Nationalists
	March	Nationalist offensive to tighten the pressure on Madrid from the north fails at the battle of Guadalajara. This was a major defeat for the Italian Army, and again Soviet equipment was vital to Republican success
	Apr	Franco unites Carlists, fascists and monarchists into one movement
	26 Apr	German Condor Legion bombs and destroys Guernica
	15 May	Fall of Largo Caballero
	17 May	Juan Negrin forms new government
	19 Jun	Fall of Bilbao to the Nationalists; end of Basque independence
	Jul	Republican offensive to break the siege of Madrid to the west fails at Brunete
	Aug	Republican offensive to break out from Madrid to the north-east fails at Belchite
	Sep–Oct	Nationalists captured rest of northern Spain
	Dec	Newly organized Republican Popular Army captures Teruel in central Spain.

Republican- and Nationalist-held territory, May 1938. ▶

1938	Feb	Nationalists retake Teruel and launch the strategically crucial advance to the Mediterranean to cut Catalonia off from the rest of Republican Spain
	Apr	Nationalists reach the Mediterranean at Vinaroz. Republican Spain cut in two
	Jul	Republican offensive on the River Ebro fails
	Nov	Nationalists drive Republicans back across River Ebro. Nationalists march on Barcelona
1939	Feb	Barcelona falls to Nationalists
	28 Mar	Nationalists enter Madrid
	1 Apr	Franco announces end of war.

Why did the Nationalists win the Spanish Civil War?

We can analyze the reasons for the Nationalist victory by considering the weaknesses of the Republicans versus the strengths of the Nationalists.

Republican weaknesses

Political disunity

Caballero became head of a coalition government in September 1936. His rule was weakened by the fact that the Republicans were politically divided. Indeed, Republicans subscribed to widely different ideologies. The key divisions were between the communists and socialists, who believed that the 'revolution' should now be postponed until the war was won, and the anarchists, who argued that the war could only be won through revolutionary policies. The anarchists, dominant in Catalonia, Aragon and Andalusia, encouraged 'revolution from below' in the areas they controlled, and some historians suggest that this added a crucial hurdle for the Republic, as they had to try to regain their centralized control. The communists/socialists had more influence in Madrid and Valencia. The regions of Catalonia, the Basque region and Asturias became virtually independent.

The war generally increased the popularity of the communists. For example, in July 1936 the Spanish Communist Party numbered around 40,000 members, but by October 1937 it had 400,000 members. The Communist Party exploited the fact that it was the only Republican group with clear foreign support – from the USSR. However, to retain control the communists often used 'terror' tactics, which led to some resistance even in sympathetic territories (for example, the 'May Days' in Barcelona in 1937 – see below). In addition, the communists and socialists wanted victory in the war to strengthen the Second Republic, whereas the anarchists wanted a new revolutionary regime.

The lack of unity between the forces of the Republic is exemplified in the four days of street fighting in Barcelona in May 1937 – communists and socialists on one side and the anarchists and POUM on the other. This fighting became known as the 'May Days'. As a result of this turmoil, Caballero was replaced by the Marxist Juan Negrin, the communists' choice, as leader. Negrin attacked the POUM and anarchist leaders, who were imprisoned or executed. His more authoritarian regime lasted until March 1939, when there was military a coup in Madrid.

Military problems

The Republic lacked strong military leadership. There was no unified command, and the communists and anarchists would not work together. Indeed, the anarchist militias and the Basques refused to be led by a central command structure. The Basques would not permit their forces to defend areas outside their own territory. In addition, loyal army officers, with potentially valuable experience, were not trusted by the Republic.

In the first vital weeks of the war, the Republic was dependent on ineffective militia units that formed haphazardly. This meant that they fought a series of local conflicts rather than one clear overall campaign. Different fronts operated separately, although to some extent this situation was due to the territory held by the Republicans. Many battlefields were not within range of their air force, and they failed to sustain offensive campaigns in 1937 at Brunete, Belchite and Teruel. Indeed, it was not until the end of 1936 that the Republicans started to replace militias with a coherent 'Popular Army'.

Economic problems

In areas under anarchist control, industries, public utilities and transport were taken over by workers' committees; in the countryside collective farms were set up. However, neither

To access worksheet 12.1 on propaganda in the Spanish Civil War, please visit www.pearsonbacconline.com and follow the on-screen instructions.

POUM
The Partido Obrero Unificación Marxista (POUM; Workers' Party of Marxist Unification) was a small influential Catalan Marxist party that was critical of the Soviet system and was often in opposition to the communists/socialists, siding with the anarchists.

of these systems could supply the needs of the Republic to fight the war. Some historians have argued that this situation was due more to the impact of the war than to a badly run government, but most believe that the collectives impaired the Republic's war effort. Production in the key area of Catalan fell by two-thirds between 1936 and 1939, and the Republic was increasingly affected by food and raw material shortages. Inflation was also a problem, reaching 300 per cent during the war. At the same time wages only increased by 15 per cent.

The international body known as the Non-Intervention Committee (NIC), established by Britain and France in 1936 for the purpose of preventing the foreign influx of support to the warring parties in Spain, also had an impact on the Republic. It starved the Republic of all credit; the USSR was the only country willing to trade with it. Even this trade had to be paid for using the entire gold reserves of Spain. Paul Preston has argued that communist control ultimately improved the situation by centralizing control, but this happened too late to save the Republic.

Foreign Assistance

STUDENT STUDY SECTION

Review activity

Look back at the timeline on pp.235–36. Identify key points where foreign intervention played a significant role in the fighting.

Foreign aid has been seen as a critical factor in determining the outcome of the Spanish Civil War. Some historians have suggested its role has been exaggerated; nevertheless, there is no doubt that the foreign assistance given to the Republic was far more limited than that afforded to the Nationalists. The main ally of the Republic was the USSR, and it was the Soviets who initially saved the Republic and enabled it to fight a civil war in 1936–37. The Soviet aircraft and tanks were better early on than their German and Italian counterparts. However, no Soviet troops were sent to fight; they committed only 1,000 aircraft, 750 tanks and some advisers. In addition, this aid had to be paid for by the Republic, which sent, as we have seen, all of its gold reserves to Moscow.

The other key allies of the Republicans were the International Brigades, which were organized by the Soviet Comintern. Some 35,000 foreign volunteers went to fight in Spain. Although their role seems to have been significant in the defence of Madrid, overall their impact was limited. In 1938, the Soviets withdrew their support and the International Brigades went home, a final blow for the Republic.

Although France sent aid initially, the support ended when it joined Britain in the policy of non-intervention. This policy was primarily driven by anti-communist sentiments, but it also meant that Hitler and Mussolini had no opposition from the Western democracies. This policy has been condemned by many historians. Francisco José Romero Salvadó writes of the NIC that:

...it was never more than a sham which actually worked in favour of the insurgents. A legal government was equated to a group of seditious generals. The Republic was hindered by an arms embargo from mounting an effective defence and a perfect cloak was provided for the Axis powers to continue their activities. Under British auspices, the committee would remain until the end of the war an empty talking shop. It was a perfect weapon to prevent France from making a more direct commitment, preserve consensus at home and avoid confrontation with Germany and Italy.

From Francisco J. Romero Salvadó, *Modern History Review*, February 1995

Document analysis

What criticisms does Salvadó make of the Non-Intervention Committee (p.238)?

Research activity

The English novelist and journalist George Orwell was one of many foreign individuals who went to Spain to join the International Brigades during the Spanish Civil War.

In small groups, research the different countries, groups and famous individuals that went to Spain to fight in the International Brigades; for example, the Abraham Lincoln Brigade from the USA.

Nationalist strengths

Political unity

The major strength of the Nationalists was unity. In July 1936, however, the Nationalists were almost as divided as the Republicans. Their only common aim was to overthrow the government. Initially, Generals Mola, Goded and Sanjurjo seemed more important than Franco, but after the first few weeks Franco had emerged as the leader. In September 1936, the generals decided that they needed a unified command. It was agreed that Franco would assume political and military control. He became head of government and head of state. This rise to power was due not only to other leaders dying, or doing badly in the war, but also to his position in command of the Army of Africa and because important German aid came through him.

To achieve political unity, Franco needed to control both the Carlists and the Falange. In 1937 their numbers were impressive: 70,000 and one million respectively. In April, Franco merged the two parties. This new party, Falange Española Tradicionalista (FET; Spanish Traditionalist Phalanax), was under his control.

Franco was also assisted by support from the church, which opposed the left and its secular ideologies. From the pulpit, church leaders would denounce atheist communism and call for a crusade to protect Christian civilization. Indeed, Franco used a mixture of propaganda and terror in the areas under his command.

Although some historians argue that the Soviet involvement in the war (which may have been Stalin's deliberate policy) led to its extension, others have suggested that Franco gained power and authority from his victories on the battlefield, and that it was he who extended the war to enhance his own dictatorial power. The nationalistic politics of Franco were not undermined by the foreign support given by Germany and Italy.

Military unity

Militarily the Nationalists initially had similar problems to the Republicans – 'columns' of Carlist and Falangist militias attempted to operate alongside regular army units. In contrast, however, these militias were effectively drawn into the regular army. The Army of Africa played a significant role. It contained the best troops in the country, and it could cover for other forces while they were being trained and equipped. In open and mobile offensive operations, the Army of Africa proved itself the most effective force in the entire Civil War.

The unified command was key to the Nationalists' success. Franco's leadership was accepted by the other generals and right-wing parties. Ultimately, the Italian forces were under his command too. They were successful in pushing on and winning offensives, and were also able to adopt effective defensive tactics during the Republican offensive campaigns of 1937.

The Nationalists had sound communications, and managed to equip their growing army throughout the civil war. They could also rely on their large number of junior officers.

Franco was an able military and political leader. He would often not pursue more radical advice given to him by his German and Italian advisers. His concern for his troops ensured that the majority was obedient.

Economic advantage

The business community backed the Nationalists, which meant they could get credit to buy war supplies. Also, by September 1936 they were in control of the main food-producing areas. After their successes in 1937 in the north, they added the main industrial areas to their control.

The Nationalists also benefited from international trade and credit, which was not restricted. It has been estimated that the USA gave $700 million in credit during the course of the war. This meant that Franco's forces could buy all the rubber and oil they needed, acquired from US companies.

Foreign assistance

As suggested above, some historians have argued that foreign aid was a crucial factor in the Nationalists' victory over the Republic. Hugh Thomas writes in his 1961 book *The Spanish Civil War* that the conflict 'became an international crisis whose solution was decided by external circumstances.' Indeed, the rebels benefited from more aid, which was of a better quality than that given to the Republicans, and its supply was continuous throughout the war. The Germans had airlifted Franco's Army from Morocco to the mainland in the first stage of the war, at a vital moment in the conflict. The Germans also committed the Condor Legion – 10,000 troops, 800 aircraft and 200 tanks. The Italians sent 70,000–75,000 troops, 750 planes and 150 tanks. The Portuguese sent 20,000 troops and permitted aid to pass over their long border with Spain. This assistance was significant in several ways. It allowed the Nationalists to fight in the first place, owing to the German airlift, but German planes also gave the Nationalists control of the air from 1937. Franco's command was not compromised, and after an Italian defeat at Guadalajara, they were taken under Spanish command. The key benefit for the Nationalists, however, was not the manpower, as most of their armies were Spanish, it was the modern equipment they received.

Review activities

Summarize the key points made in the text in a grid:

	Nationalists	Republicans
Political strengths/weaknesses		
Military strengths/weaknesses		
Economic advantages/ disadvantages		
Foreign assistance		

Class debate

Divide the class into two groups. One side will argue that the Nationalists' strengths won the Spanish Civil War, the other will argue that it was due to Republican weaknesses. The motion is:

'The strengths of the Nationalists won the Civil War.'

Each side must have a series of thematic and coherent arguments. To gain a point, they have to support arguments with clear evidence.

Overview: foreign intervention

In general, the decision by foreign governments to get involved (or not get involved) in the Spanish Civil War was a result of both ideology and self-interest. Foreign intervention had two main effects:

- It both lengthened and intensified the war
- It meant that the Spanish issues that caused the war were overtaken and submerged by the wider ideological battles taking place in Europe.

Britain

Britain took the lead in establishing the NIC in September 1936. Britain's fear was that the war would spread and become a general European conflict. However, three of the key members of the NIC – Germany, Italy and the USSR – ignored the NIC completely and became the main foreign forces in Spain. In addition, Britain's non-intervention policies were limited and tended to favour the Nationalists. They focused on preventing aid going to the Republic and allowed the Nationalists, but not the Republicans, to use Gibraltar as a communications base. In December 1936, they signed a trading agreement with the Nationalists that permitted British companies to trade with the rebel forces. The USA also allowed American companies to trade with the Nationalists, such as the Texaco oil company and General Motors. It would seem that Spain was sacrificed to the policy of appeasement in the same vein as Czechoslovakia; Britain wanted to avoid a general war at all costs, and did not want the civil war to damage its relations with Italy or Portugal.

STUDENT STUDY SECTION

Cartoon analysis

Cartoon by David Low, in the *Evening Standard*, 13 January 1937. The caption says 'Trustful Tony: "Just to discourage cheating I'll wear a strait-jacket and let you boys play my hand."'

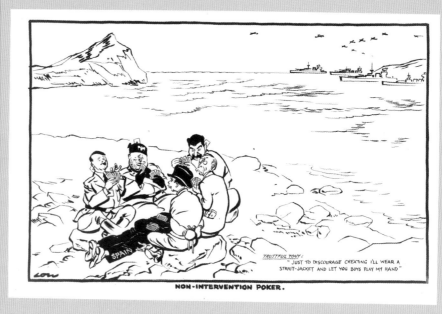

Question

What is the message of this cartoon with regard to the Non-Intervention Committee?

France

The French support for the Republic was inconsistent, and this reflected the complexity of its position towards the civil war. It was not in French interests to have a right-wing regime on its border that could join with Italy and Germany to encircle France. But French politics was also polarized, and the government feared a revolt in France should it fully commit in Spain. France was also reliant on Britain, which was more anti-Republic, for its foreign policy options. In the end, the French restricted themselves mainly to humanitarian assistance. The impact of the French pursuing non-intervention with Britain dealt a fatal blow to the Republic, which could have benefited greatly from support from this large country on its border. The resulting reliance of the Republic on the Soviets polarized the politics of the Spanish Civil War, and associated the Republic with 'Soviet communism'. Nevertheless, the French did not stop citizens from joining the International Brigades, which were mainly organized in France. In addition, France was the main centre for the coordination of Soviet aid.

USSR

The USSR's reasons for supporting the Republic were not simply ideological. The Spanish conflict in fact presented Stalin with a dilemma. The emergence of another fascist state in Europe would strengthen Hitler's position in Europe. On the other hand, a Republic victory could panic Britain and France into an alliance with Hitler against the threat of communism. Such an outcome would ruin Stalin's policy of bringing Britain and France into an alliance with the USSR to contain Hitler. Stalin was divided between these two concerns. Initially he welcomed the NIC, but seeing that Germany and Italy were able to ignore its rules, he then went on to organize the transport of international volunteers to Spain and also weapons from Russia. He actually withdrew from the NIC in October 1936.

Although some historians have argued that Franco protracted the Spanish Civil War to enhance his own power, Stalin also had a motive for dragging the fighting out. The war would drain the resources of Germany, and the longer it went on the more likely it was for the war to develop into a general war. This general war would then be waged on the other side of Europe, far from the borders of the USSR.

Nevertheless, Stalin withdrew Soviet support in June 1938. Not only did the Republic seem to be losing, but it now seemed that the Western democracies were set on appeasing the fascist dictators. Stalin's aim of creating a bloc to resist Hitler ended when Czechoslovakia was abandoned by Britain and France in the Munich Agreement in September 1938.

Germany

Hitler's Germany was cautious when the appeal for help came from the rebels. He was not yet ready for a general European war. Hermann Göring was important in the decision to support the rebels. Both he and Hitler wanted to stop the spread of communism, but Göring also wanted to test out his *Luftwaffe* in live conditions. There were economic and strategic benefits for Germany too; raw materials such as iron ore could be gained, and deploying to Spain would give Germany the potential to hamper Anglo-French maritime communications.

Hitler did not think the war would last long, and only wanted to commit limited aid. Although a member of the NIC (it left in May 1937), Germany supplied the Nationalists through Portugal. As well as its support of Franco in the initial stages of the war, the Condor Legion perpetrated the now infamous bombing of Guernica and they played a pivotal role supporting the nationalists in taking Catalonia.

German involvement was important to the outcome of the war, not only as it played crucial military roles at critical times during the fighting, but also as other governments were deterred from getting involved due to their presence.

Italy

Italy gave the most assistance of all the foreign powers. Mussolini wanted to be involved for a number of reasons. First, involvement would be in line with his anti-communist/socialist/democratic outlook and his pro-fascist stance. Second, he wished to enhance his influence as the key power in the Mediterranean and thereby demonstrate Italy's might. Third, a fascist victory would weaken France and prevent French left-wing influence in Spain. Another fascist power would encircle France and put pressure on French colonies in North Africa.

As we have seen, the Italians not only sent 70,000–75,000 troops, they contributed many planes, tanks and weapons. Italian bombers attacked Spanish cities, and their submarines were a constant threat to supplies. Italy ignored its membership of the NIC. Historians suggest that although Italy sent many troops, the significant element of its intervention was its air and naval support, which helped the Nationalists to secure victory. As a wider result, the relationship between Italy and Germany was cemented in Spain.

Portugal

Portugal was an important part of the foreign contribution to Franco's victory. Indeed, it was the only foreign force not compromised at any time by membership of the NIC. Not only did Portugal send 20,000 troops, but it was fundamental to supplying the rebels along the Spanish–Portuguese border, and provided a base for communications. Portugal's long-term alliance with Britain led to the British being reluctant to counter its support for the Nationalists. This was, of course, an important benefit for Franco's troops.

Pablo Picasso's *Guernica* has become the iconic image of the Spanish Civil War.

ToK Time

Document work – case study: Guernica

One of the most notorious events of the Spanish Civil War was the German bombing of the defenceless Basque town of Guernica. The Condor Legion were the perpetrators of the raid, in which 1,600 people were killed. Pablo Picasso's painting *Guernica* is not only the iconic image of the Spanish Civil War, but it has become one of the most powerful anti-war paintings in the history of art. Its powerful and terrifying image of the carnage wreaked by the bombing of civilians is recognized across the world. Indeed, its impact was considered so powerful that a copy of Guernica hanging in the UN was covered up when the war against Iraq was announced to the world's press.

Discuss how and why a piece of art can convey such a powerful and cross-cultural message. Consider the relative role of the different ways of knowing in your discussion.

STUDENT STUDY SECTION

Read the following sources and answer the questions:

Document A

The Nationalists maintained that Guernica had been blown up by the Basques themselves, in order to discredit the blameless Nationalists. A later version said that Republican planes dropped bombs to detonate charges of dynamite placed in the sewers. Twenty years later it was still a crime in Franco's Spain to say that Guernica had been destroyed by the Nationalists.

From David Mitchell, *The Spanish Civil War*, 1971

Document B

Our consciences were uneasy about it. After living through the raid we knew only too well that the destruction had come from the air. The Reds had hardly any planes, we knew that too. Amongst our own, we'd admit the truth: our side had bombed the town and it was a bad thing. 'But what can we do about it now?' we'd say. It was simply better to keep quiet.

From a statement by Juan Sangroniz, a Nationalist, quoted in Ronald Fraser, *Blood of Spain*, 1994

Document C

The Germans said the wind caused the bombs to drift eastwards [the target had been a bridge over the river]. In fact Guernica was a military target, being a communications centre close to the battle line. Retreating republican soldiers could only escape with any ease through Guernica because the bridge over the river was the last one before the sea. But if the aim of the Condor Legion was to destroy the bridge why did they not use their supremely accurate Stuka bombers? At least part of the aim must have been to cause maximum panic and confusion among civilians as well as soldiers. The use of incendiary bombs proves that some destruction of buildings and people other than the bridge must have been intended.

From Hugh Thomas, *The Spanish Civil War*, 1977

Questions

1   In what ways are the views expressed in Document A supported by the views in Document B?

2   What reasons are identified in Document C for the bombing of Guernica?

IBLP link – Communicators

As effective communicators, you should be able to express ideas and information confidently and creatively in a variety of ways – not just in your written work. Divide the class into groups. Within each group, someone should take on one of the following roles:

- Spanish socialist from Barcelona
- Spanish Nationalist from Madrid
- French supporter of the Republican government
- German supporter of the Nationalist government
- Italian supporter of the Nationalist government
- Russian Stalinist supporter of the Republican government
- British non-interventionist
- American supporter of the Lincoln Brigade.

You must now write a speech, which should last around one minute, rallying people to join your forces fighting 'for freedom' in Spain. You must include details of why you believe your perspective to be right, and why people should fight or not intervene. Present your speech to your group, or to the whole class.

The nature of the Spanish Civil War

Although for the foreign powers the war was 'limited', for the Spanish it was a 'total' war as well as a civil war. Propaganda was used on both sides to 'dehumanize' the enemy, even though that enemy was from the same country. Atrocities were common. Meanwhile, the targeting of civilians in bombing raids, symbolized in the attack on Guernica, offered a chilling premonition of what was to come in World War II. There were no lines drawn between civilian and combatant.

Militarily, the Spanish Civil War seems to have been fought at a 'crossroads' in the evolution of modern warfare. For example, in some cases cavalry charges proved effective, as in the Nationalist attack north of Teruel in February 1938. However, the importance of new technology – particularly the dominance of airpower – in future wars became clear in Spain, shown by the crushing of the major Republican offensives of 1937 and 1938 by the combined arms of the Condor Legion. Indeed, one of the reasons that the war lasted so long was due to the fact that neither side managed consistently to gain control of the air. Control of the sea was also important, and the Italians played a significant role in maintaining supply routes for the Nationalists.

The war on land was at times similar to the attrition and stalemate battles of World War I. Defence remained easier than attack. In repeated attacks by both sides around Madrid, casualties were high, with attackers taking little ground. In other battles, the changing nature of land warfare could be seen; the tactics of *Blitzkrieg* were evolving, with the application of tanks, artillery and air bombardment to prepare an advance.

The Spanish Civil War did not develop into a guerrilla war because, as Antony Beevor writes in *The Battle for Spain*:

The conditions for a universal guerrilla war simply did not exist. The best-suited regions, with the right terrain, were insufficient to have stretched nationalist forces beyond capacity. But on thinly held fronts, many more nationalist troops could have been held down by commando actions … Franco did not so much win the war: the republican commanders, with the odds already stacked against them, squandered the courage and sacrifice of their troops and lost it.

From Antony Beevor, *The Battle for Spain: The Spanish Civil War 1936–1939*, 2006

Effects and results of the Spanish Civil War – Spain

Scene from the film *Land & Freedom*, the story of a British communist who fights for the Republicans during the Spanish Civil War.

Human cost

The civil war had brought great human and material destruction to Spain. Around 100,000 Republicans were killed during the war, and about 70,000 Nationalists. Moreover, the killing continued after the war, as Franco launched a terror campaign to eradicate opposition. It is estimated that a further 40,000–200,000 were killed during this period, known as the 'White Terror'.

Thousands of Republicans and their sympathizers were held for years in concentration camps and prisons. Often Republican children were taken from their parents to be 're-educated'. Some were placed with reliable Nationalist/Catholic families, while others were sent to orphanages where they were indoctrinated against the views and actions of their own parents. Divisions and hatred remained in Spanish society for decades.

STUDENT STUDY SECTION

Research activity

A female combatant during the Spanish Civil War.

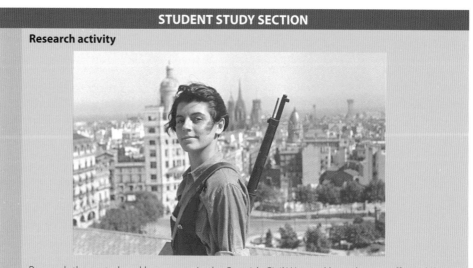

Research the part played by women in the Spanish Civil War, and how the war affected their role in society.

Economic cost

Spain's economy was devastated by the war. Some 10–15 per cent of its wealth was destroyed, and per capita income was 28 per cent lower in 1939 than in 1935. Seventy per cent of Madrid's factory machinery needed to be replaced, and its communications systems, including the city's tram network, had to be rebuilt. Around a third of its merchant shipping was out of action. There was high inflation due to the cost of fighting the war, and the method used to attempt to pay for it – printing money. The Republican land reform was reversed by Franco, and Spain's agricultural economy remained inefficient and ineffective. Labourers had to tolerate periodic unemployment, and landowners were not interested in modernization. In addition, Spain had massive debts to pay. Due to the human cost of the war, there was a corresponding lack of skilled workers, and an overriding general labour shortage. Spain attempted to find foreign loans for investment, but the British demanded that debt was paid back first, and the Germans also wanted the Spanish to repay the cost of the aid sent to them before further investment was made.

The economy may have improved due to the outbreak of World War II. Franco seems to have attempted to gain leverage over Spain's debt to Britain and France in August 1939, by offering to remain neutral and not ally Spain with Nazi Germany. He also had discussions with the Germans, presumably offering a similar exchange, in November and December. Once war broke out, Britain and France relented, and signed trade agreements with Spain (France in January, and then Britain in March 1940). But the German exploitation of Spain's resources during World War II may also have weakened the economy. The original debt remained after the war, and this gave Britain, France and the USA influence in Franco's Spain. Spain was in isolation after World War II, and suffered famine in 1946. With industrial output at a level below that of 1918, Spain's economy may have been saved by aid from the right-wing Argentine dictator, Perón.

Nevertheless, in the longer term, as the Cold War took hold, Spain became less isolated, and with some reforms in the 1950s and 1960s it developed a powerful capitalist economy. Spain industrialized and also developed a strong service industry.

Political effects

Franco emerged from the war as Spain's dictator. He remained in power until his death in 1975, ruling, as Paul Preston writes, 'as if it were a country occupied by a victorious foreign army'. Franco's regime declared that they had to save the country from communism. The White Terror that ensued led to the killing of thousands of Republicans and the exodus of half a million Spaniards, who fled to neighbouring countries. They included most of the intellectuals of Spain – teachers, lawyers, researchers, doctors and famous writers, poets, artists and musicians. Those that remained had to conform to Franco's authoritarian, Catholic and conservative views.

In 1939, the Law of Political Responsibility made supporters of the Republicans (either before or during the war) liable to punishment, including confiscation of land, large fines or even the death sentence. The law allowed for the transfer of vast amounts of land from Republicans to the state.

The key objectives of the new regime were to restore the power of the privileged class and to control the working class. Wages were cut and all industrial political activism was outlawed. The CNT and the UGT were destroyed. Employment for those Republicans who had escaped imprisonment was almost impossible. In rural areas, the inequalities and iniquities of the social and working system, described earlier in this chapter, were preserved and maintained by the Civil Guard.

All of the Republic's reforms concerning the church were repealed, and indeed the 1950s have been termed the 'era of the national church.' The historian Frances Lannon writes, 'The Catholic Church enjoyed a degree of state support that was much greater than at any time since the 18th century. Government and church combined to preach order, hierarchy and discipline. The counter-revolution had triumphed.' The church took up the cause of the workers, and created links with their movements; Patricia Knight argues this was an attempt to infiltrate and prevent any resurgent communist groups. The aspirations of the Basques and Catalans for autonomy were also ended. Use of Catalan, Basque and Galician languages was forbidden and all power was centralized in Madrid. As Preston writes, 'behind the rhetoric of national and social unity, until the death of Franco every effort was made to maintain the division between the victors and the vanquished'.

The suppression and removal of all political opposition led to a period of political stability in Spain. Fear of state repression meant that Spain appeared more unified than it had been for decades. Nevertheless, the defeat of the fascist powers in World War II made Franco more vulnerable. Under pressure from the monarchists, Franco agreed to restore the King, but kept himself as head of state. The army also lost its pre-eminence in society after Spain's last colony, Morocco, gained its independence in 1956. Without an empire to run, and with no real external or internal threat, the old-style Spanish Army became defunct.

Franco increasingly delegated control from the 1960s, and following his death a democracy was restored in 1977. But the results of the war and the Nationalist victory for Spain had meant that it was a country 'frozen in time'. No modernization took place for 36 years. The rest of Europe shunned Spain until Franco died.

Effects and results of the Spanish Civil War – international

USSR and communism

The communists had been defeated in Spain, and this undermined their international credibility. In addition, Stalin's cynical contribution to the Republican cause, and the divisions it fostered within the left wing, disillusioned many former supporters of the USSR. Thus, the Soviets lost a lot of intellectual sympathy in the West.

Although the war accentuated the hostility between the Soviets and the Germans, it also pushed Soviet foreign policy away from attempting to build an alliance with the Western powers in order to contain Germany, to one based on appeasement of Nazi Germany. It had become clear to Stalin, through their actions in the NIC, that neither Britain nor France would be a sound ally against Hitler's expansionist ambitions. Stalin began to show his interest in a possible deal with Nazi Germany as early as December 1937. His viewpoint was strengthened when Britain decided to sacrifice both Czechoslovakia and Spain in September 1938; the Munich Agreement was the turning point.

Hitler's Germany and Mussolini's Italy

Hitler was able to gain valuable military lessons from the war. The importance of air power was highlighted in the initial transport of Franco's forces to the mainland, as was the effectiveness of applying air cover for ground troops in *Blitzkrieg*. The Germans were also able to test their bullet-resistant fuel tanks, and they discovered that their armoured vehicles needed to be able to use radio contact. The bombing of civilians also seemed, to some extent, effective. These were all important factors in the success of Hitler's campaign in Europe in 1939–40. However, some drew the conclusion in March 1937, when the Italians were defeated at Guadalajara, that *Blitzkrieg* would not work.

The war brought Germany and Italy together, as it further prevented a reconciliation between the members of the Stresa Front (see p.116). Britain's and France's non-intervention policies, and pursuit of appeasement, strengthened Hitler's position. Germany also seemed to be the principal country 'defending the world from communism'.

Cooperation between Italy and Germany had far-reaching consequences, the most important of which was the removal of Italian constraint on Hitler's policy of expansion in Central Europe. Although he had clearly indicated in Mein Kampf *that he intended to construct a Greater Germany, Hitler had been impeded by Mussolini's own interest in Austria. Military involvement in Spain, however, absorbed Mussolini's attention, allowing Hitler to carry out, without Italian opposition, the annexation of Austria in 1938.*

From Stephen Lee, *Aspects of European History 1789–1980,* 1984

Britain and France

The military lesson taken by Britain, that the 'bomber will always get through', seemed to give more credibility to their policy of appeasement. The suffering and terror of Spanish civilians who had endured the bombing of their towns and cities made it clear that another general European war would witness horrors on a scale never seen before. The polarized political nature of the foreign intervention forces also led to more support for appeasement – it seemed that the warring factions would and should battle it out and exhaust one another without the democracies being dragged into the conflict. The spread of communism, as it manifested itself in Spain, still appeared the greater threat. However, the apparent 'weakness' of Britain and France over Spain, and their wider policy of appeasement, led Hitler to change his perception of Britain. Although he had initially intended to avoid a war and attempt to ally himself with the British, by 1938 he was losing his respect for Britain. Therefore, Britain's attempts to avert war by non-intervention actually encouraged Hitler to be more aggressive.

The USA

The USA remained ostensibly neutral, and although horrified by the atrocities on both sides in the Spanish Civil War, offered no tangible assistance. Indeed, the war strengthened the country's isolationist sentiment. President Roosevelt did make the 'Quarantine the Aggressors' speech in October 1937, but words meant little to the dictators in Europe and the military regime in Japan.

The UN called for economic sanctions against Franco in 1946, and all its member states broke off diplomatic relations. In addition, Spain was excluded from the USA's massive economic recovery package for post-war Europe, Marshall Aid. The initial plan in the West was to wait for a crisis in Spain to bring about the overthrow of Franco. Yet the Americans changed their perspective on Franco's Spain as the Cold War developed with the USSR. Franco was clearly a strong anti-communist force and, therefore, the 'enemy of my enemy is my friend'. This philosophy transformed into direct economic aid when the Cold War became global in 1950. In 1951, President Eisenhower agreed to the first American grant to Spain, and in return the Americans were permitted to use air bases in Spain. Spain became an ally of the USA and was permitted to join the UN.

Was the Spanish Civil War a cause of World War II?

A number of key factors suggest that the Spanish Civil War played a significant part in the causes of World War II:

- It emboldened Hitler by increasing his popularity at home and abroad.
- Hitler drew closer to his former enemy, Italy.
- Hitler gained practical military lessons that he would later apply in the campaigns of 1940. It was a distraction for Britain and France and pushed the USA further into isolation.
- It fostered a new direction for Soviet foreign policy, meaning that there could be no broad alliance in Europe to contain Hitler.

Alternatively, A.J.P. Taylor, in *The Origins of the Second World War*, concludes that the Spanish Civil War was 'without significant effect' in causing World War II.

STUDENT STUDY SECTION

Essay work

Planning essays is an essential way to revise topics as you approach examinations. In pairs or groups, plan out the essays below. Your plan should include:
- An introduction written out in full
- The opening sentence for each paragraph setting out your 'topic'
- Bullet points setting out the evidence to go in each paragraph
- A conclusion written out in full.

Each group should present its essay plan to the rest of the class. How much overlap of content is there between the different essay plans? Some hints are given for your planning in the first three essays.

Essay 1

Analyze the causes of the Spanish Civil War.

You could structure this essay thematically, and consider the key issues in the long term and the short term. Your analysis should then explain why there were tensions that intensified over time. Remember to include the 'trigger' of the civil war, as this explains why the war broke out when it did.
- Themes: 1898–1931 – Economic/Social/Political/Empire
- Themes: 1931–36 – Land reforms/Church reforms/Social unrest/Reaction of right/Popular Front
- Trigger: 1936 – The attempted coup.

Essay 2

What were the key effects of the Spanish Civil War?

You might want to include material from this chapter on the 'nature' of the war in this essay, as well as focusing on the more general results. It might be helpful for you to structure your essay in two parts: effects of the war internally on Spain, and then effects of the war externally on other countries. Remember to attempt to adopt a thematic approach.

Essay 3

What was the impact of foreign intervention in the Spanish Civil War?

You could discuss this question in terms of how the 'nature' of the war was affected by foreign intervention:
- Polarizing the complex political divisions in Spain
- Increasing the brutality and casualty rate
- Protracting the war.

You could then discuss this question in terms of how the 'outcome' of the war was affected by foreign intervention:
- Germany / Italy / Portugal: Strengthening the military capabilities of the Nationalists
- USSR: Weakening the political unity of the Republic, and then undermining its ability to wage war by withdrawing support
- NIC and Neutrals benefited the Nationalists.

Now attempt to make detailed plans for the following essay questions:

- In what ways, and to what extent, did social and religious divisions lead to war in Spain in 1936?   © IBO 2007

- To what extent was the Spanish Civil War caused by divisions in Spain and in Spanish society?   © IBO 2005

- Assess the impact of political and constitutional developments in Spain between 1930 and 1939.   © IBO M01

- Why did the Constitutional Monarchy in Spain collapse in 1931?   © IBO N00

CIVIL WAR CASE STUDY 2: THE CHINESE CIVIL WAR (1927–37 AND 1946–49)

Mao Zedong, the communist victor of the Chinese Civil War.

As you read this chapter you need to focus on the following essay questions:
- Analyze the causes of the Chinese Civil War.
- To what extent was the communist victory in China due to the use of guerrilla warfare?
- In what ways was the Chinese Civil War a revolutionary war?

For the first half of the 20th century, China faced political chaos. Following a revolution in 1911, which overthrew the Manchu dynasty, the new Republic failed to take hold and China continued to be exploited by foreign powers, lacking any strong central government. The Chinese Civil War was an attempt by two ideologically opposed forces – the nationalists and the communists – to see who would ultimately be able to restore order and regain central control over China. The struggle between these two forces, which officially started in 1927, was interrupted by the outbreak of the Sino-Japanese war in 1937, but started again in 1946 once the war with Japan was over. The results of this war were to have a major effect not just on China itself, but also on the international stage.

Timeline of events – 1911–27	
1911	Double Tenth Revolution and establishment of the Chinese Republic
1912	Dr Sun Yixian becomes Provisional President of the Republic. Guomindang (GMD) formed and wins majority in parliament. Sun resigns and Yuan Shikai declared provisional president
1915	Japan's Twenty-One Demands. Yuan attempts to become Emperor
1916	Yuan dies/warlord era begins
1917	Sun attempts to set up republic in Guangzhou. Russian Revolution
1918	Paris Peace settlement
1919	May Fourth Movement
1921	Chinese Communist Party (CCP) formed
1922	First United Front established between GMD and CCP
1925	Sun dies. National government set up under leadership of GMD
1926	Jiang Jieshi becomes leader of GMD in March. Northern Expedition launched in June. Tension increases between Jiang and Communist Central Committee. Jan–March: communist-led strikes in central China threaten Jiang. Shanghai massacre of communists in April. Communists expelled from GMD in July. Guangzhou massacre in December
1928	July: Jiang has control of Beijing, declares China now united. GMD now turns against the communists.

Long-term causes of the Chinese Civil War
Socio-economic factors

In 1900, China was ruled by the imperial Manchu dynasty. The vast majority of the population were peasants. Their life was hard, working the land, and most were extremely poor. It was the peasants who paid the taxes that in turn paid for the great Manchu imperial court. It was also the peasants who faced starvation during floods or droughts, as their subsistence farming techniques often left them with barely enough to feed their families. The population in China grew by 8 per cent in the second half of the 19th century, but the land cultivated only increased by 1 per cent. This imbalance made famines more frequent. Peasants' plots of land were reduced, although at the same time landlords increased rents; some peasants had to pay 80 per cent of their harvest. Peasants would be driven to the cities by poverty, where there was already high unemployment due to improved technology and cheap Western imports.

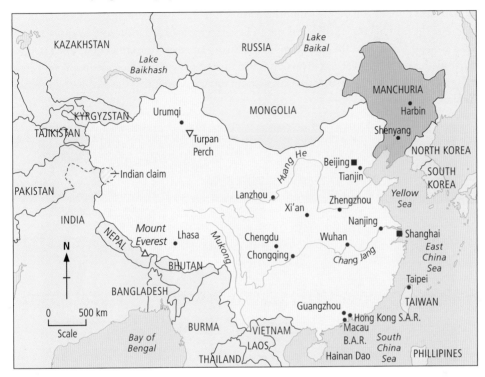

Map of China in 1900.

Political weakness and the influence of foreign powers

In the century that preceded the Chinese Civil War, the European imperialist powers had humiliated and exploited China and caused the destabilization of China's ruling Manchu regime. Britain had defeated China in the mid 19th century in the Opium Wars, and subsequently the great Chinese Empire was carved up into spheres of influence by the Europeans, Americans and, at the end of the 19th century, by Japan.

China had been forced to sign unequal treaties that gave the imperialist powers extraordinary controls over Chinese trade, territory and ultimately sovereignty. Foreigners refused to abide by Chinese laws, and they had their own extra-territorial courts. In addition, missionaries flooded into China in an attempt to spread Christianity. Inflation and corruption weakened the financial position of the Manchus. Widespread corruption among local and provincial government officials also meant that a large portion of tax revenues did not reach the central government.

STUDENT STUDY SECTION

Research question

Before the arrival of Europeans, China had been a great power in Asia for thousands of years. Research:
- Inventions associated with the Chinese
- The political relationship that China had with its neighbouring countries
- The impact of Confucianism on Chinese society
- The Qing dynasty.

In 1850, the Taiping Rebellion spread throughout southern China. The rebellion, which lasted until 1864, was part religious movement, and part political reform movement. It was only put down after the death of millions of Chinese by regional armies. This involvement of regional armies began the move away from centralized control, which would result in the Warlord Era in the 1920s.

There had been attempts to resist Western control by sections of the educated elite in China. However, the Self-Strengthening Movement was divided as to how to modernize China, and the Manchus did not coherently support reform. China remained subjugated to the West, and faced the humiliation of defeat in war to Japan in 1895. China lost more territory to Japan when it was part of the settlement in the Russo-Japanese War (1904–05). The extent of popular anti-Western feeling turned into widespread violent rebellion against Westerners in the Boxer Rebellion in 1899. However, without modern weaponry, the anti-foreign revolt was doomed to fail.

This photo of a group of Chinese Boxers illustrates their poor levels of armament compared with the contemporary European and Japanese military forces.

The overthrow of the Manchu dynasty

By the beginning of the 20th century, China was in a desperate condition, and there was a growing feeling that the ruling Manchu dynasty should be overthrown so that China could be Westernized and democracy introduced. The political weakness of the Manchu dynasty intensified with the death of the Emperor and the succession of a two-year-old boy, Pu Yi, in 1908. The former Emperor's brother, Prince Chun, ruled as regent, but was not capable of conducting the essential programme of reform. Indeed, he dismissed the potential troublemaker General Jiang Jieshi and humiliated him, and he increased taxation and frustrated the business classes without any socio-economic progress being made.

In October 1911, the ruling dynasty was overthrown in a revolution know as the Double Tenth. A republic was created. The revolution began when the government lost control of the military; soldiers in Wuchang revolted and rebellion spread quickly. Most provinces then declared themselves independent of Beijing. The key tensions and issues that led to this revolution would also be significant in the causes of the civil war 15 years later: the impact of imperialism, anti-foreign sentiment and political weakness.

In November 1911, in an attempt to seize the political initiative, delegates from the 'independent' provinces gathered in Nanjing to declare the creation of a Chinese Republic. A political exile, who had been in the USA during the revolution, was invited to be China's first President – Dr Sun Yixian.

Pu Yi, the Chinese Emperor from 1908 to 1912.

The imperial government attempted to use the former influential general of the Northern Army, Yuan Shikai, to suppress the rebellion, but he double-crossed them, arranging a deal with Sun Yixian. Sun agreed for Yuan Shikai to be President of the new republic in February 1912, in exchange for the end of Manchu rule in China. On 12 February 1912, Pu Yi abdicated.

The revolution, however, was incomplete. There was no real introduction of democracy, and most former imperial officials kept their positions. The impetus for the revolution was wholly Chinese, but had not been led by the middle classes. It had been the military who ignited the rising and Chinese radicals had joined in later. Michael Lynch argues that the revolution was fundamentally a revolt by the provinces against the centre: 'The Double Tenth was a triumph of regionalism. It represented a particular phase in the long-running contest between central autocracy and local autonomy, a contest that was to shape much of China's history during the following forty years' (*China: From Empire to People's Republic 1900–49*, 1999).

STUDENT STUDY SECTION

Review question

How had the following weakened China in the century leading up to the civil war?

- European imperialism
- Failure of modernization
- Regionalism.

The rule of Yuan Shikai

Yuan ruled China as a military dictator from 1912 until 1915. However, the key issues that had led to the revolution in 1911 remained unresolved. Regionalism continued under Yuan's rule and became the key obstacle to a united China. Sun's party reformed as the Guomindang (GMD) in 1912, and declared itself a parliamentary party.

The GMD and the Three Principles

The GMD had been set up by Sun Yixian in 1912. He wanted to create a unified modern and democratic China. He had returned to China after the Double Tenth Revolution in 1911, and established a government in southern China, in Canton. Sun was not a communist, although he was willing to cooperate with them, and the organization of the GMD was along communist lines. Sun also saw the need to develop a GMD army.

Sun stated that he and his party had three guiding principles:

- Nationalism – to rid China of foreign influence, unite China and to regain its international respect
- Democracy – the people should be educated so that they could ultimately rule themselves democratically
- People's Livelihood – this was essentially 'land reform', the redistribution of land to the peasants and economic development.

It is argued that Sun agreed to Yuan Shikai's rule in order to avert the possibility of China descending into civil war. The republicans were not powerful enough at this stage to take on the military. It was a lesson that both the GMD and the Chinese communists would take on board – to win the political battle for China you need military power.

Sun attempted to undermine Yuan's power by moving him from his power base in Beijing to the south in Nanjing to set up a new government. Yuan refused to leave. At this point the GMD were a regional power only in the southern provinces, and the republicans were not sufficiently organized to mount resistance to Yuan. A 'second revolution' failed and Sun had to flee to Japan in 1913. However, Yuan mastered his own downfall by a series of

▲ Dr Sun Yixian

ill-conceived acts. The 1912 Republican constitution had created regional assemblies, which he abolished in an attempt to centralize power. This act further alienated the provincial powers, especially as tax revenues were centrally controlled. Yuan's final miscalculation was to proclaim himself Emperor in 1916. At this point he lost the support of the military and stood down. He died three months later.

Short-term causes of the Chinese Civil War

Political weakness: regionalism – the warlords 1916–28

Map of China under the warlords. The marked borders are approximations only, and frequently changed.

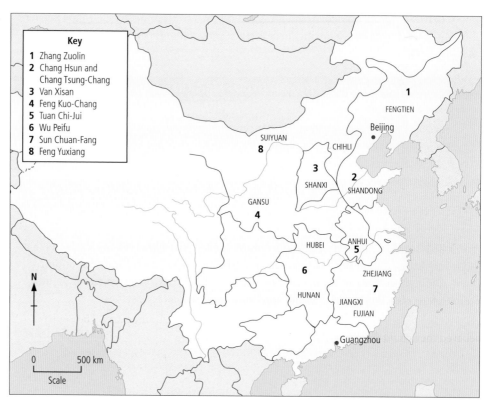

The warlords

The warlord era can be divided into two periods: the first, pre-1920, was by default rather conservative (they wanted to preserve their own power and feudal rights); the second phase, after 1920, saw the rise of new military commanders who had not been powerful under the Republic, but who became more opportunist. Although they are referred to collectively, the warlords were made up of leaders with very different aims and ambitions.

A key cause of the civil war in China was the increasing lack of unity in the country by the second decade of the 20th century. Indeed, regionalism or provincialism was to play a significant role not only in causing the war, but also in its course and outcome.

With the abdication and death of Yuan, China lost the only figure that had maintained some degree of unity. China broke up into small states and provinces, each controlled by a **warlord** and his private army. These warlords ran their territories independently, organizing and taxing the people in their domains. They had their own laws and even their own currencies. As warlords extended their power and wealth by expanding their territories, it was the peasants who suffered in their continuous wars. None of the warlords was willing to relinquish his armies or power to the central government.

The warlord period increased the sense of humiliation felt by many Chinese and, coupled with their desire to get rid of foreign influence, led to an increase in nationalism during the decade of warlord rule.

China had all but ceased to exist – it was in a state of internal anarchy. If the warlords remained, China would remain divided.

The May Fourth Movement

During this period, two political movements developed in response to both the warlords and foreign influence in China. The May Fourth Movement began in 1919. Students led a mass demonstration in Beijing against the warlords, traditional Chinese culture and the Japanese. The hostility had been ignited by the Versailles settlement, which had given to Japan Germany's former concessions in Shandong province. China, it seemed, had joined the Allies in the war only to be humiliated by them.

The significance of the May Fourth Movement was that it was dedicated to change and the rebirth of China as a proud and independent nation. Some intellectuals and students were inspired by revolutionary ideology in order to achieve these goals. The Bolshevik revolution of 1917 provided a practical example. The new Bolshevik government had also denounced the imperialists, and said that all contested border claims would be dropped. Imperialism was perceived by many as the main cause of China's problems.

Other Chinese were inspired by the GMD nationalist party, which had grown much stronger during the warlord period. These two groups – communists and nationalists – were to come together in an alliance in 1922.

Communists and nationalists

By the time Sun died in 1925, the GMD had made little progress towards fulfilling their 'Three Principles'. They had been limited by their lack of power beyond the south, and the fact they had to rely on alliances with warlords due to the weakness of their military power.

General Jiang Jieshi, leader of the nationalist forces.

After the death of Sun, a general took over leadership of the GMD, General Jiang Jieshi. Jiang was a committed nationalist, and had enthusiastically joined the GMD. He had had military training before World War I in Japan, and then in the USSR. Indeed, the Soviets had begun to invest in the GMD, providing aid and assistance to the party. The Soviets believed they could foster good relations with a nationalist China. As well as the GMD, another revolutionary party emerged during the warlord period, the Chinese Communist Party (CCP). This communist party was officially set up in 1921. Initially, its membership was mainly intellectuals, and it had no real military strength. It was due to this weakness, and some shared aims, that the CCP agreed to work with the GMD. It was also consistently encouraged to cooperate with the nationalists by the USSR.

Attempt to unify China: the First United Front

Both the GMD and the CCP wanted a unified China. They agreed that the first step to this was to get rid of the warlords, and in 1922 they formed the First United Front. Both parties also agreed that China needed to be free of the foreign imperialist powers. The Third Principle of Sun Yixian's, 'the People's Livelihood', was often called 'socialism', which convinced the Comintern that this was a party they could back. In addition, Jiang had studied in Moscow in 1923, and then ran the Whampoa Military Academy, which was set up and funded by the USSR to train GMD officers. Despite his Soviet links, however, Jiang was not a communist. Indeed, he became increasingly anti-communist, and began his leadership of the GMD by removing communists from key positions in the party. He stopped short of breaking off the alliance with the communists, as he knew that he must first take out his primary obstacle to a unified China – the warlords.

Jiang now determined to act on the first of the Three Principles and attempt to unify China by putting an end to the warlords' power. Together with the communists, the GMD set out on the 'Northern Expedition' in 1926 to crush the warlords of central and northern China. This operation was a great success; by 1927, the GMD and the communists had captured Hangzhou, Shanghai and Nanjing. They took Beijing in 1928. Within two years, the United Front of the GMD and the CCP had destroyed the power of the warlords, and the GMD announced that it was the legitimate government of China and the new capital and seat of government would be Nanjing.

Map showing the GMD's Northern Expedition, 1926–28.

Immediate cause of the Chinese Civil War: the GMD attacks the CCP

Despite the results of the Northern Expedition, China was not now unified. The United Front was only a friendship of convenience. What had united the CCP and the GMD – the fight against the warlords – was over, and ideology divided the two parties. The success of the Northern Expedition had been not only due to nationalist ambitions, it was also because of the communist promise of land to the peasants; this commitment had given them local peasant support. The communists also had support from the industrial workers. For example, Zhou Enlai, a communist member of the GMD, had organized the workers rising in Shanghai.

The popular support for the communists was a key reason that Jiang decided he could no longer tolerate them in the GMD. There could be no more cooperation. Jiang was sympathetic to landlords and the middle classes, and was far more to the right than Sun had been. Areas under communist control had seen peasants attack landlords and seize land – this could not be tolerated. It seemed to Jiang that the CCP needed to be crushed before China could truly be unified under the GMD.

Jiang now expelled all communists from the GMD, and his attacks on the communists reached a peak in Shanghai in the 'White Terror' in April 1927. A powerful 'workers' army' under Zhou Enlai had proved very effective during the Northern Expedition and Jiang turned on them, using informants from the underworld of triads and gangsters – 5,000 communists were shot. The GMD carried out similar attacks in other cities, in what became known as the 'purification movement' – 'purification' meant the massacre of thousands of communists, trade unionists and peasant leaders. About a quarter of a million people were killed. Despite attempts to resist (Mao's Autumn Harvest Rising failed), the CCP was very nearly crushed by the end of 1927.

Ignoring the orders of the Comintern to retain the United Front, the CCP decided that its only hope of survival was to flee into the mountains of Jiangsi. The GMD pursued them, determined to destroy the communists. The civil war had begun.

STUDENT STUDY SECTION

Review questions

1   Why did support for communism grow in China?

2   Why did Jiang turn against the communists?

Review activity

In groups, create a diagram (mind map or flow diagram) on a large sheet of paper to show the causes of the first period of the civil war in China. Decide what themes you want to develop, how you are going to show long-term and short-term causes, and how you are going to show any links between the causes. Each group should then present and explain its diagram to the rest of the class.

The course of the war

Timeline of events – 1930–50	
1930–31	Jiang's First Encirclement campaign attacks Jiangxi Soviet, defeated by CCP
1931	Japanese attack Manchuria. Twenty-Eight Bolsheviks take over Central Committee of CCP. Jiang launches Second and Third Encirclement Campaigns against Jiangxi Soviet; both are defeated
1932	Japanese attack Shanghai. Jiangxi Soviet declares war on Japan. Fourth Encirclement Campaign begins
1933	Truce with Japan. Fifth Encirclement Campaign
1934	Long March begins

continued overleaf

1935		Survivors of Long March reach Shaanxi Soviet base
1936		Jiang Jieshi taken hostage by warlord Zhang Xueliang in Xi'an. Second United Front established
1937	Apr	Second United Front is formed
	Jul	Japanese invade China
	Nov	Jiang Jieshi moves government to Chongqing
	Dec	Rape of Nanjing
1940	Aug	Hundred Regiments assault on Japanese by Red Army
1941	Jan	Anhui incident ends Second United Front
1944	Oct	US commander General Joseph Stilwell leaves China at Jiang Jieshi's request
1945	Aug–Oct	US Ambassador Hurley leads talks between GMD and CCP
	Oct	Agreement announced, but both sides send forces to Manchuria
	Sep	Japan formally surrenders in China theatre
	Dec	US General George C. Marshall arrives to lead negotiations
1946	Jan	Truce between CCP and GMD
	Mar	USSR begins to withdraw from Manchuria. Fighting breaks out in Manchuria between GMD and CCP
1947	Jan	Marshall leaves China
	Mar	Jiang Jieshi takes Yan'an
	Oct	Mao announces land reforms
1948	Apr	US Congress passes China Aid Act – aid sent to GMD again
	Nov	Battle of Huai-Hai begins
1949	Jan	GMD lose battle of Huai-Hai
	Apr	CCP capture Nanjing
	May	CCP take Shanghai
	Oct	Mao announces the establishment of the People's Republic of China
	Dec	Jiang flees to Taiwan

Chinese communist troops, seen here about to depart for Nanjing in 1927, generally had inferior equipment compared to the nationalists, but fought an enemy with low morale and endemic corruption amongst the officer class.

STUDENT STUDY SECTION

Review activity

Look back at Chapter 1 at the section on guerrilla tactics. The Chinese Civil War is a good example of guerrilla tactics working successfully against a stronger force. As you read through the rest of the chapter, note the rules for guerrilla fighting that were established by Mao and how and why they were so successful.

To access worksheet 13.1 on Mao's guerrilla tactics, please visit www.pearsonbacconline.com and follow the on-screen instructions.

The Jiangxi Soviet

The CCP were forced to retreat into Jiangxi province in order to survive the GMD onslaught. This territory become known as the 'Jiangxi Soviet'. Mao's writings suggest that the White Terror had only confirmed what he had already thought about the United Front, i.e. that this cooperation with the GMD would destroy the CCP. He also believed that the GMD and the Comintern had the wrong strategy for China, basing their revolution on urban areas. Mao's revolution would be based on the peasants. Essentially, this was a more realistic strategy, as the vast majority of Chinese were not urban workers but rural peasants. From a population in China of around 500 million, only 12 per cent were in urban areas, whereas 88 per cent lived in rural regions. From a total workforce of approximately 259 million, 205 million were agricultural workers and a mere 54 million were non-agricultural or industrial workers.

Mao arrived at Jiangxi and organized the Jiangxi Soviet around his idea of the central revolutionary role of the peasant – 'The peasants are the sea; we are the fish. The sea is our habitat', he stated. His ideological shift away from orthodox Marxism, which placed the proletariat at the centre of the revolution, put him at odds with more orthodox members of the CCP. But his success in recruiting and organizing the peasants in the Jiangxi Soviet began to win him the argument.

Jiangxi Soviet

The term 'Soviet' was taken from Russia. During the revolution in 1917, Russian workers and soldiers had set up soviets or councils in which discussion and debate took place.

STUDENT STUDY SECTION

Review activity

Research Marx's theory of revolution. Explain how Mao's ideas were different from Marx's belief (and thus the Soviet model) of how revolution should take place.

Division within the CCP

Both the CCP and the GMD suffered from 'internal factionalism' during this period of the civil war. Mao's views on the revolution and how the civil war should be fought could be summarized, by 1930, in the following key points:

- The revolution will be carried out by the peasant masses, thus the peasants will be mobilized and politicized by the Red Army
- The army's tactics will be guerrilla warfare
- Land reform will be carried out in their areas of control.

Yet his views were not shared by the Soviet Union and the Comintern. The USSR saw the Great Depression as the beginning of the end of capitalism, and believed that the world was on the brink of international revolution. In February 1930, the Comintern official Li Lisan issued an instruction to all CCP members to attack cities in Jiangxi and Hunan. This order was known as the 'Li Lisan Line'. All the attacks failed, and the communist army was forced into retreat. (The Comintern then blamed Li Lisan by saying he had misunderstood its orders.) The CCP in the cities was shattered, and it appeared that the Party could only hold its influence in rural areas. Li Lisan was dismissed from his leadership of the CCP in January 1931.

GMD attempts to exterminate CCP

From 1928 to 1934, Jiang had the chance to carry out Sun's Three Principles. His government was ineffective, however, and Jiang made no progress towards democracy or land reform. His support came from landlords and the rich, and so initiatives were limited to the building of some roads and the construction of more schools. From 1931, Jiang also had to face the threat of the Japanese, who invaded Manchuria in 1931.

Jiang's main goal remained the elimination of the communists, and during this time he carried out the 'Five Encirclement Campaigns' in an attempt to destroy the Jiangxi Soviet and the CCP. The GMD strategy was to encircle the Reds and cut them off from supplies and resources. The communists focused their strategy on survival, and based themselves in the mountains between Hunan and Jiangxi provinces. Here they built up their military force – the Red Army. Mao explained his strategy in a letter to Li Lisan in 1929: 'The enemy advances, we retreat; the enemy halts, we harass; the enemy tires, we attack; the enemy retreats, we pursue.'

Li Lisan was replaced by a group of Moscow graduates known as the 'Twenty-Eight Bolsheviks' and the influence of the Comintern remained strong enough to remove Mao as chief commissar of the Red Army. Mao did not like these 'inexperienced men'.

The first three Campaigns were launched between December 1930 and September 1931. The Red Army under Mao and Zhou Enlai faced increasingly strong GMD forces, first 100,000, then 200,000 and finally 300,000 men – and they defeated all three. Using Mao's strategy of revolutionary war, they allowed the GMD to enter their territory and begin to round up communists, and then they attacked the fragmented units. Their knowledge of the terrain and their use of the support of the local peasants meant that they could choose the place and timing of their engagements.

Mao was not involved in the Fourth Encirclement Campaign. Zhu De was commander-in-chief of the Red Army, and he used the same tactics as before with the same results – the GMD was forced back again in March 1933.

Mao and the Twenty-Eight Bolsheviks

During the military campaigns of the early 1930s Mao's position was being eroded and marginalized by the Twenty-Eight Bolsheviks. The *coup de grace* came in July 1934, when by order of the Comintern Mao was put on probation and barred from meetings. From July until the beginning of the Long March in October when he was released, he was under house arrest.

STUDENT STUDY SECTION

Document analysis

Document A

Kuomintang [GMD] armies all fought by the usual Japanese military tactics, always advancing in one column with front and flank guards… But we split up into small, swift combat units which got in their rear and on their flanks and attacked, cutting them into segments. There's nothing secret about such tactics … and the militarists later tried to use them against us. They failed because such guerrilla warfare requires not only a thorough knowledge of the terrain of the battle area but also the support of the common people.

Zhu De, from C. Brown and T. Edwards, *Revolution in China 1911–1949*, 1983

Document B

The eight rules of the Red Army:

Return and roll up the straw matting on which you sleep.

Be courteous and polite to the people and help them when you can.

/cont

Return all borrowed articles.
Replace all damaged articles.
Be honest in all transactions with the peasants.
Pay for all articles purchased.
Replace all doors when you leave a house.
Be sanitary, and, especially, establish latrines a safe distance from people's houses.

The Eight Rules of the Red Army (1928), quoted by the American journalist Edgar Snow

---

Document C

The GMD troops burned down all the houses in the surrounding area, seized all the food there and blockaded us…We were sick and half-starved. The peasants were no better off, and we would not touch what little they had. But the peasants encouraged us. They dug up from the ground the grain they had hidden from the GMD troops and gave it to us…they wanted us to win. Tactics are important, but we could not exist if the majority of our people did not support us. We are nothing but the fist of the people beating their oppressors.

Statement by CCP general Peng Dehuai, in 1936

Questions

1 According to Document A, how was guerrilla warfare waged?
2 According to Documents B and C, why would the CCP have the support of the peasants?
3 Why was peasant support so crucial to the CCP?
4 Using these sources and your own knowledge, explain why Mao's guerrilla tactics were successful in this first phase of the Chinese Civil War.

The Long March

Seven months later, in October, Jiang attempted his fifth and final campaign against the 'bandits'. On this occasion he had taken the advice of a German general to adopt a gradual approach. This time a force of 800,000 men was sent in, with air cover and artillery. The Red Army could not take advantage of its previous strengths of higher mobility and local support. Outnumbered and surrounded by GMD forces, it fought and lost a final battle at Ruijin in 1934.

MILITARY STRATEGY 1930–34		
1930–31	**1932–33**	**1934**
Mao in charge ↓	Zhu De in charge of Red Army ↓	Twenty-Eight Bolsheviks in charge of Red Army ↓
Guerrilla warfare ↓	Guerrilla warfare ↓	'Stand and fight' ↓
GMD Encirclement Campaigns 1–3 ↓	GMD Encirclement Campaign 4 ↓	GMD Encirclement Campaign 5 (began 1933) ↓
GMD campaigns 1–3 fail	GMD campaign 4 fails	GMD campaign 5 succeeds – German military advice. Red Army breaks out / Long March

The CCP faced annihilation. Mao decided that the only chance the CCP had was to break through the GMD's lines and set up another base. They succeeded in doing this on 19 October and then embarked on what became known as the 'Long March'. The Long March took the CCP on a seemingly impossible 9,600km trek to Shaanxi across some of the most inhospitable territory in China. It took 368 days and it led to the death of more than 90 per cent of the 90,000 communists that broke through their encirclement at Jiangxi.

ToK Time

Read the two sources here, and answer the ToK question in pairs. Write up your discussion in your ToK journal.

Well, we ourselves at the beginning did not know that we were actually on the Long March… All we knew was that we were getting out of the bases; we were surrounded and being choked; a million men against us, tanks, aeroplanes… we broke through one cordon of encirclement, then a second, then a third… We thought if we could get to Szechuan [Sichuan] all would be well; for Szechuan was not letting Jiang Kai-Shek in; the warlord of Szechuan did not want Jiang there.

A Red Army veteran quoted in Brown and Edwards, *Revolution in China 1911–1949*, 1974

Hardships and Hope

We are short of grain,
For three months we have tasted no meat;
In summer we feed on berries, in winter bamboo;
Hunting wild boars we pant over the mountains,
And after dark catch snakes.
* The enemy searches the whole mountainside,*
Trees and grass scorched and burnt;
Never before was savagery like this,
But our people resist with ever greater vigour;
We shall give battle again.
* We put our trust in the people…*
And never forget their support;
They are second parents to us,
We are good sons in the fight,
The best soldiers for the revolution.

From Chen Yi, 'Guerrillas in South Kiangsi'

Question

Can a contemporary poem or song give us a better understanding of an historical event than a contemporary diary or journalist's report? What are the Knowledge Issues involved in using imaginative literature as historical documents?

Map showing the route of the Long March. ▶

STUDENT STUDY SECTION

Review activity

What was the Long March and why was it significant to the outcome of the Chinese Civil War?

In small groups, research the course and key turning points of the Long March, using the information that follows. Your group will be writing the script of a short play or documentary based on your research. It should include the key events listed below, any extra information from your own research, and an explanation of why the Long March remains important in Chinese history. You could also include historical characters and quotations from contemporaries.

Key events of the Long March

Crossing the Xiang River

The Xiang River was strongly defended by the GMD, and Jiang was determined not to let the CCP escape. Mao criticized the strategy the CCP used at the river, where around 50,000 died. The CCP had not used his tactics of outmanoeuvring and deceiving the GMD; they had also been loaded down with furniture and other unnecessary equipment. The Twenty-Eight Bolsheviks, now in charge of the army, had simply led the CCP in a line into the river, where they were 'sitting ducks' for Jiang's forces.

Zunyi Conference

In January 1935 the CCP, this time using 'guerrilla tactics', managed to capture the town of Zunyi. The Twenty-Eight Bolsheviks had been discredited due to their disasters at Jiangxi and the Xiang River. At a party conference held here to determine future CCP policy, Mao emerged as leader.

Upper Yangtze River Crossing

At Zunyi, Mao declared that his forces 'march north to fight the Japanese', and now led the Red Army towards Sichuan to meet up with the 40,000-strong communist army under the leadership of Zhang Guotao. Jiang pursued Mao across the far western provinces of Yunnan and Tibet. The GMD destroyed all the boats at the Yangtze River crossing in an attempt to rout Mao's forces. Mao deceived the nationalists that his army was constructing a bridge to cross, but sent units to a town 136km further along. Thus, while the bridge was being built, the CCP crossed the river in another place. Mao got across before the GMD realized what was going on.

The Luding Bridge

Just two weeks later, with Mao forcing the pace, covering 134km in just 24 hours, the Red Army came to the Dadu River. Local people had built a bridge, using their own resources to pay for it, from 13 heavy iron chains covered by wooden planks. The river was very fast moving, but here was the only way to cross. The GMD could, and should, have blown the bridge, but this action would have led to local outcry. Instead Jiang's forces removed the planks that covered the chains. What took place next is disputed, but according to the CCP, 22 volunteers crossed the bridge, clinging on to the chains and lobbing hand grenades at the machine-gun posts that fired on them. Only five of the attackers survived, but they managed to take out the machine-gun posts, while those behind them laid new boards so that the Red Army could then rush across. In the ensuing battle, the GMD attempted to set fire to the bridge, but it was too late. The crossing was a great morale booster to the CCP, and their courage inspired many members of the GMD to switch sides.

The Zunyi Conference resolutions

Mao left the Zunyi Conference with a list of resolutions that almost summarized his key military ideas:

- Being weaker than the enemy, the Red Army was to concentrate its forces for selected decisive battles.
- Battles were to be avoided when victory was not certain.
- The enemy was to be lured in deep; giving up territory was not necessarily bad from a military point of view.
- The Red Army was a propagandizing team as well as a fighting force … Every soldier was to be told the aims and dangers of every move.

Adapted from Ross Terrill, *Mao: A Biography*, 2000

The Long March became a much mythologized episode in Chinese communist history. Here an idealized poster celebrates the march and its participants.

Disputes between Zhang Guotao, Zhu De and Mao

Mao had 10,000 left in his army, and this force finally met up with 45,000 men under the command of Zhang in Sichuan. The two leaders disagreed on what the Red Army's next move should be. Mao wanted to go north to the Shaanxi Soviet, where they could fight the Japanese. Zhang wanted to stay in western Sichuan, or go further west to have closer access to the USSR. They could not agree and ended up going separate ways. Zhu De decided to go with Zhang, and the two generals took the majority of forces with them. The GMD attacked them, split their forces, and Zhu fled to join Mao. Zhang's forces were virtually destroyed.

Songpan Marshes

To get to Shaanxi, Mao had to cross the unmapped and deadly Songpan marshes, where men sank into the mud and drowned, faced attack from local tribes, and ate poisonous plants in an attempt to fend off starvation. Of the 10,000 that entered the marshes, only 7,000 made it across the 400km region.

Shaanxi

After marching 9,600km, and fighting 15 major battles and many smaller skirmishes, Mao's army arrived at the Shaanxi Soviet in October 1935. Here they set up a communist base centred on the town of Yan'an.

STUDENT STUDY SECTION

Document analysis

Has there ever been in history a long march like ours? No, never. The Long March is also a manifesto. It proclaims to the world that the Red Army is an army of heroes and that the imperialists and their jackals, Jiang Jieshi and his like, are perfect nonentities. It announces the bankruptcy of the encirclement pursuit, obstruction and interception attempted by the imperialists and Jiang Jieshi. The Long March is also an agitation corps. It declares to the approximately two hundred million people of eleven provinces that only the road of the Red Army leads to their liberation. Without the Long March, how could the broad masses have known so quickly that there are such great ideas in the world as are upheld by the Red Army? The Long March is also a seeding machine. It has sown many seeds in eleven provinces, which will sprout, grow leaves, blossom into flowers, bear fruit and yield a crop in future. To sum up, the Long March ended with our victory and the enemy's defeat.

Mao reminiscing on the Long March

Question

According to Mao, what was the significance of the Long March?

Mao and revolutionary warfare

Mao's war against the GMD can be classed as a revolutionary war, as he was not only trying to defeat the GMD but also to impose a revolutionary ideology on the Chinese people. The choice the Chinese people had was between Maoism, with its total restructuring of society, economy and government, and the nationalists' policy, which basically involved maintaining the status quo. Mao believed that the peasants were central to revolutionary war, and so his priority had to be to persuade them to support the communist cause.

Mao's revolutionary warfare consisted of several stages:

- **Setting up base areas** – Mao planned to set up 'base areas' in which he would organize the peasants and educate them in communist ideology. They would then, it was hoped, accept new taxes and justice systems applied by the CCP, which would be better than those they had previously endured. These base areas would be remote and thus difficult for the GMD to interfere with during this 'education process'. Part of the 'Eight rules of the Eighth Route Army' was to treat everyone with respect, and this very powerful idea helped to gain the support and trust of the peasants.

- **The organization phase** – Once a base camp was set up, CCP leaders would be sent out to other villages to repeat the process. Mao called this the 'organization phase'. The aim was slowly to take over the countryside, thereby isolating the cities to allow the CCP ultimately to take political control of China.
- **Defending the bases** – The next stage was to defend the base areas, which would not remain free from GMD attack, especially once GMD taxes were going to the CCP. Mao organized the peasants to use hit-and-run tactics, their advantage being knowledge of terrain and support of the local population. If the GMD attempted to hunt down the CCP units, they would be drawn into hostile areas, which would enable the guerrillas to attack them again and/or disappear into the local community. In this way, the 'enemy' would become demoralized and worn down. Any attempt by the GMD to wipe out the CCP presence with massive attacks and looting of villages would only increase hostility to the nationalists and improve the position of the communists.
- **The guerrilla phase** – The communists could always survive by retreating, as they had in the Long March. Other bases could be set up as they retreated – these would then create more guerrilla fighters. This was the 'guerrilla phase' of the war.
- **Protracted war** – Mao understood that his strategy would lead to a long war; indeed, the idea of a 'protracted war' was central to his thinking. However, as the numbers of guerrillas grew, and in turn the number of attacks on the enemy increased, the balance would finally tilt in favour of the guerrillas.
- **Seizing power** – At this stage, the revolutionary war would go into the 'open or mobile phase', where guerrilla units joined together to form a conventional army. The CCP was in this last stage of guerrilla warfare when the second phase of the civil war broke out in 1946. Once in power, a period of consolidation would be needed to rid China of the remnants of the 'old regime'.

End of the first stage of the Chinese Civil War – the Second United Front, 1937

The Long March was essential for ensuring the survival of the CCP and also for making Mao the unchallenged leader. Jiang Jieshi was still determined to defeat the communists, but he also had to deal with the threat from Japan. China had been invaded in 1931 when the Japanese took over Manchuria. Jiang initially did little about this apart from appealing to the League of Nations, as he still regarded the communists as the more dangerous threat. He said that the Japanese 'were a disease of the skin while the communists were a disease of the heart'.

Jiang unsuccessfully attempted to resist the Japanese attacks on Shanghai in 1932, and in May agreed to a truce. The Japanese advanced to the Great Wall in January 1933, however, and their growing control in China led to a great increase in anti-Japanese sentiment.

Mao called for another 'United Front' to fight the Japanese, and this was supported by all who had suffered under Japanese occupation – including the northern warlords Zhang Xueliang and Yan Xishan. Yet in the end it was the Comintern and not Mao that pushed the alliance between the CCP and the GMD. Stalin was worried about Japanese expansion in and from Manchuria. By 1936 he saw Jiang Jieshi as the only leader in China who could effectively fight them. The Second United Front was sealed when Jiang Jieshi was kidnapped in Xi'an by the warlord Zhang (he had been there planning his next assault on the CCP). It shocked both the Chinese and the Soviets – and although some wanted to shoot Jiang, he was released on Comintern orders after 13 days.

In April 1937 the Second United Front was formed. The civil war was suspended, and there was instead a 'National War of Resistance'. The GMD would benefit from support from the USSR, and potentially aid from the USA. The CCP benefited from the legitimacy the alliance gave them – they could no linger by, dismissed as 'bandits'. The communists also hoped that the war against Japan would exhaust the GMD.

The Japanese responded to this new situation with a show of force – attacking the Marco Polo bridge outside Beijing in July 1937. This was the beginning of the war proper between Japan and China. In the battle for Shanghai, Jiang Jieshi's forces were forced to retreat after losing around 300,000 troops. The capital, Nanjing, was relocated 1,200km to the west to Chongqing for the remainder of the war. Nanjing was left to face the onslaught of the Japanese. The atrocities that were then perpetrated there became known as the 'Rape of Nanjing' (see p.135).

Why was the CCP able to survive the first stage of the Chinese Civil War?

The final victory of the CCP after 1945 could never have occurred had it not been for their successes between 1928 and 1936. Why were they successful in this period?

CCP successes

- The Long March ensured CCP survival and offered a defensible base in Yan'an. It was also a propaganda victory for the CCP, who were able to use the journey to proclaim their policies to many thousands of people. They also won patriotic support for their claim to be going north to fight the Japanese.
- The march also confirmed Mao as the leader of the CCP, gave the CCP a good deal of fighting experience and welded the survivors into a very tight, dedicated group of fanatical revolutionaries.
- Mao's offer to create a joint front with the GMD against the Japanese again won the CCP popularity, allowing them to pose as the true nationalists.

GMD errors

In contrast to the CCP, the GMD forces made several errors. Their decision to deal with the CCP before the Japanese lost them patriotic support. In addition, the poor treatment of peasants by the GMD forces further degraded their popularity. They had also failed to implement Sun's Three Principles (see p.255).

The Sino-Japanese War

The events of the war against Japan were key to explaining both the reasons for the outbreak of the second phase of the civil war and also the ultimate victory of the CCP.

The impact of the war on the GMD

The GMD withdraw its capital to Chongqing, but did little to resist the Japanese. Jiang Jieshi's best troops were sent to Yan'an, and he gambled on the USA winning the war against Japan for him, a choice that had a bad impact on the morale of the army.

As large areas of the GMD's support base were under Japanese occupation, Jiang Jieshi lost much-needed tax revenue. He faced the problem by printing more money, which led to high levels of inflation,

Japanese expansion in China, 1937–44.

Key
Territory conquered by Japanese, with dates

and in turn impacted badly on the middle classes, who were the natural supporters of the GMD. The peasantry were also hardest hit by taxes. Other problems facing the GMD were:

- Corruption was rife in the GMD army, and its troops were ill-treated and unmotivated (see Document Analysis exercise below). Conscription further alienated the peasantry.
- Although the USA sent aid to the GMD, Japanese control of the coastal ports and key land routes meant that only limited supplies could come in via the Himalayas.
- The GMD remained riddled with factions throughout the war. With rising discontent against his rule due to corruption, military failures and inflation, Jiang Jieshi's response was increased repression, which exacerbated hostility towards the government.
- Territorially, the GMD lacked control over many of China's provinces. It really only controlled the territory around its capital in central China and areas of the south.
- The war exhausted the GMD physically and psychologically. They bore the brunt of the Japanese attacks in the early stages of the war, and throughout they continued to meet the Japanese in conventional battles, which resulted in heavy losses. Meanwhile, the CCP was fighting a guerrilla war, incurring only light losses.
- The public lost a lot of respect for the GMD in the later stages of the war, as it appeared it was sitting back and waiting for the Americans to win the war.

STUDENT STUDY SECTION

Document analysis

The Communists got their chance because the Nationalists failed so completely … [The Nationalists'] notorious corruption resulted in hoarding and profiteering while millions of peasants starved… The Nationalist army was a scandal. It was largely led by incompetent generals who owed their position to cronyism… Soldiers died more from lack of food or medicine than from battlefield wounds; 10% of the army probably had tuberculosis. The army made enemies rather than friends out of the people. Peasants were conscripted into the ranks by force … often shackled to one another … it was so hated that peasants often killed Nationalist soldiers who fell into their hands...

From June Grasso, Jay Corrin and Michael Kort, *Modernization and Revolution In China: From the Opium Wars to the Olympics*, 2009

Questions

1 Using this source, identify the key problems within the GMD army.
2 With reference to its origin and purpose, what are the value and limitations of using this source to find out about the GMD's army?

The Dixie Mission
The US Army sent an 'Observation Group', known as the Dixie Mission, to establish relations with the CCP in July 1944. The mission lasted until March 1947. Its task was to analyze the CCP politically and militarily in order to establish whether the American war effort would benefit from working with them. John S. Service was responsible for analysing the CCP politically, and Colonel David D. Barrett was the military analyst. The Dixie Mission's initial feedback was positive; it suggested that Yan'an was more effectively governed than other GMD-held territories, and was in general less corrupt. It also suggested that the CCP could be a useful military ally in China. The Dixie Mission also hosted the failed attempts by the Americans to broker an alliance between the CCP and the GMD. Their analysis of the potential of the CCP to be a sound post-war ally was not taken on board by the US government either. Indeed, those involved with the Dixie Mission were later accused of being communist sympathizers in the 1950s, and were persecuted during the McCarthy era.

The impact of the war on the CCP

Mao used the war against the Japanese to carry out his revolutionary warfare. Indeed, Mao said that 'our fixed policy should be 70 per cent expansion, 20 per cent dealing with the GMD and 10 per cent resisting the Japanese.' By March 1945, the communists had liberated 678 out of 914 country towns and implemented their policies in them: land reform, setting up village schools and village soviets, reducing taxes and abolishing debt. The historian James Sheridan writes that the reason they achieved the enthusiastic backing of the peasants was 'by meeting the local, immediate needs of the peasants through reformist and radical social policies and by providing leadership for the defence of peasant communities against the Japanese. In this fashion the communists won peasant confidence and in the process began the transformation – the modernization – of rural China' (*China in Disintegration*, 1977).

The CCP also gained support through its egalitarian policies. Everyone had the same living conditions and the intellectuals had to work with the peasants. Women were treated as equals with men for the first time in Chinese history. Women had been seen as property

Chairman Mao shown chatting with steel workers while inspecting a factory in Anhwei Province in 1959.

The Rectification Campaigns

The Rectification Campaigns or Movement was initiated by the communists to reinforce their ideology, but quickly became a campaign against intellectuals and then anyone who was not in line with communist thinking. After approximately 10,000 people had been killed, the campaign led to Mao's position and leadership in the CCP being confirmed.

in traditional Chinese society, having no rights to divorce or inheritance, no education, no political rights and often being bought and sold to be wives, labourers or prostitutes. The communists offered them freedom to marry whom they chose and gave them the rights to divorce, education, voting at 18, military service and to form women's associations.

During the GMD's blockade of Yan'an from 1939, the CCP attempted to be self-sufficient. They held back inflation by taxing people in goods. Officials and soldiers had to contribute to agricultural production under the 'garrison' system. To a certain extent this worked, as the historian Jack Gray suggests, '… by 1945 about 40 per cent of their basic needs were supplied in this way' (*Rebellions and Revolutions: China from the 1880s to the 1980s,* 1990).

To establish unity within the party and to spread Maoist ideology further, a series of Rectification Campaigns were launched between 1941 and 1944. The 'correct ideas' were Mao's, and any deviation would not be tolerated. The primary ideas were: the 'mass line', which meant policies were to be taken to the people and ideas taken from the people, Mao's peasant-based communism and the military strategy of guerrilla warfare. The Rectification Campaigns were successful in ridding the communists of their factions, including pro-Russian groups.

Historians do not agree on the military contribution of the CCP in the war against the Japanese. Some suggest that it was rather more limited than Mao claimed. There is little doubt, however, that there was a general perception within China and internationally that the CCP gave good leadership during the war. This perception led many Chinese to see the communists as the true nationalists, and support the CCP rather than the GMD. Indeed, the CCP's Hundred Regiments Offensive in 1940 was the largest single campaign of the Sino-Japanese War and provoked a brutal retaliation from the Japanese, expressed in the 'kill all, burn all, loot all' policy.

Mao used his guerrilla assaults on the Japanese as good propaganda to promote the CCP as the *real* nationalist force defending China. He also emphasized the support that the GMD was receiving from the USA, arguing that Jiang was nothing more than a puppet of the Western imperialists. Such sentiments fed into the long-held anti-foreign and anti-imperialist popular feelings in China.

STUDENT STUDY SECTION

Review questions

1. In what ways had the CCP been strengthed by the impact of the Sino-Japanese War?

2. In what ways had the GMD been weakened by the impact of the war?

3. 'It is absurd to speak of an historical event as "inevitable", but the Communist–Guomindang civil war almost demands that adjective. It is difficult in retrospect to see how it could have been avoided. An abyss of profound hostility and distrust, and the scars of brutal conflict, separated the two parties, to say nothing of their utterly different social philosophies' (James Sheridan, *China in Disintegration*, 1977).

   Why was renewed civil war 'inevitable' at the end of the Sino-Japanese War, according to this historian?

Review activity

In pairs, discuss and make notes on the following question: 'What was the impact of foreign involvement in: a) the first phase of the Chinese Civil War, and b) the war against Japan?'

Second phase of the Civil War, 1946–49

By the end of the war with Japan, the CCP was significantly strengthened, and the GMD weakened, so much so that the communists could move from the guerrilla warfare phase of combat to a phase of more conventional fighting. The first period of civil war (1927–37) was an essentially Chinese war. The second would be more of an international affair. The polarization of the international political context through the development of the Cold War meant that China's civil war could not be an internal struggle alone. The war between nationalists and communists in China had become part of a larger Soviet–American effort to create a new post-war balance of power.

Both superpowers wanted a stable China, and a weakened Japan, and to this end they both wanted the GMD and the CCP to form a coalition government. The USSR wanted influence in Manchuria, and the USA accepted this desire to a certain extent.

Failure of the USA

The Americans worked hard to achieve a diplomatic solution between the CCP and the GMD. Yet neither side was willing to share power. General Marshall was given the responsibility of brokering a deal, and managed to get the GMD and the CCP to agree on the following terms: prepare to set up a coalition government, form a temporary state council, unite their armies in a new National Army and have free elections for local government. But as negotiations were being finalized in February 1946, both sides were moving troops into Manchuria. There would not be a diplomatic solution in China; its fate would be decided on the battlefield.

Map showing major battles and campaigns, 1946–49.

Despite the growth in strength of the CCP during the Sino-Japanese war, it is important to point out that in 1945, the GMD still had four million troops compared to the CCP's one million. The GMD also had more heavy weaponry. The events of the next three years are thus important for explaining the success of the CCP.

Initial victories for GMD (1945–47)

At first the GMD, with more troops and better equipment, forced the communists onto the defensive. Following the Japanese surrender in August 1945, the Red Army under General Lin Biao entered Manchuria to secure this important industrial region under communist control. At the Yalta Conference in February 1945, the Allies had agreed that the USSR would invade Manchuria following Germany's surrender. The Soviets had duly invaded, and were in control when the CCP forces arrived, whereupon the Soviets gave the CCP large stockpiles of Japanese weapons. The USSR was clearly not neutral. General Albert Wedemeyer, the Allied commander of the South-East Asia Theatre, authorized Jiang to resist the communists by using US ships and aircraft to transport 500,000 troops to Manchuria, and 50,000 American troops were sent north to occupy Beijing. The USA could no longer claim to be neutral either.

Although the CCP forces were better armed than before, the GMD greatly outnumbered them. The CCP also had to fight conventionally in Manchuria, defending and holding its positions and territory. The GMD was able to force the CCP out of the cities, and in December 1945 Mao reverted to his policy of creating bases outside the cities.

It seemed as though Manchuria had been won by the GMD, but despite their early military achievements they continued to govern the region as they had others during the war with Japan, and this led to political defeat. Indeed, corruption was worse than it had been before, which encouraged Manchurians to support the CCP. President Truman sent General Marshall to mediate in the conflict, attempting to prevent a civil war and to avert US involvement in the fighting. US policy continued to be to promote a coalition government. The Americans were in a difficult position, as they did not support single-party states, and wanted to retain the position of mediator – even though they continued to arm Jiang Jieshi. The truce facilitated by Marshall broke down in March 1946. By May, the GMD was in control of the central area of Manchuria. The CCP demanded a ceasefire and condemned US support for Jiang Jieshi.

CCP on the offensive (1947–48)

At this point the US intervention, according to Jiang, played a key role in the outcome of the civil war. In June, General Marshall managed to get Jiang to agree to another truce. The ceasefire worked to the CCP's advantage, as it saved them from a final assault on their headquarters. The communists used the time to train their forces and ready them for the war. Mao also introduced land reforms in the area. As it had done in Yan'an, land reform led to the peasants joining the communists, as their victory would mean they could keep their land.

Fighting resumed in July, and the Red Army (now called the People's Liberation Army; PLA) reverted to guerrilla warfare. The GMD recaptured the cities of Manchuria and went on in March 1947 to take the CCP capital, Yan'an. Yet cities in Manchuria were now isolated, and Mao could use guerrilla tactics effectively; the PLA cut the GMD forces off by targeting their supply routes, the railways.

By March 1948, the remaining American advisers told Jiang Jieshi to leave Manchuria to protect his forces. At this point, the GMD and the CCP were quite evenly matched – in terms of their military manpower and resources. Jiang refused to acknowledge that the balance had shifted unfavourably, and that the PLA now had more heavy weapons than the GMD. He fought on, but in March 1948 the CCP was in control of Manchuria. Jiang had lost 40,000 troops.

Collapse of GMD resistance

Capitalizing on its success, the PLA launched an offensive against the vital railway junction of Xuzhou. Here the communists fought a conventional battle, relying on massed heavy artillery. The defeat of the nationalists was a huge blow for Jiang's men, both strategically and psychologically. In the same month, January 1949, Lin Biao took the cities of Tianjin and then Beijing. The whole of northern China, including Manchuria, was now under communist control. In April the PLA launched the final series of offensives, taking Nanjing and then Shanghai in May. In October, Guangzhou was taken, and throughout November the communists crushed the remnants of GMD resistance.

On 1 October 1949, Mao proclaimed the establishment of the People's Republic of China in Beijing, saying: 'Our nation will never again be an insulted nation. We have stood up.'

What were the reasons for the communist success?

Strengths of the CCP

- **Guerrilla tactics and revolutionary warfare** – The CCP used guerrilla tactics successfully in the first phase of the civil war, in the fight against the Japanese and in Manchuria in the second phase of the civil war.

STUDENT STUDY SECTION

Review activity

Give specific examples from this chapter of how guerrilla tactics were used by the communists in their struggle.

- **The leadership of the PLA** – The PLA was led by Lin Biao, who was an excellent military commander and who was able to transform the PLA from a guerrilla fighting force into a regular army. The PLA was greatly strengthened in the final stages of the war by desertions from the nationalist forces and through capturing enemy weapons. Through better conditions and political indoctrination, the PLA was a much more effective fighting force, with far higher morale than the nationalist troops. In addition, the good behaviour of the communist soldiers attracted much support from the peasantry.
- **The role of Mao** – Mao's leadership was central to the communist success. It was his leadership in the Long March and his innovative guerrilla tactics that allowed the CCP to survive and then to broaden its support base in Yan'an. He was able to take advantage of the opportunity presented by the war with Japan, and also to adapt his ideas and policies to the changing military situation. For example, although revolutionary ideas involved attacking the bourgeoisie, or middle classes, during the war against Japan, he stressed the idea that this was a *national* struggle in which all classes should cooperate.
- **The spread of communist ideas** – As we have seen, the communists used the period during the war with Japan to spread communist ideas throughout the areas they captured. The policy continued in the second phase of the civil war. Land reform continued in all rural areas captured by the communists.

As the communists moved into the towns, they similarly spread communist ideas. The army would take over the control of the towns, working to prevent crime, control food distribution and establish fairer taxation systems. These activities broadened the base of support for the CCP.

- **The role of intelligence** – The superior intelligence of the communists in the second phase of the civil war played an important role in their victory. Jiang's assistant Chief of Staff, Liu Fei, was a communist spy, as was the head of the GMD's War Planning Board. This meant that the communists knew all intended GMD moves in advance. In addition, several of the nationalist commanders were in fact communist agents. In Manchuria, for example, the nationalist commander Wei Lihuang was a communist agent, and his actions helped secure the PLA victory there. In contrast to this situation, the nationalists were unable to infiltrate the communists.

Jiang Jieshi's errors

- **Political** – Jiang Jieshi continued to resist democratic changes, and his increasingly repressive regime alienated liberals and the middle classes. He failed to win mass support and his government relied on a narrow, wealthy section of businessmen and landlords for its survival. The GMD's corruption and inefficiency further alienated the middle classes and also the peasants who bore the brunt of the unfair tax system.
- **Economic** – Jiang Jieshi's support base was further damaged by rampant inflation, which had a devastating effect on the middle classes. Jiang only took decisive action to deal with this in 1948, when a new currency was introduced and rationing started. These reforms were too late, however, and there was economic collapse by 1949 in those areas under nationalist control.
- **Military** – US observers continually commented on the poor quality of many of Jiang's troops, and their low morale contributed to the high number of desertions at the end of the civil war. The behaviour of the army towards ordinary Chinese was also in sharp contrast to that of the communist army, with its strict rules of behaviour.

In terms of military leadership, Jiang also made serious mistakes – for instance choosing to pour resources into Manchuria, far from his real bases of support. His decision to fight it out at Xuzhou was also a disaster. He also tried to interfere too much in the actual running of the campaigns, even though he was far removed from the actual action.

What was the role of foreign support in the final outcome?
The USA

To access worksheet 13.2 on US involvement in the Chinese Civil War, please visit www.pearsonbacconline.com and follow the on-screen instructions.

The Americans, as discussed earlier, had economic and strategic interests in China, and they had supported the GMD from the first phase of the civil war. This support should have given the GMD key advantages over the CCP, and despite the problem of getting effective aid to the GMD, the USA provided Jiang with almost $3 billion in aid and large supplies of arms throughout World War II. At the beginning of the second stage of the civil war, the Americans transported GMD forces by sea and air to the north of China, and US troops occupied Tianjin and Beijing to hold them until the GMD were ready. In short, the USA did what it could to assist Jiang, but his regime was too ineffective to survive.

Yet some historians believe that there should have been *more* military commitment from the USA, and that this could have 'saved' China from communism. The Americans were held responsible by Jiang for pressurizing him to agree to truces at critical times during his war on the CCP. Finally, their mere presence also gave Mao excellent anti-GMD propaganda.

USSR

The Soviets had been rather reluctant to support the CCP, and did not in the end give them the military and economic assistance that the GMD received from the USA. The involvement of the Comintern in the early stages of the CCP's struggle with the GMD had led to division and near annihilation in Jiang's final Encirclement Campaign. Mao waged the Rectification Campaigns to oust Soviet supporters from the CCP. The USSR had backed both United Fronts, and Stalin did not see that the CCP could win the civil war until the later stages in 1948.

Some historians view the Soviet assistance in Manchuria, which also included establishing military training colleges and the training of CCP pilots, as essential to establishing the PLA as a more modern and effective force. Nevertheless, Stalin was worried that the USA would involve itself further in the Chinese Civil War, and attempted to limit Mao's successes in the later stages of the conflict. In 1949, Stalin told Mao to consolidate his gains in the north and not cross the Yangtze into southern China. Mao ignored his advice.

STUDENT STUDY SECTION

Document analysis

Historians, of course, often disagree on the key reasons for the CCP's victory over the GMD. Read the documents below and identify in each case what reason the historian is emphasizing as the most important for CCP victory.

Document A

The most important near cause for the downfall of the Nationalists was the eight-year Japanese war, which completely exhausted the government militarily, financially and spiritually. Had there been no Japanese war, the situation in China would have been very different ... [M]any of the disastrous repercussions of the war ... continued to plague the Nationalists during their struggle with the Communists. The price the Nationalists paid to win the Japanese war was also the first instalment toward its eventual downfall.

From Immanuel Hsu, *The Rise of Modern China*, 1995

Document B

China in fact was a classical eve-of-revolution situation. The ruling elite had lost its confidence and its will to rule. In these circumstances the final victory of the Communists, although it was gained by war, was actually a political victory. In 1947 the Communist armies faced Nationalist superiority in men and materials of two-and-a-half to one. After less than a year of fighting, they had reversed the proportion, as a result of the corruption, demoralisation and frequent defection to the nationalist armies…The actual military events of the communist conquest of China are of little interest. The Nationalist armies, as Lenin had said of the soldiers of the tsar in 1917, voted with their feet. The war-lord allies of the Guomindang retreated into their own bailiwicks and from them made their peace with Mao Zedong.

From Jack Gray, *Rebellions and Revolutions: China from the 1880s to the 1980s*, 1990

Document C

What finally undermined the Nationalist government was not war or politics but economics. The military and political success of the Communists under Mao Zedong certainly played a vital part in determining their takeover in 1949, but it is arguable that the single most powerful reason fro the failure of the GMD government was inflation…By 1949 China's monetary system had collapsed, the government was discredited, and the people of Nationalist China were demoralised. Even had the Nationalists not been defeated in civil war and driven from the mainland it is difficult to see how Jiang Jieshi and the GMD could have continued to hold power in China.

From Michael Lynch, *China: From Empire to People's Republic 1900–49*, 1999

Document D

It is clear that a host of factors went into the Communist success…But the central factor was unquestionably the mobilization of vast numbers of Chinese, primarily peasants, into new political, social, economic, and military organizations, infused with a new purpose and a new spirit. This mobilization largely accounted for the Communist victory …

From James Sheridan, *China in Disintegration*, 1977

Review questions

1   What was the impact of a) the USSR's and b) the USA's involvement in the Chinese Civil War?

2   To what extent were political/ideological factors more important to the CCP's victory than military factors?

ToK Time

How important is the study of history to our understanding of international relations today? How does our understanding of history impact on our understanding of the world today? What are the knowledge issues involved in how politicians use history? Does the study of China's relationship with the West give us a better understanding of modern foreign relations?

Results of the Chinese Civil War

For China

After the civil war, the CCP consolidated its control in China, and pursued the key ideas that they had initiated in Yan'an. The experiences of the long war were a guidebook for the new Chinese communist regime. Society had been militarized and Mao had a god-like status. Society would be changed by short and 'total' campaigns, and all obstacles would be overcome by the power of the people. One of the key legacies of the Chinese Civil War is the continued authoritarian rule by the CCP. China remains a single-party state in which individual rights and freedoms are suppressed. In 1989, when young protesters on the streets of Tiananmen Square, Beijing, were forcibly dispersed with guns and tanks, the battles of the civil war were used to justify the actions of the state.

For Asia

Mao's victory led to the globalization of the Cold War, which spread from its seedbed in Europe to Asia. Asia was now a region in which the superpowers would struggle for control and influence. The communist victory inspired insurgencies in Indonesia, Malaya, Indochina and Thailand. It also led to the first 'hot war' of the Cold War – the Korean War (1950–53).

For the USSR

Although the CCP's victory should have been viewed as a victory for the spread of communism and for the USSR, Stalin feared Mao as a rival for the leadership of the communist world, and he had not wanted the Cold War to spread to Asia. Jiang's GMD would have recognized disputed border territory along frontiers in Manchuria and Xinjiang as Soviet. Fundamentally, Stalin did not view Maoism as 'genuinely revolutionary' and did not agree with Mao's 'hybrid' ideology, which was a mix of traditional Chinese culture and Marxism.

Mao became convinced that Stalin planned to create a divided and weak China, which would leave the USSR dominant in Asia. He saw Stalin's policies as rooted in self-interest rather than true revolutionary doctrine. Mao later said that in 1945 Stalin refused China permission to carry out revolution and told him: 'Do not have a civil war: collaborate with Jiang Jieshi. Otherwise the Republic of China will collapse.' Mao believed that Stalin saw him as another Tito (the communist revolutionary who became the leader of post-war Yugoslavia).

Nevertheless, once the CCP had won the civil war, Mao visited Moscow in 1950 and this visit produced the Sino-Soviet Treaty of Alliance. This was the first treaty between the USSR and China. The USSR had become excited and enthusiastic about the CCP's victory, and the Soviet press had poured praise and admiration on Mao and the new People's Republic of China (PRC). The US State Department referred to the alliance as 'Moscow making puppets out of the Chinese'. Soviet planners and engineers in China developed 200 construction projects in the 1950s; traditional buildings were pulled down for Soviet-style constructions and Soviet scientific technology was prioritized in China over Chinese technology.

Sino-Soviet relations chilled again during the Korean War. When American forces, under the UN flag, came close to the Chinese border, Stalin encouraged the PRC to send troops into Korea. The Soviets gave material assistance to the one million Chinese troops engaged in battle, but despite this support for PRC intervention in the Korean War, Mao bitterly complained when the Soviets demanded that the Chinese pay for all weapons and materials they supplied.

Relations between the USSR and the PRC worsened dramatically after the death of Stalin. Khrushchev's attack on Stalin's cult of personality was seen by Mao as an attack on his own style of leadership, and the USSR's handling of the Cuban Missile Crisis in 1962 caused Mao to accuse Khrushchev of being a 'paper tiger'. The Sino-Soviet split worsened, culminating in border clashes in 1969.

China's relations with the USA and the West

Mao's victory led to much anxiety in the USA, and seemed at the time to shift the balance of power in the Cold War in the USSR's favour. Many in the USA initially saw the communist victory as inevitable given the lack of support that existed for the nationalists in China in 1949; nevertheless, as the Cold War intensified and **McCarthyism** took hold in the USA, state officials were accused of having 'lost' China. Stalin was now seen as having been the mastermind behind Mao's CCP. The USA failed to understand the different types of communism or that there was increasing tension and hostility between Mao and Stalin. The USA also refused to recognize the PRC as a legitimate state. Instead they backed Jiang

Jieshi and the Chinese nationalists, who had fled at the end of the civil war to the island of Taiwan, about 160km off the coast of mainland China. The Americans then ensured that Taiwan and *not* the PRC was given China's seat at the UN.

The USA initially perceived the CCP victory as opening a new 'front' in the Cold War; there was the *iron curtain* in Europe and now the *bamboo curtain* in Asia. Mao's victory was a key reason for the passing of a vast new military budget to fund the struggle against the spread of communism. It also led the USA into the Korean War and conflict over Taiwan. However, by the end of the 1960s there was a radical change by both the Americans and the communist Chinese in their policies and strategies towards one another. During the late 1960s, China and the USA entered into a period of dialogue, known as 'ping pong diplomacy'.

STUDENT STUDY SECTION

Review activity

	GMD: Policies / Actions	CCP: Policies / Actions	Foreign intervention: Policies / Actions	Historians' comments
1927–37				
1937–45				
1945–49				

Questions

Copy out the grid above and use it to help you answer the following essay questions:

1 Why did the CCP win the Chinese Civil War?
You can divide this essay into the following headings:
- Strengths/successes of the CCP, 1928–49
- Weakness/failures of the GMD, 1928–49
- The impact of the Sino-Japanese War
- The impact of foreign intervention.

2 How significant was the role of foreign intervention in the Chinese Civil War?
You can divide this essay into the following headings:
- The impact of foreign intervention (consider long-term European intervention, as well as Japanese and superpower involvement)
- Strengths/successes of the CCP, 1928–49
- Weakness/failures of the GMD, 1928–49.

3 Also try answering this question:
In what ways can the Chinese Civil War be seen as a 'revolutionary war'?
Refer back to p.266 to help you with this question.

IBLP link – Reflective

First, reflect on your understanding of the causes of war in the 20th century, and then reflect on the causes of the Chinese Civil War. Can you identify and understand the political, economic, social and military causes of a war? What factors do you find more difficult to understand?

14 ALGERIAN WAR – WAR OF DECOLONIZATION

As you read through this chapter, consider the following essay questions:
- Analyze the reasons for the outbreak of war in Algeria in 1954.
- What were the reasons for the outcome of the Algerian War?
- How important was the strategy of guerrilla warfare for ensuring that Algeria gained independence?

The Algerian War of 1954–62 was one of the most savage of Africa's struggles for independence. The war started on 1 November 1954 with an insurrection led by the Front de Libération Nationale (FLN; National Liberation Front) and it ended in 1962 when Algeria became independent. It was never a straight struggle between Algerians and the French government, however. It eventually became a four-way conflict between the Algerian nationalists, the French government, the European colonists and, in the final stage, General Charles de Gaulle.

The war was devastating for Algeria; during those eight years, at least a quarter of a million Algerians died and approximately two million had to leave their villages. It also left France deeply scarred, and was unique in colonial wars for causing a change of government in a European country, with the destruction of France's Fourth Republic. This war also stands as an example of a guerrilla war.

STUDENT STUDY SECTION

Review questions

Look back at Chapter 1 on the discussion of guerrilla warfare.

1 What are the key characteristics of guerrilla warfare?

2 What factors have made guerrilla warfare the chosen style of warfare for people struggling for independence against European powers?

Charles de Gaulle.

Charles de Gaulle
De Gaulle is one of the most influential leaders of modern France. He was a brigadier-general in World War II, and following the fall of France in 1940, he organized the Free French Forces with exiled French officers in England. He became Prime Minister in the French Provisional Government following the liberation of France in 1944, but then retired from politics in 1946. The Algerian crisis brought him out of retirement, and he was then elected President of the Fifth Republic. He finally retired in 1969.

Timeline of events – 1945–62

1945	8 May	VE Day. Algerian revolt in Sétif followed by severe reprisals
1954	Apr	End of French rule in Indochina
	Nov	FLN created. FLN insurrection and beginning of civil war
1955	Jan	Jacques Soustelle appointed as Governor-General of Algeria
	Aug	FLN massacre *pieds-noirs* at Philippeville
1956	Feb	Robert Lacoste appointed as Governor-General of Algeria
	Mar	Independence given to Tunisia and Morocco
	Sep	FLN explode bombs in fashionable cafes: battle for Algiers begins
	Oct	Suez Crisis
	Dec	Raoul Salan appointed as commander-in-chief in Algeria
1957	Jan	Jacques Massu's paras take over Algiers
	Nov	Battle for Algiers won by French
1958	May	Pierre Pflimlin new premier. French Assembly gives de Gaulle full powers for six months to make a new constitution. Committee of Public Safety set up under General Massu
	Sep	FLN announce formation of a provisional government called the GPRA based in Tunis Fehrat Abbas is Prime Minister

1959 **Sep** De Gaulle offers Algeria self-determination
1960 **Jan** *Colon* Ultras attempt coup – Barricades Week
1961 **Jan** Referendum gives de Gaulle go-ahead to work for Algerian self-determination. Both sides agree to peace talks
    Apr Generals' insurrection in Algiers; de Gaulle triumphs. Organisation de l'armée secrète (OAS; Secret Army Organization) created
    May First peace talks at Evian; failure
1962 **Feb** OAS kill 533 people
    Mar Second Evian Conference – agreement reached and ceasefire implemented OAS continues terrorist attacks and 'scorched earth policy'
    Jul Algeria becomes a sovereign state
    Sep Ben Bella becomes President of Algeria

Map of Algeria.

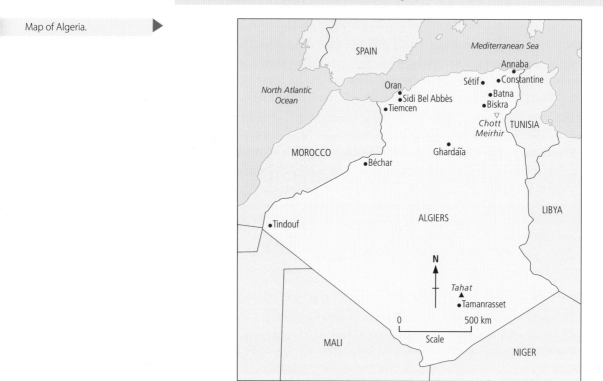

Causes of the Algerian War
Tensions in Algeria before World War II

Algeria had been colonized by France in the 19th century. By 1841 there were already 37,374 French settlers, the *colons*, later called the *pieds-noirs* (black feet) by Arabs because of the fact that they wore cheap black shoes. By 1945, there were about one million *pieds-noirs*, many of whom had been born in Algeria and who regarded it as their home. The *pieds-noirs* were an extremely diverse group both in terms of wealth and of political beliefs. The extreme conservatives among this group, who resisted all change, were known as the Ultras; there were also, however, liberals (approximately 20–25 per cent) who supported reforms of some kind.

The official French policy with regard to colonies was one of 'assimilation'. This was based on the idea that French civilization was superior to all others and that the colonies would therefore benefit from being integrated into all aspects of this civilization, its social and political institutions, French citizenship and the French language. Thus colonies were seen as *départements* ('departments'; the primary regional divisions of France itself), which, in the case of Algeria, had direct political representation in Paris. In the words of Arthur Girault, the idea of assimilation 'is not separation, but, on the contrary, an increasingly intimate union between the colonial and the metropolitan territory… The colonies are theoretically considered to be a simple extension of the soil of the mother country' (*Principes de colonisation et de législation coloniale*, 1921). This view was particularly true of Algeria, which was dominated by the French more than any of the other French colonies and which was seen as an integral part of France, with three departments.

In reality, however, French rule was racist and condescending. For the one million *colons* living in Algeria, maintaining the French connection was essential, as it gave them a social advantage over indigenous Algerians. Muslim land had been expropriated and only 2 per cent of the population owned 25 per cent of the land. *Colons* earned substantially more than the Muslims, who also suffered a high unemployment rate. This situation was not helped by the fact that the French government prevented industrialization and development of certain areas of the agricultural sector in order to prevent foreign competition with France.

With regard to education, there were 1,400 primary schools for the 200,000 Europeans and only 699 schools for the 1,250,000 Muslims. Thus the Muslim population was in a state of near illiteracy by 1945.

STUDENT STUDY SECTION

Research question

How did the idea of French assimilation compare with British methods of ruling colonies?

The impact of World War II on French rule in Algeria

World War II had a decisive impact on colonial resistance movements throughout Asia and Africa. The European colonizers had been revealed as vulnerable; France had fallen to the Germans, the British colonies of Singapore, Hong Kong and Malaya had fallen to the Japanese. The Japanese had also helped stir up nationalism through their anti-European propaganda and their promotion of local officials; their ruthless subjugation policies had also encouraged the emergence of nationalist leaders such as Ho Chi Minh in Vietnam, leaders who wanted to resist not just the Japanese but also the European rulers when they tried to return after the war.

Both the USA and the USSR after 1945 expressed their opposition to imperialism, and the founding of the UN, with its emphasis on human rights and freedoms, also undermined the whole concept of imperialism. Nevertheless, the French government had no intention of fundamentally changing its colonial policy. In 1942, Fehrat Abbas, representing Algerian Muslim political activists, had drawn up his 'Manifesto of the Algerian People'. This demanded 'the condemnation and abolition of colonization' plus self-government and a constitution, allowing for immediate participation by Algerians in their own political affairs. Yet these demands were ignored, and in fact Abbas's moderate nationalist party was dissolved in 1945.

Meanwhile, de Gaulle called a conference of colonial administrators in Brazzaville in the French Congo in 1944. The conference promised a new 'French Community' that would abolish the worst aspects of colonialism. Yet there was no suggestion of any move towards self-government. Indeed René Pleven, a prominent French politician, asserted in his speech at the Brazzaville Conference that 'there are no peoples to liberate' and that the colonial subjects 'do not want to know any other independence than the independence of France'. De Gaulle did, however, concede local assemblies.

Fehrat Abbas.

The 'era of broken promises'

Frustration at this situation exploded as early as 1945. During celebrations for VE (Victory in Europe) Day in the predominantly Muslim town of Setif, nationalist banners, which had been banned, appeared. When police tried to seize the banners, fighting broke out. The result was attacks on Europeans, including murder, rape and robbery. Throughout Algeria, about 100 people were killed. French revenge was swift and bloody. Officially, 1,005 Muslims died during the savage repression. According to Algerian nationalists, 40,000 to 50,000 died. The killings had the effect of whipping up nationalist sentiment, but the French quickly restored order and therefore believed that they could carry on with colonial rule as before.

In 1946, the Fourth Republic renamed the French Empire as the French Union. Based upon the principles of the Brazzaville Conference, it agreed greater autonomy for the colonial people – but again there was no question of decolonization. In 1947, the Muslims did get the right to vote in Algeria, but out of the elected assembly, 60 of the deputies were to be elected by the *colons* and 60 by the Muslims, who were 90 per cent of the population. *Colons* and Muslims each sent 15 deputies and senators to Paris. In 1956, only eight out of the 864 higher posts in the administration were held by Muslims. In addition, because many *colons* believed that the Muslims should not be able to vote at all, elections were rigged. The *colons*, who had immense influence through their deputies and pressure groups, also stopped any reforms that threatened their interests.

This period was known as the 'era of broken promises', and even moderates like Fehrat Abbas became disillusioned. He became a leader of the revolutionary FLN along with Ben Bella. The FLN was set up in 1954 in Cairo and aimed to wage a guerrilla war against the French. Its first proclamation stated that independence was to be reached by whatever means were necessary and that 'the struggle may be long, but the outcome is certain…'

Events outside Algeria

It is important not to look at Algeria in isolation from events that were happening elsewhere. Arab nationalism was fired by the success and the leadership of Colonel Nasser in Egypt, who had overthrown King Faroukh in 1952. In addition, the French had been defeated decisively by the Vietminh insurgents in Vietnam at the battle of Dien Bien Phu in 1954. Even before that, Cambodia and Laos had gained independence in 1953. Meanwhile, in two other French colonies in West Africa, Morocco and Tunisia, independence was gained in 1956.

STUDENT STUDY SECTION

Review question

Research and assess the impact of each of the following in the lead-up to civil war in Algeria:
- France's colonization policies
- The influence of the *colons* (*pieds-noirs*)
- World War II
- Failure of French political reform after World War II
- Events in Egypt
- Events in other French colonies – Indochina, Morocco and Tunisia.

The outbreak of war

The first attack by the FLN, launched on 1 November 1954, was immediately dismissed by the French as another uprising that could easily be contained. A far more serious attack upon *colons* and French forces was launched upon the town of Philippeville in August 1955. Here a massacre by the FLN left 123 Muslims and *pieds-noirs* dead; the French retaliatory action, according to French sources, killed 1,200 people (or 12,000 according to FLN sources).

The 50,000 French troops already in Algeria were reinforced by paratroopers and gendarmes. Jacques Soustelle was made Governor-General in January 1955. Soustelle was a liberal intellectual who hoped to carry out economic and political reform. Yet Soustelle was thwarted by the *colons*, the brutality of the fighting on both sides and the growing support for the FLN. In 1956, the French government, under pressure from the *colons*, replaced him with a less liberal governor, Robert Lacoste, who was given special powers to deal with a situation that was now spiralling out of control.

The nature of the fighting in the Algerian War

The army played a key role in the development of events in Algeria. The French defeat at Dien Bien Phu in Vietnam, they believed, was a humiliation that must not be allowed to happen again. They were thus united with the *colons* in believing that Algeria must remain under French control, although their concerns for Algeria were different from those of the *colons*: 'The day-to-day business of administering large tracts of Algeria had become the responsibility of the army, and in the course of governing their localities had acquired a proficiency, knowledge and sympathy for the people in their care which, they judged, would not easily be supplied by anybody else' (from Peter Calvocoressi, *World Politics 1945–2000*, 2001).

When the scale of the FLN operations increased in 1955, the army started to fight the guerrillas in earnest. A key aspect to French tactics was the use of helicopters, which moved troops around and attacked over large areas from the sky. Without support from a major power, the FLN lacked anti-aircraft missiles, and the open, arid terrain made conditions easier for the French Army to identify FLN forces on the ground.

Both sides targeted civilians. The FLN used terror against civilians to ensure that they did not associate with the French authorities. All Muslims were ordered to give up smoking and alcohol or face death or mutilation. The French Army purposely targeted civilians with its policy of 'collective responsibility', i.e. that all Muslims were responsible for the guerrilla attacks. As in other guerrilla wars, a cycle of retaliation emerged whereby any FLN attack on French forces would result in the French Army taking retaliatory action against civilians in an attempt to discourage support for the FLN. These actions by both sides had the effect of radicalizing both Europeans and Algerians, and also dividing the population of France.

To access worksheet 14.1 on tactics in the Algerian War, please visit www.pearsonbacconline.com and follow the on-screen instructions.

Algerian National Liberation Front fighters erect barricades on the border between Algeria and Tunisia.

STUDENT STUDY SECTION

Document work

Document A

The disfiguring of French victims, the widespread appearance of le *grand sourire (the broad smile), which was how the French macabrely described the Algerian practice of throat slitting, the bombing of civilian public places – these acts of terrorism aroused a comparable response. French soldiers began the practice of torture to obtain information and engaged in indiscriminate killing that shocked the population at home. French intellectuals vigorously protested these practices seeing that the very soul of the nation was threatened. French soldiers occasionally shivered at the thought that their behaviour was not dissimilar to that of the Nazis in occupied France. The war was thus dispiriting and disturbing, moods deepened by the lack of clearly defined military objectives, by the lack of political plan and resolve. Never recognised by the French government as a war, the struggle went on for seven years.*

From Raymond Betts, *France and Decolonisation*, 1991

Document B

Before the crisis was over, the French army in Algeria would grow to 500 000 troops, and this within a few years of the debacle at Dien Bien Phu. Moreover, the French government was forced to send conscripts to Algeria, something it had never done in the case of Indo-China. As a result, the war affected many in France who were not enthusiastic supporters of empire, and widespread dissatisfaction with the war in North Africa developed by the late 1950s. France had freed itself from one military disaster only to become embroiled in another. As late as 1958 probably a majority of French citizens still favoured protecting the interests of the colons whatever the price. But others considered that it was a lost cause, so that French politics tended to become polarized, and France itself entered upon a particularly unstable period in its history.

From T.E. Vadney, *The World Since 1945*, 1991

Document C

[Following the Vietnam War]…The FLN was able to pick up a blueprint of people's war ready made, although the war they fought was rather different. Lacking the Vietminh's regular military strength and its Chinese sanctuary and support, the FLN's campaign was more strongly marked by terrorism. The war began in 1954 with one of the most spectacularly deadly urban bombings yet seen, and was largely sustained by similar means. The French responded in kind, with a counter-terror…. The French army had bitterly concluded that defeat in Vietnam had been due to its failure to match the ruthlessness and conviction of the Communists.

From Charles Townshend (ed.), *The Oxford History of Modern War*, 2005

Review and document questions

1 From what you have read so far, why do you think that the FLN adopted guerrilla tactics to fight the French? (Also refer back to your answers to the question on p.282)

2 What kind of tactics did the FLN use?

3 What impact did these tactics have on a) the French Army, and b) France (both the government and the French population)?

The ALN

The more conventional army of the FLN became known as the ALN – the Armée de Libération Nationale. It was mainly based in Tunisia (see p.285). It never played a significant role in the war.

The international dimension of guerrilla tactics

The FLN was quick to realize the importance of international support, and worked to develop worldwide backing for its cause. Thus thanks to pressure from the Arab League, the Algerian situation was discussed at the UN and the Bandung Conference in 1955. FLN delegations were sent to Eastern and Western Europe, the USA, China, India and Latin America. This tactic resulted in both moral support for the guerrilla fighters, with the UN putting pressure on France regarding its Algerian policy, and also material support. Weapons came to the FLN from other Arab countries, but also from Britain and America.

STUDENT STUDY SECTION

Research question

There have been several references to the war in Indochina/Vietnam, where the French had been defeated by the Vietminh at the battle of Dien Bien Phu. This conflict is another excellent example of a guerrilla war.

Research:
- The reasons for this war
- The tactics used by the Vietminh
- The problems faced by the French and why they ultimately lost.

From what you have read so far, what similarities and differences existed between the situation in Indochina and that in Algeria?

The battle of Algiers

The army had the opportunity to assert its control over the direction of the war and indeed Algeria itself during the 'battle of Algiers'. In September 1956, the FLN began an attack on the capital, one that involved brutal terrorist attacks against Europeans, Arab 'collaborators' and armed forces. Here was an attempt by the FLN to gain more international attention, and particularly shocking was the placing of bombs by Muslim women in cafes that were popular with *colon* families. Yet moving their action into the cities was a high-risk strategy for the guerrilla fighters. The French General Jacques Massu and the 10th Paratroop Division, endowed by Lacoste with the powers of civilian police, used torture and terror to destroy the FLN hideouts.

The battle of Algiers is described in the following way by French historian, Benjamin Stora:

It was truly 'blood and shit,' as Colonel Marcel Bigeard said, a horrendous battle, during which bombs blew dozens of European victims to pieces while paratroopers dismantled the networks by uncovering their hierarchy, discovered caches, and flushed out the FLN leaders installed in the city. Their means? Electrodes dunking in bath tubs, beatings. Some of the torturers were sadists, to be sure. But many officers, non-commissioned officers, and soldiers would live with that nightmare for the rest of their lives. The number of attacks perpetrated fell from 112 in January to 39 in February, then to 29 in March. The FLN's command centre, run by Abbane Ramdane, was forced to leave the capital. Massu had a first victory.

From Benjamin Stora, *Algeria 1830–2000: A Short History*, 2001

What were the results of the battle of Algiers?

* The FLN was weakened militarily, but nevertheless continued to grow in political strength, and gained increasing support from the outside world, especially from the communist bloc. Following the independence of Tunisia and Morocco, the FLN was able to seek sanctuary in these two countries. In 1958, the FLN announced the formation of a provisional government called the Gouvernement Provisoire de la République Algérienne (GPRA; Provisional Government of the Republic of Algeria) based in Tunis, with Fehrat Abbas as the Prime Minister. This development obviously complicated the situation for France. To prevent FLN attacks from these countries, the French built expensive, heavily guarded security fences along the borders. The construction programme used up vital French resources and soldiers, which then could not be used in the actual fighting in Algeria.

To access worksheet 14.2 on the battle of Algiers, please visit www.pearsonbacconline.com and follow the on-screen instructions.

The Battle of Algiers
The Battle of Algiers is a famous 1966 film by Gillo Pontecorvo portraying the events that took place in Algiers in 1956. It shows that atrocities were committed on both sides, and it thus caused political controversy in France, where it was banned for five years. Scenes of torture were in fact cut from the original American and British showing of the film. The film has seen a revival in the last few years due to the similarities between the situation faced by the French in Algeria in the 1950s and the situation faced by the Americans in Iraq following the US invasion in 2003.

A scene from the influential film, *The Battle of Algiers* (1966).

- The French Army grew in influence in Algeria (see below), and both the army and the *colons* believed that they had been right in combating the FLN with their own tactics of force and ruthlessness.
- No solution to the situation in Algeria seemed in sight.
- The French faced international condemnation for their actions in Algeria and opposition to the army's methods grew within France.
- The internal crisis in Algeria precipitated a political crisis in France.

Following their victory in Algiers over the FLN, the army concluded that they could not trust the existing French government to keep Algeria under French control. The *colons* were also appalled at the apparent weakness of the French government, and a new government under Pierre Pflimlin, which included no sympathizers of the *colons*, provided the trigger for a direct challenge to the young French administration. On 13 May 1958, those opposed to the French government instigated a mass demonstration in Algiers in an attempt to intimidate Pflimlin's government. Violence broke out and a Committee of Public Safety took over political power under the control of General Massu. It was clear that the army and *colons* were united in direct and open opposition to the government in Paris.

French protesters in Algeria vent their anger against the policies of the French government.

What was the role of de Gaulle in the crisis?

There was confusion and panic in Paris at the situation in Algeria, and fears of a military coup in Paris itself as extremists considered launching a paratroop attack on the French capital. In this situation, the National Assembly voted to end the Fourth Republic and to invite de Gaulle to take power. De Gaulle was a favourite of the *colons*, who believed that he would crush the FLN and keep Algeria French. Muslims also wanted his return; de Gaulle was on good terms with the Moroccans and the Tunisians, and it was thought that he would give a settlement generous to Algeria. French politicians, meanwhile, concluded that the return of de Gaulle was the only solution to the Algerian crisis. Under a new constitution, de Gaulle was given wide powers for at least six months to restore order and authority.

Despite the support that de Gaulle had from the army and the *colons*, he understood that France could not be involved indefinitely in a never-ending guerrilla war in Algeria. His primary goal was to re-establish France as a world power, and in this context maintaining Algeria was costly; it impeded economic modernization and it distracted France from taking a lead in Europe. He thus concluded that negotiations and concessions to the FLN were necessary, and he also gradually realized that the terms would have to involve full independence.

Cartoon analysis

A British cartoon from the *Manchester Guardian*, 3 June 1958, depicts the problems assailing Charles de Gaulle's leadership.

Question

What does this cartoon reveal about the difficulties facing de Gaulle?

De Gaulle started off by bringing Algeria back under the control of the civilian government in Paris. He allowed the army to continue to attack FLN bases. However, this was not in order to gain total control over the FLN, but rather to weaken them in order to get them to negotiate. In a major radio broadcast of 16 September 1959, de Gaulle made a speech that was a turning point in Franco-Algerian relations. In this broadcast, he announced three alternatives to the Algerian people: secession, integration or a federal relationship in which France would provide assistance with the economy and education, and direction in matters of defence and foreign affairs. De Gaulle was thus now talking about an Algerian Algeria, and ignoring the possibility of an *Algérie française*.

Barricades Week and the Generals' Insurrection

De Gaulle's new policy was too extreme for the *colons* and the army. In January 1960, the *colon* Ultras rioted in Algeria, erecting barricades in what became known as 'Barricades Week'. The army took no action to stop the ensuing violence against the police and distanced themselves from the situation. Yet there was no outright rebellion; de Gaulle gave a dramatic TV address in which he made it clear that he would not give way, and in which he reminded the army that this was France's war and that 'in your mission there is no room for equivocation or interpretation'.

Barricades Week was a clear failure for the *colon* leaders. However, although the army had not directly gone against de Gaulle, the hostility of the army leaders towards de Gaulle's plans continued to grow. On 4 November 1960, de Gaulle made it clear that his plans were heading 'not to an Algeria governed by Metropolitan France but to an Algerian Algeria'. This declaration was followed by a referendum on his policy, in which the French voted overwhelmingly in favour of de Gaulle's position, giving him a free hand to deal with Algeria. On 15 March 1961, it was announced that peace talks between France and the FLN were to take place.

These developments were too much for the French generals. Before the peace talks could begin, the 'Generals' Insurrection' occurred when the 1st Foreign Paratroop Regiment led by General Maurice Challe seized control of Algiers. Once again, de Gaulle used the media to end the crisis, making a radio broadcast to appeal directly to the troops.

STUDENT STUDY SECTION

Document analysis

Officers, non-commissioned officers, policemen, sailors, soldiers and airmen, I am in Algiers with Generals Zeller and Jounard and in touch with General Salan so as to keep the army's oath to ensure a French Algeria, so that our dead may not have died in vain. A government of abandonment is preparing to hand over the departments of Algeria to the external organisation of the rebellion. Do you want Mers-el-Kebir and Algiers to become Soviet bases tomorrow? I know your courage, your pride, your discipline. The army shall not fail in its mission.

Radio broadcast by General Challe on the day of the Generals' Insurrection, April 1960

Question

What does this source reveal about the aims of the French Army in Algeria?

The formation of the OAS

With the failure of the conspiracy, the Ultras formed an underground army known as the Organisation de l'armée secrète (OAS; Organization of the Secret Army) which, composed of civilians and military deserters, would use terror tactics to disrupt Algeria and France. Their actions included an assassination attempt on de Gaulle's life and a plan to bomb the Eiffel Tower. They also involved assassinations and bombings within Algeria, which continued with brutal ferocity during and after the peace talks. In fact, French disgust and condemnation of the OAS bombing of Paris – which resulted, amongst other casualties, in the maiming of a four-year-old girl – meant that there was a resolve amongst the French population to end the war and restore Algeria to the Algerians.

The peace talks

Meanwhile, despite the activities of the OAS, the peace talks started at Evian. The first talks failed because of problems over whether Algeria included the Sahara. However, by the second Evian conference, de Gaulle was impatient to end a war so damaging to France's international standing, and so made far-reaching concessions. Instead of permanent guarantees for minorities, the rights of French citizens were protected for a period of three years, after which they could opt for Algerian citizenship. (If they decided to keep French citizenship, they would not enjoy full civil rights in Algeria.) Existing levels of French economic and technical assistance were guaranteed for the same three-year period and French armed forces were also to withdraw after three years (though France could retain the lease of the Mers-el-Kabir base for 15 years). Most important of all, France recognized the territorial integrity of Algeria and so gave up any hope of getting control of the Sahara and its oil (though French companies were allowed leasing rights to continue to develop oilfields).

De Gaulle said: 'We must concede these details rather than reject an agreement; for there is no comparison between the primary interest, which consists of reaching an agreement, and the secondary interest, which consists of holding a little longer certain things which, anyway, we do not reckon to hold for ever.' Algeria became a sovereign state on 1 July 1962.

Photo analysis

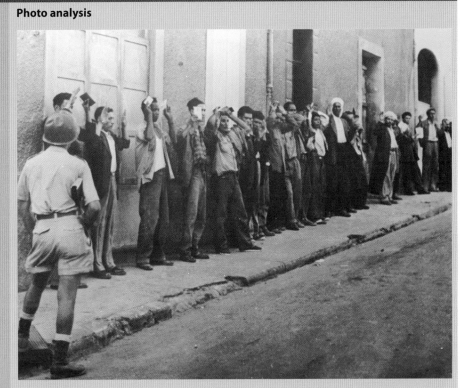

French security forces round up suspected insurgents during the Algerian Civil War.

Question

What is the message of this photograph?

IBLP link – Principled

Discuss the extent to which the French public felt that the way war was being waged in Algeria was no longer in line with their principles. How far can a government act with 'integrity and honesty, with a strong sense of fairness, justice and respect for the dignity of the individual, groups and communities' (IBLP) when fighting a war?

● **Examiner's hint**
Photos can be very useful for giving us a visual image of events. However, they do not have to be an accurate representation of the events they are showing. When analyzing a photo for value and limitations you still need to ask key questions: Do we know who took the photo and for what purpose? Is there any suggestion that it was taken for propaganda purposes? Does it show the whole scene, or only part of a scene?

What were the results of the Algerian Civil War?

For Algeria

The Algerian conflict was one of the most violent of the post-1945 colonial wars; more than 250,000 Algerians were killed in the war – with possibly as many as 12,000 being killed in the last attempts of the OAS to prevent a settlement. In addition, thousands suffered through being uprooted from their homes and through the massive destruction of property. The departing *colons* also destroyed buildings and facilities before they left.

Politically, the government of the FLN did not produce stability. There was another civil war following the Evian agreement, a conflict that decided which Muslim group was to rule. It was only by the end of the summer and after another 15,000 had died that Ben Bella took control. Ben Bella established a dictatorial system, purging former resistance fighters such as Fehrat Abbas, who was expelled from the FLN in 1963. In 1965, Houari Boumediène and the army overthrew Ben Bella, who was then put in prison. Boumediène ran a one-party state for 13 years, but his authoritarian socialism did not deliver the promises of higher living standards.

In 1991, the Islamic Salvation Front won that year's elections. However, the results were cancelled and military rule was imposed. A new civil war began as a result between the Algerian government and various Islamist rebel groups. It is estimated to have cost between 150,000 and 200,000 lives.

For the *colons*

The European population of Algeria departed en masse; nearly one million returned to France (including most of the country's senior administrators). The mass exodus of the *pieds-noirs* left a vacuum in administration and business in Algeria that was exacerbated by the departure or killing of those who had cooperated with the *colons* (see below). Ben Bella, who was elected first President of Algeria in 1963, legalized the expropriation of most foreign-owned land and hundreds of businesses that had been abandoned by the French.

For the *harkis*

The *harkis* were Algerians who had worked with the French. A report given to the UN assessed the number of pro-French Muslims at 263,000 men, working in all areas of administration and living in all areas of Algeria. At the end of the war, however, as the *pieds-noirs* fled to France, these people were largely forgotten. Thousands were massacred after Algerian independence, while those that did get to France (some 90,000) found great difficulties integrating into French society.

For France

Algeria was France's last major act of decolonization. Official French casualties were put at 17,456 dead, 64,985 injured and 1,000 missing. The war consumed 50–60 per cent of the French military budget and 10–15 per cent of the total French budget for 1954–62. Yet with the end of its overseas conflicts and renewed focus on Europe, France then experienced a period of prosperity.

French links with Algeria continued as Boumediène concluded a series of agreements with France for the development of mining and other industries. Many Algerians, particularly the *harkis*, also emigrated to France.

Nevertheless, bitterness and controversy still exists between France and Algeria, with continuing debate over issues such as how the war is portrayed in French school textbooks, torture used by the French during the war, and the lack of recognition for the *harkis*.

ToK Time

There remains much debate in France over the causes, nature and rights of the Algerian War. Professional historians using at least some of the same sources of evidence have reached different conclusions about the conflict. As this is the case, what knowledge issues are there in the methods used by historians to reach conclusions about past events? Would you be more likely to believe the theories of historians who used their emotions to draw conclusions, or the theories of historians who used their reason? Explain your answer thoroughly, and write up your response in your ToK journal.

STUDENT STUDY SECTION

Research question

Using the internet, research news articles from the past ten years showing the continued debate over the Algerian War in France.

Review questions

1   Explain briefly who or what the following were, and what impact they had on the course of events in the Algerian War:
   - *Colons*
   - FLN
   - Committee of Public Safety
   - Generals' Insurrection
   - OAS
   - Battle of Dien Bien Phu
   - Battle of Algiers
   - Barricades Week
   - De Gaulle
   - Evian conferences

2   Go back to the notes you made to the questions on p.284 on guerrilla war, and add more examples to the question on tactics used by the FLN and on the response of the French Army.

3 From what you have read so far, what problems did the French face in fighting the guerrilla tactics? Read the extract below and add to your answer:

A summary of this conflict illustrates the general difficulty of mounting effective counter-insurgency operations. Tough anti-insurrectionary measures, including widespread torture, which was seen as a justified response to FLN atrocities, gave the French control of the capital, in 1957. However although undefeated in battle, and making effective use of helicopter-borne units, the French were unable to end guerrilla action in what was a very costly struggle. And French moves were often counter-productive in winning the loyalty of the bulk of the population. There were also operational problems: aside from the difficulty of operating active counter-insurgency policies there was also a need to tie up large numbers of troops in protecting settlers and in trying to close the frontiers to the movement of guerrilla reinforcements, so that much of the army was not available for offensive purposes, a situation that helped the insurgents.

From Jeremy Black, *Introduction to Global Military History*, 2005

Essay question

Use the answers to Questions 2 and 3 above to help you answer the following essay question:

How important was the strategy of guerrilla warfare for ensuring that Algeria gained independence?

Introduction

As in all introductions, you need to explain any key terms in the question. Here you need to give a brief definition of guerrilla warfare (go back to Chapter 1 to remind yourself again of the key characteristics). You also need to put the conflict into context – provide dates and explain that the FLN was the Algerian group carrying out the guerrilla tactics. Also set out your key argument.

Section 1

Always deal first with the issue that is given to you in the title. Thus here you need to look at the FLN's strategy of guerrilla warfare. Remember that you are not just describing the guerrilla tactics, but assessing their effectiveness. The key issue here is the impact that guerrilla warfare had on the tactics of the French Army. Although guerrilla tactics were not successful in defeating the French forces or in winning the battle of Algiers, the fact that they forced the army into retaliating with similar tactics (e.g. torture) alienated French public opinion against the war. It was also difficult for the French Army to destroy the guerrilla forces completely or to win the support of the Algerian population, and they were forced into a costly and drawn-out struggle (see Black's comment above on this).

Section 2

Interestingly, in this war the OAS also used guerrilla warfare. How did this help the Algerian cause of independence?

Section 3

The question is asking you to make an assessment of the effectiveness of guerrilla warfare, and so you need to assess the contribution of any other factors to FLN success. Thus you may also want to consider here the actions of de Gaulle.

Essay question

Analyze the reasons for the outbreak of war in Algeria in 1954.

For this question you need to consider whether you are going to divide the causes of the war into long-term and short-term causes, or whether you are going to structure your answer around the different issues that led to conflict (e.g. as identified in the Student Review Activity on p.282).

To access worksheet 14.3 on photographic representations of the Algerian War, please visit www.pearsonbacconline.com and follow the on-screen instructions.

Essay question

What were the reasons for the outcome of the Algerian War?

This question is very similar to the question on guerrilla warfare, except here you can decide the order in which you deal with the different factors. The order you choose might depend on what you consider to be the most important factor – a good idea might be to deal with this factor first.

As above, points to consider include:
- The role of de Gaulle
- The effectiveness of the FLN's guerrilla tactics
- The impact of the French Army's tactics, e.g. in the battle of Algiers and the use of torture, particularly the effect that these tactics had on French public opinion
- The effect of the OAS, and again how this affected French public opinion.

15 WHICH WAR FOR WHICH QUESTION?

Map illustrating the IB regions.

Legend:
- The Americas
- Africa
- Europe and the Middle East
- Asia and Oceania

© International Baccalaureate Organization

All of the wars in this book are specified on the IB syllabus for Topic 1 of Paper 2. Therefore, as you have seen at the end of each chapter, you may get specific questions on these wars. You will also get 'general' questions, where you can choose which war to use as an example. Sometimes you will have to compare two wars.

General questions need careful planning before you start writing.

- You have to decide first which war/s are appropriate for the question and will allow you to answer the question effectively.
- You need to look carefully at the question: how many wars? Do they have to be from different regions? Do you have to deal with two aspects of the war (e.g. both causes and results)? If dealing with two wars, do you have to compare and contrast them directly or can you deal with each one separately?

Questions on 'causes' and 'results'

The first set of questions below is on causes and results. Decide in pairs which wars would be appropriate for each question. In questions where there are TWO wars, you need to consider the following:

- How much you have to write for each war; make sure you choose examples that you can deal with effectively in the time available.
- If you need to compare and contrast, they need to be wars that have obvious comparisons and contrasts. For instance, for the first question below, the two world wars work well because historians have already made comparisons on the causes that you could use as your starting point. Alternatively, choose two of the same type of war, e.g. two limited wars or two civil wars, as there are more likely to be obvious comparisons/contrasts.

- If the question specifies different regions, it is vital that you cover them. The map showing the different regions specified by the IB is shown above on p.293.

For questions on causes, make sure you distinguish between long-term, short-term and immediate causes for the wars that you choose. Also, where appropriate, identify economic, political, social and religious causes. These categories will help you keep an analytical focus.

Questions

1   Compare and contrast the causes of two wars (excluding the First World War), each chosen from a different region.   © IBO 2003

2   Analyze the results of two wars, each chosen from a different region.   © IBO 2004

3   How far is it true to say that economic resources, rather than a belief in a cause, win wars?
                                                                                      © IBO 1999

4   'Wars create more problems than they solve.' Discuss this claim with reference to the causes and results of two wars (each chosen from a different region) during the 20th century.
                                                                                      © IBO 1992

Questions on total wars

For any question specifically on total war, your best examples are World War I or World War II. Note that World War II includes the war in the Pacific, which can be used as an example of a war in Asia if you need a different region from Europe.

For a question that asks about the contribution of civilians or propaganda to wars, you can choose any war for which you can give good examples.

Questions

1   What do you understand by 'total war'? Select one 20th-century war to illustrate your understanding.   © IBO 1997

2   Evaluate the contribution made towards the war effort by civilians on both the home front and the battlefront in two wars, each chosen from a different region.   © IBO 2005

3   Examine the effects of war and the fear of war on the civilian population of two countries, each chosen from a different region.   © IBO 2002

4   Analyze the use and effects of propaganda in two wars, each chosen from a different region.
                                                                                      © IBO 2002

Refugees displaced by the fighting in World War II.

Questions on limited wars

Question

For what reasons, and with what results, was 'limited' warfare a feature of the second half of the 20th century?   © IBO 2005

Some points you could consider in this essay are listed below. You must back up each point, though, with specific examples, e.g. from the Falklands War and the Gulf War:

Reasons for limited war
- Aims
- Nuclear weapons
- Role of superpowers
- Role of UN
- Geography
- Role of democracy
- Role of the media.

Results
- Limited use of weapons
- Limited casualties
- Limited length
- Limited cost to economy
- Limited international impact
- Limited involvement of civilians
- Limited impact on home front
- Limited peace terms (no peace treaty)
- Swift restoration of diplomatic links.

Now have a go at planning the following essays.

Questions

1   Define the term 'limited war'. With reference to two wars, each chosen from a different region, explain why they remained limited.   © IBO 2007

2   'No 20th-century war could be called a limited war.' To what extent do you agree with this assertion?   © IBO 2006

Questions on civil wars

Question

Analyze the causes of two 20th-century civil wars, each chosen from a different region.

Again, with causation questions such as this one, it is important not to get caught up in a description of the lead-up to each war. Keep a thematic approach so that you maintain an analytical focus.

In pairs, apply the following themes to the Spanish Civil War and the Chinese Civil War to help you answer the question:

Political
- Failure of monarchy/ruling dynasty
- Republican attempts at government
- Role of the military.

Regionalism
- Lack of unity/central authority
- Nationalism.

Economic
- Gap between wealthy and poor urban workers/peasants
- Lack of economic development and modernization
- Taxation
- Economic crises.

Social/Religious
- Lack of modernization and education
- Power of church/traditional or orthodox belief.

Now have a go at planning the following essays. For Question 1 use both the Spanish and the Chinese Civil Wars. For Questions 2 and 3 decide which of these two wars would be most appropriate for the question.

Questions
1 Why did foreign intervention occur so frequently in civil wars of the 20th century and what impact did this intervention have on two civil wars each chosen from a different region? © IBO 2004
2 Analyze the reasons for the outcome of one civil war. How did the outcome affect the country in which the war was fought? © IBO 2003
3 To what extent has any civil war in the 20th century settled the issues that caused it? © IBO 1990

Questions on guerrilla wars

Question
Examine the reasons for, and the contribution of, guerrilla warfare to the outcome of *one* 20th-century war. © IBO 2007

Work in pairs. One of you use the Chinese Civil War as an example for this question. The other should try using Algeria as an example. Below are some points you could consider – not all are appropriate for both wars.

Reasons for adopting guerrilla warfare
- Lack of resources, arms, training and conventional military experience compared to opponent
- Physical terrain limits conventional military operations and gives advantage to guerrilla activities
- Ideological support: revolutionary/people's war
- Practical need to win time, so that ideology can spread
- Need to shock, and generate publicity
- Opposing side's aversion to a long war
- Local traditions of resistance to authority
- Local traditions of resistance against foreign influence.

Contribution of guerrilla warfare to victory
- Mass mobilization of people behind insurgency – 'hearts and minds' effects
- Major campaigns and turning-point battles
- Impact of political campaigns

- Produces social and economic reform
- Anti-imperialism and nationalism.

There are other factors that contribute to victory that you might also want to mention. Then, in your conclusion, you can assess the actual impact that guerrilla tactics had in your chosen conflict.

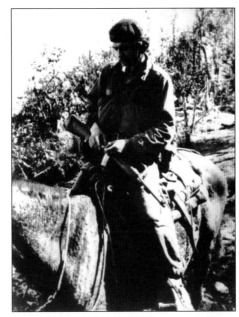

The Cuban revolutionary Che Guevara, often held up as the model guerrilla leader.

Question

With reference to specific examples, account for the adoption of guerrilla warfare and assess its effectiveness.   © IBO 2006

In this question, you can use both wars. Look back to Chapter 1 for ideas on why guerrilla warfare was used in the 20th century. However, make sure you back up each point you make with evidence from the specific wars.

Questions on peace settlements

Not all wars ended with official treaties, so you need to go back through all of the wars that you have studied and identify those that actually concluded with a treaty. What difference does the implementation of a treaty make to the results of a war?

The Versailles settlement is always a good example of a peace settlement that had profound results. A good contrast, i.e. one that did not cause future conflicts, is the Treaty of San Francisco signed between Japan and the Allied powers in 1951. Note that Question 2 below requires you to identify first the problems that caused the conflict.

Questions

1 Analyze the results of one 20th-century treaty or peace settlement.   © IBO 2008

2 In what ways, and with what success, did post-war peacemakers attempt to deal with the problems which produced the conflict? Specific reference should be made to two peace settlements.   © IBO 2006

3 'Peace settlements create conditions for new conflicts.' With reference to at least two settlements explain to what extent you agree with this statement.   © IBO 2005

Questions on technology

> **Question**
>
> To what extent did technological developments ensure victory in 20th-century wars?
>
> © IBO 2006

This question is not just about technology, but also about other factors that result in victory – for instance, the success of guerrilla tactics in the Chinese Civil War and Algerian War, which brought victory over technologically superior opponents. On the other hand, technology was central to the outcome of the Gulf War of 1990–91 and provides a good alternative case study.

> **Question**
>
> Compare and contrast the role of technology in two wars of your choice.

Again, you could here compare one war in which technology was of little importance, with a war such as the Gulf War, where it was vital in ensuring victory for the coalition forces.

> **Question**
>
> How and why did technological developments play an important part in 20th-century wars?
>
> © IBO 2003

Questions on tactics on land/sea/air

Throughout this book, we have explored wars in terms of how they were fought on land, sea and air. In pairs, discuss the best examples for each question. Refer back to your planning grids (e.g. the one on p.174 of Chapter 8) to refresh your mind on the key features of war on land/sea/air.

> **Questions**
>
> 1 Examine the role of warfare either at sea or in the air in two wars, each chosen from a different region. © IBO 2008
> 2 Compare and contrast the use of naval warfare in two wars, each chosen from a different region. © IBO 2005
> 3 Assess the role of air power in two 20th-century wars. © IBO 2004

The following question is on tactics in general, and allows you to choose as many examples as you want.

> **Question**
>
> In what ways, and with what results for 20th-century wars, did tactics change? © IBO 2002

Which wars would you choose here to give a good idea of how tactics have changed? Note that there are two parts to the question: 'How' and 'What results'.

Questions on social and economic factors

Make sure that you have specific examples to back up your answers for these types of question. Questions 1 and 4 below, for example, are quite vague in the way they are worded; you therefore need to be clear about which countries you are going to talk about and you need to structure your answer carefully to address a range of social results and a range of economic results.

ToK Time: The 'What ifs …' of History

War is a brutalising experience for all involved. Innocents suffer and young men die in combat, resources are wasted and the social and economic fabric of the countries involved is disrupted and sometimes impaired for years. It is also normally avoidable. A point can often be identified in the development of a conflict when firm action might have resolved a dispute coming to the boil or warned off a potential aggressor. In the aftermath of any war it is natural to look for such points in an effort to learn how to avoid similar tragedies in the future and to assign blame for the past. If wars are like road accidents, as historian A.J.P. Taylor argued, then more skilful 'driving' can surely help avert some of them.

From L. Freedman and E. Karsh, *The Gulf Conflict, 1990–1991*, 1995

Go back over all the wars in this book and think at what point different action/s could have avoided war? Looking at what could have happened if a different action been taken is called counterfactual history. Do you think it is useful to look at the 'What ifs …' of history? Is it possible, as Freedman and Karsh claim, that by doing this it is possible 'to learn how to avoid similar tragedies in the future'?

Revision techniques

- It is important that you develop a technique for summarizing information thematically in ways that will help you to revise. In most chapters in this book, we have given you suggestions for mind maps and grids to help you organize the information for revision. You should go back over these; complete them if you have not done so (or develop your own system). You can then use these grids/mind maps to help you identify the key points necessary for essay questions.
- For each topic, also summarize the key points made by different historians, so that you can bring in historiography where appropriate to your essay.
- Plan as many essays as possible. Also practise writing out introductions.
- Look at past IB papers. Work out which questions you could do. Also work out which questions you are NOT prepared to answer.

Chapter 16
Theory of Knowledge

Why study History?

Many elements of the IB History course link in well to exploring Theory of Knowledge, including the question of why it is important to study history at all.

American historian John Lewis Gaddis argues:

> **… the study of history is … to achieve the optimal balance, first within ourselves, but then within society, between the polarities of oppression and liberation.**
> John Lewis Gaddis, *The Landscape of History*, 2002

Over 60 years ago the British philosopher and historian R.G. Collingwood also defended the study of history, saying:

> **What is history for? … Knowing yourself means knowing, first, what it is to be a man; secondly, knowing what it is to be the kind of man you are; and thirdly, knowing what it is to be the man YOU are and nobody else is. Knowing yourself means knowing what you can do; and since nobody knows what he can do until he tries, the only clue to what man can do is what man has done. The value of history, then, is that it teaches us what man has done and thus what man is.**
> R.G. Collingwood, *The Idea of History*, 1946

So, history helps us understand ourselves and our own individual 'histories', and is, therefore, important in helping us clarify our understanding of the world in which we live. History is used to argue and justify political positions, economic policies, international relations between countries and religious perspectives. In fact, most other areas of knowledge rely to a certain extent on the use and application of history. For example, it would be almost impossible for a scientist to add to the body of knowledge in his or her subject in a meaningful way without knowing what had come before, that is, the history of science.

Question

How do you think a ToK teacher or student today would react to the sexist language of Collingwood's time? Does the gender bias in the language he uses mean that the points he puts across are less valid?

▲
British philosopher and historian, R.G. Collingwood (1889–1943).

What is the historian's methodology? How do historians work?

An important question for ToK students to examine is to what extent history is discovered or invented. Below is a list of some of the steps an historian might go through in attempting to find 'historical truth':

- Plan research
- Decide on a line of enquiry
- Research/investigate evidence
- Build a body of evidence
- Cross-reference evidence from a variety of sources – corroboration
- Evaluate sources for value and limitations
- Consider different perspectives
- Apply methodology from different areas of knowledge, such as the sciences or economics
- Consider which lines of argument seem most important, or where there is more weight of supporting evidence
- Select evidence and lines of argument.

Questions

1 How far does opinion impact on each part of the methodology?
2 New evidence leads to new historical interpretations. However, should you also consider the extent to which the 'context' of the historian leads to new historical interpretations?

Question

'…if there is to be an acceptable bias in the writing and teaching of history, let it tilt towards liberation.' What do you think John Lewis Gaddis meant in this quote?

Can we find historical truth?

- What is the difference between known facts, like the exact date of a battle, and the background 'facts', e.g. what caused the battle?
- Sometimes the evidence is rather scarce, and the historian may have to 'fill in the gaps'. Where there seems to be too much detailed evidence, the historian may have to be more 'selective' to build a line of argument with the information chosen.
- The problem of source reliability is key to the work and method of the historian. Historians acknowledge these problems and attempt to limit them as much as possible, through cross-referencing and judging the limitations of each source.
- The role of the historian in attempting to identify 'themes' and 'categories' in his or her research is likely to be affected by the historian's own cultural paradigms and/or religious context. Indeed, any 'selection' of evidence is always be open to some degree of bias.

Historians are dangerous people. They are capable of upsetting everything.
Nikita Khrushchev

British historian E.H. Carr described the problems that historians have with 'catching' the facts in this way:

The facts are like fish swimming in a vast murky ocean, and what the historian catches will depend partly on chance, but mainly on what part of the ocean he chooses to fish in and what bait he chooses – these two facts of course being determined by the type of fish he wants to catch. By and large the historian will get the facts he wants.
From E.H. Carr, 'What is History?' (a lecture given in 1982)

The Wall Street Crash

Treaty of Versailles is too harsh on Germany

Treaty of Locarno

Germany invades Poland

French invasion of the Ruhr

Americans enjoy a jazz festival in 1931

August 1939

August 1938

The 1936 Olympics are held in Germany

Stalin initiates collectivization in the USSR in 1928

January 1933

Anglo-German Naval Agreement

Abyssinia appeals to the League of Nations

Munich Agreement in September 1938

Japanese invasion of Manchuria

League of Nations and economic sanctions

Washington Agreements

The USA pursues a policy of isolation

Questions

1 Which five key dates and events would you choose in attempting to explain why World War II broke out in Europe in 1939?
2 Why might other people select differently from you?

It is surprising that history is so dull considering that so much of it is invented.
British novelist Jane Austen (1775–1817)

Question

To what extent is history invented or discovered?

Problems of knowledge

History has, of course, already happened, and so you might therefore reason that the 'truth' in history should be clear. Yet there are similar problems of knowledge in history as there are with the other areas of knowledge. As already discussed, there are problems with the process of researching evidence, the evidence itself, and the selection and interpretation of the evidence. It must also be considered that most sources of evidence are themselves interpretations. This is because the sources have been created by individuals, and these individuals are liable to bias due to their own backgrounds, views and opinions.

The ways of knowing: reason, emotion, language and sense perception

Questions

1 Which of the four 'ways of knowing', listed in the heading above, are used by historians when attempting to find historical truth?
2 What problems are associated with these ways of knowing?
3 Which of these four is the most important to the historian?
4 Historians put history into periods or thematic areas. It has also been done in this book – for example, 'Origins of World War I' or 'The inter-war years'. Why do historians do this? Would people who lived through these events recognize these labels?
5 'Historians seek to be detached, impassionate, impartial. In fact, however, no historian starts with his mind a blank, to be gradually filled by the evidence' (historian A.J.P. Taylor, in *The Times Literary Supplement*, 6 January1956). What does Taylor mean by 'no historian starts with his mind a blank'?

History is as much an art as a science.
French philosopher Ernest Renan (1823–92)

Links with other areas of knowledge

Historians have their theories, their arguments and accounts 'tested' by other historians in their field. Perhaps in this way history can be considered similar to science, in that it is open to criticism, correction and revision. In addition, scientific methods can be used to support historical theories, for example, to test the authenticity or age of documents.

Also, history, like the Natural Sciences, uses deconstructions, and macro and micro scales. In science, there are 'general laws', but also specific experimentation, while in history you might consider broader factors, for example, causations (macro). These factors could then be used to consider causal developments in one country, or even one city (micro) as a case study.

Historical evidence, however, can also be viewed as different from scientific evidence in the way it is 'found'. Scientific experimentation, 'double blind testing' and so on, are not methodologies available to the historian.

Case study

Briefly research the impact of Marshall Aid money on one European country. While you are researching consider the following:

- The language used by the historians
- Information included or omitted by the historians
- Details emphasized by each historian
- Analytical concepts used by each historian, and whether such concepts are liable to change over time.

Then find an example from this book, or another resource from your IB History course, and consider the extent to which history can be seen as 'changing' within new theoretical frameworks.

Challenges for historians

Historians, like scientists, search for cause and effect. Most history examination essay questions will ask you to find a number of key causes and analyze their relative importance. The main cause may be found by assessing the most important evidence, and the factor with the greatest amount of relevant evidence.

There are also problems in terms both of scope and depth of causation. For example, how far back do we go to look for causes? How much detail is relevant? This is also a problem in analyzing the effects of a past historical episode – when do we judge the consequences of an event to end? How much detail should we attempt to include as evidence to support our views?

It is also important to consider the role of 'accident' and 'chance' in history. Can you identify any events in the wars you have studied where there was an element of 'chance' in the factors that caused them? How useful is the consideration of 'accidental' causation to an historian?

Perhaps history has more in common with the Arts than with the Natural Sciences. Is history really more about highlighting and emphasizing the nature of humankind and the human condition in the way that the Arts attempt to?

Do historians paint pictures with their words, highlighting issues and events in ways that might mirror the power that artists can command with their images? If so, does the artistic method have any similarities to the research methods employed by historians?

British soldiers go 'over the top' during World War I, moving out of their positions to attack the German trenches opposite.

The difference between history and historiography

In history, there is the narrative, a description of the events that took place. There is also the historiography, the analysis and interpretation of these events.

There are problems with facts in both cases. When writing a descriptive account of events, or even a chronological timeline, the historian might have to be selective, omitting some events that others might think relevant or significant. These additions and omissions create a personal interpretation of the event. A further step away from objectivity is taken when an historian then has to select or identify different themes, causes and effects. The choice of language in which these selections are presented will also impact on any attempts to maintain objectivity when presenting historical 'truths'.

The belief in a hard core of historical facts existing objectively and independently of the historian is a preposterous fallacy, but one which it is very hard to eradicate.
From E.H. Carr, 'What is History?', 1961

Questions

1 How far do you agree with Carr's assertion that 'The belief in a hard core of historical facts existing objectively and independently of the historian is a preposterous fallacy'?
2 Why does Carr say this view is 'very hard to eradicate'?

History is written by the winners.
English novelist and social commentator George Orwell in his essay 'On Revising History', 1944

History, power and elites

History often focuses on the roles of great leaders in important world events. But it has been suggested that this perspective adds to the limitations of historians' craft. They not only need to have an understanding of the background and context of any individual leader or person of influence, but also need to use this information to interpret the individual's motivations.

A further problem is that, particularly before mass literacy, much of what we know about the past was recorded by the literate elites in society. In the brave new world of the IT revolution, we will have video footage of average families on holiday, at weddings and at school. There will be emails, voicemails and online images of a cross-section of Western society. But again, just as the voices of

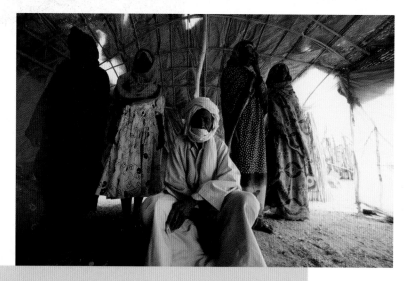

Each person's perspective on life is shaped by his or her individual circumstances, upbringing and society. Think of ways in which the culture of a specific people has shaped its sense of history and politics.

the poor and of the majority of women were unrecorded in the past, so in our technological age the lives of the dispossessed in the developing world will, to a greater extent, be left unrecorded. As American historian Barbara Tuchman explained: 'each man is a package of variables impossible to duplicate.' Tuchman argued that everything about an individual, from his parents, food, home and school to his first job and first girlfriend, combine to make up his personality. All these factors also combine with 'another set of variables: country, climate, time and historical circumstance.' Each person, including historians, consequently has his or her own unique perspective or 'bias' on life.

If a certain degree of bias is impossible to avoid completely, how then can an historian attempt to write objective history? Indeed, historians need to have a viewpoint or a paradigm to provide a structure for their selections of data. Some historians attempt a number of approaches, consciously or not, in an attempt to address different perspectives.

Social determinism

It has been said that any event, once it has occurred, can be made to appear inevitable by a competent historian. Those historians who use the model of 'social determinism' to inform their analysis believe that the 'laws of history' are independent of the actions of individuals or regimes.

Karl Marx believed this. He asserted that the important factors in historical causation are the socio-economic conditions. He was convinced that the development of these factors follows a certain course, which ultimately and inevitably leads to a new society.

Historians recognize the problems of their methodology and attempt to limit and overcome them. As we have seen, evidence is often central to reasoning, so the problem of evidence is central to all areas of knowledge. It is not only new evidence that changes our perspective of the past, but our own current world that changes what we consider to be 'historical truth'.

Question

Have you learned in your IB History course that history is driven more by socio-economic factors, or by individuals and regimes?

Intrinsically it is not a question of the higher or lower degree of development of the social antagonisms that result from the natural laws of capitalist production. It is a question of these laws themselves, of these tendencies working with iron necessity towards inevitable results. The country that is more developed industrially only shows, to the less developed, the image of its own future.

Karl Marx in *Das Kapital*, vol. 1 (Preface to the First German Edition, 1867)

Reading the perspectives and arguments of 21st-century historians on the 20th-century wars will tell us not only about the history of the 20th century, but also about the world we live in today. Current attitudes often shape how historians think, and this then shapes our understanding of the 'historical truth'.

▲ Karl Marx, seen by many as the founder of modern communism.

Russian writer Leo Tolstoy (1828–1910) also believed in history being inevitably determined. This passage refers to the Napoleonic Wars:

The causes of this war seem innumerable in their multiplicity. The more deeply we search out the causes the more of them we discover … And consequently nothing was exclusively the cause of the war, and the war was bound to happen, simply because it was bound to happen.

From Leo Tolstoy, *War and Peace*, 1869

Questions

1 Consider the above quote from Tolstoy – is the idea that history is 'determined' useful to historians or the student of history? Perhaps it is more useful to suggest that history is about the interplay of social and economic forces *and* the actions of individual men, women and regimes.

2 Consider the events during the July Crisis before World War I. Which were more important – socio-economic factors or the actions of individuals?

FURTHER READING

Books

World War I

Albertini, Luigi, *The Origins of the War of 1914*, vol. 1, trans. by Isabella Massey (Enigma, 2005)

Beckett, Ian, *The Great War 1914–1918* (Pearson, 2001)

Bell, P.M.H., *Twentieth Century Europe* (Hodder Arnold, 2006)

Breach, R.W., *Documents and Descriptions in European History 1815–1939* (Oxford University Press, 1976)

Cawood, Ian J. and David McKinnon-Bell, *The First World War (Questions and analysis in History)* (Routledge, 2000)

Ferguson, Niall, *The Pity of War* (Penguin, 2006)

Ferguson, Niall, *The War of the World: History's Age of Hatred* (Penguin, 2006)

Fischer, Fritz, *Germany's Aims in the First World War* (Chatto & Windus, 1967)

Geiss, Immanuel (ed.), *July 1914: The Outbreak of the First World War – Selected Documents* (Batsford, 1967)

Henig, Ruth, *The Origins of the First World War* (Routledge, 1993)

Hobsbawm, Eric, *Age of Extremes: The Short Twentieth Century* (Michael Joseph, 1994)

Iriye, Akira, *The Cambridge History of American Foreign Relations*, vol. 3: *The Globalising of America 1913–1945* (Cambridge University Press, 1993)

Joll, James, *The Origins of the First World War* (Longman, 1992)

Keegan, John, *The First World War* (Pimlico, 1999)

Keynes, John Maynard, *The Economic Consequences of the Peace* (Skyhorse Publishing, 2007)

Laffin, John, *British Butchers and Bunglers of World War One* (Sutton Publishing, 2003)

Lee, Stephen J., *Aspects of European History 1789–1980* (Routledge, 1988)

Lowe, John and Robert Pearce, *Rivalry and Accord: International Relations 1870–1914* (Hodder & Stoughton, 2001)

Lowe, Norman, *Mastering Modern World History* (Palgrave Macmillan, 1995)

Martel, Gordon, *The Origins of the First World War* (Longman, 1987)

Strachan, Hew, *The Oxford Illustrated History of the First World War* (OUP, 2000)

Taylor, A.J.P., *How Wars Begin* (Hamish Hamilton, 1979)

Townshend, Charles (ed.), *The Oxford History of Modern War* (OUP, 2005)

Tuchman, Barbara, *The Guns of August* (Ballantine Books, 1994)

Woodward, L, *Great Britain and the War 1914–1918* (Methuen, 1967)

Wroughton, J., *Documents on World History 1: 1870–1918* (Macmillan, 1976)

The inter-war years

Brogan, Hugh, *The Penguin History of the USA* (Penguin, 2001)

Culpin, Christopher and Ruth Henig, *Modern Europe 1870–1945* (Longman, 2007)

Farmer, Alan, *Introduction to Modern European History 1890–1990* (Hodder & Stoughton, 2005)

Henig, Ruth, *Versailles and After 1919–1933* (Routledge, 1995)

Henig, Ruth, *The Origins of the Second World War* (Routledge, 1992)

Lentin, A., *The Versailles Peace Settlement* (Historical Association, 1991)

Overy, Richard, *Origins of the Second World War* (Longman, 1992)

Rayner, R.M., *The Twenty Years' Truce* (Longman, 1943)

Williamson, D.G., *War and Peace: International Relations 1914–1945* (Hodder & Stoughton, 1994)

Wilson, Sandra, *The Manchurian Crisis and Japanese Society, 1931–33* (Routledge, 2003)

World War II

Adamthwaite, A.P., *The Making of the Second World War* (Routledge, 1989)

Bergamini, David, *Japan's Imperial Conspiracy* (William Morrow, 1971)

Buchanan, Patrick, *Churchill, Hitler and the Unnecessary War: How Britain Lost its Empire and the West Lost the World* (Crown, 2008)

Calvocoressi, Peter, Guy Wint and John Pritchard, *Total War: The Causes and Course of the Second World War*, vol. 1 (Penguin, 1989)

Darby, Graham, *Europe at War 1939–45* (Hodder Murray, 2003)

Davies, Norman, *Europe at War 1939–1945* (PanBooks, 2006)

Goldston, Robert, *The Road Between the Wars, 1918–1941* (Dial Press, 1978)

Ienaga, Saburo, *The Pacific War* (Tokyo, 1968)

Iriye, Akira, *The Origins of the Second World War in Asia and in the Pacific* (Longman, 1987)

Keegan, John, *The Second World War* (Pimlico, 1997)

Lee, Stephen, *Aspects of European History 1789–1980* (Routledge, 1984)

Overy, Richard, *Why the Allies Won* (Pimlico, 2006)

Overy, Richard, *Russia's War* (Penguin, 1997)

Sheehan, James, *The Monopoly of Violence: Why Europeans Hate Going to War* (Faber & Faber, 2008)

Shirer, William, *The Rise and Fall of the Third Reich* (Simon & Schuster, 1990)

Townley, Ted, *Hitler and the Road to War* (HarperCollins, 1998)

The post-war world

Best, Antony et al., *International History of the Twentieth Century* (Routledge, 2004)

Judt, Tony, *Postwar: A History of Europe Since 1945* (Heinemann, 2005)

Malvinas/Falklands War

Anderson, Duncan, *The Falkands War 1982*, Essential Histories (Osprey, 2002)

Middlebrook, Martin, *The Argentine Fight for the Falklands* (Pen & Sword Books, 2003)

Vinen, Richard, *Thatcher's Britain* (Simon & Schuster, 2009)

Gulf War

Alchin, Nick, *Theory of Knowledge* (Hodder Education, 2006)

Black, Jeremy, *Introduction to Global Military History* (Routledge, 2005)

Finlan, Alastair, *The Gulf War 1991* (Osprey, 2003)

Freedman, Lawrence and Efraim Karsh, *The Gulf Conflict, 1990–1991* (Faber & Faber, 1995)

Snow, Donald and Dennis Drew, *From Lexington to Desert Storm: War and Politics in the American Experience* (M.E. Sharpe, 1994)

Stoessinger, J.G., *Why Nations Go to War* (St Martin's Press, 1998)

Tyler, Patrick, *A World of Trouble: America in the Middle East* (Portobello Books, 2009)

Vadney, T.E., *The World Since 1945* (Penguin, 1998)

Spanish Civil War

Beevor, Antony, *The Battle for Spain: The Spanish Civil War 1936–1939* (Penguin, 2007)

Fraser, Ronald, *Blood of Spain: Oral History of the Spanish Civil War* (Pimlico, 1994)

Knight, Patricia, *The Spanish Civil War* (Hodder & Stoughton, 1998)

Lannon, Frances, *The Spanish Civil War,* Essential Histories (Osprey, 2002)

Lee, Stephen J., *Aspects of European History 1789–1980* (Routledge, 1984)

Mitchell, David, *The Spanish Civil War* (Grenada, 1971)

Preston, Paul, *The Spanish Civil War: Reaction, Revolution and Revenge* (Harper Perennial, 2006)

Thomas, Hugh, *The Spanish Civil War* (Penguin, 1977)

Chinese Civil War

Brown, C. and T. Edwards, *Revolution in China 1911–1949* (Heinemann, 1974)

Grasso, June, Jay Corrin and Michael Kort, *Modernization and Revolution in China: From the Opium Wars to the Olympics* (M.E.Sharpe, 2009)

Gray, Jack, *Rebellions and Revolutions: China from the 1880s to the 1980s* (Oxford University Press, 1990)

Hsu, Immanuel, *The Rise of Modern China* (Oxford University Press, 1995)

Lynch, Michael, *China: From Empire to People's Republic 1900–49* (Hodder & Stoughton, 1999)

Sheridan, James, *China in Disintegration* (The Free Press, 1977)

Terrill, Ross, *Mao: A Biography* (Stanford University Press, 2000)

Westad, Odd Arne, *Decisive Encounters* (Stanford, 2003)

Algerian War

Betts, Raymond, *France and Decolonisation* (Macmillan, 1991)

Black, Jeremy, *Introduction to Global Military History* (Routledge, 2005)

Calvorocessi, Peter, *World Politics 1945–2000* (Pearson, 2001)

Gildea, Robert, *France Since 1945* (Oxford University Press, 2009)

Horne, Alistair, *A Savage War of Peace: Algeria 1954–1962* (New York Review Books, 2006)

Stora, Benjamin, *Algeria 1830–2000: A Short History* (Cornell University Press, 2001)

Thorn, Gary, *End of Empires* (Hodder & Stoughton, 2001)

Vadney, T.E., *The World Since 1945* (Penguin, 1991)

Websites

To visit the following websites, go to www.pearsonhotlinks.com, enter the express code 4433P and click on the relevant weblink.

General websites

The following websites cover both of the world wars, plus the interwar years:

Spartacus Schoolnet

A history site with good summaries on key individuals and events – click on Weblink 1.

The History Learning Site

Includes major sections on 20th-century history – click on Weblink 2.

The Avalon Project

Useful for primary source government documents – click on Weblink 3.

World War I and the League of Nations

First World War multimedia history

General World War I resources – click on Weblink 4.

World War I – Trenches on the web

An 'Internet History of the Great War' – click on Weblink 5.

BBC History (WWI)
The World War I section of the BBC History website – click on Weblink 6.

Eyewitness to History
Featuring numerous first-hand accounts of the war – click on Weblink 7.

World War I
General World War I information site – click on Weblink 8.

The Great War and the Shaping of the 20th Century
An extensive internet resource from PBS – click on Weblink 9.

World War I art
Excellent site for studying the art of World War I – click on Weblink 10.

The Covenant of the League of Nations
Full text of this important convenant – click on Weblink 11.

World War II

BBC History (WWII)
The World War II section of the BBC History website – click on Weblink 12.

worldwar-2.net
Major World War II website – click on Weblink 13.

world-war-2.info
Includes links to features on weaponry, campaigns and personalities, plus a timeline – click on Weblink 14.

ibiblio.org
Major collections of World War II primary sources – click on Weblink 15.

Spanish Civil War

Spanish Civil War 1936–39
A website featuring comprehensive links to other Spanish Civil War websites. A good starting point for your online research – click on Weblink 16.

Abraham Lincoln Brigade Archives
Website exploring the Abraham Lincoln Brigade – click on Weblink 17.

Essays on the Spanish Civil War
Collections of useful essays on this conflict – click on Weblink 18.

Gulf War

The Gulf War
A major PBS resource for studying the 1990–91 conflict – click on Weblink 19.

CBC Digital Archives
A CBC site on the Gulf War – click on Weblink 20.

Falklands War

The Falklands Conflict 1982
Major site on the Falklands War, including weapons data, chronology of events and useful links – click on Weblink 21.

Fight for the Falklands – 20 Years On
A BBC History website – click on Weblink 22.

Britain's Small Wars
An extensive website with a dedicated Falklands War section – click on Weblink 23.

Chinese Civil War

Selected works of Mao Zedong
Translations of Mao Zedong's most important works – click on Weblink 24.

Moving the Enemy: Operational Art in the Chinese PLA's Huai Hai Campaign
An online book by Dr Gary J. Bjorge, with chapters on the development of the communist forces – click on Weblink 25.

Algerian War of Independence

Pacification in Algeria, 1956–58
A downloadable report from the Rand Corporation – click on Weblink 26.

War of Independence
A history of the Algerian War of Independence from the University of San Francisco – click on Weblink 27.

GLOSSARY

Anarchist Someone who believes that government and law should be abolished.

Anschluss The union of Austria and Germany, which took place in 1938.

Appeasement Achieving peace by giving concessions or by satisfying demands. It was the policy followed by the British government in the 1930s towards Nazi Germany.

Arbitration The act of settling disputes through a neutral intermediary.

Area bombing The policy of indiscriminate bombing of an enemy's cities, with the aim of destroying the enemy's means of producing military material, plus communications, government centres and civilian morale.

Armistice An agreement to end fighting so that peace negotiations can begin.

Autarky The policy of economic self-sufficiency.

Ballistic missile A missile that is guided in the first part of its flight but falls freely as it approaches its target. It is used to deliver one or more warheads (often nuclear) to a predetermined target.

Blitzkrieg This term means 'lightning war' and is used to describe the German offensive tactics in the early stages of World War II.

Blockade An action to prevent goods from entering or leaving a country.

Bolshevik A member of the Bolshevik Party, which was a political party founded by Lenin in 1912. It followed the ideas Karl Marx and seized power in Russia in October 1917.

Bourgeois Relating to the 'middle classes' (bourgeoisie). It is usually used in a negative way in the context of Marxist writings, where the bourgeoisie are contrasted with the proletariat, or working classes.

Capitalist Someone who believes that trade and industry should be controlled by private owners and for profit (as opposed to being controlled by the government).

Civil war When fighting takes place within one country between two or more different factions.

Client states States that are controlled or influenced by another larger and more powerful state, or which are dependent on this state for support and protection.

Coalition government A government made up of members of two or more different political parties.

Cold War The period of international tension from the end of World War II in 1945 to the collapse of the Soviet domination of Eastern Europe in 1990.

Collectivization (USSR) The process by which private farms are confiscated by the state and collective communal farms created instead. This took place in the Soviet Union under Stalin in the 1930s.

Colonial Relating to countries that are colonies (controlled by another country), or to colonialism.

Communism A political theory that emerged in the 19th century based on the writings of Karl Marx. It claimed that all property should be owned by the community and labour should be organized for the common benefit.

Conscription Compulsory military service.

Conservative Someone who follows the ideas of conservatism. This is a political philosophy that wishes to preserve and keep intact institutions, practices and traditions. It is 'right wing'.

Constitutional monarchy A monarchy that does not have unlimited power, but rather is restrained by written laws and has to share power with an elected parliament.

Coup d'état A violent or illegal seizure of power.

Deductive reasoning Making conclusions logically from other things that are already known.

Demilitarized zone An area in which the deployment of military forces is not permitted.

Democratic Describing a country governed by representatives who are elected by the people.

Democratic monarchy See above – constitutional monarchy.

Diktat A 'dictated' agreement in which there has been no discussion or mutual agreement.

Diplomacy Managing relations between governments of different countries by discussion and peaceful means.

EEC European Economic Community, an inter-governmental organization that fostered economic integration and mutually beneficial trade arrangements between European member states.

Entente French word for an 'understanding', e.g. the Anglo-French Entente of 1904.

Fascism Fascism is rooted in ideas that are the very opposite of liberalism. Fascists believe in limiting individual freedoms (in the interest of the state), extreme nationalism, the use of violence to achieve ends, keeping power in the hands of an elite group or leader, and an aggressive foreign policy.

Feudal Relates to the system of feudalism that existed in Europe in medieval times. In theory, the King owned all or most of the land and gave it to his leading nobles in return for their loyalty and military service. The nobles in turn held land that peasants, including serfs, were allowed to farm in return for the peasants' labour and a portion of their produce. Under feudalism, people were born with a permanent position in society.

Fire-control The means by which artillery, missile or tank fire is accurately guided to the target.

Franchise The right to vote.

Free trade Trade without government interference – e.g. without tariffs or customs barriers.

Friendly fire When soldiers are mistakenly injured or killed by soldiers fighting on the same side.

Front (military) The line where two opposing armies are facing each other.

General Agreement on Tariffs and Trade (GATT) GATT was set up in 1947; its objective was the reduction of barriers to international trade such as tariff barriers and subsidies. The functions of GATT were taken over by the World Trade Organization in 1994.

Genocide The deliberate extermination of a race of people.

Globalization Describes an ongoing process by which regional economies, societies and cultures have become integrated through a globe-spanning network of communication and exchange.

GNP Gross National Product – the market value of all goods and services produced in one year by a country.

Great Depression The world economic recession that took place after the Wall Street Crash in America in October 1929.

Guerrilla warfare Irregular warfare and combat in which a small group of combatants uses mobile military tactics in the form of ambushes and raids to combat a larger and less mobile formal army.

House of Representatives Part of the US government that makes and passes laws. The House of Representatives and Senate make up Congress.

Hyper-inflation A rise in prices that becomes totally out of control.

Idealism The beliefs and behaviour of someone who has ideals and who tries to base his or her behaviour on these ideals.

Ideology A set of political beliefs.

Imperialism Empire building; the gaining of colonies.

Incumbent Someone who holds an official post at a particular time; combatants in a civil war who side with the government.

Indemnity An amount of money or goods that is received as compensation by someone for damage or loss that they have suffered, or legal protection against future losses.

Inductive reasoning A method of reasoning in which you use individual facts or ideas to give you a general rule or conclusion.

Infantry The foot soldiers of an army.

Inflation A general increase in the price of goods and services in a country.

Insurgents People who are fighting against the government or army of their own country.

International Monetary Fund (IMF) An international organization that oversees the global financial system.

Isolationism A policy that involves not getting involved with other countries or international problems.

Junta A military government that has taken power by force.

Landed aristocracy A category of nobility in various countries over history, for which land-ownership was part of their noble privilege.

League of Nations Organization set up after World War I to ensure that international disputes were solved without recourse to war.

Lebensraum German for 'living space'. Hitler wanted to expand eastwards in order to gain living space for the German nation.

Left wing Term given to progressive parties, socialists and communists.

Lend-Lease US aid to Britain in World War II. It enabled Britain to obtain war supplies for which it could not pay, under the agreement that these supplies would be returned or paid for after the war.

Liberal Someone who has liberal views is tolerant of different behaviour or opinions.

Limited war War that is not total war. It is limited by the weaponry used, by its geographical location or by its impact on the country fighting the war.

Mandate In the context of 20th-century international affairs, a mandate is a territory placed under the authority or tutelage of a European power.

Marxism Political and economic theory of Karl Marx, which holds that human actions and institutions are economically determined and that class struggle is needed to create historical change – capitalism will ultimately be superseded by communism.

McCarthyism A vehemently anti-communist movement in the USA during the 1950s, associated with US Senator Joseph McCarthy.

Militarism When there is an emphasis in a country on the importance of the military.

Monarchy A system of government where the ruler is a King or Queen.

Nationalism Can mean pride for one's nation or a desire for national independence.

Nationalization When a government takes over private industry or land so that it is owned by the state.

NATO North Atlantic Treaty Organization. An association of European and North American states set up in 1949 for defence against any Soviet attack.

Neo-colonial The policy of a strong nation seeking political and/or economic control over an independent nation.

Non-commissioned officer (NCO) A term used in the armed forces for leadership ranks that are junior to 'commissioned officers'. Sometimes the term is used to describe conscripted officers.

Nuclear submarine A submarine that uses nuclear power.

Occupied Territories Refers to the territories retained by Israel after its victories in the 1967 Six-Day War. They are (post-1982) the West Bank, East Jerusalem, the Gaza Strip and the Golan Heights.

OPEC Organization of Petroleum Exporting Countries – an organization founded in 1960 from nations that export large quantities of oil. The organization was formed to establish policies and prices.

Pacifist A person who is opposed to war or violence.

Parliamentary democracy A democracy that has an elected parliament.

Pincer movement A military manoeuvre in which both flanks of an enemy force are attacked with the aim of attaining complete encirclement or a collapse in the enemy defence.

Plebiscite A direct vote by the public on a specific issue/question.

Post-traumatic stress disorder The psychological and/or physical effects of experiencing extreme conditions, often associated with war; for example nightmares, depression and panic attacks.

Private sector The area of the nation's economy under private rather than governmental control.

Proletariat The working class, those that earn their living from manual labour. In Marxist terms the proletariat are those who must sell their labour to survive, as they own no personal capital or property.

Propaganda The particular doctrines deliberately spread by an organization or movement.

Protectionism The promotion or development of domestic industries by protecting them from foreign competition.

Public sector The area of the nation's affairs under governmental rather than private control.

Republic A state where power rests in a body of citizens that have gained power democratically.

Reservist A person who belongs to a reserve military force of a country.

Revanche Revenge or retaliation, often in the political context of regaining lost territory.

Revisionist An advocate of theories that are different from established theories or doctrines.

Right wing Conservative or reactionary political views, or in opposition to extensive political reform.

Sanctions An action by one or more states towards another state, calculated to force it to comply with legal obligations.

Satellite state A political term that refers to a country that is formally independent, but under heavy influence or control by another country.

Savings bonds A bond that may be underwritten by the government.

Senate The US Senate is the Upper House of the US Congress, which along with the House of Representatives forms the main legislative apparatus of the USA.

Shi'ite A member of one of the two great religious divisions of Islam. It regards Ali, the son-in-law of Muhammad, as the legitimate successor of Muhammad, and disregards the three caliphs who succeeded him.

Slavic Relating to the Slavs or their languages.

Small arms Firearms designed to be held in one or both hands while being fired.

Socialism A system of social organization that to a greater or lesser extent attempts to give the community as a whole ownership of the means of production, capital, land and so on.

Socio-economic The combination or interaction of social and economic factors.

Standing army A permanently organized military force maintained by a nation.

Stealth technology The use of advanced design and specialized materials to make an aircraft difficult or even impossible to detect by radar.

Strategic bombing A military strategy associated with total war, involving the bombing of targets that are deemed vital to an enemy's war-making capacity.

Sunni A member of one of the two great religious divisions of Islam, regarding the first four caliphs as legitimate successors of Muhammad.

Superpower A nation that is sufficiently powerful to dominate international events and the policies of other nations. Used specifically to refer to the USA and the USSR after 1945.

Tariff Duties or customs imposed by a government on imports or exports.

Total war A war in which a state uses all its human and material resources to fight.

Totalitarian A centralized government that tolerates no opposition to its control.

Truman Doctrine Policy of President Truman (announced in March 1947) to provide military and economic aid to Greece and Turkey and, by extension, to any country threatened by communism or any totalitarian ideology.

U-boat A German military submarine of the world wars era. The word derives from the German *Unterseeboot* (under-sea boat).

Ultimatum A final demand or set of terms, the rejection of which would have consequences.

United Nations An international organization formed in 1945 to promote international peace, security and cooperation.

Veto The power to cancel or postpone decisions or actions.

Wall Street Crash A devastating collapse of the US stock market in October 1929, which led to a global economic crisis.

Warlord A military commander who has seized power, usually in a region or specific area of a country.

Weapons of Mass Destruction Weapons that can produce devastating results when delivered in a single strike. They include nuclear, chemical and biological weapons.

Weimar Republic The German republic that was founded at Weimar (1919–33).

Weltpolitik 'World Policy', pursued by Kaiser Wilhelm II's Germany, which aimed to build an overseas empire and a strong German navy.

Index

The arrangement is word-by-word. Italic page numbers indicate illustrations not included in the text page range.
Bold page numbers indicate interesting facts boxes.

machine guns 51
McKinnon-Bell, David 65
Maginot Line 126, 145
Malaya 156, 277
Malmedy 76, 97
Malvinas/Falklands War
　　brinkmanship 192
　　British mobilization 191
　　course of 193–9
　　diplomacy 190
　　immediate causes 189
　　impact on home front 199–200
　　invasion 190
　　limited war 3
　　long-term causes 186–7
　　map 6
　　reasons for victory 202–3
　　results of 203–6
　　short-term causes 187–8
　　timeline 185–6
　　war at sea 194–6
　　war in the air 193–4
　　war on land 196–9
Manchu dynasty 252, 254
Manchuria 131, 134–5, 271, 272
Manchurian Crisis 100–2, 140
mandates 76–7
Manhattan Project 159
Mannock, 'Micky' **57**
manpower control 65
Mao Zedong 3, 182, *252*, **261**, 262,
　　265–70
Marco Polo incident **135**, 268
Marks, Sally 80
the Marne, battle of 41
Marshall, George 272
Marshall Plan **179**, 180, 181, 249
Martel, Gordan 35
Marx, Karl 307
Marxism 3
Massu, Jacques 285, 286
May Days fighting 237
McCarthyism 277
the media
　　censorship 200
　　Gulf War (1990–91) **220**
the Mediterranean, World War II 148
Mein Kampf 112–13, 122
Méndez, Costa 192
Menen, Carlos 204
Menéndez, Mario 191, 192, 193, 198,
　　199, 202
Messerschmitt Bf-109 fighter plane 147
Mexican Revolution 6
Michiko Hasegawa 140
Middle East
　　and Gulf War (1990–91) 223
　　map *207*
　　and USA 210
　　and USSR 210

Midway, battle of 157, 163
militarism 25
military expenditure, Germany 115
minority groups 63
Mirage planes 194
missiles 194
Mitchell, David 244
Mitterand, François 202
Mola, Emilio 235, 239
Moltke, Helmuth von 26, 32
Moore, Jeremy 198
morale
　　and *Blitzkrieg* 161
　　in Britain 147
　　control of 2, 65
　　Malvinas/Falklands War 202
　　and propaganda 173
　　and strategic bombing 163
Moravia 82
Moresnet 76
Moroccan Crisis 18–19
Mosul 93
Mountbatten, Louis 158
Muhammad VI 83
Mujahideen warriors *4*
multi-party democracies 179
Munich Agreement 120, 126
Munich beer hall putsch **112**
Muslim radicals 223
Muslims 208
Mussolini, Benito 103, 148, 152, 243,
　　249
mustard gas 52

N

Nagasaki 159, 165
Nanjing *135*, 142, 170, 268
National Confederation of Labour
　　(CNT) **228**, 247
National Health Service 172
National Liberation Front (FLN) 279
National Origins Act 138
National Socialist German Workers'
　　Party (Nationalsozialistische
　　Deutsche Arbeiterpartei) *see* Nazi
　　Party
nationalism 62, 112, 205
'Nationalists' 235
nationalization 65, 172, 180
NATO (North Atlantic Treaty
　　Organization) 180
naval armament 107
naval engagements *54*
naval race 16, 25
naval warfare 53–6, 161–3, 194–6
Nazi Party
　　25-point programme 112
　　and reparations 114
Nazi–Soviet Pact 120–1, 123, 137
Negrin, Juan 237

the Netherlands, and Indonesia 183
Neurath, Baron von 119
neutrality **43**
New Zealand 48, 76
New Zealanders (Anzacs) 47
NIC (Non-Intervention Committee)
　　238, 241–2
Nicaraguan Revolution 6
Nicholas II *12*
Nicolson, Harold 78
Nigerian Civil War *6*
night fighting **198**
night-vision devices 216, 217, 218
Nimitz, Chester 157–8
Nine Power Treaty 107, 133
Nivelle Offensive 42
Non-Agression Pact 115, 139
Non-Intervention Committee (NIC)
　　238, 241–2
Normandy landings 153
North Atlantic Treaty Organization
　　(NATO) 180
North Schleswig 76
Northern Expedition 258
Norway 143
Nott, John 187, 189
NSDAP (National Socialist German
　　Workers' Party) *see* Nazi Party
nuclear weapons 1, 2, 180, 183, 189, 205
Nuremberg Tribunal 183

O

OAS (Organization of the Secret Army)
　　288, 289
occupation zones, Germany 176–7
Office of War Information 173
oil production 211, *213*
oil spillages 222–3
Okinawa 158
Operation *Azul* 189
Operation *Barbarossa* 138, 148–51, 161
Operation *Desert Shield* 213
Operation *Desert Storm* 215–20, *218*,
　　223
Operation *Overlord* 153
Operation *Rosario* 189
Operation *Sealion* 146
Operation *Torch* 152
Opium Wars 253
Organization of the Secret Army (OAS)
　　288, 289
'organization phase' 267
Orlando, Vittorio 71, 72, 73
Osachi Hamaguchi 134
Oslo Accords 223
Ottawa Agreements 100
Ottoman Empire *9*, 11, 12–13, 19
Overy, Richard 101–2, 124, 146, 151,
　　155, 156, 162, 165, 171, 179

Watson, Alexander 59
weaponry
    and guerilla warfare 4
    World War I 50–3
    World War II 168
weapons of mass destruction (WMD)
    210, 223
Wedemeyer, Albert 272
Wei Lihuang 274
Weimar government **99**
Weinberger, Caspar 202
Weisbaden Accords 94
welfare 86, 172
Welfare State 179
Weltpolitik 14, 15
Western Europe 179–80
Western Front 39–44, 49–50, 63
'White Terror' 246, 247, 259
Wilhelm I 13
Wilhelm II **14**, *14*, 69
Wilson, Sandra 102
Wilson, Woodrow **43**, 53, 56, 71–2, 73
Wilson's Fourteen Points 71
Winter War **143**
WMD (weapons of mass destruction)
    210, 223
women
    and CCP 269–70
    Hitler on 171
    post-World War II **180**
    rape of **169**
    rights issues 86, **180**
    Spanish Civil War *246*
    and war effort 61, 64, 65, 86, 171
    World War I 61
Woodward, Sandy 193, 195
Workers' Party of Marxist Unification
    (POUM) **237**
World War I
    aircraft 56–7, *58*

Allied strengths 60
Balkan Front 47
bombing raids 56–7
breakdown of events 38
colonial territories 48
death toll 68–9
Eastern Front 45–7, 63
and Franco-Prussian War 8–9
Germany's defeat 59–60
historiography: causes 31–4
human cost 68–9
immediate causes 27–31
impact on Europe 68–70
impact outside of Europe 70–1
Italian Front 47
and Japan 132
long-term causes of 13–18
Middle East Fronts 47–8
militarism 25
nationalism 24
naval warfare 53–6
short-term causes 18–24
tactics change 50–3
timeline 7
as total war 61–4
Turkey 47–8
war at sea 53–6
war in the air 56–9
war on land 49–53
war plans 25–6
weaponry 50–3
Western Front 39–44, 49–50, 63
World War II
    appeasement 122–5
    causes 125–6
    'collective security' 87–9
    death toll 1
    economic cost 176
    in Europe 143–55
    human cost 175

immediate causes 120–2
impact in Algeria 281
impact in Asia 181–3
impact in Europe 175–80
and international relations 177–80
in the Pacific *see* Pacific War
political consequences 176–7
refugees *294*
short-term causes 114–20
and Spanish Civil War 249–50
total war *2*
war at sea 161–3
war in the air 163–6
war on land 160–1

X

Xiang River crossing 265

Y

Yalta conference 176, 272
Yamamoto, Isoroku 156
Yan Xishan 267
Young Plan 97–8
'Young Turks' 12, 19
Ypres 41, 42, 52
Yuan Shikai 255–6
Yugoslavia 82, 85, 148

Z

Zeppelin airships 56, *57*
Zhang Guotao 265, 266
Zhang Xueliang 267
Zhou Enlai 259, 262
Zhu De 262, 266
Zhukov, Georgy 149, 151
Zimmerman telegram 42, **43**
Zunyi Conference **265**
Zweites Buch (Secret Book) 113